THE PRACTICE
OF SUPERVISION
AND MANAGEMENT

THE PRACTICE OF SUPERVISION AND MANAGEMENT

Fred Luthans
College of Business
University of Nebraska

Mark J. Martinko
College of Business
Florida State University

McGraw-Hill Book Company

New York   St. Louis   San Francisco
Auckland   Bogotá   Düsseldorf   Johannesburg
London   Madrid   Mexico   Montreal   New Delhi
Panama   Paris   São Paulo   Singapore   Sydney   Tokyo   Toronto

234567890DODO 832

This book was set in Helvetica, by Black Dot, Inc. (ECU).
The editors were John F. Carleo and David Dunham;
the designer was Jo Jones;
the production supervisor was Leroy A. Young.
The drawings were done by J & R Services, Inc.
R. R. Donnelley & Sons Company was printer and binder.

Library of Congress Cataloging in Publication Data

Luthans, Fred.
    The practice of supervision and management.

    Includes index.
    1. Supervision of employees. I. Martinko,
Mark J., joint author. II. Title.
HF5549.L83   658.3′02   78-12166
ISBN 0-07-039123-8

This book is dedicated to the many outstanding supervisors
whom we have had the pleasure to work for and with through the years.
These men and women have taught us a great deal about effective supervision.
Their influence is found throughout the book.
We thank all of you.

CONTENTS

PREFACE

The old saying that the supervisor is the person caught in the middle is true. The supervisor plays the pivotal role between largely abstract top management on the one hand and largely operational personnel on the other. How supervisors perform in this often frustrating but nevertheless crucial role is probably the biggest single factor in the success or failure of modern organizations.

In recent years, an emerging body of knowledge and practical experience clearly points to certain concepts and techniques that can be used to make supervision more effective. This book presents, analyzes, and demonstrates these basic concepts and specific skills. After defining the role of modern supervisors and discussing the increasingly complex and changing internal and external environment facing them, the book is broken down into two major parts. The first part concentrates on the basic functions and related techniques of effective supervision (planning, delegating, organizing, staffing, training, controlling, disciplining, and appraising). The second part then gives more direct attention to the human relations aspects of effective supervision (communicating, motivating, and leading). Having grasped this blend of conceptual/functional and human relations insights and skills, the present or potential supervisor should be able to meet the challenges of supervision as effectively as possible.

We have given our "best shot" to making this book as up to date and relevant to the effective practice of supervision and management as possible. We have drawn from the rapidly expanding research literature and our own practical experiences in a wide variety of organizations. We have made a concerted effort to take the very best, and often very sophisticated, research and experience and write it up in a very straightforward, readable manner. Our goal throughout has been to make our text understandable, interesting, and applicable. To make this book as student-oriented as possible, we have included a number of end-of-chapter learning aids (key concepts, exercises, and cases) and a Glossary and chapter-by-chapter Self-Review Guide at the end of the book. Although many of the cases and examples are from business and industry, we recognize and our book reflects the growing importance of supervision in nonbusiness organizations. *The Practice of Supervision and Management* should be well suited for supervision and management courses that contain a mixture of people from, or going to, a variety of organizations, as well as those courses/programs that have a homogeneous group from business or nonbusiness organizations. We have aimed our work primarily at lower-level supervision. However, the book is also suitable—because of the nature of the material—for those who are currently or hope soon to be in mid-level management positions.

We would like to acknowledge the excellent administrative support and encouragement we received from Dr. Sang Lee, Chairman of the Department of Management at the University of Nebraska, and, of course, our families, who helped to make this book a reality.

Fred Luthans
Mark J. Martinko

THE PRACTICE
OF SUPERVISION
AND MANAGEMENT

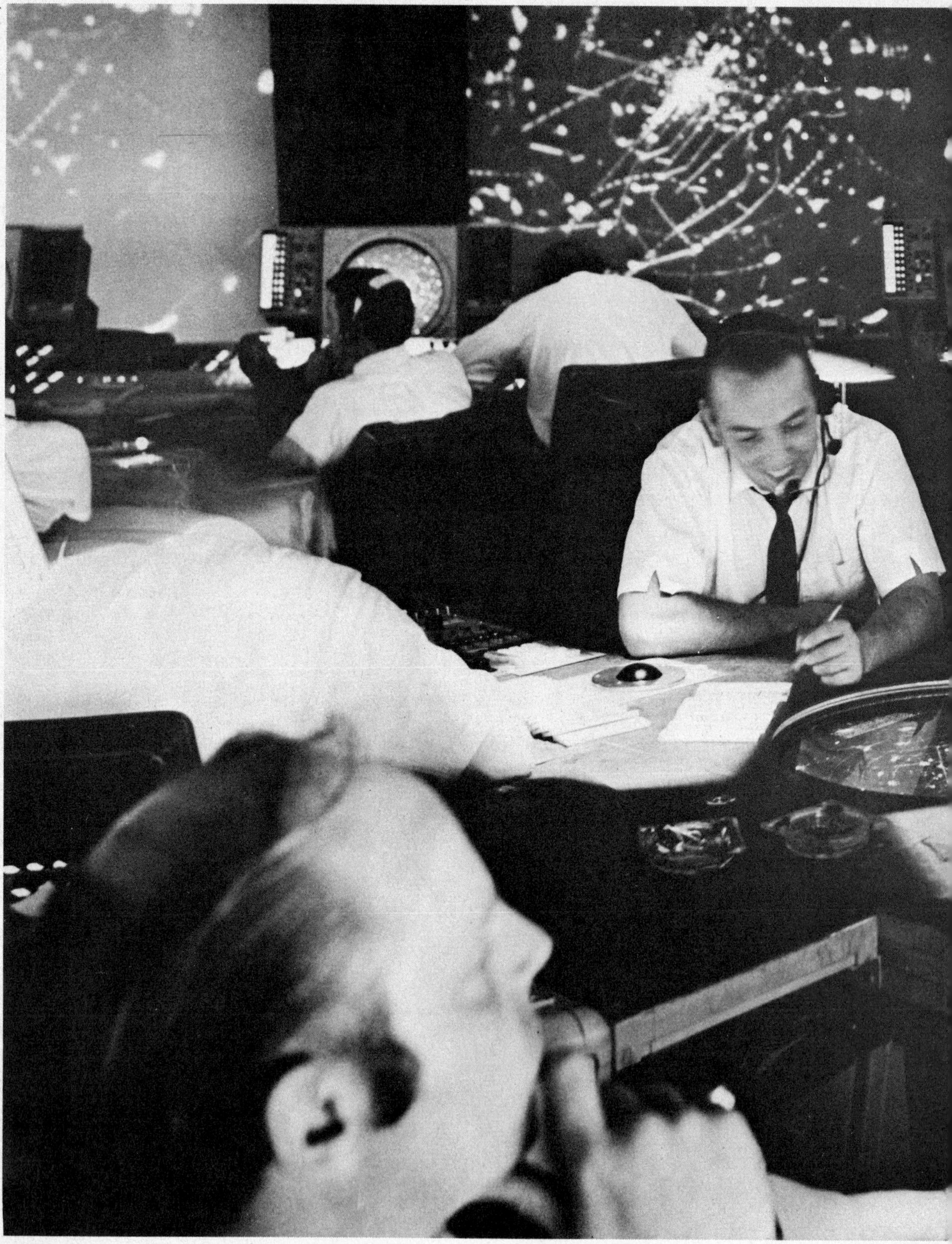

(United Nations)

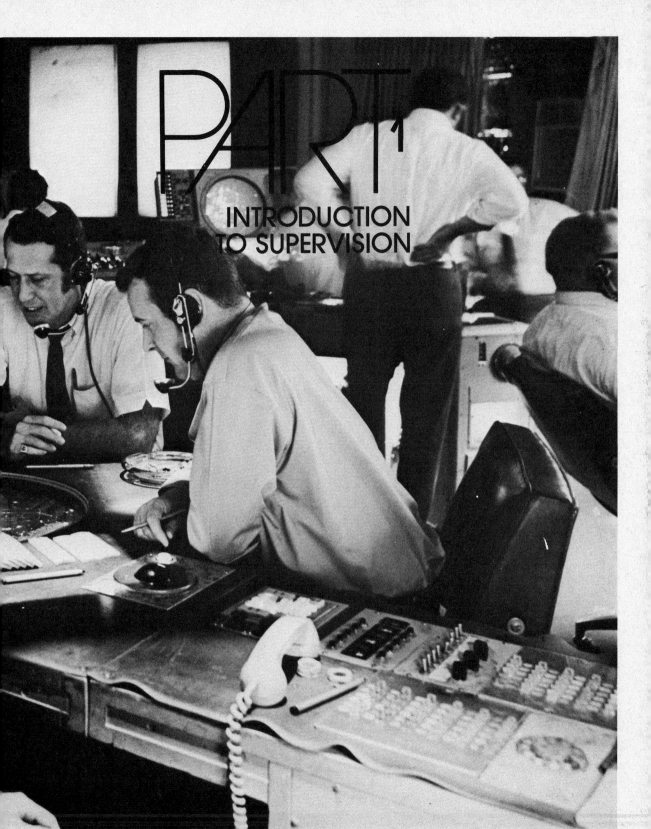

PART 1

INTRODUCTION TO SUPERVISION

THE ROLE OF THE MODERN SUPERVISOR

CHAPTER 1

Gary Edwards was 28 years old and had been selling Universal insurance for over seven years. During that time, Universal had more than tripled the amount of insurance sold; it now had more than 650 full-time employees in five locations throughout the Northwest. While the company was growing, Gary was learning the sales end of the insurance business. In his seven years of experience, he had learned just about everything, he thought, that a person could know about selling insurance. Last week, Helen Allen, the director of sales, asked Gary if he would consider being the supervisor for the central sales office. Without hesitation, Gary accepted the new position. Soon afterward, his friends and colleagues were full of advice and questions. Was he going to be a "tough nut" like old Jim? Would he remember his old friends, or would he forget about them, like all the others who had become supervisors? Did he think he could take the reins and establish an effective sales program in his area? What types of changes did he plan to make, if any? At first, Gary laughed good-naturedly at these questions. Now, one week later, the full impact of the decision to become a supervisor was beginning to worry Gary. Suddenly, he realized that there was a lot more to supervising the sales group than knowing the mechanics and techniques of sales. He wished he had a real understanding of the role of a supervisor and more knowledge and skills for the difficult but challenging job that he was about to undertake.

LEARNING OBJECTIVES

After reading this chapter, you should have:

A good understanding of the scientific-management, human relations, universal principles, and contingency approaches to supervision

An understanding and definition of the scientific-management role of modern supervision

An understanding and definition of the human relations role of modern supervision

An understanding and definition of the functional roles of modern supervision

A knowledge of the contingency applications of the various roles of supervision

A knowledge of the reasons supervisors fail

Most people probably feel they have a good idea of who supervisors are and what they do. For example, some may picture the supervisor as the person at the fast-food chain down the street who runs frantically from one work station to another shouting "Faster!" "Faster!" Others may visualize as a supervisor the person behind the serving line in the cafeteria, arms folded and frowning, who berates the cooks and helpers every time the servers run out of an entree. Still others may picture the person in authority at the local factory, who collects the time cards, assigns the daily work orders, orders raw materials, schedules machines for maintenance, and passes out the weekly paycheck. Another view of a supervisor can be found in the local hospital. The nurse in charge of the floor station, who holds meetings with the floor nurses at the beginning of each shift and chides the aides for not answering the patients' signals faster, is a good example. Despite the obvious differences and inaccuracies in these various pictures of supervisors, they all have at least two things in common:

1 Supervisors seldom or never actually perform the physical or manual work they oversee.

2 Supervisors are *directly responsible* for accomplishing the goals of their respective organizations through the management of the human and physical resources under their control.

These two significant aspects of the supervisor's job are sometimes difficult to resolve; they pose a dilemma. On the one hand, supervisors are responsible for all the work in their areas of responsibility; on the other, they are restricted from actually doing the work themselves. This unique situation has stimulated much attention over the years from researchers and writers on management theory and practice. The resulting literature varies considerably in the approaches it suggests for coping with the daily problems of supervision successfully. Yet despite these differences, some definite categories of tested approaches to supervision are beginning to emerge.

VARIOUS APPROACHES TO SUPERVISION

Through the years, a number of major theories or viewpoints of the supervisor's job have emerged. The most widely recognized include the scientific-management, human relations, universal principles, and contingency approaches to supervision. Each of these theoretical approaches has been thoroughly discussed, analyzed, and researched; all are considered to be effective by both practicing supervisors and management scholars.

The Scientific-Management Approach

This was one of the first comprehensive theories of supervision. Very simply, the scientific-management approach says that there is one best way to do each of the jobs the supervisor oversees. The task of the supervisor becomes one of studying the jobs carefully (scientifically), determining the proper work methods, and ensuring that the workers follow the procedures which have been decided upon.

A good illustration of how scientific management works is provided in the works of Frederick Taylor, the recognized father of this approach to supervision. Taylor's earliest and most important work was conducted at Bethlehem Steel Company at the turn of the twentieth century. After observing a group of workers handling pig iron (pieces of iron shaped like pigs, weighing about 92 pounds each), using various different methods, Taylor reasoned that there must be a better way. He decided to study this job in a more detailed, scientific way. In his writings, he used an actual worker given the name Schmidt as an example. Taylor gave Schmidt a very precise set of instructions which were derived from an analysis of rest breaks, methods of handling the pig iron, and payment methods. Specifically, Schmidt rested an almost unheard of 58 percent of the time and based his pay on the amount of pig iron loaded onto a boxcar. The average man was loading $12\frac{1}{2}$ tons per day; but at the end of the first day under Taylor's supervision, Schmidt had loaded 47 1/2 tons. The entire work group was then trained in Taylor's method, and productivity increased almost fourfold in the pig-iron-handling operation at Bethlehem. Taylor was equally successful in other areas (e.g., in the shoveling operation at Bethlehem), and he gained worldwide fame.

Today "Taylorism," or scientific management, is still very much in evidence in our factories. One example is the modern automobile assembly plant. The entire assembly process is carefully analyzed and divided into a specified number of jobs. After the jobs have been thoroughly studied, precise routines, standards, and methods are prescribed for each worker. If all workers perform their jobs according to this approach, the auto assembly plant is extremely efficient and profitable. The catch, however, is that it is not uncommon for workers to refuse to follow the rigid procedures and methods inherent in such a scientific-management approach. The Chevrolet Vega plant in Lordstown, Ohio, has provided a widely publicized example of workers' refusal to be pigeonholed into the routines dictated by a scientific-management approach. Even when only a minority of workers refuse to follow the prescribed work methods, the results can be devastating, because each job in the factory depends on all the other jobs. A breakdown in a single job can cripple the entire production process. This is the major criticism to be leveled against the scientific-management approach. It assumes that people will accept the rigid structure of "scientifically" designed jobs, and that this acceptance can be ensured through payment on a piecework basis. Thus, the theory has been severely criticized for overlooking the human needs of the workers, who are essential to the accomplishment of any organization's goals.

The Human Relations Approach

This approach to supervision initially came about in reaction to the scientific-management movement. The supervisor who has adopted the human relations approach is mainly concerned with employee needs, taking into account the human element in the assignment of jobs, determination of work procedures, and so forth. The reasoning behind this approach is that the supervisors must be considerate and fair in their relationships with employees and must integrate their personal needs with the goals of the organization. The assumption is that if the supervisor treats employees well and provides the personal attention that is necessary, they will respond favorably and be highly productive in their work efforts.

Perhaps the pioneering studies conducted at the Hawthorne Works of the Western Electric Company in the late twenties and early thirties provide the best illustration of this approach. The original study was intended to find out what lighting conditions would raise the productivity of a group of women assemblers to the highest possible level. It was a typical scientific-management type of study.

The experimenters found that regardless of the intensity of light, the productivity of the work group increased. When the intensity was increased, productivity increased. When the intensity was decreased, productivity also increased. In other words, no matter how the intensity of light was varied, the experimenters recorded continuous increases in productivity. The researchers were completely baffled by these results.

In order to investigate these findings further, more studies were conducted at Hawthorne. The researchers varied things such as lunch breaks, coffee breaks, length of work day, length of work week, rest periods, and methods of payment. But again, they found that no matter what they changed or how they changed it, productivity continued to increase. This was true even when the original factory conditions were reinstituted. Of course, this is a problem that all supervisors would like to have. The researchers wanted to find out what was going on, so they analyzed the results carefully to isolate the cause for the increased productivity.

Through a series of intensive interviews, this cause eventually became clear. It was simply that someone was finally paying attention to the workers! What the researchers had forgotten was that each time a change was made, the workers were interviewed either formally or informally to see what they thought about it. In other words, for the first time, someone asked for their opinions, listened carefully to the answers, and acted upon them. It was concluded that the novelty and attention created by the experimental situations—coupled with the increased attention from the experimenters—were the major factors accounting for the increased productivity.

Today, a significant proportion of supervisors and management scholars advocate a human relations approach. To these supervisors, the most important aspect of the job is their daily interactions with their people. They are particularly concerned with establishing effective communications throughout their work groups. Similarly, they emphasize employee participation in all aspects of the job, including the design of work procedures and methods, planning, decision making, and performance appraisals. This approach has further expanded and can be seen as the impetus behind employee-attitude surveys and team-building techniques—both of which are mechanisms for increasing the employee's motivation and ability to provide input toward the accomplishment of organizational goals.

Like the scientific-management approach, human relations has had its critics. For example, in the academic world, there have been a number of studies which show that employee attitudes have little or no impact on, or relationship to, productivity. Moreover, on the practical side, most of us can probably recall a supervisor who was extremely gruff and aloof in relationships with people but who, by most standards, would have to be considered extremely effective. Similarly, we can probably recall a number of fellow employees who felt highly disgruntled and unhappy with their supervision but who were nonetheless extremely productive and hard workers.

The Universal Principles Approach

A third approach to supervision can be called the universal principles approach. It is so named because it is based on the premise that there are some universal principles of management which, if carefully followed by the supervisor, will result in the efficient operation of the organization. While these principles may be expressed somewhat differently by different authors, they generally include such basics as planning, organizing, coordinating, communicating, directing, and controlling. The idea is that supervisors must develop approaches and specific techniques to ensure the occurrence of these universal functions. For example, to ensure that planning occurs in the organization, supervisors may be required to complete a budget every six months or to submit a list of objectives to top management. Similarly, communications within the organization can be encouraged by establishing a system of production schedules which are delivered to key personnel each week. According to this theory, then, supervisors should be concerned with the "big picture" and view the organization from the larger perspective. Human and technological problems are inevitable but will be worked out if the proper processes or systems are designed for the long-range health and functioning of the organization.

Like the others, this approach has a number of inadequacies. Although general principles of supervision can serve as useful guidelines, the specifics of application vary considerably depending upon the particular situations in which supervisors find themselves. Thus, although the principles approach tells supervisors that it is important to plan and organize, it often fails to provide any specific recommendations for initiating or carrying out the activities recommended. Moreover, when the authors who stress principles have tried to be more specific, they have often been criticized because their principles do not apply to all supervisory groups. For example, one author stated that the greatest number of subordinates a supervisor can manage efficiently is five. Yet it is commonplace in many types of organizations (e.g., factories or hospitals) for supervisors to handle twenty or thirty people effectively. Thus, the critics of this approach admit that the functions have value, but they feel that the assumption of universality is unrealistic and that this approach therefore fails to provide direction for solving the complex day-to-day problems facing today's supervisor.

The New Contingency Approach

The word "contingent" means "depending on something else"; it describes the newest approach to supervision. In a nutshell, it says that the techniques and philosophy of effective supervision depend upon the circumstances that supervisors find themselves in. Thus, in some cases, the most effective supervisory approach may be scientific management, which systematically analyzes jobs and enforces work rules and procedures. However, in a different situation, supervisory effectiveness may call for the human relations approach or perhaps the application of one or another of the principles.

One of the best examples of the contingency approach deals with leadership. Professor Fred Fiedler of the University of Washington has provided a major breakthrough for leadership theory and practice. Before Fiedler, many leadership experts strongly encouraged the use of concepts and techniques such as democracy and participation *without* any reference to the supervisor's particular situation. Fiedler, on the other hand, undertook a rigorous analysis of many different kinds of leadership situations before recommending any particular style. From his research, he found that in extremely good or extremely poor situations (according to things like the formal position that the supervisor held, how well-defined the job was, and how well the supervisor got along with the people), the very directive, scientific-management type of supervisor was most effective. On the other hand, for the majority of situations—which are not extremely favorable or unfavorable—he found that the human relations approach to supervision was most effective. Later, this contingency approach will be expanded upon and explained further. For the present, however, the contingency approach can be thought of as a technique whereby the supervisor selects and applies from the scientific-management, human relations, and/or principles of management approaches the appropriate concept or procedure for the situation at hand.

The contingency approach is rapidly becoming the most widely accepted conceptual and practical method of supervision. It is realistic and, of course, many successful supervisors have used and will use the contingency approach without realizing it. The approach recognizes the complexity of the supervisory process and the need to remain flexible and adapt to the particular circumstances of the job. It is not a simple approach. While the other approaches recommend one course of action covering all situations, the contingency approach requires supervisors to remain constantly aware of their circumstances, to analyze them, and to change their methods when appropriate.

In some cases, which will be mentioned throughout this book, some fairly solid recommendations are given for analyzing the situation and determining the most effective supervisory approach. However, it must be realized that the supervisor is often confronted with many unique and challenging situations for which there are no simple answers. This, then, is the perspective that will be taken in the following chapters. Accordingly, this book will avoid many of the simplistic recommendations and guidelines that are all too common to books on supervision.

This book will be a deliberate blend of what is known about effective supervision from careful research conducted by behavioral scientists and management experts. It will also draw heavily upon the experience of the many thousands of effective practicing supervisors. Particular attention will be given to the basic elements of supervision, drawn from the scientific-management and the universal functions of management (e.g., planning, organizing, and controlling) approaches as well as from the human relations (e.g., communicating, motivating, and leading) approaches. However, these basic elements and human relations aspects of supervision will always be discussed within the contingency framework. In other words, whether, when, and how a particular approach or technique can be effectively applied will depend upon the given situation.

DEFINING THE ROLE OF THE SUPERVISOR

Closely related to the various conceptual approaches to supervision are the several roles which supervisors are expected to play. For example, the supervisor's role reflects the way in which other members of the organization (e.g., employees, other supervisors, and top-level management) expect the supervisor to behave and perform in his or her job.

Scientific-Management Roles

As suggested by the discussion of the contingency approach, every effective supervisor will need to use scientific management under certain conditions. Again, this assumes that there is one best way to do the job and that it is the supervisor's responsibility to analyze the jobs carefully to determine the appropriate work methods. Provided that employees follow these procedures and are paid accordingly, it is expected that productivity will be high. According to this scientific-management perspective, the supervisor's boss, employees, and cosupervisors will expect the supervisor to assume the following types of roles:

1 *Technician.* Frequently, employees look to their supervisors to solve their technical problems. As a result, supervisors often become involved in extremely challenging and complex problems. For example the supervisor of an engineering group might be expected to help subordinates solve extremely complex and intricate design problems. Similarly, the supervisor of a customer complaint department may be expected to handle the really tough customers. Supervisors derive many advantages from engaging in these types of problems. It provides the opportunity to continually refine technical skills and often gains for supervisors the personal respect of the work group. However, there are also some disadvantages. The most obvious is that a supervisor may become overburdened with the work of subordinates. Moreover, doing the work of subordinates may rob these people of important developmental opportunities and deprive them of some of the important things suggested by the human relations approach.

2 *Researcher/Analyst.* Another scientific-management role supervisors are expected to perform is that of the researcher and job analyst. The employees expect supervisors to design new job procedures and to implement them when they prove to be effective. Today, at least some of this responsibility has been taken over by staff experts such as systems analysts and industrial engineers.

3 *Controller.* Another important role of supervisors is controlling the work group to ensure that the appropriate work methods are utilized. The supervisor is also expected to provide rewards for productive workers, such as pay increases and promotions. Moreover, employees also anticipate that the supervisor will provide sanctions or punishments when they deviate from accepted work procedures.

Human Relations Roles

According to the human relations approach, the supervisor must be a person who is sensitive to employee needs and who carefully integrates these needs with the goals of the organization. There are a number of specific roles which the supervisor assumes as a result of this viewpoint.

1 *Counselor.* One of the major responsibilities of the supervisor is to provide the employees with the opportunity to air their problems. Frequently, patient listening by an objective person can help the employees gain perspective on their difficulties. If the problem is work-related, the supervisor may be able to make an adjustment or a suggestion which can solve the problem. However, even when the problem is not directly related to work, counseling is warranted, since the problem may, now or in the future, affect the productivity of the employee. Supervisors should be cautioned, however, not to assume the role of psychologist or psychiatrist. When serious personal problems arise, the supervisor should be prepared to refer the individual to a professional. An increasing number of large organizations are including professional counselors on their staffs.

2 *Linking Pin.* Both employees and top management view supervisors as the key linking pins in the organization. To the supervisors' own subordinates, *they are management.* For management, the supervisors represent the critical link to the operating employees. This relationship is illustrated in Figure 1-1.

3 *Human Relations Expert.* The linking-pin role implies that the supervisor will serve as a negotiator, communicator, buffer, and compromiser. All these indicate that supervisors need a large measure of interpersonal or human relations skills. They must be skilled

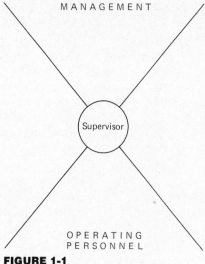

FIGURE 1-1
The supervisor as a linking pin.

at defining, translating, and carrying out the objectives of management. Similarly, they must be able to communicate the needs, problems, and concerns of employees to management.

4 *"The Person Caught in the Middle."* Besides being the human relations expert implied in the linking pin role, the supervisor is also the person caught in the middle. On the negative side, this role may be seen as creating severe stress and anxiety for supervisors. Quite often, supervisors are viewed as being on the fringe of both management and employee groups. Top management often view supervisors as operative employees, and the employees view supervisors as members of management. Thus, being a supervisor can be a lonely occupation, since it may involve less than full acceptance by either top management or the work group. On the positive side, supervisors who are able to provide the human relations skills necessary in this role become indispensable to both management and the employees under them. Thus, both managers and employees may come to depend upon and respect the supervisory function.

5 *Motivator.* Certainly one of the key functions of supervisors is to motivate their people. As pointed out in the discussion of the Hawthorne studies, the environment created by the supervisor is critical to the motivation of employees. Successful supervisors listen carefully to employee needs and design the environment to fulfill these needs. Moreover, in all phases of their operations, they are constantly striving to renew the employees' interest in their work by providing the proper working conditions. At times, the supervisor will need to offer tangible rewards, such as pay increases and promotions. Similarly, productivity may be stimulated by providing opportunities that allow the employee to develop new skills or assume additional responsibility. Most often, however, workers will be motivated if the supervisor gives them the attention and recognition that should reward good performance.

6 *Trainer.* Training is a critical human relations skill. Supervisors must be aware of the differences among employees and capable of responding to each person as an individual. They must carefully analyze the needs of the employees through counseling and/or careful observation. Based on this needs analysis, the supervisor can provide the opportunity for employees to make the most of their skills and abilities by making the right job and position assignments or offering individualized training and instruction. Although many organizations provide a staff of training experts, it is not usually possible to respond to all the needs of employees with specialized training programs. Thus, the supervisor bears the major responsibility for the day-to-day training and coaching of rank-and-file employees.

Functional Roles

The discussion of the universal principles approach emphasized the broad perspective, or view of "the big picture," that supervisors have to maintain. It follows that they must be responsible for interpreting overall goals and specifically defining the objectives of the particular operating unit of which they are in charge. They must organize and coordinate the unit's human and physical resources to achieve the objectives. Four primary roles evolve out of these expectations:

1 *Leader.* Employees look to the supervisor for direction. The supervisor is expected to assign the daily tasks and resolve both personal and operating problems, using the unit's objectives as the standard. In performing the leadership functions, the supervisor can be either task- or people-oriented. According to the task-directed style, the supervisor's main considerations are the work goals of the operating unit. This approach, of course, is closely related to the scientific-management philosophy. The people-oriented style, on the other hand, is closely related to the human relations approach. This latter style implies that the feelings and concerns of the work group are highly important to the supervisor. There are advantages and disadvantages to both approaches, which will be discussed in detail in later chapters. However, regardless of the approach used, the supervisor is expected (i.e., it is his or her role) to assume the appropriate leadership functions for the group.

2 *Organizer.* The supervisor's world can be viewed as a complex network of people, jobs, machines, paperwork, materials, objectives, and goals. Each of these factors must be carefully brought together in an organized, coordinated manner to create a smooth-running organization. In this organizer role, the supervisor is much like the conductor of a symphony orchestra, bringing into play each of the instruments at just the right moment to produce beautiful music.

3 *Planner.* Purposes, goals, and directions are characteristics of all functioning groups. As a planner, the supervisor has the major responsibility for determining exactly what these goals are, evaluating them, and changing the direction of the work group if necessary. Coupled with this responsibility for providing the workers with the "big picture" is the planning to achieve the objectives. The members of the work group have to know what direction they are to take before they can accomplish their goals. The supervisor can point the way by planning step by step and determining how to get there from here. Thus, supervisors break major overall objectives down into intermediate or smaller steps, ensuring that the long-run goals of the organization as a whole and the particular unit will be achieved.

4 *Decision Maker.* Another important functional role of the supervisor is that of decision maker. Supervisors are viewed by employees and top management as having the most direct access to information on which to base important operational decisions—on-the-spot decisions. Because of supervisors' positions in organizations, they are most likely to be the first to identify potential problem areas. Similarly, they can analyze the problem directly and propose the course of action that must be taken to solve the problem before it gets out of hand. Finally, they are in the position to implement the decision and follow-up to make sure that the appropriate actions are taken. Once again, this role illustrates the fact that the supervisor is in a critical position for making the many decisions required for the successful day-to-day operation of any modern organization.

CONTINGENCY APPLICATION OF SUPERVISORY ROLES

As previously discussed, the contingency approach to supervision would say that there is no one best way. The scientific-management, human relations, and universal principles approaches are all appropriate and effective *depending upon* the situation confronting the supervisor. This contingency perspective holds true for the various roles which supervisors must adopt. At one time or another, supervisors are expected to perform each of the various roles described so far, but always within a particular set of circumstances. Thus, one of the greatest challenges of supervision is deciding which role will be the most effective in a given situation. Although emphasis will be placed on describing the particular situation in which the concepts or skills discussed in the text are applicable, some general guidelines are also needed.

One important analysis of the supervisor's role is provided by Robert Kahn, a professor at the University of Michigan. He views the supervisory function as a combination of technical, human and conceptual roles. His definitions of these terms correspond basically to scientific management (for "technical"), human relations (for "human"), and universal principles (for "conceptual"). He studied these roles in relation to organizational level. The results are presented in Figure 1-2.

From this figure, it can be seen that first-line supervisory approaches should be about equally distributed among the technical, human, and conceptual roles. In other words, Kahn has found that effective first-line supervisors give equal emphasis and attention to all three roles. The figure also interestingly points out that, for middle- and upper-level managers, the technical aspects of their jobs becomes less and less important. As one progresses up the management ladder, the human and conceptual roles become relatively more important.

Kahn's analysis of the relative importance of the supervisor's roles is worth noting for several reasons. First, as supervisors receive more responsibility, their roles become increasingly oriented toward human relations and the conceptual approach and less technical in nature. Second, supervisors must continually switch roles as the demands of their jobs change. Sometimes they must use their human relations skills, and at other times they need their technical expertise. The important question becomes *when* and *how* a supervisor should change roles. While there are no simple answers to this complex question, some guidelines are available.

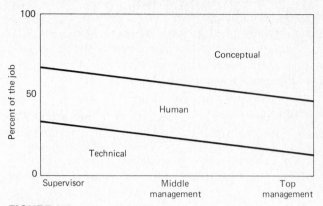

FIGURE 1-2
Breakdown of the roles for effective
supervision.

According to one model, the supervisor will assume the appropriate role by responding to the expectations and behavior of the other members of the work environment. Whenever employees interact with their supervisors, they are sending subtle role messages. For example, if the employees bring personal problems to their supervisors, they influence them to adopt the human relations role of a counselor. Similarly, when employees ask for the next job assignment, they are asking the supervisor to adopt the leadership role. On the other hand, the resulting behavior of these employees may also modify the supervisor's role perception. For example, if an employee tells a supervisor to mind his or her own business after the supervisor inquires about an employee's personal problem, this obviously means that the employee rejects the supervisor's assumption of the counseling role. Similarly, the supervisor's boss's acceptance or rejection of proposals for new work methods or changes can also be viewed as shaping the supervisor's role. In the same manner, supervisors establish their roles through their behavior toward the people in their work organization. The entire process of role taking can be viewed as an exchange of expectations and behaviors, where a bargain is struck between the role taker and the role senders.

In the initial stages of role definition, there is bound to be confusion and conflict as the supervisor gives and receives contradictory role messages. Eventually, however, both supervisor, employee, and top management learn what to expect, and the role is defined.

Some supervisors will have negotiated roles that lead to effective results. Others will be dissatisfied with the outcome of the roles that they have assumed.

WHY SUPERVISORS FAIL

Besides the work that has been done on supervisory roles, there have been a number of studies of why supervisors fail. These studies are extremely important for new supervisors, since they emphasize the roles they will need to stress and concentrate on in order to become effective. One such study surveyed the supervisory personnel of 100 major companies to find out why things go wrong. The results of the survey are summarized in Table 1-1. Clearly, the results indicate that supervisors fail because they do not assume the responsibility for

TABLE 1-1
WHY MANAGERS FAIL
A recent survey of managers indicated failure due to weaknesses in the following areas:

Technical	Percent mentioning each
Marketing and distribution	28
Products and procedures	25
Accounting	15
Labor law	10
Conceptual	
Formulating organizational objectives	85
Analyzing problems	84
Making decisions	71
Organizing	23
Human	
Delegating work	91
Evaluating people	81
Cooperating with others	79
Administering personnel matters	69
Motivating subordinates	60
Assuming responsibility	47
Persevering	23

their important conceptual and human relations roles. The top three causes of supervisory failure—inability to delegate, failure to become aware of organizational objectives, and failure to analyze problems—are related to the conceptual role. Similarly, human relations dimensions of evaluating people and cooperating with others were rated high on the list. Another important finding is that technical skills were not seen as strongly related to supervisory failures. This is explained by the selection process in the majority of companies, where almost 90 percent of the supervisors are promoted from within. Because these supervisors are promoted as a result of their technical abilities, they rarely fail in this area of their jobs. Unfortunately, human relations and conceptual skills are seldom considered in selection decisions for supervisory positions. These findings are an important point of departure for the rest of the book, in helping supervisors bridge the gap between their existing technical abilities and the much-needed conceptual and human relations skills.

■ KEY CONCEPTS

Scientific management
Human relations
Universal principles
Contingency management
Role expectations
Supervisory failures

■ PRACTICAL EXERCISES

(These can be performed by individuals or by groups.)

1 Identify the characteristics of a supervisor, using the role expectations of: *(a)* scientific management, *(b)* human relations, and *(c)* universal principles. Discuss the differences in the approaches of each role and explain how the contingency approach would apply.

2 If you now have or have had supervisory responsibilities, compile a list of your daily duties and indicate the approximate percentage of time spent on each task. Classify each of these tasks according to the three approaches to supervision: scientific management, human relations, and universal principles. Add the total time in each of these categories and discuss the contingency implications of your time allotment.

■ DISCUSSION INCIDENTS

Jim Bates had graduated from high school and attended community college in his home town. Jim had held a wide variety of summer and part-time jobs while he was attending school. Now it was about time to graduate, and he began thinking about the type of permanent job he would take. One thing was sure: he was tired of taking orders and wanted to be in a position of giving them to others. In his first interview for a supervisor's job, the interviewer asked him, "Jim, what do you think the role of a supervisor should be? What approach would you use if you were hired by our organization?"

1 How would you answer the interviewer's first question? How would you answer the second question?

2 What do you think about Jim's reason for pursuing a supervisor's job? Does he have the needed background to become a good supervisor?

Jane Ortega has been a very successful supervisor for a number of years at the XYZ organization. Over coffee one day, a cosupervisor in another department said to Jane, "You have been at this longer than I have, and for the life of me I can't figure out what approach to use with my people. Sometimes I feel that all I am supposed to do is give directions to my people and see that they know the procedures. Other times, though, I feel I have to listen to their problems and see if I can't motivate them a little more. At still other times, I feel I have to set some objectives and see that they are carried out. Frankly, I am confused and I am afraid I am not doing any of the things I should. Do you have any suggestions that may help me out of this fix I'm in?"

1 What answer should Jane give? How can the confusion be eliminated for this supervisor?

2 What roles are found in this incident? Do you think that Jane uses these roles? Why is she successful while the other supervisor is not?

THE SUPERVISOR'S ENVIRONMENT

②CHAPTER

D on Walker is a supervisor in a small plant that manufactures plastic and foam rubber products for the automobile industry (e.g., padded dashboards, steering wheels, and armrests). Don's department produces armrests, a process which is fairly simple. The raw materials are the plastic skins which form the outside of the armrests, metal inserts which fit inside the plastic skins, and the foam rubber compound used to fill the armrests. The workers put the metal inserts inside the plastic skins and then place the shells in molds on a small conveyor belt. The conveyor takes the shells through a small metal housing, where they are automatically filled with foam rubber. As the armrests come out the other side of the housing, the workers remove the finished products. Each of the eight assembly lines which Don supervises has three people. In addition, Don also supervises six materials handlers, who are responsible for bringing the raw materials to the line and removing the finished products. Thus, Don supervises a total of thirty employees.

At first glance, Don's job looks like a breeze. The manufacturing process is very simple; usually only a few hours are required to train a new worker. However, if we are fortunate enough to get Don really talking about his job, we find that he has a vast number of concerns and unresolved problems which he feels are beyond his control. Below is a list of these:

1 *Turnover, Absenteeism, and Poor Motivation.* Almost 50 percent of the workers in Don's area leave or are terminated within the first year. Moreover, he has five employees who are averaging more than three days' absence per month, an average of thirty-six days per year. The biggest problem of all, however, is that many of Don's people are giving eight hours and nothing more to the job. Many have, in effect, retired, even though they have many years to go until they will be eligible for their pensions. Don attributes much of the problem to the younger workers, who appear to be unmotivated and unwilling to make the sacrifices that his generation made.

2 *Layoffs.* In spite of Don's difficulties in keeping workers, almost half were laid off last year. He is told by top management that the oil embargo had a severe impact. It lessened the demand for cars; as a result, there was very little demand for armrests. He was also told that as the price of oil increased, the cost of the company's petroleum-based raw materials (e.g., plastic) skyrocketed. This led to a greater demand for cost cutting and increased production efficiency in the plant and delayed workers callbacks.

3 *Discrimination Problems.* A year ago, a female worker on the production line applied for a job as materials handler. Since the job would have required her to lift boxes of finished products weighing up to 60 pounds, Don turned down the application explaining that, in his opinion, a woman would not be able to handle the job. Much to Don's surprise, the woman filed a charge of discrimination against the company. Although the case never went to court, the company's top management made an agreement with federal officials and awarded the woman the job with back pay. Today, the woman is on the job and performing poorly. Don feels his hands are tied and that he has to accept the poor performance.

4 *Safety Problems.* Several employees within the plant, including one of Don's workers, have filed complaints with federal agencies about working conditions at the plant. Most of the complaints concern the chemicals released into the air by the foam rubber production process. The workers say that they frequently get sore throats at work. Don has also noticed this but does not feel it is harmful. At any rate, a number of state and federal officials have been sampling the air in the plant. Workers have been told by management to wear face masks, but Don has had difficulty enforcing this rule.

5 *Production Planning.* Another major concern is the way production is scheduled. Last week there was almost nothing to do and Don had to keep pushing the workers to do menial tasks such as cleaning the conveyor belt, sweeping the floor, and painting the metal housings. Yet the week before, he had extreme difficulty meeting the production schedule, and some of the workers put in almost sixteen hours of overtime. It seemed ridiculous.

6 *Paperwork.* Every day Don runs through a maze of paperwork: daily and weekly time-card reports; reports on materials received; amount of scrap, finished product, and inventory. This he can understand. But the many other incidental reports do not make sense to Don. For example, every time a worker is hired or fired, there is a great deal of paperwork: interview forms, medical forms, compensation sheets, etc. Special forms are also required every time an employee has even a very minor injury, requests a leave of absence, or uses a company vehicle. It goes on and on. Some of the forms he fills out regularly and has little trouble with. Others he uses only once or twice a year, and he never really does learn how to fill them out. Much of this endless paperwork seems to be an unnecessary burden.

7 *Engineering Problems.* The production process is primarily determined by the engineering design and research department. Every month or so, they change the production process slightly. It might be a new tool for scraping residue off the molds, a change in the makeup of the foam rubber that fills the armrests, or a new kind of wax for the molds. Seldom, if ever, do the engineers consult Don on these changes, and they are often very disruptive to the entire department. Once a new foam rubber compound was put into the automatic fillers. It created quite a disturbance. The smell of the new compound was obnoxious, and the foam stuck to the molds and the outside of the armrests. This is only one example of a number of similar engineering foul-ups. Don avoids the engineering staff whenever possible.

8 *Other Problems.* In addition to these complaints, Don also enumerates a number of other factors which influence his ability to maintain a productive department: the factory down the street, which pays 50 cents more an hour; the local action group that is complaining about the pollution the factory emits; his boss, who plays politics with the engineering department; the austerity crisis that hits each December, causing him to count pens, papers, and elementary items such as gloves and putty knives; and the worsening of the community drug situation, which he believes may be causing some of the absenteeism and turnover. Don indicates that there are other problems as well.

■ LEARNING OBJECTIVES

After reading this chapter, you should have:

A knowledge of the changing attitudes toward work

An understanding of equal opportunity and other employment laws

An awareness of other relevant laws, such as consumer and environmental protection and safety and health laws

An appreciation of the impact of the economy

An awareness of technological change

An understanding of the more direct, internal environment, including private and public sectors, technology, size, and other variables

The introductory case pointed out that although the supervisor's job appears to be fairly simple at first, it becomes increasingly more complex as the constantly changing factors in the environment are considered. This portrait is the rule, not the exception. All supervisory jobs—regardless of whether they are in other manufacturing organizations, government, retail stores, or the military—involve similar problems and environmental influences.

The purpose of this chapter is to review and discuss some of these important external and internal environmental influences affecting the modern supervisor.

THE EXTERNAL ENVIRONMENT

The external environment affects the supervisor's organization and the way he or she performs on the job. Generally, these external forces are beyond the direct control of the organization and the individual supervisor, but many of the problems that face Don, the supervisor in the introductory discussion, stem from the external environment. Effective supervisors must have some understanding of these forces so that they may adapt their supervisory practices accordingly. Some of the most important forces of the external environment which the supervisor will have to contend with include societal values, laws and regulations, the economy, and technology.

Changing Values with Regard to Work

Today's employees are certainly different from those at the turn of the century. They are generally better educated, more inquisitive, and less willing to accept authoritarian patterns of supervision. Moreover, they are much more likely than in previous decades to be female and from a minority race. Some interesting statistics which help to characterize this new work force and the changing times are the following:

1 Eleven percent of today's work force is nonwhite.

2 Forty percent of the work force is female.

3 Almost 40 percent of all operating employees at the beginning of the decade had completed twelve to fifteen years of formal education. This figure is expected to increase to 55 percent by 1985.

4 By 1985, one out of every ten managers will be female.

5 One out of every fifteen blue-collar workers is black or Spanish-speaking.

6 Recent surveys of college students indicate that over 60 percent have tried marijuana at least once.

Value systems by ages of employees Apart from these statistics, there are also some historically significant factors which have influenced the nature and values of today's work force. Employees in their fifties grew up during the Great Depression of the 1930s. These people were often deprived—many of their basic needs went unfulfilled. Today, as workers, they want job security above all. To these workers, pensions, promotions based on seniority, and protection from arbitrary layoffs or dismissals are extremely important. They expect their supervisors to establish guidelines for conduct and behavior and to enforce them fairly.

People in their forties grew up during the 1940s, which, of course, were dominated by World War II. The war years were characterized by sacrifice and patriotism. As workers, these people have a moderate concern for security, but mostly they tend to want as much in the way of personal freedom and financial rewards as possible. They tend to feel that supervisors should allow them free rein while also ensuring that they will be rewarded for exceptional performance.

Younger employees, in their late twenties and their thirties, are products of the 1950s and 1960s. Most of these people had the benefit of the "good life" in America. Their parents all had pretty good-paying jobs; new products such as television sets, transistor radios, fancy automobiles, and so on were at the disposal of these young people. Through an odd turn of events, many members of this generation eventually turned their backs on their material blessings and became much more interested in pressing social concerns such as poverty, civil rights, and the Vietnam war. In today's work force, this generation of employees is vitally concerned with the quality of working life. To them, work must provide chances for meaningful interaction with peers as well as opportunities for growth and challenge. They feel that supervisors should make special efforts to see that all employees are getting the maximum opportunities for self-development.

Now, very young people who grew up during the late 1960s and early 1970s are taking their first jobs. Many of these young people experienced a period of "future shock" (too much change in too short a time) at a very impressionable age. To some of them, the end of the world—through nuclear attack, pollution, the population explosion, or world starvation—often seemed inevitable. Today, many characterize these employees as the "live now" generation, interested only in immediate gratification. These very young employees expect a supervisor to be understanding, but they are likely to reject attempts to try to get them more involved in their work than they wish to be.

The loss of trust Table 2-1 summarizes the various value systems discussed so far. More recently, the social environment has been dominated by Watergate and scandals of political bribery and highly questionable ethics among some of America's top leaders in business and government. These widely publicized incidents have contributed to the erosion of trust in business and government. Because the situation has become so critical, one large advertising agency has turned to using rank-and-file employees like car mechanics and janitors in its commercials, claiming that such people have more credibility than do corporation executives. Certainly, the forces operating today will have some long-range effects on our present and future work force.

The complexity of values Although classifying people's values by their age has some value, it must be emphasized that there are many other factors that enter into this. For example, many first-generation Americans today probably have values much closer to those of people raised during the Depression than of Americans who grew up in the 1950s and 1960s. Generally, their parents had a somewhat difficult time becoming acclimated to their new environment and were not able to give them many of the advantages enjoyed by other children their age. Similarly, a person growing up in an urban ghetto during the 1960s might be more conformist than socially oriented because of the deprivation he or she experienced while growing up. On the other hand, even during the Depression, there were those who had wealthy parents and all the advantages of life, and who may therefore have adopted socially oriented values. Thus, a value system cannot be assigned to a particular individual merely as a function of age.

By the same token, the economic conditions which individuals experience are only a partial explanation. Certainly there are people who have experienced severe economic difficulties in their formative years but who have nevertheless managed to develop value systems oriented either toward social consciousness or opportunities for personal advancement. Thus, the historical method of classifying value systems merely illustrates how these systems might develop for

TABLE 2-1

EMPLOYEES' VALUES

Value system	Developmental background	Values with regard to work	Expectations of the supervisor
Conformity	Depression of the thirties. Second-generation Americans' strong religious background. People growing up in a world of "hard knocks."	Value a steady job which insures against misfortune. Accept work with specified routines and expect promotions to be based on seniority.	Expect a strong leader who establishes and enforces work procedures and rules. Discipline should be consistent and should be based on established rules.
Opportunism	Grew up during the war years. Physical needs cared for but many sacrifices and delays for many of the better things of life.	See work as a challenging game through which many of the better things in life can be won. Like freedom to operate and experiment with different approaches.	Prefer to be left alone but expect the supervisor to be open-minded. Discipline should only be initiated when a worker clearly endangers the safety of coworkers.
Social consciousness	Grew up during fifties and sixties. Physical, social, and psychological needs all adequately provided for. Children of successful parents and well-educated.	See work as an opportunity to engage in meaningful interaction. Get along well with coworkers; concerned about the equity and fairness of the workplace.	Prefer a democratic style of supervision. Very opposed to arbitrary discipline and layoffs. Wish to be consulted on any changes affecting themselves and coworkers.
Future shock	Turbulent late sixties and seventies. Wants and needs provided but constant threats posed by the environment: racial disturbances, nuclear war, ecology, and overpopulation.	Work is a temporary necessity. Do not expect to stay in any one job too long. Expect immediate recognition, promotion, and pay increases. Live for today, not tomorrow.	Not concerned about the supervisor. See supervisor as temporary. Enjoy a good "rap" with supervisor about things in general, but do not take the supervisor too seriously.

some people. Each individual, with a unique combination of historical and personal experiences, will develop somewhat differently.

Chapter 12, "Understanding Employee Behavior," will go into a more detailed explanation of how personality characteristics and values are formed; for now, however, it is important to note that the supervisor is affected by the social values of his or her subordinates. These employee values compound the complexity of the supervisor's job. Each person must be treated somewhat differently by the supervisor depending on his or her social value system. Even when two employees seem to have had identical history, their values will often differ and they will respond very differently to supervision. From the human relations role perspective, this is a vital key to effective supervision: the continuing challenge of determining employee values and developing methods of supervision which will be compatible with these values.

THE LEGAL ENVIRONMENT

Constantly changing laws and regulations governing areas such as employment practices, safety, consumer liability, and environmental pollution have been a dominant part of the supervisors' external environment in recent years.

Equal Opportunity

Perhaps the most significant part of the legal environment affecting the supervisor involves the civil rights and equal opportunity aspects of employment. The purpose of these laws is to ensure that non-whites, females, the handicapped, older people, and Vietnam-era veterans are competing in the job market on an equal basis with white males. Some of the more important laws are these:

1 *The Equal Pay Act of 1963.* This law forbids an employer to pay different wages for the same jobs on the basis of sex. Thus, if women are doing the same job as men, they must be paid the same wages. The Wage and Hour Division of the Department of Labor has the responsibility for enforcing this law.

2 *The 1964 Civil Rights Act, Title VII, as Amended by the Equal Opportunity Act of 1972.* This law prohibits discrimination in employment because of race, color, sex, religion, or national origin. The Equal Employment Opportunity Commission (EEOC) is empowered to investigate unlawful employment practices.

3 *Age Discrimination in Employment Act.* This law forbids discrimination in employment with regard to anyone above 40 and below 65.
4 *Rehabilitation Act.* This law bans discrimination in the employment of the handicapped.
5 *Vietnam-Era Veterans Readjustment Act.* This act requires employers to take affirmative action in employing all veterans of the Vietnam war.

The impact of the above laws on employment practices has been profound. Many organizations have lost costly lawsuits because the tests administered during the selection or promotion process were found to be discriminatory and unrelated to the requirements of the job. Similarly, questions on application blanks and in interviews regarding the applicants' age, arrests/convictions, nationality, and provisions for child care have been found to be illegal. Some of the publicized awards provided by the courts include the following:
1 American Telephone and Telegraph was fined $15 million in backpay for females and minority males, with an additional $23 million awarded for raises.
2 Detroit Edison was fined $4 million and one of the unions in the company was fined $250,000.
3 Wheaton Glass Company was fined $100,000 in backpay and pay raises for female packers who had not received equal pay.

While such financial awards have been substantial, the courts have also demanded that changes be made in organizational policies and practices and all terms and conditions of employment. Areas of employment that have been affected include hiring, promotion, transfers, locker facilities, termination, dress codes, training, leaves of absence, hours of work, and even smoking privileges.

While at face value many of these practices may not appear to be discriminatory, the courts have ruled that the effect of organizational practices is much more important than their intent. Thus, a requirement that all operating employees must have high school diplomas may be determined to be discriminatory if this practice screens out a disproportionate number of minority applicants and if it can be shown that a high school diploma is not necessary for the performance of the job. Moreover, even if no overt discriminatory practices are found, organizations may still be found to be in violation of the law if the percentage of minority people and women on their work forces is substantially lower than the representation of these groups in the surrounding area. Thus, the external legal environment has a direct impact on the *way* in which an organization and the individual supervisor handles the employment function.

Other Employment Laws

In addition to the laws governing equal opportunity, there are many other laws that govern how the supervisor performs on the job. Among the more important ones are these:

1 The National Labor Relations Act, passed in 1935, which forbids discrimination by the employer to encourage or discourage employee participation in labor unions.

2 The Fair Labor Standards Act, which established minimum wages and standards for working hours and child labor.

3 The Welfare Pension and Disclosure Act, which establishes guidelines and reporting arrangements for retirement, health, and other types of insurance plans.

These laws, like the others governing equal opportunity employment practices, are constantly changing as their meanings are being reinterpreted and tested through court decisions. Obviously, the supervisor cannot possibly keep abreast of all these legalities. Thus, most of the larger organizations retain either legal or personnel specialists to aid in the interpretation of and compliance with these laws. Many times, these staff specialists may make recommendations with which supervisors do not agree. For example, they may restrict all operating managers from interviewing prospective job candidates. Similarly, this may require a highly documented appraisal of each employee's performance, which is reviewed and signed by the employee being appraised.

Although these recommendations sometimes appear to obstruct the performance of supervisors. compliance is often absolutely necessary according to the law. It should be understood that these staff specialists can help keep supervisors out of trouble; it is not their business to create problems and obstacles.

Consumer Protection Laws

A relatively new area of legislation deals with protecting consumers. This protection actually goes as far back as 1906, when the Food and Drug Administration was established, but it has received renewed attention recently, with the passage of the Truth in Lending and the Truth in Packaging acts. While these consumer protection laws do not directly affect many supervisors, they are indicative of the trend toward increased scrutiny of the internal affairs of organizations from the general public.

Environmental Protection

Finally, the increasing concern for the quality of the environment has generated two important pieces of legislation: the Water Quality Act and the National Air Quality Standards Act. As a result of these acts, organizations have had to change their methods of disposing of liquid, solid, and gaseous wastes.

Again, most supervisors will, as a rule, not have direct responsibilities for interpreting these laws or implementing actions for compliance. Yet because of increasing public awareness and concern, supervisors who are familiar with their organizations' efforts to comply with these regulations can provide important information to their employees and the public at large.

Safety and Health Laws and Regulations

The most important piece of legislation regulating the safety and health of employees is the Occupational Safety and Health Act (commonly known as OSHA), passed in 1970. This law empowers the Secretary of Labor to set standards for both safety and health. Included in the bill is the provision for on-site inspections and the levying of fines on employers who are not in compliance.

Unlike many of the other laws, this law directly affects a large number of supervisors. In most cases, management provides supervisors with specialized training in order to comply with those OSHA standards that are applicable in their areas of responsibility. Moreover, specific instruction will also be given on the organization's policies for responding to audits by OSHA officials. Again, it is important that supervisors comply with these recommendations, because failure to comply with OSHA standards can result in substantial fines and embarrassment to the employer.

ECONOMIC FORCES

Forces in the economy—such as inflation, unemployment, recession, and the energy crisis—affect the health and vitality of all organizations. When the economy is in a downturn and unemployment is high, companies producing goods and services that are not basic necessities usually suffer considerably. For example, manufacturers of cosmetics and recreational equipment and those that provide unessential services (e.g., photography studios, car washes) usually have considerable difficulty during an economic downturn. The demand for their products can be characterized as highly elastic (the quantity sold is greatly affected by the price), with the demand increasing when people have more "extra money" and decreasing when things are tight. On the other hand, organizations providing essential services (e.g., hospitals, electric and gas utilities, grocery stores) do not suffer as much. Their demand is inelastic (the quantity sold is not greatly affected by the price). Regardless of people's economic circumstances, they still need and will continue to buy the essential goods or services. Thus, these latter types of organizations have the advantage of being able to pass their increased costs of doing business on to their customers without experiencing a decrease in the demand for their products. However, in recent years, when economic conditions have been sufficiently severe, even these companies have been experiencing some difficulties. Recently, consumer activism has been directed against the electric and gas utilities, the oil industry, and the health-care industries for price gouging and inefficiency. This shows that no organization is immune from the scrutiny of an increasingly active consuming public.

At present, it appears that many of the economic problems facing business organizations will continue into the foreseeable future. The costs of energy in the forms of electricity, natural gas, petroleum, and nuclear fuel give every indication of continuing to rise sharply in the coming years. As a result, organizations requiring large expenditures of energy in order to produce products and services will continue to experience severe economic problems. Even though a national policy on energy is anticipated, it appears unlikely that the dramatic trend toward increasing energy costs will be reversed.

In addition to energy, the costs of basic raw materials—such as wood and paper and basic minerals such as lead, zinc, tin, copper, and iron ore—are expected to continue to increase as these limited resources become scarcer. Thus, unless the use of these resources is carefully controlled, continual price increases are inevitable. Of course, as the basic costs rise, it is likely that inflation will continue. Organizations which are not able to anticipate these price increases and pass them on will suffer severe economic consequences. A recent example of the failure to pass on price increases can be found in the paint industry. As the cost of lead pigments, turpentine, and other raw materials for paint increased dramatically, many paint companies were reluctant to increase their prices. As a result, paints were being sold beneath the combined cost of production and raw materials, and many companies experienced severe economic setbacks. Those that increased their prices in response to the costs of their raw materials suffered through a period of reduced sales, but they eventually emerged as financially solvent. Those companies that refused to increase their prices often worked their way into bankruptcy. In all organizations, competition in pricing will continue and pressure for cost reduction will become more intense. The supervisor often bears the brunt of an organization's drive to cut costs.

Another economic consideration is the cost of money or capital. As inflation continues to rise and interest on loans increases, the cost of capital becomes an increasingly important factor in doing business. For example, in the electric utility business today, it is not unusual for interest costs to amount to almost a third of the total cost of doing business. Thus, financial expertise in the ability to negotiate reasonable interest rates in the money market is becoming more critical to organizational growth and even survival.

TECHNOLOGICAL CHANGE

Technological change is occurring at a faster pace than ever before. In fact, it is estimated that the entire body of scientific knowledge doubles about every ten years. Similarly, applied technical capabilities are constantly increasing; for example, satellites relay television programs around the world, computers sign our paychecks, and we can cross the country by commercial airline in less than six hours. Thus the combination of technological knowledge and technology itself is advancing at an accelerated, future-shock pace.

Some rather interesting and amazing examples of technology are these:

The income from long-distance phone calls placed by computers is larger than that for such calls placed by people.

We have now been able to land a man on the moon and a vehicle on Mars.

One computer specialist claims that if advances in commercial transportation were as great as those in the computer industry, a person could fly around the world in less than two hours and at a cost of only $1.75.

Supervisors are living in a computer world. Computers produce production schedules, deposit paychecks in the bank, and decide when to change drill bits. Although most technological changes

Computer technology is becoming
increasingly sophisticated and is
having a direct impact on supervision
(Cornell Capa/Magnum Photos).

37

affecting the supervisor will be initiated by people outside his or her immediate situation (top management, outside consultants, or staff specialists), supervisors are usually responsible for implementing the new technology, which includes selling their people on its benefits and training them in its use. Therefore supervisors should try to keep up with impending technological developments wherever possible. In giving their people advance notice of technological change, supervisors will allow them to consider both the implied benefits and the disadvantages of such innovations. Imposing technology on people without warning can often have detrimental effects on performance and produce outright resistance. In one case, for example, a company switched from having the supervisors deliver paychecks directly to employees to direct deposit by a computer in a local bank. The employees reacted with extreme indignance and caused disruptions for several months. A little advance information and consultation from the supervisor could, in this case, have helped to avoid the problem.

THE INTERNAL ENVIRONMENT

The internal environment consists of the characteristics of the organization (hospital, office, store, manufacturing plant, military unit, public agency, educational institution, police department, etc.) which have a direct impact on all supervisors. Included would be such factors as whether the organization is public (i.e., nonprofit) or private (privately owned, with a profit motive); the type of technology that is used; the size of the organization; the competitive position in relation to other organizations; and the managment style or climate that dominates.

Public- or Private-Sector Environment

Whether an organization is in the public or private sector has a significant impact on the internal environment. In the past, the private sector has dominated, but recently the public sector has become increasingly important in our society. Everyone now realizes that there are more white-collar workers than blue-collar workers. Not so well known is the fact that most people now work for service industries, and that the number of professionals exceeds that of line business executives by two to one. Most of these white-collar and professional employees are found in the public sector. We now live in a postindustrial society. The top management of public-sector organizations is elected by the citizens within a particular voting district. City and state government are good examples. Private organizations, on the other hand, are owned by individual entrepreneurs or stockholders and constitute the majority of all business organizations. The management of these business firms is usually selected by a board of directors, which, in turn, is selected by the stockholders. Ford Motor Company, Gulf Oil, and the local machine shop are all examples of privately held companies.

Within the private sector, organizations can be broadly characterized as either manufacturing or service organizations. Manufacturing organizations produce tangible products such as cars, furniture, or plumbing fixtures. Service organizations provide intangible services such as life insurance, health care, merchandise, and transportation.

Public-sector organizations are primarily service-oriented. Examples of public-sector services includes education, defense, welfare, licensing of automobiles, provisions for recreational facilities, garbage removal, maintenance of roads, drug and alcohol rehabilitation programs, social security, and systems of criminal justice. Each of these services is generally dependent on taxes, which come from the public.

Public officials are elected on the basis of the quality or kind of service they promise to provide to the public. The public then judges their ability to deliver during their term in office. If the people do not believe they are getting the most for their tax dollars, different officials are elected and the emphasis on programs shifts. This is perhaps the greatest challenge to supervisors and employees working in public-sector organizations: the constant changes and shifts in emphasis in the nature of the programs for which they are responsible. Supervisors in public organizations must be constantly aware of changes in public sentiment. They have to be extremely careful not to offend the public and must live with the constant realization that their organizations' plans and goals will constantly change with changes in public sentiment and the election of new officials. These supervisors in the public sector have the constant responsibility of gauging the political environment and keeping their people informed on possible changes. Those who are astute at assessing this ever-changing environment are able to survive and adapt their programs to whatever changes may arise.

Private-sector firms have the advantage of greater continuity and an agreed-upon overall objective: profit. They are unlike organizations in the public sector in that the goals and tenure of their top managements and their stockholders are usually fairly stable, and their supervisors usually have a reasonable time in which to develop and achieve the firm's goals. In the private sector, supervisors are supposedly judged on their ability to achieve established, profit-related goals, although they generally have little latitude in selecting the goals, objectives, and specific programs and tasks which they will supervise.

Private-sector organizations are also markedly influenced by competition. Companies are successful only to the extent that they can provide a product or service at a lower price and of better quality than that which the competition can offer. This competitive environment provides some objective yardsticks (costs, sales volume, and eventually profit) by which private-sector supervision and management can be objectively measured. Such quantitative measures are not yet in existence in the public sector. However, with the increasing demand for accountability, such measures are beginning to be developed in all public-sector organizations.

Organizational Technology

Many organizations have a knowledge-based technology; today, these are becoming increasingly dominant in our future-shock society. However, more traditional organizational technologies can be classified as craft, assembly, and process.

Craft technology Under a craft system of technology, employees must possess a relatively high level of skill and are largely responsible for the total end product or service. Machinists, medical technicians, electricians, bricklayers, welders, nurses, chefs, police detectives, sellers of insurance, people who do drafting, and rehabilitation counselors are examples of craft workers. Each of them has a particular skill or ability which is applied to produce an end result. Generally, these workers consider themselves professionals and do not require close supervision. They need to know what is required— the results expected—but they generally prefer to achieve them in their own way.

Mass-production technology The second kind of technology is characterized by the assembly line. Here the jobs are highly simplified and broken down into direct parts for mass production. Usually, the jobs are interdependent, with one department producing the outputs that will be used as the raw materials for another department. Examples of organizations having an assembly line, mass-production technology can be found in the automobile, meat-packing, electronics, and furniture industries.

Because of the highly specialized nature of the jobs (e.g., installing a given bolt on part after part, all day long, or performing a very simple procedure time after time) and the interdependencies inherent in assembly-line technology, there are many problems for the supervisor. The high degree of specialization leads to boredom and the so-called "blue-collar blues" that plague assembly-line supervisors, and the interdependent nature of this technology leads to conflicts. An example of the latter problem is that of the supervisor described at the beginning of the chapter. His assembly-line workers were dependent upon the materials handlers to provide raw materials and remove finished goods. If the materials handler did not do the job correctly, the productivity of the workers on the entire line would suffer. A breakdown in any of the jobs in an assembly-line process has a fairly direct impact within the given department; it also, of course, affects the other departments in the organization. This characteristic of assembly-line technology—coupled with the highly specialized, routine nature of the jobs—is considered by many organizational psychologists to be the root of the conflict and dissatisfaction common among assembly-line operators. Motivating, stimulating, and supervising employees in an assembly-line type of technological environment can be one of the most difficult and challenging jobs in supervision.

Process technology A process technology is characterized by highly automated systems which refine or change raw materials into a finished good through a process flow. Examples are oil refineries, chemical companies, waterworks, electric utilities, canneries, and breweries. Because the process for producing the end product is usually highly automated and technologically sophisticated, most of the employees possess high levels of skill. For example, a high proportion of the employees in a nuclear generating plant are nuclear, electrical, mechanical, or environmental engineers, and the remaining employees are highly skilled craftspeople.

The main function of most of the employees is the maintenance of an automated system. When problems do arise, they are frequently fairly sophisticated and challenging. Because of this, motivation is less of a problem in process industries than in assembly-line industries. Moreover, because of the relatively small payroll as compared to the plant investment, the employees can usually be paid well without any great impact on the cost of doing business. The supervisor's job within such companies is not usually as tedious as in others. When the plant is operating smoothly, the workers are on a relatively lax schedule. However, when problems arise, they are prepared and can provide the immediate attention which is required. In process-technology types of organizations, the supervisor often serves much more as a lead technician and teacher/coach than a taskmaster.

The different types of technological environment lead to different types of supervisory styles and techniques for effectiveness. This is a basic premise of the contingency role of supervision, discussed in the last chapter. Chapter 16, "Leading Employees," will go into the details of contingency patterns of leadership.

Organizational Size

The size of the organization is an aspect of the internal environment that is important to supervisors. Large organizations (with some 1,500 or more employees) usually specialize and departmentalize many functions which were traditionally the territory of supervisors. For example, many supervisors in large organizations will not see their new employees until the first day the employees report for work. The employment interviewing, selection, and placement process will all have taken place in the personnel department. This procedure ensures that the selection of new employees is within legal guidelines and is based on objective standards rather than the personal biases of supervisors. In addition, many other phases of the supervisor's job will be monitored or controlled by other functions. Some representative areas that are handled by functional or staff specialists in large organizations include the following:

1 *Promotions, transfers,* and *raises* will frequently be monitored and approved by upper-level management, personnel specialists, and union officials.

2 *Planning* and *scheduling* of production or services will often be provided by upper management or a department such as engineering with the specific responsibilities for this function.

3 *Job design, work methods,* and *procedures* will frequently be regulated by an engineering department. Deviations from suggested procedures may require the approval of this department.

4 *Quality control* may be assigned to a special department which has the function of monitoring the quality of goods or services produced.
5 *Purchasing* of materials usually must be approved by an upper level manager and/or a member of the purchasing department.
6 The use of new procedures or materials will often be determined by a *research and development* function. This group must be consulted if any deviation from suggested procedures is attempted.
7 A *safety* department will usually be responsible for ensuring that all operations are in compliance with federal and state laws. The safety director will have the authority to require changes in operations if safety hazards are identified.
8 If the organization is unionized, then the *labor relations* function, concerned with union-management relations, will involve a designated representative of management and a corresponding union official. Management's labor relations specialist will also become involved when grievances are filed.
9 Frequently at least part of the *training* of employees will be done by professional trainers. The supervisor, however, will usually have input into the content of the training programs.

The rationale for taking these functions away from supervisors is that each one of them calls for specialized skills or expertise if it is to be performed effectively. For example, a specialized purchasing function has the advantage of comparing quality and price for even small items like gloves. If, by buying an item like gloves in quantity, the company can save 25 cents per pair, it will be able to realize a savings of $350 on 1,400 pairs. The economics and purposes of these specialized functions, however, are rarely apparent to the individual supervisor, who may need the gloves for the workers right away and cannot wait for the purchasing order to be delivered. Yet regardless of the many complications that may arise when functions become specialized, more and more functions are of necessity assigned to staff specialists as organizations become larger.

Rather than always diminishing the importance of supervision, specialization can actually magnify its importance. Regardless of the number of responsibilities which are stripped away from supervisors, they still maintain the only direct link between the management of the organization and the operating employees who are getting the work done. They still have the ultimate responsibility for *implementing* the suggestions of the staff specialists. For example, if a new procedure is suggested by a safety expert, it will be implemented by the workers only if the supervisor cooperates and effectively communicates the new procedure to the employees. Thus, despite what may appear as encroachment on the supervisory function by staff specialists, supervisors still maintain their responsibilities of planning, directing, and controlling work assignments as well as leadership and motivation of their work groups. The staff functions are only effective when the supervisors will need to use the recommendations of staff personnel if they are to function at their maximum capability.

The supervisors in smaller organizations usually have a much wider range of responsibilities than their counterparts in large organizations. For example, a person supervising a gas station will usually be the final authority for hiring, firing, purchasing tools, training workers, and seeing to it that the work is done in a safe manner. The advantage here is that supervisors have much more direct control over their employees. They are performing both supervisory and staff functions and can create a very favorable work environment, free of red tape, if they perform with competence in each area. However, because the supervisor's time, skills, and priorities are limited, it often occurs that some areas are neglected. For example, if the supervisor in the gas station did not place a high priority on safety and the company did not carry the proper disability insurance, this supervisor could be found liable for a disability injury of one of the employees.

Similarly, if the supervisor of a small restaurant did not consider health and sanitation as high-priority matters, public health officials might revoke the restaurant's license and the supervisor would be blamed for the forced closing of the restaurant. Thus, even though a supervisor may be extremely competent in most areas, a breakdown in any of the others may become critical to the very survival of his or her organization. Moreover, as each of the peripheral functions of supervision become more complicated and legislated, it becomes much more likely that costly mistakes will, in fact, be made. On the positive side, a supervisor in a small organization finds it much easier to take corrective action when problem areas are identified.

Research has generally demonstrated that there are relationships between the size of an organization and the satisfaction, turnover, and absenteeism among its employees. Not so clear is the direction that these relationships take. Although there are mixed results, most studies show that employees are more satisfied and there is less turnover and absenteeism in smaller organizations. The exceptions to these findings are usually explained if size is considered in terms of the number of people under a supervisor rather than the total number of people in the organization. Even in extremely large organizations, satisfaction may be high and turnover and absentee-ism low if the immediate supervisory groups are small. However, there are still a number of exceptions to this theory, and it is still not entirely clear which specific factor or combination of factors contrib-utes to absenteeism, turnover, and satisfaction.

Other Aspects of the Internal Environment

This discussion does not, of course, begin to include all the factors which contribute to the internal climate of an organization. Below is a partial list of other factors that may be considered critical. However, because of the lack of research, it is not clear what their specific effects on supervision may be. Thus, these factors are presented with the full realization that further research is needed to determine their impact on supervision more precisely.

1 *Goals.* It is commonly agreed that the goal of all private organiza-tions is profit. Not so clear are the goals of organizations in the public sector. Moreover, even in profit-oriented organizations in the private sector, there are often other implicit goals such as prestige, success, status, the provision of unique services, or personal growth and development. Each organization (private or public) will have a differ-ent mix of goals and priorities, and many of the differences in the internal environment can be explained in terms of these goals. Some contrasts which emphasize the influence of goals on the internal environment might be *(a)* an army boot camp versus a seminary; *(b)* a hospital versus a steel mill; *(c)* an alcoholism rehabilitation center versus a prison; and *(d)* a PTA versus a local citizens' group formed to stop a new highway. Thus, while the exact influence of different types of goals cannot be entirely specified, it is certain that the varying goals do influence the internal environment within organizations and that this, in turn, affects supervisors and the way they do their jobs.

2 *Time Perspective.* The time perspective of an organization can also be important to the internal environment. For instance, a cut-rate retail organization which buys merchandise in bulk quantities and sells at reduced rates is most often oriented toward a small, short-term profit. It treats its customers much differently than an exclusive retail organization like Neiman-Marcus or Tiffany's, which attempts to cultivate a clientele that will provide patronage over an extended period of time. Similarly, a small electronics firm manufacturing CB radios usually has a much shorter time orientation and treats its employees much differently than a company producing sophisticated biomedical equipment that is trying to build a reputation in the medical field. It is generally agreed that organizations oriented toward the longer time spans produce a climate that is more conducive to employee satisfaction.

3 *Product or Service.* The product or service an organization produces may also influence the internal environment. For example, employees of a physical rehabilitation center will usually have a much different attitude toward their jobs and the service they provide than persons employed in garbage collection. Similarly, in an organization producing pacemakers for individuals with heart conditions, the attitude of workers toward quality control will probably be more favorable than it would be if they were producing vacuum cleaners.

4 *Management Style.* The style of management in an organization can vary on a continuum from very directive/authoritarian to very participative/democratic. It is generally thought that these styles are a significant factor of the internal environment. An example can be found in a company that produces mirrors for the automobile manufacturers. Producing mirrors could be a very tedious, typical assembly-line process. However, within this company, no distinctions are made between management and employees. All employees have equal status. Within departments, decisions to hire, promote, and grant salary increases are almost completely democratic, with all participating on an equal basis. Outsiders have great difficulty in imagining a company that can function without a designated management. However, this company claims that, through the years, its people have become more and more responsible and efficient. In fact, this company's competition is almost nonexistent because it has become so efficient at producing the highest-quality mirrors at the lowest possible prices. At least one feature that helps to account for this company's success it that the employees' wages are directly dependent on the success of the company. There are also many other notable examples of organizations which have had great success with the participative style (e.g., Lincoln Electric Corporation in Cleveland, Ohio; Texas Instruments; and a dog-food processing factory in the General Foods system, located in Topeka, Kansas). Within these companies, the opportunity for employees to participate in the decision-making processes is seen as one of the most important determinants of the organizational environment.

5 *Pride and Tradition.* Certainly the public's regard for an organization and its products influences the environment within the organization. Employees of companies which are leaders in their fields often feel a pride in their work or profession that contributes to a favorable organizational environment. Employees in a top-quality image organization (e.g., Rolls-Royce or Harvard University) probably have a different internal environment than those in organizations having a negative public image. Similarly, a family-owned diner which has established a tradition of quick service and home cooking over a number of decades will usually have a much different atmosphere than a newly established, franchised, fast-service restaurant.

6 *Status.* Many organizations discriminate among employees and among managers on the basis of their placement within the organizational hierarchy. There may be differences in parking facilities, locker rooms, bathrooms, lunchrooms, fringe benefits, and privileges—all depending on organizational status. Similarly, depending upon a supervisor or manager's rank within the organizational hierarchy, they may be assigned different types of stationery, company cars, office furniture, office space, and expense-account privileges. The general feeling is that employees at the bottom of the status hierarchy are frequently dissatisfied, while satisfaction increases along with increased status.

7 *Physical Environment.* The physical layout will similarly influence the organizational environment. In some organizations, there is very little consideration even for basic human needs. Rest rooms and cafeterias may be inconveniently located; locker rooms may be filthy; and even work stations may be constructed in aversive ways, with chairs that are uncomfortable or with physical characteristics that force employees into unnatural working positions. In short, it may become very apparent to employees that the physical facilities were constructed with only economic factors in mind, ignoring basic human needs. Of course, employees usually reciprocate this attitude, creating an atmosphere which is continuously distrustful of management. On the other hand, where the physical conditions of the workplace are arranged with workers' needs in mind, the resulting environment is usually much more favorable.

Again, this list is only partially complete. Additionally, no single factor can be cited as being the most critical to the internal environment. Rather, it is the unique combination of all these factors, as well as many others not mentioned, that goes into the makeup of the internal environment.

In the subsequent chapters of this book, present or future supervisors will have to choose those ideas, concepts, and techniques which make the most sense for their individual situations. Some of the concepts will prove worthwhile, others will not. The supervisor must take a contingency approach based on the external and internal environmental factors that have been discussed in this chapter.

■ KEY WORDS AND CONCEPTS

Elastic demand
Inelastic demand
OSHA
Public/private sector
EEOC
Craft technology
Mass-production technology
Process technology

■ PRACTICAL EXERCISES

(These can be performed by individuals or by groups.)
1 List and discuss the key factors in the external environment which affect the organization in which your class is being conducted. Discuss how these external factors have changed over the last few years and how these changes affect the organization in question.
2 List and discuss the various types of status symbols which characterize the organization in which your class is being conducted. Do these status symbols serve any useful purpose?
3 Examine the internal environment of an organization in which you have recently worked or are currently working. Identify specific variables such as public/private, technology, size, goals, product, management style, tradition, and physical environment. What implications do these factors have on the type of supervision that takes place? Explain.

■ DISCUSSION INCIDENTS

Harry Marlow was enrolled in a supervision course. Since Harry wanted to be a supervisor, he felt that this course would be directly relevant to giving him the answers on how to be a good supervisor. About the second class period, the instructor said, "supervisors must realize they operate in an extremely complex environment. Things outside the walls of the organization will indirectly and in many cases directly affect the way supervisors perform." The instructor then started to discuss the legal environment of supervisors. Harry became upset. He said to himself, "Here we go again, another course on theory. What I want is to be a good supervisor, and this guy starts telling us about the laws."

1 Is Harry's reasoning correct? Do supervisors have to have knowledge of the external environment to be effective? Why or why not?

2 Besides the law, what other things will this instructor discuss? Are these important to good supervision?

Mary Henry had just read the chapter called "The Supervisor's Environment" for her class in supervision. She was having coffee with a fellow student at the hospital where they worked and said, "Jane, I can see how the environment, both external and internal, is important to business firms, but I don't see how it really affects the supervision of a hospital. We are pretty much doing our own thing when it comes to patient care. Sure, there are laws and so forth, but who is going to tell us from the outside what is the best way to accomplish our goals? I think that studying the environment is a waste of time for those of us who work in nonbusiness organizations."

1 Do you agree with Mary?

2 What are some examples of the environmental impact on supervisors in a hospital setting? In other nonbusiness organizations?

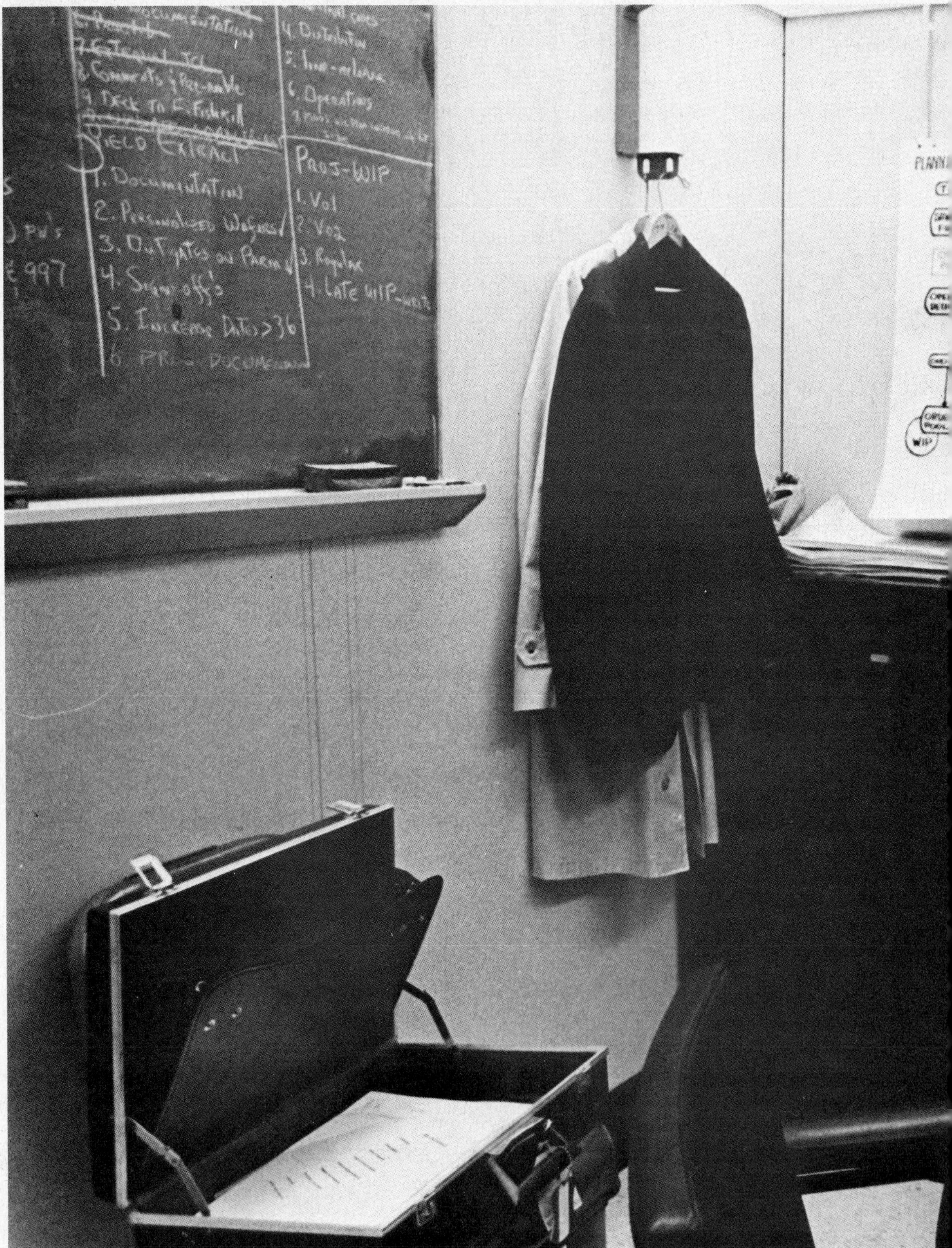

(Freelance Photo Guild)

PART²

BASIC ELEMENTS
OF EFFECTIVE SUPERVISION

PLANNING THE WORK

③ CHAPTER

Frank Powers has just been promoted to supervisor of accounts receivable for a medium-sized department store. He knew the job inside and out, having been head clerk for eight years. Right now he was at home discussing the new job with his wife, Karen. In particular, he was questioning his first assignment: "The first thing the boss did was tell me to establish plans and set goals for the coming year. That would be okay if I was in sales or some area where I could control the numbers. But on my job, I really don't have any control over our work. We do everything on a demand basis, and planning makes almost no sense at all." His wife replied, "Frank, I appreciate your concern, but isn't that the difference between being a clerk and being the supervisor?" Frank shook his head slowly and said, "I guess you're right. I sure wish I knew more about exactly what is meant by 'planning' and had some guidelines I could follow to get this assignment done effectively."

After reading this chapter, you should have:

A realistic and concrete conceptual framework for the planning process

An understanding and appreciation of the need for long-range planning

The techniques and skills necessary for utilizing and interpreting long-range planning methods such as MBO, budgeting, network planning, and statistical planning

An understanding and appreciation of short-range planning

The techniques and skills for short-range planning, such as planning checklists, Gantt charts, and real-time systems

An awareness of all of the available planning options that will lead to effective performance

THE NATURE OF THE PLANNING PROCESS

Planning is a basic supervisory function. It is a process whereby a future state is compared with the present one and specific steps are formulated and selected to achieve the future state. For example, a restaurant owner may project a goal of a 15 percent growth in sales and a 10 percent increase in profit for the coming year. To achieve this goal, a wide range of alternatives will be considered (e.g., changing the menu, expanding kitchen and/or dining facilities, increasing the number of employees, changing the decor of the dining area, increasing the amount of advertising, changing menu prices, and possibly even changing location). Although several combinations of these possible actions may achieve the stated goals, there are also some combinations that will definitely not work. Effective planning would involve evaluating each possible action carefully with a view of its impact on all other factors. The planner must call on all the experience gained in the restaurant business to eventually determine a feasible set of action plans that will result in goal attainment. Finally, once a workable set of action plans has been determined, the planner must follow through. The plans must be communicated to the employees and resources must be allocated to make the necessary changes. Throughout the year, the plan must be continually reassessed and modified to make sure that the projected goals are in fact being achieved.

A similar example, but with a shorter time frame, can be used for a manufacturing supervisor. At the beginning of the week, the supervisor receives a production schedule indicating that the section must produce 600 units of product X, 450 units of product Y, and 350 units of product Z by the end of the week. The supervisor then figures out the combination of workers, machines, and materials that will be needed to meet this goal. After considering a number of alternatives, the supervisor finally arrives at a plan which specifies the workers that will be assigned to particular tasks, machines, and materials. If all goes well, the production goals for the week will be achieved.

Inherent in the definition of planning and the above examples are the following aspects of the planning process:

1 *Goal Setting.* People need something to shoot for. Countless studies have clearly demonstrated that when goals are challenging and acceptable, people are motivated to achieve them. Similarly, when goals are unrealistic or fail to challenge a person's skills and abilities, they are frequently not attained. Increasing sales in the restaurant and boosting profit by 50 percent—or an absolutely unrealistic schedule in the production example—would have defeated the entire purpose of planning for both the restaurant owner and the production supervisor.

2 *Making Measurements and Establishing Standards.* Plans, goals, and activities should always be stated in terms that are observable and measurable. This requirement of the planning process serves several functions. First, it is vital to the initial phase of comparing the present state with a desired future state. Only when these conditions can be specified can the difference between the two be identified and recorded and can goals be outlined. Similarly, there can be consensus on the meaning of goals and the direction toward achieving them only when the goals are objectively defined. Finally, the standard of measurement serves both a control and a feedback function. Both supervisors and employees in general are able to evaluate their progress when objective standards have been specified. Particular techniques for measurement will be presented and discussed in the following pages.

3 *Maintaining a Time Perspective.* All plans are designed to provide guidance through some time period. Short-range day-to-day and week-to-week plans are frequently called *operational,* because they emphasize the immediate activities which must be performed. Long-range plans spanning a year or more are usually called *strategic* plans, because they identify goals and objectives which are critical to the health and survival of the entire organization. This distinction, of course, is somewhat artificial. As strategic plans approach implementation, they are reduced to operational day-to-day activities. Therefore, most planning procedures such as MBO (management by objectives, which is explained later) and budgeting have elements of both strategic and operational planning. But regardless of the type of plan, the specific time periods are specified and serve as objective goals for the planner and participants.

4 *Specifying Alternatives.* As shown in the examples, there is a wide range and many combinations of variables which may affect the achievement of a goal. Many experts believe that the planner's ability to specify the entire range of alternatives is the most important aspect of the planning process. According to this viewpoint, planners must be creative, open-minded, and willing to consider all options. Creative techniques such as brainstorming (discussed in Chapter 13) emphasize this aspect of the planning process.

5 *Analyzing Alternatives.* This is another critical stage in the planning process. Here all the variables and alternatives which have been defined are carefully weighed to determine some combination or subset which will lead to the achievement of the desired future state. Computers, mathematical techniques, and various decision-making methods such as Delphi (which will be reviewed in Chapter 13) can all aid in this process. Yet even with these sophisticated aids, the seasoned and rational judgment of the experienced decision maker is still a necessary component of this process.

6 *Elaborating Plans and Specifying Details.* Strategic, long-range plans are usually specified in global terms at the top level of an organization. However, as they filter down to the operational levels, they become much more specific and detailed. For example, a general manager may state the goal of increasing sales by 15 percent in the coming year. The next level (i.e., the major departments) may define this goal in terms of specific increased levels of production, human resources, or advertising. At the lowest operating level, the salesperson may define the goal in terms of increasing the sales calls from eighteen to thirty-three per week. Thus, effective plans are intertwined at all levels and become much more specific as one goes down the organization ladder.

7 *Ensuring Participation.* Carrying out the plan requires the cooperation and participation of those members of the organization who are affected by it. Several methods and philosophies of planning, such as MBO, emphasize the need for participation throughout the planning process (i.e., goal setting, defining alternatives, evaluating alternatives, and implementing the plan). There is ample research to demonstrate that both the quality of the plans attained and the motivation to achieve these plans increase when employees participate in the planning process.

8 *Maintaining Communication.* Only when organizational goals and the plans to achieve them are effectively communicated to those involved can they be achieved. Yet many plans are still relegated to filing cabinets or placed under lock and key. Similarly, there are many planning departments in large organizations which function as autonomous units without any communication links to the operating units. In all cases, the operating units should know how the data they furnish to the planning process are utilized. Similarly, they should receive a copy of the plans which are eventually based on the data they have provided. Effective planning is a down-to-earth process that can be communicated and understood at all levels of the organization.

9 *Organizing.* Our description of the planning process so far has carried the implication, throughout, that all activities within the organization are carried out in a rational and organized fashion. Each activity is evaluated to determine its effect on the organization's goals—or, more simply, all activities are planned. If the restaurant owner did not plan and changed the menu, prices, or location in a haphazard fashion, it is very likely that the business would not succeed. Similarly, the idea behind any planning process is the organization of the activities into an integrated and unified pattern that guides everyone toward the desired objectives.

10 *Implementing.* Plans are useless unless they are followed. The plan must have the complete and total support of top management, supervision, and the employees carrying it out. The plan must be viewed as an integral part of everyone's job if it is to be implemented. Provided that the users have had adequate input into all phases of the plan, it will naturally follow that the goals, objectives, and activities which are specified in the plan are viewed by the participants as their operational goals.

11 *Following Up.* Every plan must have provisions for periodic follow-up and review. As plans become more specific, measurable guideposts for achievement should be indicated so that individuals know where they are in relation to achieving the overall objectives. Where deviations are noted, alternative courses of action may be warranted or the overall goals may be modified. Again, this process will be achieved only when the plan is considered an important part of the job.

12 *Providing for Flexibility.* Closely related to follow-up is the concept of flexibility. As the saying goes, "The best laid plans of mice and men ofttimes go astray." Deviations from the plan should be expected and anticipated. Plans were never made to be "chiseled in stone."

Rather, they must be viewed as dynamic and ever-changing. Even the major objectives and goals for an entire organization must be viewed as flexible and subject to change when warranted by circumstances and conditions. Thus, planning is not a process with a defined beginning and end but a *continuing* process which is part of the supervisor's everyday responsibilities.

13 *Planning for Unpredictable Contingencies.* Because planning hinges on the future, it is subject to all the hazards of any type of forecasting procedure. These unpredictable factors include *(a)* lack of sufficient information or data; *(b)* unprecedented changes in such supply or demand characteristics as personnel, raw materials, or products; *(c)* suboptimization of planning efforts where subunits within the organization attempt to optimize unit goals at the expense of overall goals; *(d)* lack of time perspective, where organization members attempt to maximize short-term goals at the expense of long-term objectives; and *(e)* synergism, which refers to the unique and unanticipated combination of any of the above variables into conditions that are unanticipated. However, even though these factors may markedly affect supervisory plans, their impact is much more critical when no attempt has been made to assess them. The planning process helps supervisors to anticipate and account for these variables rather than react to them helplessly.

The remainder of this chapter will be devoted to the presentation and discussion of specific techniques and methods that will be of help to the supervisor in planning. For ease of discussion, the planning techniques are categorized into two areas: (1) long-range strategic planning and (2) short-range operational planning. However, as noted in the introductory comments, this classification is somewhat artificial, because any complete planning technique encompasses all three areas. Finally, it should be emphasized that supervisors have the major responsibility for determining and selecting the techniques that are most useful for their particular situations. Some of the techniques may not be viewed as immediately applicable, but knowledge of a particular technique may be critical to the supervisor's understanding and interpretation of the plans originating from other areas of the organization.

LONG-RANGE PLANNING

The planning approaches described in this section usually encompass time spans of a year or more. They are most frequently

Planning is a necessary function of
effective supervision (Ray Ellis
from Rapho/Photo Researchers, Inc.).

implemented by the top levels of the organization and are designed to
integrate the activities of each subunit for coordinated goal achievement. Sometimes supervisors are not directly included in the design
of these plans. However, at least within larger organizations, a basic
understanding of these systems is critical to the survival and success
of individual supervisors.

Budgets

Budgets are among the most important and common planning
devices for most organizations. Very simply, a budget is a systematic

statement of the financial resources required within a specified time period for a particular subunit of an organization. Although a budget may be presented in one lump sum, supervisors are most frequently required to itemize specific expenditures so that the spending can be better controlled. Common expenditure categories that are itemized include wages and salaries, equipment, maintenance, and raw materials. The actual format for the budget differs in almost every organization. Figure 3-1 shows a typical budget.

The budget serves two major functions. First, it allows the management of the organization to evaluate and assess the efficiency and contributions of each unit in the organization. Obviously, the areas receiving the highest expenditures are also expected to make the most significant contributions. Second and most important from the perspective of planning, budgets provide a pooled estimate of the organization's capital needs over a period of time. Accordingly the financial people in the organization can manage money to ensure that it will be available when needed. When budgets are overestimated, it can be extremely costly for the organization. Just as individuals must pay interest to finance automobiles and homes, so organizations must finance their needs through stocks, bonds, loans, and mortgages.

Accurate budgets become critical to the health and survival of organizations, and significant pressure is placed on supervisors and managers who exceed or overestimate their budget. These pressures, in turn, have created many curious but certainly not humorous games which are often played with budgets. For example, sometimes budgets are seemingly cut, say, 10 percent with no apparent justification. The affected supervisor learns this game quickly and subsequently overestimates his or her budget by at least 10 percent. This forces top management to redefine its rules and escalate cuts to, say, 20 percent. As the game continues, the overall organization becomes the big loser.

Another potential problem with budgets is that supervisors' salaries are sometimes tied to the size of their budgets. Thus, supervisors learn to strive for budget increases and see no rewards in budget- or cost-reduction programs. Some organizations, however, are beginning to provide substantial rewards and recognition for budget and cost reductions. Supervisors must attempt to cope with these potential problems with budgets because, regardless of some of the seemingly ridiculous things that go on, the budget will have a significant impact on their planning effectiveness and the organization's future fiscal health.

Item	Projected Cost	Actual Cost
Raw Materials		
1. No. 1 wire — 400 ft @ 20¢/ft	$ 800.00	
2. No. 2 wire — 10,000 ft @ 24¢/ft	2400.00	
3. No. 3 wire — 24,000 ft @ 11¢/ft	2640.00	
4. No. 4 wire — 20,000 ft @ 8¢/ft	1600.00	
5. No. 5 wire — 12,000 ft @ 7¢/ft	840.00	
6. No. 6 wire — 2,000 ft @ 23¢/ft	460.00	
7. Oil — 15 gal @ 2.10/gal	31.50	
Total	$ 8771.50	
Maintenance		
1. Routine maintenance — 20 hours @ $8/hr	$ 160.00	
2. Downtime maintenance — 40 hours @ $8/hr	320.00	
3. Special projects — 20 hours @ $8/hr	160.00	
Total	$ 640.00	
Wages and Salary		
1. Henry M. — 160 hr x 6.30	$ 1008.00	
2. Tony T. — 160 hr x 5.30	848.00	
3. Sue S. — 160 hr x 5.60	896.00	
4. Al R. — 160 hr x 7.00	1120.00	
5. Donna W. — 160 hr x 6.50	1040.00	
6. Glenn M. — 160 hr x 6.20	992.00	
7. Jack K. — 160 x 6.10	976.00	
8. Overtime — 40 hours @ average 6.14/hr	245.60	
Total	$ 7125.60	
Miscellaneous		
1. Gloves and work supplies	$ 50.00	
2. Office supplies	50.00	
Total	$ 100.00	
Grand total	$16,637.10	

FIGURE 3-1
A budget.

Management by Objectives

Management by objectives, or MBO, as it is commonly called, is a relatively recent and much popularized technique. Although MBO can be thought of as a total philosophy of management and incorporates all the supervisory functions, it is also a planning tool. Despite the mystique surrounding it, MBO is really quite simple. Very briefly, MBO can be defined as setting of objectives and appraising them by results. The objective-setting part of MBO is what ties most closely into planning. Ideally, the objective-setting process starts at the top level of the organization and is defined in terms of results. The managers at the next level of the organization then set their objectives in line with the overall objectives. The process continues in this way throughout all levels of the organization. As shown in Figure 3-2, each manager becomes a linking pin, and the entire organization and management structure is linked together by objectives that are all pointed upward toward the overall objectives of the organization.

Operating within this overall process of objective setting are several major characteristics of the MBO approach to planning:

1 *Specific Measures.* Each objective is stated in observable and measurable terms. Whenever possible, the objectives are quantified. For example, an objective may state that production will increase by 10 percent. When goals are difficult to quantify, they can often be stated in terms of tangible end results that are desired. For example, a supervisor may want to improve the competence and expertise of subordinates. This objective could be quantified by defining it in terms of conducting at least eight hours of training for ten subordinates during the year. Similarly, a supervisor who wants to improve employee attitudes may use turnover, absenteeism, grievance, or attitude-survey results statistics as specific benchmarks for measuring the attitudes.

2 *Results Orientation.* Besides being stated in measurable terms, the objectives are also always stated in terms of results rather than activities. Inherent within this results orientation is the idea that supervisors are free to develop their own strategies and utilize their personal styles in achieving the desired results.

3 *Role Clarity.* Through the process of setting objectives, each supervisor clearly identifies an area of responsibility and accountability. Under many traditional planning processes, it is difficult to pinpoint responsibility. With written statements of responsibility under an MBO approach, all accountabilities and responsibilities within the organization are clarified.

4 *Adaptability.* At the top level of an organization, objectives are usually more general and long range and are reviewed on a yearly basis. Thus, MBO provides strategic plans at top organizational levels. However, as the objectives filter through the organization, they are further defined and much more specific. For example, lower-level objectives could be set at six-month or even quarterly periods and may be considered more operational in nature.

5 *Feedback and Communication.* An MBO approach ensures both feedback and communication throughout the organization. Inherent in every MBO system are the objective-setting process, measurable

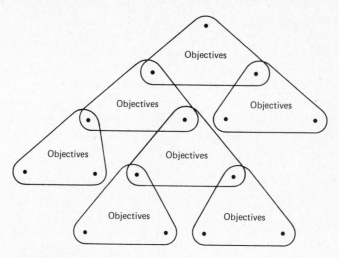

FIGURE 3-2
The MBO objective-setting process.

standards, and target dates for follow-up. Periodic reviews of progress are a natural part of the process and provide both upper-level management and supervisors with the information needed to ensure achievement of results. On the basis of the feedback, objectives may be modified or reordered, resources reallocated, or responsibilities redistributed. Obviously, this aspect of MBO shows that it is an important control device as well as being beneficial for effective planning.

6 *Participation.* Throughout the MBO process, participation and collaboration by supervisor and subordinate pairs at all levels is emphasized. Although upper-level organizational objectives are used as a basis for setting those at lower levels, the idea is that supervisors have a fairly wide range of freedom within the specified constraints. Sometimes, however, lower-level objectives may significantly alter upper-level objectives. In essence, MBO is a top-down–bottom-up system. Recent studies have clearly demonstrated that when individuals become meaningfully involved in setting their work objectives, they demonstrate increased commitment and motivation in achieving these objectives.

7 *Upward Perspective.* Within a MBO system, each participant's objectives are interlocked with the other objectives of the organization (see Figure 3-2). If desired, employees at even the lowest level of the organization should be able to trace the contribution of their objectives through each successive level. Thus, MBO provides participants with a systematic way of assessing the meaningfulness of their jobs in an upward and (it is hoped) unified direction.

8 *Top-Management Support.* The critical variable for the success of an MBO system, as with any other long-range planning mechanism, is the participation and support of top management. This support occurs within MBO because top management really initiates the entire process through its definition of major organizational objectives. Following the definition of these objectives, however, top management must maintain support for the system through its daily use in the planning and review of organizational activities.

Although MBO is usually viewed (as in the above discussion) as a process which incorporates the entire organization, it can be successfully implemented at any level downward. Thus, an individual supervisor could implement MBO in his or her particular department. In this case the first step would be setting overall objectives for the department. These would be set by the supervisor in conjunction with the key people in the department and sent to the next level for review and approval. After this set of overall departmental objectives was agreed upon, the supervisor would then begin the process with the next level in the department and work through successively lower levels until all members of the department had participated. An example of the type of form that the supervisor could use is shown in Figure 3-3. In the first column, the area of responsibility is identified. An example might be: "To ensure that a quality product is produced." In the second column, a specific objective is stated in terms of an observable and measurable standard of performance. For example: "Reduce scrap by 10 percent over the next fiscal year." The third column indicates specific actions that will be taken to achieve the objective, such as: *(a)* establish a daily tally of scrap rates, *(b)* provide a copy of specifications and tolerances for each job to the operators, *(c)* establish a weekly award for operators with the best production-to-scrap ratio, and *(d)* allow machine operators direct contact with maintenance personnel when machine breakdowns occur. The final column specifies the exact date on which it is expected that each of the action plans will be implemented and the overall objective will be accomplished.

Throughout this MBO process, the supervisor must recognize the contributions each of the participants makes to the plan and must remain flexible.

Area of responsibility	Quantitative objective	Action plan	Target date

FIGURE 3-3
MBO worksheet.

Network Planning

Network planning involves the charting of activities and accomplishments. The result is a graphic illustration of interdependent relationships. A number of variations of the network planning technique have emerged in recent years: program evaluation and review technique (PERT), critical path method (CPM), milestone control procedure (MCP), program evaluation procedure (PEP), and program and operations planning and scheduling (PROPS). However, regardless of the variant of the network method used, there are usually four major elements to the network planning method:

1 *Accomplishments.* The first step in network planning is the listing of all intermediate accomplishments or milestones which must be achieved to reach the final major accomplishment. For example, building a new office building will involve a number of accomplishments (e.g., contracts signed, building permits approved, foundation poured, pilings erected, walls completed, and so forth). Thus accomplishments are completed objectives which can be pointed to and do not in themselves consume time.

2 *Activities.* In order to achieve each accomplishment, work will have to be performed which will consume a definite period of time. For example, the pouring of concrete for a large office building may require several days, or a period of several months may pass until all building permits have been approved. Thus, activities indicate the nature of the work which must occur and the amount of time which must be assigned to the achievement of a particular accomplishment.

3 *Integration.* After each accomplishment has been listed and the activities associated with it have been assigned time estimates, a network is constructed showing interrelationships of all activities and accomplishments. An example of such a network is illustrated in Figure 3-4. The large circles with the numbers indicate accomplishments and the numbers on the lines between the circles indicate the estimated time needed to complete the activities that will lead to the goal. Reading the chart from left to right, the sequence of activities is apparent. The network also illustrates the interdependencies. For example, accomplishments 5 and 6 must be completed before 9 can be achieved. Another feature of the chart is that, by adding the activity times along each path, the completion times can be derived. The path highlighted by the heavy markings is the longest path in the network and takes 40 days to complete. It is called the critical path, because any delay on it will cause a delay in the completion date of the entire project. Similarly, if the times on the path at the bottom of the network are added, the total is 21 days. This is called the slack path, where any delay up to 19 days (40 − 21) will not affect the completion date of the project.

4 *Network Analysis.* After the network has been outlined and the slack and critical paths have been determined, the real work of the network analyst begins. Each of the slack paths should be analyzed to determine if any of the materials or resources can be shifted to the critical path to reduce activity times and bring the completion date of the project closer. Similarly, the critical path should be analyzed carefully to determine methods for reducing activity times. After this analysis, the network may be redrawn and activity-time estimates may be changed before the final network is agreed upon. Finally, it is the job of the supervisor using this approach to monitor activities through to the completion of the project. Particular attention is given to activities on the critical path to ensure their timely completion. Sometimes unscheduled delays occur and shift the critical path to another part of the network.

Traditionally, network analysis has been used for one-of-a-kind projects such as assembling large jetliners, erecting office and factory buildings, or installing computer systems. However, through the years, they have been adapted to many other applications. For

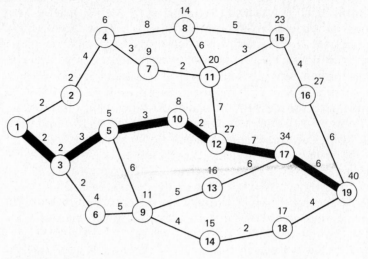

FIGURE 3-4
A complex network plan.

example, large customer-service organizations (in the utility industry, for example) use network planning programs to allocate personnel and equipment for routine additions to their systems. Similarly, manufacturing organizations may use elements of network planning to schedule production and allocate personnel, equipment, and physical facilities within their organizations. At times, supervisors may also find that a simple planning network can help them plan and schedule some of the more complex projects they receive. In other words, network planning can be a very helpful planning technique for supervisors in all types of organizations.

Statistical Techniques

Although sophisticated statistical models and techniques are beyond the scope of this text, there are some relatively simple techniques that can help supervisors to improve their planning.

Projection techniques In most cases, the past is a pretty good predictor of the future. For example, if, over the past ten years, sales, caseloads, patients, or enrollments have increased 10 percent a year, it is reasonable to assume that there will be a 10 percent increase the coming year. Therefore, a supervisor may be able to predict the future performance of some important variable by calculating its performance in the past and applying the past performance to the future. For example, if work-force levels in the department increased, on the average, five persons per year, it would be reasonable to assume that there would be twenty additional workers four years into the future.

The critical disadvantage of this statistical projection, of course, is that it assumes that future conditions will be identical to those in the past. Recently, those who have used this method to predict costs of basic raw materials such as wood, paper, oil, plastic, and coal have found their forecasts to be very far off.

Trend analysis One way to avoid some of the pitfalls of straight projections is through trend analysis. To perform this process, the levels of the index are plotted on graph paper over a period of time. The idea is that the best prediction of the future will be the curve that fits between the historical levels of the index and continues into future periods of time.

An example of trend analysis is given in Figure 3-5. As shown, it appears, without any sophisticated analysis, that work-force levels in 1980 will be somewhere between 650 and 700. This projection is probably much more valid than the projection derived by the previous method, where the average increase of 75 people per year for the four-year period would have projected a work force of 950.

Although sophisticated mathematical techniques can be used to calculate curves of best fit, the data can frequently be accurately "eyeballed," as in the above example. Similar trend analyses could be made of budgets, performance figures, or wages. However, trend-analysis techniques also have drawbacks. A well-known example is the predictions that were made for increased levels of teachers, students, and building programs in public education. Through historical trend analysis, most school districts saw enrollments increasing in larger proportions each year and concluded that this trend would continue. Colleges were geared up to train teachers and new schools were still being built when a sudden and *unanticipated* drop in enrollment occurred. Today, there are both vacant school buildings and jobless teachers which tell the story. What happened, of course, was that the planners were not aware of—or at least did not consider—the impact of population trends. Their historical trend analysis was sound, but an important variable that influenced the trend was not given enough attention.

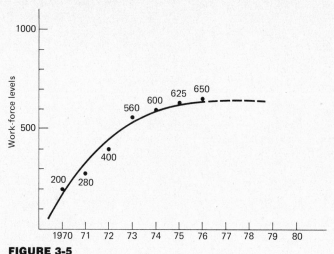

FIGURE 3-5
An example of trend analysis.

Correlational techniques The third major statistical technique for planning is correlational analysis. It takes into consideration the relationship between variables like school enrollments and population trends. Very simply, a correlation is the degree of relationship between two variables. Significantly, a correlation does not imply that one of the variables *causes* the other. Instead, correlation simply means that the variables move together in a predictable direction. If the supervisor knows that two variables are highly correlated, then knowledge of one of the variables can be used to predict the other. For example, the concession supervisor at the public stadium knows that the number of hot dogs sold is going to depend on the size of the crowd: more people means more hot dogs and less people means less hot dogs. If the supervisor wanted, a statistical equation could be developed to predict hot dog sales based on ticket sales. But it is probably unnecessary to go this far. Only rarely will supervisors need to compute the actual statistical relationship, but they can frequently make effective use of informal correlational analysis. For example, when production schedules go up in a manufacturing situation, the supervisor knows that more workers will be needed. If there is a major fire in the local community, the nursing supervisor of the burn unit in the local hospital knows she will need more help.

Some possible pitfalls of the correlational method are that the relationships between the variables are often imperfect and may even change. For example, as skiing became a popular winter sport, some organizations saw a decrease in summer vacation requests (which are generally expected to be much greater in number than those for other seasons) and an increase in winter requests.

Organizations which use complex statistical correlational models to determine relationships between variables such as sales, production, revenues, and budgets (i.e., businesses) or patient loads, drug inventories, and costs (i.e., hospitals) have the same inherent problems. Thus, despite the sophisticated mathematical techniques utilized in these forecasts, they are still subject to the drawbacks of the simpler correlational procedures.

Steps supervisors should take The following five points describe how supervisors can utilize statistical techniques for their own forecasts and projections:

1 *State problem.* State the variable to be forecasted and the time frame for the projection; list all other variables that may be related to the forecast.

2 *Compute average change.* Compute the average change in the variable over the years and project the future level based on this average.

3 *Do trend analysis.* Graph the variable over time and explain any recent trends in the data which may influence the projection made in step 2.

4 *Correlate.* State any other relevant variables which may be related to the variable to be forecasted. Indicate the influence these variables may have on the projection.

5 *Summarize.* Give your final projection along with your reasoning. Include any factors which may influence the accuracy of the forecast in the future.

An example of this application of the statistical process is contained in the memorandum of Figure 3-6. This is a very simplified example and many supervisors will be able to perform much more detailed analyses when they are needed. In addition, an understanding of the statistical techniques is needed to interpret information which supervisors receive from upper-level management.

Computer Simulations

Another method of generating alternative courses of action and assessing the impact of future conditions for the planning process is

MEMO TO: Jake Jones, Personnel Manager
    FROM: Bob Smith, Production Supervisor
SUBJECT: Workforce planning

Jake, my projection for work-force needs in the coming year is 27 employees. Over the previous eight years, we have maintained, on the average, 21 people per year. However, the figures for the past two years are 27 and 28 people because of our heavy production schedule. It is anticipated that the schedule will be about the same for next year. If there are any changes in production scheduling for our department, I will let you know.

FIGURE 3-6
A simplified example of utilizing
statistical procedures.

the use of computer simulation. According to this approach, computer programmers interrelate all relevant variables with correlational analysis and construct a mathematical model of the unit in question. The resulting model can predict the impact that a change in any single variable or combination of variables will have on all other variables. For example, it can predict the impact that a specific level of sales will have on work-force levels, profits, and the long-term debt of a business firm. Most often, an individual supervisor would not be involved in the direct application of a computer simulation model, but a supervisor might be asked to provide some inputs or be given some outputs to improve his or her planning effectiveness. It should be remembered that there is nothing magical about computers. Because these models use correlational analysis as their basic foundation, they are subject to the same kinds of errors as the correlational methods previously reviewed.

In summary, there are a wide variety of long-range techniques that organizations and individual supervisors can use to improve planning. Supervisors usually find the simpler operational techniques that are covered in the next section most useful. However, the principles of the more complex methods, such as correlational and network analysis, can also be incorporated into supervisory planning and the assessment of plans made at higher levels. Similarly, although MBO ideally begins at the top of the organization, supervisors may find this technique very useful after they modify it for use in their own areas.

The general description of the planning process that was used to introduce this chapter should also be helpful. It provides the basic elements for planning. Within this process, supervisors may include and/or modify any of the techniques discussed here to develop their own particular systems for planning and forecasting.

**Basic Elements
of Effective Supervision**

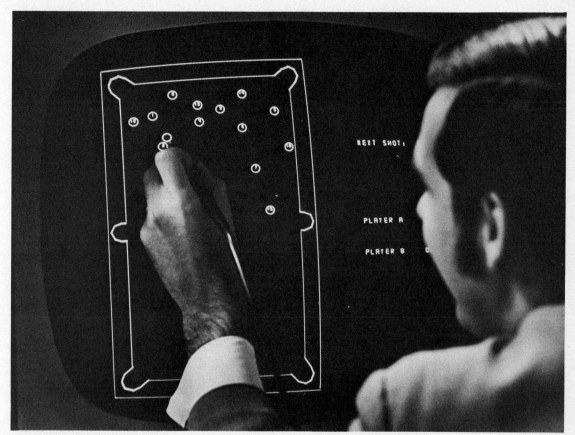

NEXT SHOT:

PLAYER A

PLAYER B

The computer is capable of sophisticated game playing or simulating important organizational decisions to help in the planning and control process (Roger Malloch/ Magnum Photos).

DAY-TO-DAY OPERATIONAL PLANNING

Whereas the long-range techniques are helpful to supervisors in the general sense, it is the day-to-day operational techniques that are most directly useful and practical for first-line supervisors. The operational techniques emphasize methods for planning and scheduling the routine day-to-day activities that are the domain of the practicing supervisor.

Checklists

All people have days when they are frantically busy but fail to accomplish anything significant. You may start on one activity only to hear the phone ring, and just as you are putting the phone down, you remember something else. Halfway into the new project, an employee enters the office with a new problem. The phone rings again, and so the day goes. At the end of the day, the desk is cluttered with a dozen projects, none of which is completed.

The simplest and most direct device for daily planning and time management is a checklist of daily activities. In the morning, the supervisor takes ten minutes to jot down on paper the things that need to be done that day. After the list is made, each item is ranked in terms of priority. The priorities should consider both the time requirements and the importance of each task. Once the priorities are assigned, the supervisor works through the list in the determined order. As items are completed, they are crossed off the list. Similarly, when "hot" new problems arise, they are added to the list but are not worked on unless it can be determined that they are top-priority items. At the end of the day, the supervisor has a record of the day's activities and accomplishments which can be reviewed to see whether most of the time has been spent on tasks which are consistent with overall objectives and goals.

If the supervisor finds that, despite this orderly approach to daily tasks and duties, significant portions of the work load are still not being accomplished, priorities must be reevaluated or additional assignments delegated. The next chapter—on time management and delegation—will provide additional information and techniques for designing checklists and managing personal time.

Calendars

A desk or pocket calendar can be an indispensable tool for daily planning. Many supervisors prefer calendars that have a space for each time of the day on the left-hand side and a blank page on the right. Tasks and meetings that must be conducted at particular times of the day are recorded in the time slots, and the supervisory checklist discussed in the last section is written down on the blank page. Similarly, supervisors can put short notes on the calendar prior to the due dates for critical events, such as monthly reports and performance appraisals. The calendar can also serve as a document of and guide to important duties in the event that the supervisor is late or absent.

Regardless of the type of calendar used, care should be taken to make sure that its use is integrated into the normal pattern of the supervisor's work day. Although a calendar aid is very basic and simple, it serves no purpose if it is not consulted frequently and routinely. Similarly, supervisors should make a choice of the aid to be used and stick with it. There has been more than one supervisor who has kept a pocket notebook, desk calendar, and checklist but failed to coordinate them, thus only increasing his or her disorganization and confusion.

Gantt Charts

Another useful mechanism for daily planning and scheduling is the Gantt chart. Named after the famous scientific management expert Henry L. Gantt, this chart illustrates planning in relation to time. The Gantt chart can help the supervisor ensure that each worker's day is fully scheduled. An example of a Gantt chart is shown in Figure 3-7. In the example, the supervisor has written in the work-order numbers corresponding to the work that has been assigned to each employee. The crosshatched section indicates work that has already been completed. As can be seen, D. Walher is far ahead of schedule by comparison with the others; therefore Walher may be reassigned to more critical jobs.

An additional benefit of the Gantt chart is that when the work of one person is the input for another person's job, this work can be tracked closely to ensure that it does not hold up anyone else's activity. In addition to scheduling tasks for individual workers, similar charts can serve to keep track of work orders assigned to particular machines, work assigned to teams of employees, and even particular sections of the unit assigned to segments of the work order.

Like all planning procedures, Gantt charts should be viewed as flexible planning devices. A major prerequisite for designing these charts is a pencil with a large eraser, as the charts will change continually as absenteeism, unforseen problems such as machine breakdowns, and rush orders of various kinds change the priorities of the schedule.

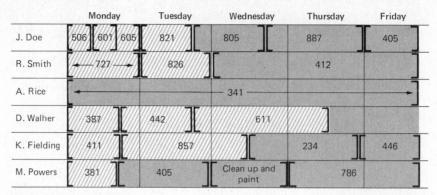

	Monday	Tuesday	Wednesday	Thursday	Friday
J. Doe	506 601 605	821	805	887	405
R. Smith	←— 727 —→	826		412	
A. Rice	←——————————— 341 ———————————→				
D. Walher	387	442	611		
K. Fielding	411	857		234	446
M. Powers	381	405	Clean up and paint	786	

FIGURE 3-7
A Gantt chart.

Real-Time Systems

A recent development, aided by the computer, is the real-time system. These systems record all transactions (e.g., inventory or purchases) immediately; they are also able to provide immediate summaries of all previous transactions. Today, these real-time systems are commonly used for airline reservations and inventory control. Very recently, a large number of retail organizations have adopted these systems, using the cash register for the primary input function into the computer. In these systems, as the salesclerk rings up the merchandise, the transaction is relayed to a central processing unit, where it is recorded. The computer can even be programmed to have the item reordered and shipped when a sufficient number of sales are recorded.

Supervisors will usually have little input to the technical side of these real-time computer systems. However, these systems can change supervisory functions significantly. For example, many supervisors in retail organizations are finding that the functions of planning, inventorying, and ordering of merchandise have been completely taken over by the computer. Even so, the planning by the computer is only as good as the data inputs originating from each supervisor. Thus, supervisors must monitor the inputs carefully if these planning systems are to be successful. Sabotage of such a system (either deliberately or by accident) is a common "war story" among the data processing specialists who work on real-time systems.

Other Operational Techniques

The operational planning mechanisms discussed so far are only a few of the many possibilities available to today's supervisors. Frequently, different types of organizations and even different supervisors develop their own simple, specialized techniques for operational planning. For example, truckers have an over-the-road itinerary, cab drivers usually have a radio-dispatching unit which directs their pickups, and short-order restaurants often use a little clothesline with paper clips or a carousel to convey orders to the chef. Examples of some other unique operational planning tools that are tailored specifically to particular needs are the following:

1 A public utility uses a 40 × 10 foot board with hundreds of small plastic clips which are hung on the board to schedule maintenance activities during nuclear-plant shutdowns. On each clip is written a different maintenance activity. The clips are also color-coded to indicate different work groups. By arranging these clips across the horizontal time dimension on the board, each of the hundreds of required activities can be coordinated and planned for every day.

2 Nursing supervisors in a large metropolitan hospital use a system of color-coded cards to relay doctors' orders and patient-care needs to the nurses assigned to each patient. White cards indicate that the treatment is routine, red cards indicate that it is a surgical preparation, a green card flags one-time treatments such as a shot, and a yellow card calls for traction or physical therapy.

3 A manager of a computer organization receives a daily printout which lists each job, employees working on the job, and the part of the job that has been completed.

4 A public relations director has a calendar the size of the entire wall on which are printed important speaking engagements and events which will occur in the coming year.

5 A roofing company employing over a hundred workers in a large metropolitan area uses a steel board with movable magnetic rectangles to plan daily activities. On the rectangles are employee names, crew numbers, supervisors' names, names of major pieces of equipment, and special categories such as vacation, sick leave, and jury duty. Each morning, the board is arranged and rearranged. Supervisors and employees can then tell at a glance what equipment, workers, and supervisors are assigned to each crew. Changes are made simply by rearranging the movable magnetic parts.

These examples illustrate that each supervisor and type of situation requires somewhat different day-to-day operational planning mechanisms.

It is hoped that, through this broad survey of long-range and operational techniques, each supervisor or potential supervisor will find one or more techniques that can be directly adapted or slightly modified to meet his or her particular requirements for effective planning.

■ KEY CONCEPTS

Budgeting
Management by objectives
Network planning
Statistical projection
Trend analysis
Correlation
Simulation
Gantt chart
Real time

■ PRACTICAL EXERCISES

(These can be performed by individuals or by groups.)
1 Suppose you were given the job of developing the long-range plan for a small factory that produces water beds and sells them directly to the customer. Briefly describe the process you would go through and what specific techniques you could use.
2 In this same water-bed operation, what technique(s) would you use in the day-to-day operational planning?
3 Supervisors are often accused of managing by crisis. They spend their whole day going from one crisis to the next. From the perspective of operational planning, how can crisis management be avoided?

■ DISCUSSION INCIDENTS

Jim Spence, a supervisor in a regional vocational rehabilitation unit, was convinced that planning was a waste of time. One day, over lunch with his boss, he said, "I've had it with the state office. They want plans for this, that, and the other thing but no one ever knows what happens to them. I asked a friend I have up there and she responded, 'I guess they're all poured down the bureaucratic hole.' Well, I'll tell you what. I am going to just copy something randomly out of a book the next time they ask me for a plan. No one reads them, so why should I put a lot of effort into these plans?"

1 How would you respond to Jim if you were his boss?

2 Does Jim really understand the planning process and how it can help him be a more effective supervisor?

3 What planning techniques can help Jim do his job more effectively?

Alice Ritter was office manager for the Angle Company. Her boss summoned her in one day and said: "As you know, we are growing by leaps and bounds and your work load out in the office has probably doubled in recent months. I have had several of your people come in to complain that they are overworked and there is no hope in sight. I am willing to increase your budget for the next fiscal year, but you are going to have to show me how the money will be spent. I want you to submit long- and short-range plans for the office operation." Alice said OK and left. She went back to her desk and pondered to herself, "This is a new ballgame. I have never been asked to submit any plans. I wonder how I go about it and what techniques I can use? I'd better get hold of a textbook and find out."

1 What will Alice find in the textbook on planning? Will this help her in developing her plans? How?

2 Has Alice been negligent in the past by not doing any formal planning?

TIME MANAGEMENT AND DELEGATION

CHAPTER 4

Harold Werner is the supervisor of engineering for a progressive design and building firm which specializes in agricultural structures such as grain silos. Besides being a supervisor, his only other noteworthy characteristic is that he is a workaholic. Each day he goes to work at 6:30 A.M., about 1 1/2 hours before his employees. His office looks like a collection point for a recycling center, with pile upon pile of papers and documents cluttering his hidden desk. During the morning, he checks all of the drawings, prints, contracts, and specifications provided by his engineers. Frequently he makes changes in the originals and notifies the buyer but forgets to tell his engineers. In the afternoon, he personally checks on each project, sometimes driving over 200 miles to ensure that the construction crews are meeting the engineering specifications. He leaves the office around 6:30 P.M., at least 1 1/2 hours after his employees have left. Although his employees respect Harold's technical expertise, they are highly critical of his supervisory style. Many accuse him of not trusting his people and treating them like children. He rarely gives them any real decision-making responsibility or authority and is extremely arbitrary in revising his employees' original designs. One employee sums up these criticisms by saying: "If he's going to entirely revise our designs, what are we even hanging around for?" Besides Harold's work habits, the employees have also become critical of his personal habits. Some say he is cheap, because he rarely buys or eats lunch and has not bought a new suit for several years. Others say he's just old-fashioned and refuses to change. The truth, of course, is that Harold has been so busy for so long that he has neglected his personal appearance very severely. The saddest part of it, however, is that Harold does not recognize his problems at all. Rather, like most workaholics, he feels that he is extremely dedicated and efficient. His employees, on the other hand, feel that he completely lacks all the important techniques and skills for analyzing his use of time and for delegating work.

■ LEARNING OBJECTIVES

After reading this chapter, you should be able to:

Develop an analytical perspective of time and its usage

Debunk the myths about time and time management

Identify and analyze the reasons supervisors fail to delegate, in order to correct this problem

Apply the methodology and specific tools for:
  Critically analyzing time usage
  Determining priorities for delegation
  Budgeting and allocating time

Identify significant time wasters and provide techniques for their control

In our society, very little separates success from failure. In 1977, the leading money winner on the Professional Golf Association tour grossed over $310,653 but averaged only 1.5 strokes better than the pro who took fortieth place and a scant $76,417. Thus, although the difference in performance between the two pros was slight, this slight edge was worth over $234,236. Like professional golfers, matters of inches and seconds have a critical impact on our daily lives. Collisions in both land and air travel are frequently avoided by split-second timing and, although the differences between proceeding safely and having tragic accidents are slight, these actually represent the critical edge between life and death. Supervisors' use of time and the resultant success or failure can be viewed in a similar manner. All supervisors have exactly the same amount of time in a day: twenty-four hours, sixty minutes per hour, and sixty seconds per minute. As in the case of the pro golfer, the critical difference in performance may be due to the slight edge that some supervisors are able to develop in the utilization and management of time.

In this chapter, two specific areas for developing the critical edge for improved supervisory effectiveness will be reviewed: delegation and personal time management. Delegation involves the assignment of tasks and duties which are frequently considered part of the supervisor's job to members of the work group. Obviously, if supervisors can assign some of their work load to subordinates, a substantial amount of their own time can be better utilized on top-priority activities. Personal time management is closely intertwined with delegation and is concerned with specific skills for analyzing time usage and spelling out the specific ways in which time can best be utilized.

As in other chapters, not all suggestions and information will be relevant for every supervisory position. However, if, by studying this chapter, the reader is able to gain some insights and at least a few specific suggestions that results in the better utilization of supervisory time, the slight edge discussed in the introductory comments may be realized.

POOR TIME UTILIZATION AND THE FAILURE TO DELEGATE

Before looking at specific techniques for effective time management and delegation, it will be beneficial to look at some of the reasons why supervisors fail to manage their time properly and to delegate.

Myths about Time

Frequently, supervisors have beliefs and ideas about the nature of time which create barriers to efficient time management. Some of the more common misconceptions about time include the following:

Time can be saved Many supervisors operate under the misconception that time can be saved. They streamline an operation and, instead of using the additional time more productively, squander it on longer lunch or coffee breaks. They fail to realize that time is an intangible resource which is expanded immediately. Once time passes, it is lost forever. Thus, time cannot be saved but only utilized and managed more efficiently. Where activities which consume supervisory time are eliminated or delegated, they must be replaced with higher-level functions or the time is lost forever. Supervisors should remember that time can be used or abused but never saved.

Good supervisors always have time One common belief is that good supervisors always have time to do what is necessary. Because they are so efficient at delegation and personal time management, their desks are neat and clean and they always have time for lengthy conversations with other employees or supervisors. There is undoubtly some truth to this view. Most successful supervisors are very active people, engaging in new tasks and problems at each hour of the day. A major reason they are successful and appear so active is because they manage their time effectively and are able to set aside a portion of their day for important activities such as planning, catching up with new developments in their field, and holding conversations with other key personnel. They consider these activities as essential to their own professional development as well as the development of their units. To them, time management and delegation are distinctly different from busy work.

Good supervisors never have enough time The other side of the coin from the preceding view is that effective supervisors never have enough time; they are workaholics who arrive at 6 A.M. and leave at 6 P.M., avoid lunch and coffee breaks, and chain smoke three packs a day while answering telephones with both ears. Some people call this the "buckets-of-blood syndrome," where supervisors feel that their productivity is a direct function of the amount of time they spend and the activity they produce. The idea is that if they can spend more time and become engaged in more activities, they will automatically be more productive. Actually, the reverse may be true. Just as machines and equipment have tolerances and needs for maintenance, so do people. Supervisors who burn themselves out on low-level activities and work needlessly long hours sometimes end up ignoring their important responsibilities. Effective supervisors learn to manage their time and to delegate, so that the most important functions, the high priorities, are carried out efficiently.

Other people waste time When most supervisors are asked to identify their major time wasters, they invariably point to other people. Specifically, they list things like unavoidable conversations, non-job-related conversations with friends, unnecessary meetings and reports, and telephone interruptions. However, when these same supervisors are forced to analyze their time usage carefully, most agree with Pogo, the cartoon character, who said, "We has met the enemy, and they is us." Although we are sometimes unaware, we frequently make the choice to engage in unnecessary conversations or allow telephone interruptions to consume too much of our time. Similarly, although we have less personal control over meetings and reports, we either act in ways which condone their overuse or fail to take positive steps for correction. Some specific techniques and methods for overcoming these common time wasters are reviewed later in this chapter. Most importantly, however, these techniques must be utilized and applied if supervisors are to gain control and effective use of their time. Where supervisors fail to use these techniques to manage their time, others will manage it for them.

The busy supervisor can become more effective by following the guidelines suggested by time management (Terry Evans/Magnum Photos).

Reasons for Not Delegating

Closely connected to the myths and fallacies about time are the reasons supervisors give for not entrusting members of their work groups with more significant parts of the work loads. In many cases, the reasons are irrational and create additional pressures and barriers to the efficient use of supervisory time. Some of the more common reasons supervisors do not delegate include the following:

Lack of trust Many supervisors feel there are tasks which their subordinates simply cannot perform adequately. They justify their own involvement in the task by reasoning that they can do it better themselves and that training others to perform competently would be more trouble than it is worth. For example, one supervisor in a bank still continues to balance the books personally at the end of the day for all tellers even though she does not supervise them directly. By refusing to delegate this duty, this supervisor has an excuse for being the last one to leave every evening as well as being the only one who does not take a vacation. Her continued insistence on performing the task severely limits her flexibility in managing her own time and life. More importantly, however, by not delegating, this supervisor is robbing her subordinates of important motivational and growth opportunities as well as possible bottom-line effectiveness for the overall organization.

Vocational hobbies As noted in our introductory chapter, supervisors are often promoted because of the excellent technical jobs they have done. For example, the sales supervisor was the top salesperson, the head nurse had the most training in patient-care techniques, and the office supervisor was the best stenographer. Unfortunately, many supervisors bring these "vocational hobbies" and nothing else to their new jobs. "Vocational hobbies" refers to the work in which supervisors excelled at their old jobs. The vocational hobby is very comfortable and familiar to the new supervisor, and most often he or she continues to gain admiration and appreciation from others because of obvious competence at these tasks. More often, however, direct subordinates become upset with supervisors who continue to hoard these activities. For example, one sales supervisor in a large medical supply company still continues to call on some very large and preferred sales accounts. The supervisor reasons that these customers have established a feeling toward him personally that, if broken, could cost his company a major account. Moreover, he feels that competition with his own salespeople is minimal because he does not get direct commissions for these accounts while in his supervisory position. Of course, his salespeople see this situation very differently. They feel that their supervisor is robbing them of important developmental opportunities as well as potential commissions. In addition, because this supervisor spends considerable time providing service to these accounts, the employees feel that he is neglecting important supervisory duties.

Loss of control Another major roadblock is that supervisors may fear that by delegating responsibility to subordinates they will lose control over their work units. Their reasoning is that if subordinates make decisions concerning the work, the supervisor may not be kept informed and will thus lose authority. It is extremely embarassing for many supervisors to be questioned by their bosses and appear ignorant because they do not know what their employees did in accomplishing a particular task. Rather than being proud of their people and taking credit for developing them, some supervisors become jealous and even try to hide their subordinates' involvement. More effective supervisors learn to set up reporting mechanisms to keep themselves informed and to encourage recognition of their work group from upper management. Supervisors who are hoping to get ahead should remember that one of the first questions that is always asked is: "Who can take the supervisor's place if he or she is promoted?" If the supervisor has not delegated responsibility and thus developed a replacement, he or she may not get the promotion. Pragmatically, supervisors should not be afraid of being replaced by subordinates who outshine them; rather, they should be grooming subordinates to take their places in case they themselves are given the opportunity to advance.

Role clarity A final major roadblock to delegation is role clarity. This simply means that many supervisors are not sure what their responsibilities and duties really are. They do not know which tasks and duties can and/or should be delegated to their subordinates. Supervisors often become confused and fail to delegate properly because the responsibility and authority for duties and tasks are not clearly defined. An example could be the new supervisor (let us call him Frank) of the payroll department of an insurance company. When Frank inherited the job, he took on the tasks and duties of his predecessor. In particular, Frank's previous supervisor used to spend every Friday walking through the central office personally distributing paychecks to department heads. Frank had always considered this practice a waste of time, but he has continued it because people seemed to expect it and he believed it to be part of his job. Once he suggested that one of the more experienced assistants in payroll might perform this duty, but people were shocked by the suggestion. They were obviously surprised that Frank would even consider letting someone else do this important job. When Frank asked what was so important about it, he was told simply that this job had always been done by the payroll supervisor and not by an assistant. Frank let it drop there and never brought it up again.

Today Frank, like many other supervisors, continues to perform such nonsensical but very time-consuming tasks because he has never clearly formulated the divisions of responsibility and authority in his department. Supervisors must have a very clear idea of what their role is all about.

THE NEED TO ANALYZE THE JOB

The first step in effective time management and delegation is analyzing the supervisor's job. The object of this analysis is to ascertain the supervisor's major tasks and duties. These must be evaluated to determine which may be better managed or delegated. Several techniques can be used to aid this analysis.

The Use of Activities Lists

The easiest way to begin time analysis is simply to list all the tasks, duties, and activities which are performed. This can be done by mentally tracing the supervisor's activities through the day or by completing forms shown in Figures 4-1 and 4-2.

In Figure 4-1, a time table, the supervisor would trace through the hour slots in the left-hand column and jot down a short note about specific activities during the time periods. After about ten or twelve of these daily checklists are completed, the results can be compiled to identify time usage. The method illustrated in Figure 4-2 is also a single and straightforward way to analyze time usage. Along the top of the table, the supervisor lists some major categories to which time is allocated. Tracing through the day in the left-hand column, the supervisor places a tick mark for each ten-minute period in the appropriate square on the table to indicate the activity being performed. The check marks are then tallied for the entire day to indicate time usage. After supervisors have tallied their time usage for a couple of weeks, they will have a reasonably accurate analysis of how their time is being utilized.

Tables like these can also be compiled for weekly, monthly, and yearly activities. It should be noted that compiling these activities lists is very similar to compiling the priorities lists described in Chapter 3. The major difference is that here, the activities lists are saved over a

FIGURE 4-1

A chart for the time analysis of daily activities.

DATE	NAME
Time	Activity
8:00	
8:30	
9:00	
9:30	
10:00	
10:30	
11:00	
11:30	
12:00	
12:30	
1:00	
1:30	
2:00	
2:30	
3:00	
3:30	
4:00	
4:30	
5:00	

FIGURE 4-2

A worksheet for the time analysis of categories of activities.

	Meeting	Inventory	Telephone	Conversation	Training	Paperwork	Planning	Communicating assignments and instructions	Other: Describe
8:00 - 8:30	X							X X	
8:30 - 9:00	X X								
9:00 - 9:30			X						
9:30 - 10:00	X X		X						
10:00 - 10:30		XXX							
10:30 - 11:00		X X	X						
11:00 - 11:30		X		X		X			
11:30 - 12:00	XXX								
12:00 - 12:30									Lunch
12:30 - 1:00									Lunch
1:00 - 1:30			X			X X			
1:30 - 2:00						XXX			
2:00 - 2:30				X		X X			
2:30 - 3:00				X X		X			
3:00 - 3:30			X X			X			
3:30 - 4:00		X		X		X			
4:00 - 4:30				X			X X		
4:30 - 5:00									Went home
Total minutes	80	70	60	60	0	110	20	20	

**Basic Elements
of Effective Supervision**

period of time and carefully analyzed to lead to more efficient delegation and time management.

Random Sampling Technique of Analysis

Random sampling is a scientific way of analyzing the supervisor's usage of time. When supervisors use the activity checklist discussed in the last section, they are sometimes biased and forget to include some activities. Most importantly, deliberately or by oversight, they exlude their major time wasters from the record of their daily activities. Use of the random-sampling process avoids these pitfalls. Very simply, random sampling is a process whereby samples of supervisory activity are recorded at random times during the day in order to gain a record of total time usage patterns.

To use this method, the supervisor may select an outside observer (e.g., a secretary or senior, trusted subordinate who has intimate knowledge of the supervisor's daily activities). The observer would then randomly select specific times during the day when the supervisor's activity is observed and recorded. A random-number table is shown in Figure 4-3. This table provides the observer with a random distribution of observation times (usually eight to ten observations suffice). Because these times are randomly selected, neither the supervisor nor the observer can bias the results of the time study. It is expected, at least over two to three weeks, that a realistic picture will emerge of how the supervisor spends time.

The form illustrated in Figure 4-4 is an example of how the observer can record the supervisor's activity. In this example, the observer simply checks the activity being performed and attempts to describe its purpose. After a sufficient number of observations have been made, the results can be tallied in the manner shown in Figure 4-5.

Supervisors who use the random-sampling technique with an outside observer have a reasonably accurate record of how their time is being spent. If it is determined that any particular category is out of line, the daily records can be checked to determine the purpose—and consequently the usefulness—of each activity.

ESTABLISHING PRIORITIES AND ANALYZING JOBS FOR TIME MANAGEMENT AND DELEGATION

The techniques for personal time analysis enable supervisors to gain a realistic perspective of how they are using their time. The next

```
60  36  59  46  53     35  07  53  39  49     42  61  42  92  97     01  91  82  83  16     98  95  37  32  31
83  79  94  24  02     56  62  33  44  42     34  99  44  13  74     70  07  11  47  36     09  95  81  80  65
32  96  00  74  05     36  40  98  32  32     99  38  54  16  00     11  13  30  75  86     15  91  70  62  53
19  32  25  38  45     57  62  05  26  06     66  49  76  86  46     78  13  86  65  59     19  64  09  94  13
11  22  09  47  47     07  39  93  74  08     48  50  92  39  29     27  48  24  54  76     85  24  43  51  59

31  75  15  72  60     68  98  00  53  39     15  47  04  83  55     88  65  12  25  96     03  15  21  91  21
88  49  29  93  82     14  45  40  45  04     20  09  49  89  77     74  84  39  34  13     22  10  97  85  08
30  93  44  77  44     07  48  18  38  28     73  78  80  64  33     28  59  72  04  05     94  20  52  03  80
22  88  84  88  93     27  49  99  87  48     60  53  04  51  28     74  02  28  46  17     82  03  71  02  68
78  21  21  69  93     35  90  29  13  86     44  37  21  54  86     65  74  11  40  14     87  48  13  72  20

41  84  98  45  47     46  85  05  23  26     34  67  75  83  00     74  91  06  43  45     19  32  58  15  49
46  35  23  30  49     69  24  89  34  60     45  30  50  75  21     61  31  83  18  55     14  41  37  09  51
11  08  79  62  94     14  01  33  17  92     59  74  76  72  77     76  50  33  45  13     39  66  37  75  44
52  70  10  83  37     56  30  38  73  15     16  52  06  96  76     11  65  49  98  93     02  18  16  81  61
57  27  53  68  98     81  30  44  85  85     68  65  22  73  76     92  85  25  58  66     88  44  80  35  84

20  85  77  31  56     70  28  42  43  26     79  37  59  52  20     01  15  96  32  67     10  62  24  83  91
15  63  38  49  24     90  41  59  36  14     33  52  12  66  65     55  82  34  76  41     86  22  53  17  04
92  69  44  82  97     39  90  40  21  15     59  58  94  90  67     66  82  14  15  75     49  76  70  40  37
77  61  31  90  19     88  15  20  00  80     20  55  49  14  09     96  27  74  82  57     50  81  69  76  16
38  68  83  24  86     45  13  46  35  45     59  40  47  20  59     43  94  75  16  80     43  85  25  96  93

25  16  30  18  89     70  01  41  50  21     41  29  06  73  12     71  85  71  59  57     68  97  11  14  30
65  25  10  76  29     37  23  93  32  95     05  87  00  11  19     92  78  42  65  40     18  47  76  56  22
36  81  54  36  25     18  63  73  75  09     82  44  49  90  05     04  92  17  37  01     14  70  79  39  97
64  39  71  16  92     05  32  78  21  62     20  24  78  17  59     45  19  72  53  32     83  74  52  25  67
04  51  52  56  24     95  09  66  79  46     48  46  08  55  58     15  19  11  87  82     16  93  03  33  61

83  76  16  08  73     43  25  38  41  45     60  83  32  59  83     01  29  14  13  49     20  36  80  71  26
14  38  70  63  45     80  85  40  92  79     43  52  90  63  18     38  38  47  47  61     41  19  63  74  80
51  32  19  22  46     80  08  87  70  74     88  72  25  67  36     66  16  44  94  31     66  91  93  16  78
72  47  20  00  08     80  89  01  80  02     94  81  33  19  00     54  15  58  34  36     35  35  25  41  31
05  46  65  53  06     93  12  81  84  64     74  45  79  05  61     72  84  81  18  34     79  98  26  84  16

39  52  87  24  84     82  47  42  55  93     48  54  53  52  47     18  61  91  36  74     18  61  11  92  41
81  61  61  87  11     53  34  24  42  76     75  12  21  17  24     74  62  77  37  07     58  31  91  59  97
07  58  61  61  20     82  64  12  28  20     92  90  41  34  41     32  39  21  97  63     61  19  96  79  40
90  76  70  42  35     13  57  41  72  00     69  90  26  37  42     78  46  42  25  01     18  62  79  08  72
40  18  82  81  93     29  59  38  86  27     94  97  21  15  98     62  09  53  67  87     00  44  15  89  97

34  41  48  21  57     86  88  75  50  87     19  15  20  00  23     12  30  28  07  83     32  62  46  86  91
63  43  97  53  63     44  98  91  68  22     36  02  40  08  67     76  37  84  16  05     65  96  17  34  88
67  04  90  90  70     93  39  94  55  47     94  45  87  42  84     05  04  14  98  07     20  28  83  40  60
79  49  50  41  46     52  16  29  02  86     54  15  83  42  43     46  97  83  54  82     59  36  29  59  38
91  70  43  05  52     04  73  72  10  31     75  05  19  30  29     47  66  56  43  82     99  78  29  34  78

09  18  82  00  97     32  82  53  95  27     04  22  08  63  04     83  38  98  73  74     64  27  85  80  44
90  04  58  54  97     51  98  15  06  54     94  93  88  19  97     91  87  07  61  50     68  47  66  46  59
73  18  95  02  07     47  67  72  62  69     62  29  06  44  64     27  12  46  70  18     41  36  18  27  60
75  76  87  64  90     20  97  18  17  49     90  42  91  22  72     95  37  50  58  71     93  82  34  31  78
54  01  64  40  56     66  28  13  10  03     00  68  22  73  98     20  71  45  32  95     07  70  61  78  13
```

FIGURE 4-3

Table of random numbers.

Date_____	Observer_____
Random time: _10:27_	Supervisor_____

Category: _____ Doing bookwork
_____ Planning
_____ Socializing
_____ Meeting
_____ Telephoning
_____ Training
_✔_ Directing
_____ Inspecting
_____ Other_____

Purpose: The supervisor was demonstrating a new procedure to a subordinate.

FIGURE 4-4
Randoming sampling observation form.

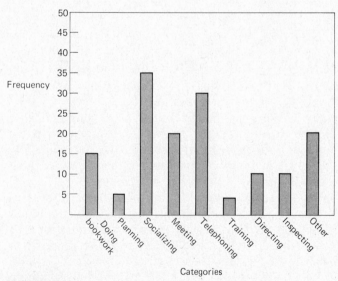

FIGURE 4-5
Summary profile form of time usage.

important step in effective time management is to establish priorities. Supervisors must determine the relative amount of time they *should* devote to each of the activities they have identified. There are at least four major considerations or criteria that must be applied to establish these priorities.

The Amount of Time Consumed

Routine tasks which recur frequently are almost always the most time-consuming activities. The time-usage lists generated in the first step should be carefully analyzed to identify the time-consuming activities. Where possible, supervisors should consider delegating these tasks to subordinates or formulating a policy or rule for dispensing with these activities. For example, one sales supervisor spent a major part of his day writing contracts for work that his employees had sold. The contracts were all very similar except for some important rarities. Generally, however, volume to be sold, delivery dates, and penalties for nondelivery were the basis of all contracts. In this case, the supervisor established a standard form for all contracts and published a set of policy guidelines for the exceptional areas. Today, the supervisor reviews completed contracts periodically instead of writing them himself and has freed up a substantial proportion of his time for higher-priority areas of his job.

The Importance of the Activity

All tasks and duties of supervisors are not equally important. Each activity should be carefully evaluated and the degree of importance designated with something like the following:

1 *Critical Activities.* These are activities that, at a minimum, must be completed before the work group can begin to accomplish its basic goals. For example, a production supervisor must see to it that parts are ordered, workers are scheduled, and paychecks are distributed if the work group is to continue to perform its basic functions.

2 *Needed Activities.* These are activities that should be performed so that the work group can approach maximum efficiency. For a nursing supervisor, these activities might include in-service training for new treatment procedures, performance appraisals, and long-range planning. Although failure to perform these activities may not have an immediate impact on patient care, it probably will have a significant impact on the long-run effectiveness of the supervisor's unit.

3 *Peripheral Activities.* These are activities which are not directly related to major goals. For example, serving on an organizationwide job enrichment or salary evaluation committee would usually have no direct impact on most supervisors' specific work-unit goals. Thus, the supervisor may rightly give many of these peripheral activities a lower priority than the critical and needed functions.

After evaluating activities according to the above criteria, supervisors must, of course, monitor the critical activities most carefully. However, it does not necessarily follow that the critical activities must all be performed by the supervisor. For example, it may be possible to delegate responsibilities for ordering necessary supplies to a subordinate, provided that adequate reporting and control mechanisms are established by the supervisor. Similarly, because needed activities will not seriously cripple an operation if temporarily neglected, this does not mean that they should necessarily be delegated. A needed activity such as performance appraisals is a good example. Appraisals provide employees with needed feedback from supervisors as well as plans for employee development. Delegating the appraisal responsibilities would be very unwise and would undoubtedly result in poor performance in the long run. Moreover, if a needed activity (such as appraisals) is neglected long enough, it may actually move to the critical activities list. Finally, peripheral activities such as collecting charitable contributions, serving on various organizationwide committees, or organizing picnics may be considered as prime targets for delegation or even elimination. On the other hand, some of these peripheral activities may also be necessary for political reasons; that is, they may eventually help the supervisor's unit and contribute to the supervisor's own personal growth and development.

Determining the Degree of Delegation

This step in time management is designed to establish guidelines for the degree of delegation. To begin this part of the analysis, each activity should be considered a potential candidate for delegation. After working through possible ways in which the tasks might be delegated, the actual degree of delegation can be designated according to categories such as the following:

1 *Authority is retained by the supervisor.* In this case the supervisor judges that the activity is an integral part of his or her job and cannot be delegated to a subordinate.

2 *Subordinate can act after the supervisor's approval.* Here the supervisor decides that an experienced and trusted subordinate may analyze the particular situation at hand and submit a recommendation. If the recommendation is approved by the supervisor, then the subordinate can act.

3 *Subordinate acts and then reports to the supervisor.* Here the subordinate may assume complete authority for accomplishing tasks but must report on activities when they are completed.

4 *Complete authority is delegated to the subordinate.* In this case, the supervisor judges that the subordinate can have complete authority for the task in question without even advising the supervisor, but the supervisor realizes that he or she will still have the responsibility for the actions of the subordinate.

The degree of delegation is assigned according to the judgment of the supervisor. Different supervisors will undoubtedly assign different degrees of delegation to tasks. Moreover, the type of delegation should not be considered as fixed and static. In many cases, there may be a logical progression through the degrees of delegation. For example, responsibilities for purchasing items may at first be delegated to the point where the subordinate analyzes the purchase and gives the recommendation to the supervisor. After a period of time, however, the supervisor's confidence may increase to the extent that complete authority and responsibility for purchases are delegated to this subordinate.

Delegation as a Method of Employee Development

Being allowed to make decisions and perform important duties (i.e., gaining meaningful experience) is a major way in which both supervisors and subordinates develop and grow in their jobs. Each activity and the potential for delegation should be carefully analyzed by supervisors with regard to their own possible growth as well as that of their subordinates. In cases where supervisors are confident in performing a particular task and feel they cannot develop themselves further by performing this task, they should consider delegating it to subordinates for their development. Similarly, a supervisor may assign a high priority for delegating a task because it under- or overspecializes the supervisor or can offer the subordinate some added variety and interest.

ESTABLISHING THE OVERALL PLAN FOR TIME MANAGEMENT AND DELEGATION

After supervisors have analyzed their jobs in the ways that have been discussed so far, they can illustrate their overall evaluation with a chart such as the one shown in Table 4-1. In this example, the supervisor listed major job activities. Each of these was then rated

TABLE 4-1

OVERALL ACTIVITY ANALYSIS FOR TIME MANAGEMENT AND DELEGATION

	Time consumption	Nature	Importance	Degree of Delegation	Developmental potential for subordinate
1. Daily inventory	10 hours/week	Routine	Critical	Act and report daily	Moderate
2. Performance appraisals	2 hours/employee every 6 months	Nonroutine	Needed	Retain	Not applicable
3. Work scheduling	1½ hours/day	Both	Critical	Act after approval	Moderate
4. Flower fund	2 hours/month	Nonroutine	Peripheral	Complete authority	Low
5. Check attendance	5 minutes/day	Routine	Critical	Act and report	Low
6. Time-sheet reports	30 minutes/day	Routine	Critical	Act and report	Moderate
7. Prepare monthly budget	2 hours/month	Nonroutine	Needed	Act after approval	High
8. Weekly production report	3 hours/week	Routine	Needed	Act and report	Moderate
9. Process grievances	2 hours/month	Nonroutine	Critical	Retain	Not applicable
10. Analyze work flow	6 hours/month	Nonroutine	Needed	Retain/solicit recommendations and suggestions	High
11. Conversations with boss	2 hours/day	Both	Needed	Retain	High
12. Conversations with vendors	1 hour/day	Routine	Needed	Act after approved	High
13. Job-enrichment committee	3 hours/week	Nonroutine	Peripheral	Unsure	High

according to the criteria described in the preceding sections on consumption, nature of the task, importance of the task, degree of delegation, and developmental potential. Scanning the chart, the supervisor can readily determine functions which cannot be delegated (e.g., conversations with the boss and processing grievances). However, the chart also shows a number of time-consuming functions (e.g., the daily inventory, conversations with vendors, and time-sheet reports) which, if delegated, could save the supervisor in this case almost twenty hours per week. In addition, the chart helps isolate time-consuming activities such as conversations with the boss, which cannot be delegated but must be carefully managed to ensure that time is spent in the most productive way.

Once the supervisors have made an overall analysis of their time usage, they should have isolated at least several activities that can be delegated or managed more efficiently. Specific plans for both delegating and managing these functions should be integrated into the activities lists, MBO plans, and other planning mechanisms previously described in this and other chapters. The following considerations will aid supervisors in actually implementing their time usage plans.

Realistic Implementation of the Plan

The analysis of a supervisory job usually identifies many activities which can be delegated or managed more efficiently. However, it may not be possible or desirable to delegate all these activities immediately and change personal habits so abruptly. For example, sudden changes may lead to disorientation and resistance in the work group. On the other hand, gradual changes are usually accepted more readily. Second, as supervisors experience difficulty or outright failure in implementing some items in the plan for time usage and delegation, they may become discouraged and abandon the entire thing. A more realistic and successful approach would be to identify one or two high-priority items to be implemented immediately. When these items have been successfully integrated into the work system, then the supervisor should move on to the items with the next highest priority, and so forth.

Similar guidelines should be followed in implementing activities checklists and planning mechanisms such as the time budget illustrated in Table 4-2. If such time budgets and other checklists are worked out on too optimistic a basis, supervisors may find that they are behind very early in the day, become discouraged, and abandon their plans completely. Most time-management experts recommend that a supervisor's schedule include at least $1\frac{1}{2}$ to 2 hours of slack (free time) to provide for unanticipated demands. In this way, they are

TABLE 4-2

WEEKLY TIME BUDGET FOR A RESTAURANT SUPERVISOR

Time	Monday	Tuesday	Wednesday	Thursday	Friday
8–9	Check inventory, place orders to vendors, and check work schedule				
	Take delivery, most items	Take delivery, potatoes	Compute payroll information	Pay all out-standing bills	Make tartar sauce for week
9–10	Change grease in french fryers, assemble milkshake machine, turn on grill, turn on fryers, check on linen supply, fill all condiment dispensers, etc.				
10–11	Check for attendance, give daily work assignments, and call replacements if necessary				
11–12					
12–1	W O R K R U S H H O U R				
1–2	L U N C H				
2–3		Train new employee	Meeting with owner	Work progress reviews—Allen	Visit 43d st. location
3–4		Work progress reviews— Joe and Mary		Meet with vendor on new microwave system	

able to maintain their plans and achieve their goals within a realistic framework.

The Use of Phased Delegation

Frequently delegating the complete authority and responsibility for a task will challenge subordinates beyond their capabilities, so that they become frustrated and fail to do the job. One way of overcoming this problem is for the supervisor to use a phased delegation process where the subordinate begins by recommending actions to the supervisor and proceeds only when approval is given. When the subordinate has gained relevant experience and is more confident, then the supervisor can begin to let the subordinate perform entire tasks with the stipulation that a report be submitted at completion. In the final phase, the subordinate may be given total authority and responsibility for the job.

Another way of achieving the same result is to break tasks down and gradually delegate the segments. For example, a daily inventory process may include the recording of all materials in process, all raw materials, all materials ordered, and all materials shipped, as well as some mathematical calculations to balance the records in each phase of the inventory. The supervisor might assign any part of this inventory process to a subordinate. Gradually, as the subordinate became more adept, additional parts of the job might be assigned until the entire task had been delegated.

Take the Time and Follow Up

Supervisors are sometimes discouraged from implementing time-management and delegation procedures because they require an initial investment of time. For example, the daily priority checklist requires at least fifteen minutes per day to make up. Similarly, teaching a subordinate to perform a complex task such as taking inventory may take several hours per week over a period of months. Thus, at least initially, these approaches take time, and the supervisor may reason that time can be saved by avoiding the time-management and delegation procedures. However, the supervisor must realize that this time is well spent. It is cost-benefit use of time to develop the necessary procedures and tools for effective time management and delegation.

Time-management tools such as priority checklists and time budgets and plans for delegation serve no purpose unless they are followed. Like other planning mechanisms, these systems must be integrated into and become an integral part of the supervisor's daily operations. When time budgets and priorities checklists are first implemented, the supervisor will find it helpful to follow up by saving these plans over a period of time. Accomplishment can then be checked with supervisory goals to ensure that the process is working correctly. This is simply a way of making sure that the time-management techniques and delegation procedures are working as intended. All aspects of supervision should be controlled. Chapter 8 is specifically devoted to this important supervisory function.

SPECIFIC TIME WASTERS AND HOW TO DEAL WITH THEM

Time-management experts have identified some specific time wasters of which supervisors are most frequently guilty, and they have suggested ways in which such time wasters may be dealt with effectively. These are discussed in the balance of this chapter. If these difficulties are recognized and the guidelines suggested for overcoming them are followed, more effective supervision may be achieved.

Unnecessary Conversations

Among the most frequent time wasters are unnecessary, unexpected, and unwanted conversations with other supervisors, bosses, subordinates, and outsiders. The following guidelines and specific suggestions can help cut down on unnecessary conversations:

1 Excuse yourself and go to the bathroom.
2 Remove all of the chairs from the office. Most people like to sit when they engage in unnecessary conversation.
3 Stand up as soon as you see the time wasters coming and do not sit down until they leave. Most people do not feel comfortable sitting when the other person is standing.
4 Tell the other person that you are busy at the moment but will schedule an appointment.
5 Schedule appointments in the other person's office. It is easier to leave someone else's office than your own.
6 End the conversation with a statement such as, "I know you're busy and I don't want to take up any more of your time."
7 Watch and listen for cues to end the conversation. Quite often, an incoming phone call or a brief interruption by another employee can serve to end the conversation if you take advantage of the moment.

Of course, some of the above approaches are radical and might even be considered rude. However, these suggestions do effectively illustrate how supervisors can reduce unnecessary conversations if they really want to. Each supervisor should develop his or her own methods for dealing with unnecessary conversations. Common sense must be used so as to better use time without being rude.

Telephone Interruptions

Telephone calls are among the most common and unwanted time wasters. The following suggestions can help the supervisor to manage this time waster more effectively.

1 Tell the person that you are busy but will call back.
2 Have your secretary tactfully screen calls. Example: "He is busy right now, but if you give me your name I will see if he can take the call"; or "She is tied up right now, but I can tell her you are on the line

if you wish." Most people will not interrupt unless it is something really important.

3 Disconnect the phone while you are in the middle of a sentence. Call back and apologize for the interruption in service but ask if there is anything else that needs to be discussed.

4 Put off all calls until a convenient time of the day.

5 Avoid letting the telephone take precedence over ongoing face-to-face conversations. One of the most irritating situations for employees is to have a supervisor interrupt a personal meeting by answering the phone and discussing some unimportant business. If answering the telephone cannot be avoided, the person on the other end of the line should be told that a meeting is in progress and that he or she will be called back as soon as possible.

Procrastination

Procrastination frequently takes up a lot of the supervisor's time. There are two simple rules that can help you avoid this time waster.

1 If you have all the information possible and do not anticipate new inputs, make the decision immediately. Delays that do not offer the opportunity to gain additional information will not increase the quality of the decision.

2 Balance decision-making time with cost. For example, the supervisory time expended in making a decision on inexpensive purchases such as office supplies frequently does not justify the cost saving realized by a full investigation. A supervisor cannot save the organization money in a $25 purchase at a 10 percent discount if it takes one hour to investigate suppliers. The supervisor's salary for the amount of time spent in the investigation would far exceed the small savings realized.

Reading Selectively

A highly touted strategy for managing personal time is faster reading. Although most supervisors could greatly benefit from taking a speed-reading course, in many cases what is needed is simply more selective reading. The basic idea here is that much reading material can be eliminated if the reader can learn to identify the important correspondence quickly and disregard unimportant reading. The following guidelines should prove helpful in identifying the importance of the reading material:

1 Look at the mailing envelope. If it has not been sent first class and has a mass-produced address label, it can probably be thrown away immediately.

2 Is the information handwritten, typed, or mass-produced? Handwritten information is usually the most important; it is followed in importance by typewritten information. Mass-produced information is frequently unimportant.

3 Who is the information addressed to? When information is addressed to all supervisors in general or the supervisor of a function rather than directly to an individual, it is frequently less important.

4 Look at the first sentence. This should state the purpose of the correspondence. If this purpose is not important, the reading material should be discarded.

5 Look at the last sentence. This should indicate whether any action or reply is required.

6 Who signed the letter? When an important individual within the management structure has signed the letter, it is usually important. On outside correspondence, many advertising firms produce letters that are signed by presidents, vice-presidents, or celebrities connected with advertising campaigns. Most often, this correspondence has limited value and should be discarded.

Individual supervisors, of course, should arrive at their own criteria for evaluating the importance of written correspondence. The main point, however, is that once one has decided that information is unimportant, no further time should be spent on it. At first, it may be difficult for supervisors to throw correspondence away without reading it or to limit themselves to skimming it lightly. After some experience, this becomes much easier.

The Gourmet Chef Approach to Time Management

Anyone who has ever observed a good gourmet chef at work can gain a true appreciation of effective time management. A good chef is amazingly adept at keeping many irons in the fire at once. In the course of an hour, he or she may complete several main dishes. Each of these dishes is a major task in and of itself. Yet by carefully dividing each course into a number of successive stages, the chef is able to complete several major jobs simultaneously.

Supervisors can learn an important lesson from the gourmet chef. For example, one of the most common time-management problems is that certain large jobs stay on the priorities checklist week after week. The rationale often given is that these jobs are so large and time-consuming that it is impossible to allocate the block of time needed for achieving them. It follows that unimportant tasks are accomplished first because they are less time-consuming, and the important, priority tasks remain undone week after week.

Taking the lead of the gourmet chef, however, these jobs could be scaled down to size. Most important jobs have several stages: planning, proposals, gathering or ordering materials, pilot projects, and so forth. When each of these stages is considered a separate task, supervisors can accomplish the really big and important task much as a gourmet chef would produce meals, by keeping several pots on the stove at once.

Paperwork

Another common time waster that is growing all the time is paperwork and reports. Supervisors who do not keep up with their mounting paperwork soon lose sight of their desks. Most of their time is taken up with shuffling papers from pile to pile and searching through the mess for something they need. Here are some specific suggestions for dispatching paperwork efficiently:

1 Write answers and replies to letters or memos in longhand on the original request. This procedure is becoming an accepted practice in many organizations.

2 At the maximum, papers should be handled twice. First, they should be screened according to the selective reading techniques discussed earlier. If the paperwork can be taken care of immediately, it should be. If additional work is required, the item should be entered on the priority list and not handled again until it can be completed and disposed of.

3 Develop form and model letters. Frequently, much of a supervisor's correspondence is of a routine and repetitive nature. If copies of previous reports and letters are saved, small changes in these letters can often be made that will provide suitable responses and save the trouble of composing an entirely new letter.

4 When unnecessary reports and letters become a problem, some supervisors have reported dealing with the situation successfully by simply ignoring it. If the requests are important, they will be repeated. If not, the problem is solved. Obviously, this strategy involves some risks, especially when the letters or reports are requested by the supervisor's boss or someone important in the organization. As with the other suggestions, common sense must be used and the trade-offs carefully evaluated.

Meetings

One of the most frustrating time wasters for most supervisors are the numerous meetings that they attend. It is getting so bad that some supervisors are spending up to two thirds of their total time in meetings, and they estimate that almost half this time is totally wasted. There are many jokes about committees, but unfortunately they often reflect the truth. The one saying that a committee "takes minutes but wastes hours" tells it all.

Some of the most common problems with meetings and some possible solutions are summarized in Table 4-3.

Most of the suggestions offered in Table 4-3 apply to the meeting leader. When supervisors do not have the responsibility for leading the meeting and they are required to attend, they may find it difficult but not impossible to manage their meeting time more effectively. Some of the following suggestions may be applied when the supervisor is not the meeting leader:

1 *Ask for time limits.* When the meeting leader arranges the meeting, supervisors should ask what the required time commitment will be. In the event that the meeting runs overtime, the supervisor will then have a valid excuse for leaving or calling for the meeting to end.

2 *Ask for a statement of contributions.* Supervisors should ask the meeting leader what the purpose of the meeting is and whether any planning or preparation will be required of those attending. Questions of this type will help motivate the meeting leader to define the purpose of the meeting more specifically and have at least a mental agenda if not a formal one.

3 *Provide leadership functions.* Where meeting leaders do not conduct the meeting appropriately, supervisors may exert themselves to provide some of these functions. For example, they may take on the responsibility for preparing the agenda or calling for specific plans of action at the conclusion of the meeting. Supervisors, of course, must be particularly careful to ensure that this behavior is not interpreted as an attempt to warp the leader's prerogatives.

4 *Don't go.* Another viable alternative is staying away from meetings which are unproductive. Once again this is a strategy which involves

TABLE 4-3
PROBLEMS CONCERNING MEETINGS AND POSSIBLE SOLUTIONS

Problem	Solution
1. Meetings are called without a specific purpose.	**1.** All meetings should be preceded by a statement of purpose and an agenda that is communicated in writing or at least verbally.
2. Inappropriate persons attend the meeting or persons with vital information are not invited.	**2.** Carefully consider who should be invited. Some individuals may be invited to attend only a portion of the meeting.
3. Meetings do not start on time.	**3.** Begin meeting on time regardless of the number of persons present. Delaying meetings rewards latecomers while punishing those who have arrived on time.
4. Meetings do not end on time.	**4.** A specific time for ending the meeting should be communicated by the leader at the beginning of the meeting. The leader should also list, with their respective time limits, the topics and issues to be discussed. When the group goes beyond these limits, the leader has the responsibility to call this to the attention of the group. The meeting should be ended on time, as the quality of participation drops rapidly as the meeting goes beyond its designated time limits.
5. Some individuals dominate the conversation.	**5.** It is the leader's responsibility to control the meeting. Tactful remarks can be made to control overambitious participants. For example, "Thank you, Henry. I'm also interested in what John and Mary feel about this issue."
6. Discussion of particular issues continues without resolution.	**6.** Most often, unresolvable issues stem from differences in values rather than facts. The leader might point this out and move on by saying "I think our differences on this issue have more to do with our

Problem	Solution
	personal feelings than with factual information. I'm sure we could continue to discuss this issue, but I am going to ask that we move on from here."
7. The leader becomes trapped into defending a position.	**7.** The leader should be a facilitator, guide, and director rather than a partisan. Leaders should avoid being trapped. When loaded questions are asked, the leader can respond by directing the problem back into the group. Example: "Yes I do have some feeling on that, but I'd like to hear what the other people have to say first."
8. Meetings may be very effective in producing considerable discussion but nothing ever comes of them.	**8.** The leader must call for a decision at the conclusion of the meeting. This is often a difficult task because it means changing the mood of the group. The leader should anticipate and be prepared for some resistance when the action-plan stage of the meeting begins. A very direct statement may help to move the group to this stage; for example: "O.K. we've got our options on the table. Now we must make a choice or we'll have been wasting our time."
9. Decisions made in meetings are not carried out.	**9.** The leader must plan for follow-through. This includes identifying parties responsible for carrying out actions, establishing specific dates and a timetable for completion, and stating how progress will be evaluated. All this should be included in the summary which ends the meeting.

some risks, but at least some supervisors have felt the trade-offs were worth it in terms of effectiveness.

Learn to Say No

There are many supervisors who just cannot say no and therefore become overburdened. Each request supervisors receive should be carefully considered to make sure that it is in line with unit goals. When it is not, the supervisor should not feel guilty for saying no. Frequently, even the supervisor's boss will back off from requests when they interfere with work-unit responsibilities and priorities.

In total then, there are a wide variety of strategies from which supervisors may choose in order to analyze, plan, and manage their time commitments. These strategies will undoubtedly be modified by each supervisor until he or she finds methods which are most effective for a particular situation.

■ KEY CONCEPTS

Time management
Delegation
Time wasters
Job analysis
Prioritizing for time management
Planning for time management

■ PRACTICAL EXERCISES

(These can be performed by individuals or by groups.)

1 Keep a log for a typical day and/or week. Analyze this list in terms of (a) the most probable time wasters; (b) things that might be delegated or eliminated; and (c) possible suggestions for how and to whom these things could be delegated for more effective time management.

2 Break up into small groups or pairs. Have each member design a weekly time budget. Exchange and critique each other's time budgets.

3 Identify four or five major time wasters you are intimately familiar with from your past or present job experience. Discuss ways in which these time wasters could be overcome or eliminated.

■ DISCUSSION INCIDENTS

Paul Dawson is the supervisor of sales for Allison Moving Systems. Allison manufactures to order all types of moving and handling systems. Their systems often involve multiple conveyor belts and sophisticated electronic equipment. A separate contract is written for each moving system sold. The problems between Paul and his salespeople revolve around the writing of the contract. To understand these problems, Paul's history with the company is important. He began working with Allison as an electrical technician and was actually involved in designing the moving systems for a period of time. As the systems became more complex, however, there arose a great need for someone with technical expertise in the sales force, so that customers who required very sophisticated systems could have a qualified person to talk to. Paul was this person, and he began and maintained an effective sales career for over ten years before becoming supervisor. About two years before his appointment to supervision, he was also given the responsibility for writing all final contracts, because there had been so many misunderstandings in the past. Paul took on this new duty with relish and has held on to it ever since his supervisory appointment almost six years ago. In that same time period, the sales force has almost doubled and many of the salespeople have begun to complain. Their major grievance was that sales were being delayed because Paul was unable to write the contracts when they were needed. Paul's response to their complaint was that it was impossible to delegate this assignment because of its highly technical nature.

1 Discuss the reasons and justifications for Paul's failure to delegate this task.

2 Can time management benefit Paul? Can you suggest a time plan for Paul? Delegating contract-writing responsibilities should be given special attention. Anything else?

At Metropolitan Hospital, Betty Sayer and Ruth O'Malia, the two charge nurses, were just leaving the two-hour-long monthly meeting held by Linda Mathews, the head nurse. "That was just about the worst yet," said Betty; "The meeting was totally useless . . . a complete waste of time. Can you believe that she went all through room-cleaning procedures for the orderlies with everyone else in the room?" "Well, the thing I couldn't believe," said Ruth, "is that she went all the way through the drug checkout procedure when only five people in the room have the authority to check out drugs. I also got a kick when she asked Carol Kelly to talk about the new surgery preparation techniques and Carol couldn't explain them. Carol really gets upset when she's taken by surprise like that." "That was kind of entertaining, but really something has got to be done to end these meeting marathons. I just can't take much more of this."

1 Discuss some constructive approaches that Betty and Ruth, as well as other employees in similar situations, might take to help make their supervisor aware of the "meeting problem."

2 What specific things could Betty and Ruth do to reduce lost time in their supervisor's meeting? What could the supervisor do to make these meetings more efficient?

ORGANIZING RESOURCES

5 CHAPTER

Helen Brady is the supervisor of the claims adjustment department for an insurance corporation. Before she took over, Phil Thompson was supervisor of the department. Phil had been with the company almost thirty years at the time he retired last month. According to Helen and most of the other employees in claims, Phil really retired on-the-job at least five years ago. However, his lack of action only began to show when Helen inherited the job. It was most apparent in the organization of the work group. Here the problems were closely related to the nature of the work. First, there are many different types of policies that need to be serviced, such as life, accident, disability, auto, and property insurance. Second, there are a number of different classifications of clients which relate to the way a claim is serviced. These types of customers include commercial accounts, homeowners, professional people, single people, and the disabled. Finally, there are a number of geographic and demographic factors that affect the servicing of accounts. Age and sex, for example, are closely related to the service required and the rates which correspond to life, accident, and health insurance policies. In addition, geographical areas are closely related to auto accident frequencies, rates, and even the size of settlements for particular kinds of claims. Thus, there are some very natural work divisions. Unfortunately, the department itself is not organized around these natural work breakdowns. Rather, it seems that people have been allowed to structure their jobs according to their personal whims. An example is Gregg Dobbins, who works only on automobile settlements regardless of the location, whereas Craig Sims services all types of claims as long as they are in Saunders County. Finally, Ted Carter, who thinks he is "Mr. Important," insists on being involved only in claims over $250,000. Helen knows that even a few simple changes could increase the efficiency of her department greatly, but she does not quite know how or where to begin to organize.

■ LEARNING OBJECTIVES

After reading this chapter, you should have:

An understanding of the bureaucratic theory of structuring organizations

A grasp of the various methods that can be used to departmentalize work

An awareness of the advantages and disadvantages of specialization

Knowledge of and the ability to apply traditional organizational principles such as unity of command, equal authority and responsibility, and hierarchy

An acquaintance with alternatives to traditional principles of organization such as project, matrix, and free-form structural arrangements

An awareness of the differences between line and staff functions and applications

Supervisors are confronted daily with questions of organization like those facing the supervisor in the opening case. Here are some common examples of similar concerns that face supervisors in all types of organizations:

Who should report to whom?

Can all paperwork be assigned to one person?

Can one person be made responsible for distributing and handling all necessary materials?

Is it appropriate to call the manager of the other division or does my boss have to do it?

Can I buy the office furniture myself or does someone else have that responsibility?

Do I *have* to listen to personnel's recommendations on hiring someone?

How many people can I supervise effectively?

Should we have one person to do just maintenance and cleanup?

This list could go on and on. Common to all the questions, however, is the implication that the resources (both human and physical) within the organization are or should be arranged in some planned and organized fashion. The responsibility and authority for particular relationships and activities should be spelled out and made explicit. This implies some master plan which specifies how different parts of the organization interact and relate. More specifically, this concept can be called organizational structure, the purposeful and systematic arrangement and relationship of physical and human

113

resources. This chapter will be concerned with the principles of organization and the ways in which supervisors can use these principles in structuring their own specific work groups. It must be remembered, however, that supervisors are operating in the context of the overall organizational structure. Supervisory work units are dependent upon and at least partially defined by their relationship to the larger organization. Thus, it is imperative that supervisors also have an understanding of structure from the overall organizational perspective in order to operate effectively.

THE BUREAUCRATIC THEORY OF ORGANIZATION

The first formal theory of organization was proposed in the late 1800s by Max Weber, the famous German sociologist, who searched for the ideal organizational form. He believed that organizations could maximize efficiency if they adopted the following rational guidelines:

1 Work should be divided and distributed throughout the organization in a rational and logical manner. For example, work that is similar in purpose, method, or function should be assigned to the same groups, and this work should be broken down into its component parts and simplified, since it is easier for people to learn and become proficient within a narrow range of responsibilities than a broad one. In other words, organizations should be highly *specialized.*
2 Organizations should establish an explicit chain of command so that communications can be relayed effectively and problems can be resolved authoritatively. In other words, an organization should have a well-established *hierarchy.*
3 There must be a set of *rules* to ensure rational and uniform behavior within the organization. For example, all members of an organization should arrive and leave at the same time, so that they can transact their daily business with one another on a consistent basis.
4 Relationships should be *impersonal* to ensure that decisions are made on objective rather than subjective criteria. For example, a supervisor should not become emotionally involved with a subordinate.

To Weber, organizations that were able to follow these few simple prescriptions would ensure the most efficient use of their resources. He called this approach to organization "bureaucracy."

Today, bureaucracy is a word that does not have the connotation of efficiency but instead conjures up any number of negative features such as inefficiency, red tape, impersonality, and basic ignorance of human needs. Yet many of the bureaucratic concepts and principles proposed by Weber remain as the cornerstones of modern, large organizations. Weber's theory was a pure type. We now know that although many of his basic principles were correct, especially under certain circumstances such as large size and a stable environment, the time has now come to recognize some necessary extensions, modifications, and—in certain situations—alternatives to bureaucratic principles of organization.

THE DEPARTMENTATION PRINCIPLE

"Departmentation" refers to the methods used for establishing the division of labor within the work force and organizing any given level of the organizational structure. The basic premise of this principle is that the tasks and functions within organizations are extremely varied and complex. It follows that it would be virtually impossible for any single individual or department to perform, at even minimum standards, every activity that is required. Therefore tasks, responsibilities, and functions must be grouped into some logical arrangement for assignment to both individuals and work groups.

Most of the methods for organizing work are self-explanatory. Some of the major ways of departmentalizing include the following:

1 *Functional departmentation* is perhaps the most widely utilized method. Here responsibilities and tasks which are directed toward achieving a common purpose are grouped together. Most organizations divide work along functional lines, such as production, personnel, marketing, finance, engineering, and public relations (in an industrial firm) or medical services, housekeeping, dietary services, personnel, nursing, pharmacy, and finance (in a general hospital).
2 *Customer/client organization* divides tasks and responsibilities according to the types of customers or clients served. A prison, for example, may have wards for lifers, those condemned to death, first-time offenders, and trustees; or a passenger ship may be organized into first class, second class, and tourist class.
3 *Alpha numerical* departmentation arbitrarily splits work load according to numerical or alphabetical listings. A university, for example, may assign professors as advisers according to the students' social security numbers; or the telephone company may assign maintenance crews to certain sets of phone numbers.
4 *Equipment* is used as the basis for departmentalizing in some

115

types of organizations. For example, a fast-food restaurant may divide work between the grill, french fryers, shake machines, and cash registers; or a manufacturing plant may have drill-press and polishing departments.

5 The *product* form of departmentation may be used in a department store, dividing areas into men's clothing, women's clothing, sporting goods, household fixtures, and appliances; or an automobile company may be divided according to its various makes and models.

6 *Time* can be used to departmentalize workers into various shifts, such as 7 A.M. to 3 P.M., 3 P.M. to 11 P.M., and 11 P.M. to 7 A.M.

7 *Geographic* departmentation is frequently used to divide work into different locales or parts of the country. For example, there may be the eastern and western divisions.

8 *Service* may be used to departmentalize. A hospital, for example, may be divided into departments such as Orthopedics, Coronary Care, Surgical Care, and Intensive Care.

A supervisor's unit may be organized in one or more of the ways described above. Figure 5-1 shows how a large business firm may be departmentalized. Another example might be a supervisor in a telephone company who is described as the night shift supervisor of the operations unit charged with trouble calls for the northwest district for numbers 0000000–4999999. Similarly, supervisors may organize within their own work units with one or more of the methods of departmentation. For example, the supervisor of a customer complaint department in a utility uses four guidelines to distribute the work load:

1 Function—credit calls, high bill complaints, and orders to connect or disconnect service

2 Type of customer—commercial or residential

3 Service—in-house or field representative

4 Geographical area—north, south, east, or west

Thus, at least one subordinate is a field representative who handles complaints about high residential bills in the east section.

Most often departmentation and division of labor evolve naturally or by default as the organization grows. For example, a janitorial service may begin as a one-person, owner-operated business. As the owner acquires new business and adds new people, divisions of labor may begin to evolve. Specific individuals may take responsibilities for bookkeeping, selling new business, commercial cleaning, residential cleaning, and so on. Although the owner may not have formal departmentation specifically in mind when the assignment of functions and responsibilities is made, this is actually what is occurring.

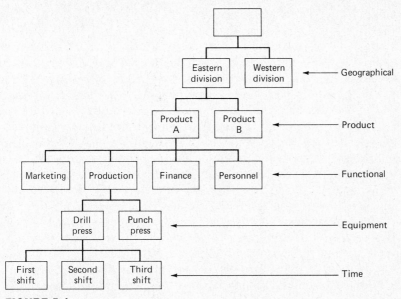

FIGURE 5-1
An example of departmentation of a
large firm.

In general, supervisors may increase their effectiveness by deliberately reviewing and implementing formal departmentation methods as described above. The various types of departmentation may suggest a way of organizing not previously considered. Moreover, supervisors should consider several alternatives for dividing the work; they can weigh the respective advantages and disadvantages of each method of departmentation to ensure that they arrive at the most effective organizational structure.

THE SPECIALIZATION PRINCIPLE

Very closely related to the principle of departmentation is specialization. Departmentation is one way to specialize. The basic premise of specialization is that employees become more efficient as they become more specialized. According to this principle, the supervisor's unit can become more effective by simplifying work and allowing employees to become highly skilled and specialized within a narrow range of responsibilities.

117

The classic example of specialization is the automobile assembly line. Each worker has a specialized job, such as bolting on doors, mounting engines, or lining up front ends. Because these tasks and responsibilities are narrowly defined, workers are able to develop highly efficient skills in accomplishing their tasks. When the entire group of specialized workers is combined on the assembly line, complete cars can be produced in a matter of minutes. On the other hand, if each worker had to build the entire car from scratch, the process would take months or years to accomplish. It is doubtful that very many of the workers could even develop the necessary skills to carry out all the tasks performed by the specialized workers on the assembly line. Moreover, the amount of time that it would take a worker to complete one task and prepare for and complete another would be prohibitive. The major advantage of specialization is that workers can develop high levels of skill for particular tasks and do not lose time as they change from one task to another.

High degrees of specialization can and are used in many organizational settings besides the assembly line in manufacturing. One example is the large family restaurant. If, for instance, the person responsible for setting tables were also responsible for seating customers, taking orders, cooking food, washing dishes, cleaning tables, and ringing up the bills, utter chaos would result, Thus, at least in this business, a high degree of specialization and division of labor is necessary. The same is true in office situations, hospitals, educational institutions, and every other large, complex organization.

At this point, however, a warning is in order: work can become *too* specialized. Again, the most visible example of the misuse of specialization is the automobile assembly line, where a worker may stand in one place for eight hours a day tightening lug nuts on wheels. The problem, of course, is that such specialized work does not challenge the worker's capabilities. Workers' skills are underutilized under high degrees of specialization and their jobs become very boring and uninteresting. High degrees of specialization contribute heavily to the widely publicized "blue-collar blues" affecting many of today's manufacturing firms. Similarly, a dishwasher in a restaurant is likely to become discouraged because the work is so routine and offers no challenge. The same holds true for office workers (who suffer from "white-collar woes") and employees in nonbusiness organizations. The supervisor has to look at the specialization principle in terms of striking a delicate balance between task breakdowns that over-specialize workers, thus creating boredom and drudgery, and under-specializing tasks, which leads to inefficiencies. Realizing that the productive/technological process is often beyond the direct control of individual supervisors, they can strive for a middle ground of specialization within their own unit. Motivational strategies such as job enrichment and job rotation, which will be discussed in Chapter 15, provide some help to supervisors in overcoming the human problems inherent in overspecialization.

THE SPAN-OF-CONTROL PRINCIPLE

Another important consideration in organizing is the span of control, defined as the number of employees who report directly to the supervisor. Some of these organizing principles go far back in history; for example, specific reference to span of control is made in the Bible. When Moses was leading his followers out of Egypt, there were many disputes over property and possessions. Moses tried to deal with these by mediating and judging each case individually. After several sessions lasting from sunup until sundown, Moses became haggard and worn. This led his father-in-law Jethro to remark, "What you are doing is not good, you and the people will wear yourselves out; for the thing is too heavy for you; you are not able to perform it alone." Jethro went on to suggest that Moses develop an organization with a more limited span of control. Moses listened and "chose able men out of all Israel, and made them heads over the people, rulers of thousands, of hundreds, of fifties, and of tens . . . hard cases they brought to Moses, but any smaller matter they decided themselves." This reference from the Bible summarizes very well the principle of span of control—which refers to the number of direct subordinates a supervisor can effectively manage.

Most classical discussions of span of control revolve around the precise number of workers a supervisor should take charge of. Management writers and practitioners through the years have offered a variety of answers. For example, in the early part of the present century, a British general, Sir Ian Hamilton, concluded after a lengthy study of military organizations that the span of control should be somewhere between three and six. He believed that the span should be smaller at the top of the organization, where thought processes were more complicated, and that it should get progressively larger toward the lower levels of the organization, where thought processes were less complicated and more routine. However, Hamilton felt that the maximum span should at no time exceed six persons.

Another interesting historical contribution on span of control was provided by V. A. Graicunas, a management consultant. To Graicunas, the important consideration in establishing span of control was the number of different social relationships the supervisor is required to manage. For example, Graicunas points out that if a supervisor (A in Figure 5-2) manages two employees (B and C), there are actually six different relationships:

1 A with B
2 A with C
3 A with B while C is present
4 A with C while B is present
5 B to C
6 C to B

As more employees are added, the number of relationships which have to be managed multiplies. Thus, a supervisor with only twelve employees will have an almost unbelievable 20,000+ relationships to manage. The point Graicunas was trying to make was that it was not enough to count only the number of bodies in a span of control; that the numerous relationships also had to be recognized.

Today, we know that there is no universal formula to determine the correct span of control. The number of people who can be supervised effectively depends on variables such as the abilities and personalities of individual supervisors and subordinates, the nature of the tasks to be performed, the overall environment of the organization, and the attitude of top management. In other words, only very general guidelines for effective span of control can be suggested. Each supervisor will need to consider guidelines such as the following in light of his or her own particular personal and organizational circumstances. This is the contingency approach that was discussed in Chapter 1. Some things to consider would be:

1 *Task Complexity.* Generally more complex tasks require narrower spans of control than less complex tasks.

2 *Similarity of Tasks.* If all employees within the work unit are performing similar tasks, then the span of control can usually be larger than when employees are performing a wide range of different activities.

3 *Routine/Exceptional.* Supervisors with workers performing routine and standardized tasks (e.g., assembly-line jobs) can usually have greater spans of control than supervisors of workers whose tasks are constantly changing (e.g., appliance repairers).

4 *Line/Staff.* Generally, spans of control in operating line units can be larger than those in support staff units. The staff concept is covered later in this chapter.

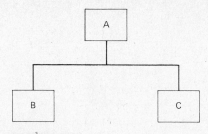

FIGURE 5-2
The span of control.

5 *Education.* In organizations whose personnel are highly educated, there is a tendency to have smaller spans of control because of the complexity of jobs. However, this may be a case where larger spans could be more effective, since they would give highly educated people more autonomy.

6 *Organization Level.* Spans of control are generally narrower at the top and broader at the bottom of the hierarchy. Like the highly educated, upper-level managers may be candidates for larger spans of control.

As in the case of the principle of specialization, there are some important behavioral implications inherent in wide (sometimes called "flat") spans of control and narrow (sometimes called "tall") spans. Figure 5-3 shows flat and tall structures for a personnel unit. From a behavioral perspective, flat organizations are generally considered to be advantageous in that they force more responsibility onto subordinates. This results in greater employee development, more decision making at lower levels, and consequently greater employee satisfaction and motivation. Taller organizations have the advantage of closer control of subordinates' activities, more routes to promotion, and more supervisor/employee contact. It should be noted, however, that tall organizations also result in more administrative levels and activities, which may detract from getting the actual work done. In the example of the personnel unit in Figure 5-3, each of the functions in the flat organization is assigned to an individual. That individual then has responsibility for a given function. Also, in the flat structure, the personnel manager is not able to keep close control over subordinates, and they therefore have more autonomy to make decisions and to develop. In the tall structure, the extra layer of supervision strips some of the responsibilities away from the functional personnel. Since the supervisors in such a structure have smaller spans of

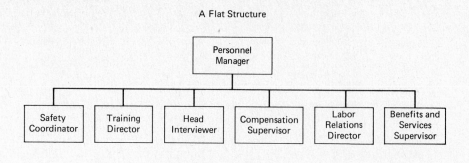

A Flat Structure

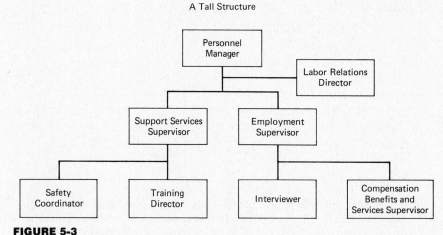

A Tall Structure

FIGURE 5-3
Examples of flat and tall structures in a
personnel unit.

control, they can keep closer watch over their subordinates. This may
rob the latter of opportunities for decision making and development.

THE SCALAR PRINCIPLE

Another major principle emphasizes the hierarchy of responsibility
and authority. According to this scalar or hierarchy principle, authority and responsibility go from the top down and define the specific
relationships between superior-subordinate pairs in each succeeding
level of the organization.

Perhaps the best illustration of this principle is a typical organization chart, such as those shown in Figures 5-4 A and B. In these two charts, authority can be traced through all lines which directly connect the boxes. In the manufacturing example, the general manager has direct authority over the finance director, purchasing agent, sales manager, and personnel manager. These positions can be labeled as staff because they serve in an advisory capacity to the general manager and do not directly supervise anyone in the line manufacturing area. This staff concept will be given specific attention later in this chapter. The scalar chain of command can also be traced through the line organization. The general manager has direct authority over the plant superintendent, who, in turn, has direct authority over the maintenance and engineering supervisors and the general supervisor. The maintenance and engineering personnel serve the plant superintendent in a staff capacity. Continuing down the scalar chain is the general supervisor, who has direct authority over the three manufacturing lines. In this hierarchical organizational structure, each person has one and only one person to whom he or she is directly responsible. The same analysis can be made of the hospital organization shown in Figure 5-4B.

Apart from its implications for authority, the scalar principle can be used to trace the flow of formal communication through the organization. For example, if one of the mechanics in the maintenance unit wanted the machine operators on line 2 to inform the maintenance department whenever the bearings on their machines began to squeak, this mechanic would, theoretically, have to follow the entire chain of command to communicate this. That is, the mechanic would be required to relay this suggestion to the maintenance supervisor, who, in turn, would have to relay it to the plant superintendent. If the superintendent agreed, he or she would then issue a direct order to the general supervisor, who would then pass the order on down to the supervisor of line 2. A similar sequence of communications would have to be followed if the dietitian wanted to have something done about patient care in the third shift.

This discussion points to the fact that the scalar chain of authority and/or communication cannot be followed religiously, since this would quickly become a rather tedious and lengthy process. In practice, this formal chain of command often is (and must be) short-circuited. For example, the mechanic may go directly to the machine operator and informally request to be informed immediately when the bearings are heard to squeak, and the dietitian may give a

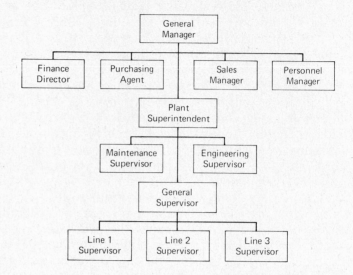

A. A Manufacturing Organization

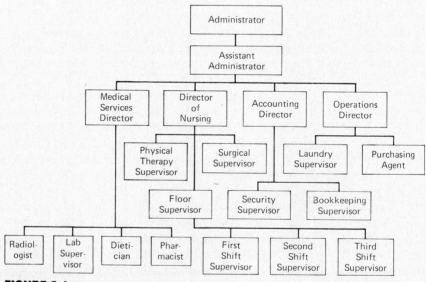

B. A Hospital Organization

FIGURE 5-4
Organization charts illustrating the
scalar principle.

**Basic Elements
of Effective Supervision**

call to the second-shift supervisor suggesting that a bedtime snack be given to certain patients. If there is voluntary compliance, then the problem is solved. However, if some of the workers choose not to comply, then the mechanic or dietitian would have to revert to formal channels in order to have the conflict resolved by the person having combined authority over both groups (the plant superintendent in the manufacturing example and the assistant administrator in the case of the hospital).

OTHER PRINCIPLES OF ORGANIZATION USEFUL TO THE SUPERVISOR

Besides the major principles of deparmentation, specialization/ division of labor, span of control, and hierarchy there are some other principles that supervisors must understand and selectively use in order to organize their resources effectively. Four of the more important are equal authority and responsibility, unity of command, functional authority, and staff.

Equal Authority and Responsibility

This organizational principle means that when individuals are assigned particular responsibilities, they must have the authority required to carry them out. One of the most common complaints is that people are assigned responsibilities without the commensurate authority. A typical example is the individual who is told to assign daily tasks and check up on workers periodically to make sure they are performing properly. Yet, despite this large burden of responsibility, such an individual may have no power to reprimand or fire others or to provide rewards such as pay increases. Quite often, unless such supervisors are very skillful at negotiating and dealing with people, they find that they cannot carry out their responsibilities adequately and therefore become very disgruntled with the person who saddled them with their burdens. The principle to be followed is that if a person is to be responsible for accomplishing particular tasks, then he or she must be given the power and authority required to carry out the orders. In some cases, principles such as this are successfully violated, but any failure to follow them must be carefully explained and justified.

Unity of Command

Henry Valentine was a pathetic person: 5 feet 2 inches tall, 190 pounds, deaf in one ear, and suffering from asthma and recurrent heart problems. Despite his sixty years, his boyish round face and short stature made him look like some kind of dwarf or elf from a Walt Disney production. He had been working in the XYZ organization for almost thirty years and had never progressed beyond the lowest pay grade. Everybody kicked Henry around, from the other rank-and-file employees to the top managers. He never said a word; with his droopy head, he would sweep away whatever mess someone else had made. Then, one momentous day, he took his stand, albeit it lasted only a few seconds. The incident began when one of the employees told Henry to clean up a mess which had been left in his work area. Henry began to clean it up, but then another employee jumped into the act, yelling at Henry to clean up another mess around *his* area. There were orange peels, coffee cups, and even half a sandwich on the floor where some employee had missed a couple of long shots from the lunch table 15 feet away. Henry started sweeping, but in no time at all the first employee was forcefully pacing toward him. At almost the same instant, the supervisor was just beginning to light into Henry because he had not yet picked up the supervisor's coffee for the afternoon break. As all three converged on him, Henry stood up (that is, he was already standing, but he now seemed to grow almost 6 inches), raised his index finger forcefully over his head, and yelled "One man, one boss!" Of course, everyone, including the supervisor, was taken aback. After almost thirty years of playing door mat, Henry Valentine had taken a stand.

In his moment of glory, Henry actually stated one of the most widely recognized principles of organization, unity of command. The concept is self-explanatory and simply means that each person within an organization should have one and only one person to whom he or she is responsible. Following this principle minimizes the conflicts and anxieties employees would otherwise have—that is, if they were required to report and be responsible to more than one supervisor. In addition, such an arrangement is helpful to supervisors, since it enables them to know exactly who is responsible to them and over whom they have direct authority.

As with the other principles of organization, there are some noteworthy exceptions to the rule of unity of command. For example, most professionals are directly responsible to their peers as much as they are to their administrators for their actions and performance, and the chief operating executive of every type of organization is almost always answerable to a board composed of several persons. Another common example where unity of command is violated is in nursing, where the floor supervisor may be responsible to the head nurse for areas such as staffing, scheduling, discipline, and training, but at the same time this supervisor may receive specific, binding, and sometimes even contradictory directions from patients' doctors. Similarly, although most supervisors in large organizations are directly responsible to their immediate bosses for operating problems, they may also have to make monthly reports to and follow directions (sometimes contradictory) from other functions such as purchasing or personnel.

These dual responsibilities seem to be on the increase as organizations become more complex and outside influences affect them. Like the other principles, unity of command should be followed unless there are unique circumstances (as in the case of medical authority in the nursing example) preventing it. When the principle is violated, it should be justified and fully explained to the persons affected.

Functional Authority

Functional authority is a more recent organizational principle which plugs some of the holes created when unity of command is violated. This principle is that the supervisor can have clearly defined authority over certain functions when interacting with other parts of the organization. According to this principle, it is possible to make supervisors responsible and have authority over particular functional areas of the entire organization as well as having the usual authority over their own work units. If this principle is to work, the reporting relationships must be clearly defined and care must be taken to ensure that the authority does not overlap.

An example of functional authority would be the rule that anyone who wants to fire an employee must first get an OK from the personnel director. In this case, the personnel director has functional authority over employee dismissal. Another example may be a regulation that any purchase exceeding $150 must be approved by the finance director. In both these examples, no supervisor in any department has the authority to fire or to make purchases over $150. Other functional areas besides personnel and finance which typically have some authority over supervisory activities are labor relations and purchasing. Regardless of the type of authority the other functions exercise over these activities, it is important for supervisors to remember that the authority applies only to the specific, stated areas. There must be well-understood guidelines, so that supervisors know when they may act freely and have the authority to make a decision and when they do not have the authority and must request approval.

Although functional authority may seem like an encroachment upon supervisors' rights and privileges, there are usually some good reasons for granting functional authority. For example, many actions by supervisors in both the areas of personnel and labor relations are regulated by federal and state laws and can involve an organization in some very embarrassing and costly legal entanglements if supervisors are unaware of these laws. Because these and other laws (as discussed in Chapter 2, on the supervisor's environment) are changing so frequently and becoming more difficult to understand, staff specialists are needed to keep up with the legislation. These people are, therefore, much more aware of potential problems and can help supervisors avoid costly and embarrassing mistakes.

The Staff Principle

The staff principle of organization was first developed in the military. Military leaders usually have relatively large spans of control, with widely divergent functions reporting to them. To compensate for this problem of size and complexity, staff specialists are utilized. The staff personnel are charged with the responsibility of analyzing problems, developing alternative courses of action, and making specific recommendations. Importantly, the staff specialists do not give orders to line personnel; they can only advise. Line commanders will listen to staff advice, but only they can issue the orders necessary to implement the recommended actions. Thus, while all orders are issued by the line commanders, they are actually the result of inputs from the staff specialists. This staff principle allows high degrees of specialization but maintains unity of command.

Most modern, large organizations have adopted the military staff principle. Top management may have a specialized staff organization. Figure 5-5 shows a line-staff organization for a typical business firm and a regional office for Housing and Urban Development. In the manufacturing example, the staff positions are those along the top (contracting, work-force planning, finance/accounting, personnel/

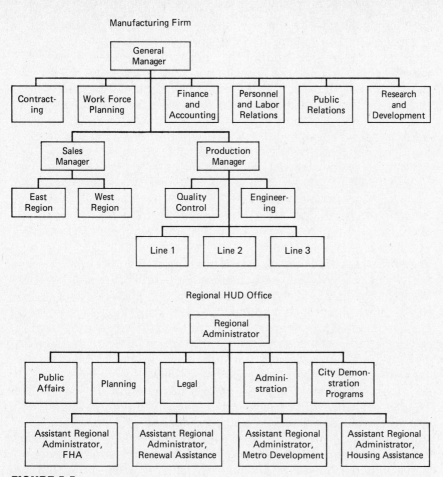

FIGURE 5-5
Examples of staff structures.

labor relations, public relations, and research and development). Importantly, it should be noted that one of the major line departments, production, also has staff backup (quality control and engineering). In the example from the public sector, the staff departments are also along the top (public affairs, planning, legal, administration, and city demonstration programs).

Except in cases of spelled-out functional authority (as discussed earlier), the staff personnel have no direct authority over the operating line departments. The staff's role is advisory; they make recommendations which, if approved, result in specific directives from top management. For example, after carefully analyzing growth and technological requirements, the work-force planning expert may recommend to the general manager that there be a systematic cutback in the number of employees. The general manager may, in turn, issue this as a specific directive to the operating departments. The work-force planning expert could go directly to the production department with this recommendation, but technically the production people could ignore it. Realistically, however, because the work-force planning expert is part of the general manager's staff, he or she would have a lot of "implied authority," and the production people would have to have very good justification for ignoring the recommendation. The work-force planner could always revert to formal channels and inform the general manager that the production people were not cooperating.

Another example may be drawn from the staff engineers, who can, technically, only recommend changes to operating supervisors. If the recommendation is accepted and it works out, the supervisor generally receives most of the credit for increases in productivity. However, if the recommendation does not work out and productivity decreases, the supervisor will also receive most of the blame. Importantly, however, the supervisor has full authority to accept or reject recommendations. If engineering recommends a change which a supervisor does not accept, engineering has no authority to impose the change. Its only option is to go through an informal negotiating process with supervisors in both engineering and operating functions and/or to revert to formal channels. Only when the issue reaches a manager with authority over both engineering and operations, which is usually the general manager, can the operating supervisors be forced to comply with the recommendations of engineering.

Another source of confusion is the problem of determining when a department is line or staff. Even though the departments in the manufacturing and HUD examples were identified as line or staff, this distinction is not always clear either by looking at an organization chart or, in many cases, talking to the people themselves. One view is that all functions which do not produce specific goods or services are considered staff. Accordingly, in a manufacturing firm, functions such as personnel, finance, engineering, accounting, maintenance, and purchasing are often considered staff functions because they do not produce a tangible product or service. Similarly, in a small building and design firm, the office personnel—such as the secretary, bookkeeper, and architect—would be considered staff, while the field people—such as carpenters, electricians, bricklayers, and plumbers—would usually be considered operating line personnel. Exceptions would come from functional authority. For example, the architects and draftspersons would frequently have functional authority over field personnel with regard to work procedures and methods utilized to achieve the design.

The above examples point to the many "gray areas" found in line-staff relations. Besides the "implied authority" that staff possess, they can also gain respect and attention by repeatedly demonstrating that their recommendations contribute to increased productivity and cost savings. After a line supervisor repeatedly rejects staff recommendations only to have them approved by higher-level management, it becomes exceedingly clear that staff personnel can and do have real power. Line supervisors who repeatedly reject valid staff recommendations soon find themselves playing a weak role and lose much of their legitimate authority. Similarly, staff people who attempt to exercise authority that they do not have soon find that they lose their informal authority and power. To have the best of both worlds, line and staff personnel must make a determined effort to utilize each other's expertise to achieve effective results, and the staff should take a "sell" rather than "tell" approach to line supervisors.

CONTEMPORARY PERSPECTIVES OF STRUCTURING ORGANIZATIONS

The concepts and principles discussed so far are largely based on bureaucratic theory and its extensions and modifications. For the most part, these principles have withstood the continuous scrutiny and criticisms of both organizational theorists and practitioners. Only recently have these traditional principles of organization been seriously challenged. First are the criticisms that bureaucratic principles and their extensions (e.g., staff) are no longer the most efficient for the modern scene. Closely related is the second major criticism—that the traditional principles at a minimum deemphasize and at most completely ignore many of the human dynamics found in today's organizations. These two important challenges to traditional organizations have resulted in project, matrix, and free-form alternative structures. Their behavioral implications can be found in an analysis of the informal organization.

Project Organizational Structures

Project organizational structures were devised to provide more flexibility than could be found in traditional forms. Generally project organizations focus resources toward the achievement of organization goals rather than the provision of a particular function. Some examples of project organizations will clarify what this means. Figure 5-6 illustrates a project organization for a moderate-sized building and design firm. The projects in this firm have been assigned to project managers or supervisors. They are responsible for all aspects of the given project. Much to their displeasure, they do not have direct authority over the functional people. This, of course, directly violates the traditional principle of equal authority and responsibility. On the other hand, although they do not have direct authority over the line organizations, project supervisors usually have very significant informal power via their recommendations to functional supervisors and, if necessary, to top management.

The important distinction between project structuring and traditional approaches is that, within the project structures, human and physical resources are directed toward completing a particular project rather than providing a function for the organization. Other examples of project management include the following:

1 A catering firm with a stable number of cooks and waitresses but with several other individuals who are responsible for organizing banquets and coordinating all the necessary resources

2 A management consulting firm where particular persons design and coordinate training programs with various firms and draw from a pool of experienced trainers and course designers to meet their particular needs

3 A computer programming organization with a specified number of individuals who are responsible for designing and coordinating different projects and use any number of a large group of programmers to implement projects

4 An employment agency with a staff of interviewers but also a group of specialists responsible for coordinating projects like the staffing of an entire manufacturing facility

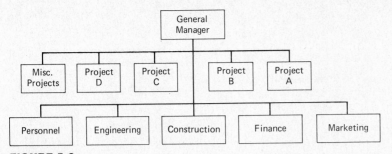

FIGURE 5-6
An example of project organization.

5 A military unit with the traditional functional areas but also designated project people to oversee civilian contracts

Project structures obviously have much greater flexibility than traditional forms. Projects can be added or eliminated with little disruption to the rest of the organization. Although project structures have been most frequently used for large concerns such as shipbuilders, aircraft manufacturers, and construction firms, the same principles can be and are used by smaller organizations. Moreover, even if the entire organization does not have a project structure, particular parts of it may utilize project concepts. For example, a project coordinator might be designated to help supervise a move to a new facility, help in the development of a new product or service, or even supervise the development of an entirely new function (e.g., maintenance or quality control) within the organization.

Matrix Organizations

A similar and somewhat related organizational form is the matrix structure. As shown in Figure 5-7, the matrix organization consists of a traditional functional structure with a project overlay. The project supervisors are given direct authority over functional personnel in a matrix structure. As a result, each person on the third level of the organization in Figure 5-7 has two bosses, a functional boss and a project boss. Of course, this matrix organization directly violates the classical principle of unity of command. As a result, there are frequent conflicts in project organizations, and project supervisors must be exceptionally skilled in human relations and conflict resolu-

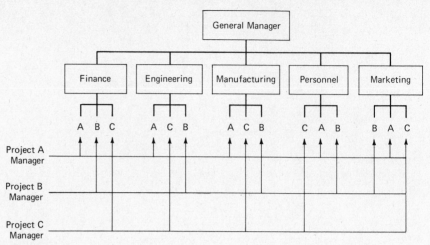

FIGURE 5-7
An example of a matrix organization.

tion. The general manager must also act strongly and decisively to resolve conflicts between functional supervisors and project supervisors. Despite the conflict inherent in matrix structures, many organizations that have used them feel that their advantages outweight the problems. Such a structure is flexible and formalizes important and necessary horizontal communication flows. It designates specific responsibilities for projects within functional structures. It is the best of both worlds: project and functional.

Some examples of how various kinds of organizations might use matrix structures are given below:

1 A rehabilitation center may have a functional breakdown into interviewers, counselors, and outreach workers. Each of these functional employees might also report to persons coordinating programs dealing with, for example, alcoholism, financial problems, drug addiction, marital problems, or child-abuse problems.

2 An advertising agency may have functional departments composed of salespersons, writers, and photographers while also having project coordinators who organize the functional personnel for particular clients or advertising campaigns.

3 A contractor may have departments of salespersons, draftspersons, engineers, electricians, plumbers, carpenters, bricklayers, etc.

People within these functional departments may also report to coordinators for specific projects.

4 A college of business administration may have functional departments of finance, marketing, accounting, economics, and management as well as directors for the various programs such as the undergraduate, graduate, continuing education, and research programs.

These suggested matrix structures are alternatives to traditional structures and they would have to be analyzed in light of the specific situation. In some situations they would be more effective than traditional structures; in others, they would not be as effective as traditional ways of organizing.

Free-Form Structures

In the free form, structure follows purpose. The structure can take any form or even no form. As the goals and purposes of an organization change, the structure also changes. If the purposes and goals are changing too rapidly, the decision may be made to abandon a formal structure altogether. Most often, however, free-form structures can be viewed as rapidly changing project organizations.

Free-form structures are most often associated with the so-called "go-go" conglomerates such as Litton Industries, LTV, and Xerox Corporation. The free form, however, also closely approximates newly developing organizations. At first, many new organizations have no idea how to departmentalize or specialize work. Responsibilities are often grouped around people possessing particular kinds of expertise. Gradually, the more skilled individuals gain responsibilities that match their abilities. In this manner, the organization forms around people rather than functions; it changes as people within the organization change.

While it has many disadvantages in terms of organizational stability and formal authority and communication, the free form's advantages in terms of meeting human needs, adaptability, and flexibility to change cannot be ignored in certain situations. Finally, it should be noted and emphasized that no one form of organizational design is optimal. Traditional, project, matrix, and free forms may all be appropriate at one stage or another within the life of an overall organization or a supervisor's given unit of responsibility. Although the traditional form has been severely criticized in recent years, it remains as the most effective structure under certain conditions. The alternative forms should not be seen as the answer to all organizational problems but rather as other effective options. It is hoped that, by examining these options, supervisors will be able to determine the most effective way to structure their own units and that they will understand their overall organizations better.

THE INFORMAL ORGANIZATION

So far, the discussion has centered around formal organizational structure. Perhaps the most valid criticism of this approach to organization is that it does not adequately account for human dynamics. Some modern critics have gone as far as to say that very little of how the organization really functions can be specified by the formal organizational structure. They carefully point out that an informal structure is inherent in every formal one. The informal structure represents the true power relationships and shows how the organization really functions. This informal structure contains informal leaders, agreements, and communication among the participants in the organization. For example, within a department of twenty-five employees, you might find the following types of informal roles, each of which serves a particular function for the work group:

1 *Old timers* who know their jobs inside out and can show new workers shortcuts which can cut corners and improve their work considerably.

2 *Social leaders* who can unify the group or can exclude group members. They can have considerable control over the attitudes and behaviors of the work group.

3 *Chronic complainers* who consistently point out supervisory and management mistakes to both coworkers and supervisors.

4 *Spokespersons* who are aware of group sentiments and have been given authority by the others in the group to relay their feelings to supervisors.

In addition to the above roles played by individuals in the informal structure, work groups also display informally sanctioned behaviors and attitudes. Some examples of informally sanctioned behaviors are the following:

1 Collections and donations for special occasions such as illnesses and weddings.

2 Informal standards specifying the amount of work that can be expected from members of the group.

3 Informal agreements between members of departments regarding division of labor. Often, these actually work out better than the formal organizational arrangements.
4 Informal agreements with other departments regarding priorities and prerogatives.
5 Expected privileges which deviate from policies, such as twenty-minute coffee breaks instead of the specified ten-minute breaks, or fifteen minutes wash-up time at the end of the day, etc.
6 Work procedures which deviate from specified procedures but which often lead to greater efficiency.

At times, the informal group roles and specified behaviors may appear to supervisors to be disruptive and ineffective. Actually, however, organizational researchers are now coming to the conclusion that many of these informal types of arrangements can actually benefit the organization and make the formal structure workable. For example, an extended cleanup time may be viewed by the workers as a reward for a productive day. When they do not meet their informal standards, they may take it upon themselves to work right up to quitting time. Moreover, when the supervisor has a rush order, task, or assignment that is beyond the employees' normal work load, they may be much more receptive to the idea of making an extra effort if their supervisor has granted privileges (such as the extended cleanup time) freely.

Another good example of how the informal structure works can be found in the deviations from the formal communication channels and reporting procedures specified by the organization charts. Theoretically, employees only have to follow the formal lines of authority and communication. For example, they do not have to comply with directions issued by any supervisors other than their own. Yet many times supervisors or even employees from other departments must make reasonable requests to all employees of the organization. If each of these requests had to go through all formal chains of command before they were carried out, organizations would come to a standstill. In fact, this is often a tactic that is used when workers or the union want to have a slowdown; they simply follow the formal channels rigorously and the work does not get done. It is clear that both the supervisor and the organization benefit from the informal organization.

The grapevine is often associated with the informal organization. Although the grapevine is most often thought of in negative terms and is associated with rumors, Keith Davis, a professor at Arizona State University, has discovered through his research that this image of the grapevine may not be true to the facts. Some of his more important findings about the grapevine are that:

1 Usually about 80 to 90 percent of the information on the grapevine is accurate.

2 The grapevine becomes active when information is timely and interesting but dies as the importance of the information diminishes.

3 Participation in the grapevine is more a function of people's positions than their personalities. When an active participant is fired, the replacement usually becomes just as active in the grapevine as if there had been no change.

Rather than viewing the grapevine as a detriment, these findings would suggest that it can be very beneficial if used properly. Anyone who has worked in an organization can also attest to the fact that the grapevine provides a much faster way to disseminate information than the formal channels of communication. Supervisors should realize that information on the grapevine, whether accurate or not, is about an issue that employees consider important. The fact that the grapevine has taken up an issue suggests that the formal organization is handling it incorrectly and must take some corrective action before problems become critical. In addition, supervisors can use the grapevine to communicate important information which cannot go through formal channels. In one case, a company, without telling the workers beforehand, contracted with local banks to have all paychecks deposited directly. When this action became known, the employees were exceedingly irate. For instance, there were some whose spouses had no idea of the amount of their weekly paychecks. Many supervisors informally expressed their disagreement with this new policy and also made informal arrangements to have the paychecks delivered directly to certain employees. While these supervisors' actions definitely represented a deviation from formal policy, the problems they avoided and the loyalty that resulted was probably worth it. In other words, the informal organization can help smooth out many of the rough edges inherent in the formal organization.

In conclusion, supervisors must be continuously aware of the informal organization underlying and supporting formal organizational structures. Although the informal organization may at times appear to work against the grain of formal organizational purposes, most organizational experts have concluded that it is an integral part of organizational functioning and that it will continue as long as the formal organization is inadequate. Supervisors who are careful observers of the informal organization can see both its limitations and advantages and may use the informal organization to their benefit. One thing is certain—coexisting with every formal organizational structure is an informal one; the supervisor should attempt to use it for goal attainment and increased effectiveness instead of trying to ignore or eliminate it.

■ KEY CONCEPTS

Bureaucratic theory
Departmentation
Specialization
Span of control
Hierarchy
Equal authority and responsibility
Unity of command
Functional authority
Staff structure
Project organization
Matrix organization
Free-form organization
Informal organization

■ PRACTICAL EXERCISES

(These can be performed by individuals or by groups.)
1 Discuss the structure of your educational institution or some other relevant organization according to the four characteristics of bureaucracy (i.e., specialization, hierarchy, rules, and impersonalization). What are some of the disadvantages of this structure? What are some of the advantages? Are there any alternatives that would avoid the problems inherent in this structure?
2 Divide into two groups (or four) and debate the following: "Resolved: The bureaucratic model is the most efficient structure possible." One group will be assigned the affirmative and one the negative. Allow opening statements and a rebuttal.
3 Discuss the evolution of structure within any of the small discussion groups formed over the class periods. What hierarchy has evolved? Are there members who now have functional authority in particular areas? Do people charged with responsibilities have the authority and resources to carry them out? Is there a better way to organize or departmentalize the class discussion groups?

■ DISCUSSION INCIDENTS

Allen James was furious. The personnel manager had just overturned his decision to fire Harry White. From Allen's perspective, Harry had been agitating him for nearly a year, mostly by talking back and responding to instructions in a belligerent manner. Yet up until last Thursday, he had done nothing serious enough to justify his dismissal. Then, last Thursday, he walked off the job after he had been refused permission to keep an appointment with his real estate agent. Allen fired him on the spot. Now personnel was overturning Allen's decision, awarding Harry back pay, and putting Harry back on his old job. Allen thought he—not somebody up in personnel—was the boss.

1 Who is line and who is staff in this incident? Is there conflict between line and staff authority? How can this type of conflict be resolved?

2 Is Allen's power to supervise effectively being eroded by giving him responsibilities without commensurate authority? Are there any alternative organizational arrangements that could be made here?

Sue Davis is the owner-manager of her own advertising agency. To the casual observer, her office and its organization are in utter chaos. She has six people working for her, none with any apparent assignments or responsibilities. Her people just take the projects as they come along. Most often one person gets the ball rolling and follows a project through to its completion. If help is needed, it is usually provided by the other group members on an informal basis. Most often, the employees are more than happy to help each other out when needed. Sue's successful operation was a real dilemma to her competitors, who carefully organized their work according to functions such as account management, artwork, layout, and writing. Yet despite Sue's apparent lack of organization, she had some of the most motivated people and one of the most successful advertising agencies around.

1 What type(s) of organization is (are) apparent in Sue's agency? Do you suppose they are labeled as such by Sue?

2 How do you explain the success of this agency? How can you account for the extremely high levels of motivation in Sue's organization?

3 Can you suggest any alternative structural forms that would make Sue's organization more effective? Do you think a more classical bureaucratic structure would work here? Why or why not?

140

STAFFING THE ORGANIZATION

6 CHAPTER

L aser Techtronics has one product: a small laser sensor beam that automatically reads price tags and enters them into a cash register which, in turn, computes a customer's total purchases. The heavy demand for the product in all types of retail firms accounts for the unprecedented growth and excitement of Laser Techtronics. Corresponding with this growth in demand for the laser is a rapid expansion of the company labor force. In particular, this rapid growth and change is the problem of Jan Spence, the supervisor of assembly. Jan now has over thirty assemblers; but there is a turnover rate of almost 200 percent per year, with four or more employees leaving each month. Jan is sure the problem is not pay, since Techtronics pays better than any competitors in the area and also has excellent fringe benefits. Moreover, training does not seem to be the problem, because the job is so simple. To a great extent, Jan feels that most of the workers who leave do so because of disappointment with the job and boredom. It is simply not a very interesting job, and there appears to be no way to improve it. On the other hand, those who stay appear to like the routine, repetitive work. Jan believes that much of the turnover could be reduced if she had the ability to select the proper applicants and orient them to their work appropriately. With a little more knowledge and experience in interviewing and orienting new employees, Jan feels that she might be able to screen out the job leavers and retain employees for longer periods. She only wished that she knew where to begin, because the situation is beginning to deteriorate.

■ LEARNING OBJECTIVES

After reading this chapter, you should have:

An overall framework and model for understanding the employment function of supervision

The necessary information and techniques to conduct a lawful employment interview

Sufficient knowledge of equal opportunity employment laws and guidelines to implement an affirmative action approach to minority and women employees

The necessary tips, pointers, and information on how to conduct an effective employee orientation

In this chapter, the staffing function of supervision is reviewed. The overall employment process is illustrated in Figure 6-1. After a general overview, the staffing process in terms of selection and orientation is given specific attention.

THE EMPLOYMENT PROCESS

As indicated in Figure 6-1, the process begins with a selection interview, followed by an orientation of the new employee. Once the employee has come on board, an assessment of his or her knowledge, skills, and abilities is made in light of job requirements. If the new employee's characteristics closely match those required by the new position, very little training will be needed. However, if they do not match up, then the deficiencies must be eliminated through the proper training and development. The removal of the deficiencies becomes the goals of the training and development process covered in the next chapter.

The next step is to identify the specific actions that will be needed to accomplish the goals. There is a wide variety of action plans which could be implemented. It should be emphasized at the outset, however, that the employees' job assignments and their work experiences on the job are almost always the most important opportunities for achieving developmental goals. While education and training and other developmental strategies are available, they are usually supplemental to the work experience itself. Supervisors, then, should be particularly careful to give work assignments that are consistent with their employees' developmental goals and help accomplish them.

In the next phase, job performance is measured. This step, which is

143

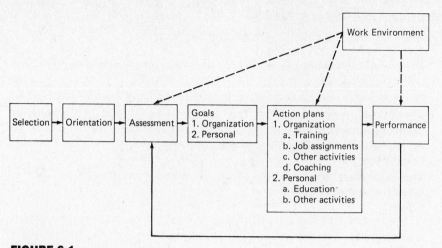

FIGURE 6-1
The employment, training, and
development process for supervisors.

the subject of Chapter 10, is critical, because it becomes the basic checkpoint for future assessment and developmental plans. The feedback loop in Figure 6-1 should also be noted. This loop closes the circuit and indicates that the employment process is a continuous and ongoing one. The following sections of this chapter will discuss the initial aspects of the employment process (selection and orientation); later chapters will examine the later phases (training, development, and appraisal).

THE STAFFING FUNCTION

Staffing involves mainly selection and orientation. The supervisor's role in staffing will depend on organizational policies and practices. In many large organizations, the personnel department both interviews and provides a formal orientation program for new employees. A supervisor may not even see new employees until they show up for the first day of work. In smaller organizations, supervisors may bear the entire responsibility for locating job applicants, making the selection decision, and orienting new employees to the organization and their specific jobs. Apart from their role at these two extremes, most supervisors will become involved in the staffing function during the selection interview and job orientation.

The Selection Interview

The first time most supervisors become involved with the staffing process is during the selection interview. This interview is essentially a matching process, where the objective is to find the employee whose knowledge, skills, abilities, and motivation most closely match the knowledge, abilities, skills, and motivation required in the job. To be effective, the selection interviewing process must go through several stages.

Establish criteria This first step is critical to the objective of obtaining qualified applicants and matching them to the position. The supervisor may list the major duties and responsibilities for the job and the qualifications which successful applicants will need. Where position descriptions are available, they can serve as good guidelines for determining job responsibilities and qualifications. Examples of how the qualifications and responsibilities of a position might be stated are provided in Table 6-1. Only those qualifications which are directly related to job performance—bona fide occupational qualifications (BFOQ)—should be listed and considered. Qualifications which are not related to job performance may be judged discriminatory by the courts and can result in costly lawsuits. In large organizations, the supervisor may be required to fill out a requisition form similar to the one in Figure 6-2. Supervisors who do not have a personnel department or are not required to fill out a requisition can use Figure 6-2 as a guideline.

Prepare for the interview There are many things a supervisor must consider in preparing for an effective selection interview: scheduling; finding a quiet room where there will be no interruptions; canceling phone calls; preparing possible questions; doing homework on starting wages, benefits, etc.; reviewing the applicant's resume; reviewing job qualifications; and so on.

Depending on the type of position the supervisor is filling, these considerations will vary somewhat. However, there are two overriding considerations in preparing for the interview. First, supervisors must be able to give and receive the information that will allow them and the job applicants to determine whether they have mutual interests. Second, and just as important, is the awareness that a job interview is a two-way process—that while the supervisor is assessing an appli-

TABLE 6-1

QUALIFICATIONS AND RESPONSIBILITIES—MECHANIC'S JOB

Responsibilites

Inspect, maintain, and repair automobiles including:

Body work and welding

Operations and/or use of diagnostic machinery, charts, and manuals

Overhauling engines, pumps, generators, transmissions, etc.

Maintenance activities such as repairing tires, lubrication, changing oil, and checking batteries

Planning and directing the work of part-time employees

Qualifications

Mechanical ability

Training or experience equal to one year of vocational school in automotive care

Ability to work with people and direct their activities

Willingness to work a ten-hour day

---

cant, the latter is also sizing up the employer's ability to match his or her own needs. Thus, supervisors should attempt to make a favorable impression on applicants. A good rule of thumb is that a job interview deserves preparation and a job applicant deserves to be received with the courtesy that one would extend to any important guest.

Begin the interview The first objective of the interview is to put the candidate at ease. One way to do this is to start by mentioning a topic of mutual interest such as a recent election, the score of a ballgame, or even a question such as "Did you have any trouble finding our building?" After a couple of minutes, the candidate will usually be ready to begin the job interview. A warning at this point, however, is that with many candidates, this warm-up stage may be unnecessary and can lead to an aimless discussion which only heightens rather than decreases anxiety.

A good way to get into the actual interview is to offer a short description of the job, noting the major responsibilities it entails and the qualifications it calls for. Supervisors should let the interviewees know that they are interested in learning as much as possible about them and that they also want to give the applicants as much information about the job as they can so that they can make a good selection decision.

146

Please be explicit. Because the quality of personnel referred to you largely depends on the information provided by this form, anticipate your needs as far in advance as possible.

For employment department use requisition number.

Classification/title	Department	Division
Proposed wage or salary	Date to start	Location

Position is: ( ) Addition to staff
         ( ) Replacement
         ( ) Regular (permanent)
         ( ) Other (part-time, summer, etc.)

Why needed?

Duties and responsibilities in detail: Include any unusual features—work weeks, etc.

Will employee be expected to drive a vehicle?   ( ) yes   ( ) no
If yes   ( ) car   ( ) light truck   ( ) heavy truck

Will employee be assigned shift work in this classification immediately?   ( ) yes   ( ) no
Eventually   ( ) yes   ( ) no

Position qualifications: For education, experience, special training, etc., use bona fide occupational requirements only.

APPROVALS		EMPLOYEE RELATIONS DIVISION	
		( ) Labor Relations	Date
Department Manager	Date	( ) Compensation	Date
Division Manager	Date	Division Manager, Employee Relations	Date

FIGURE 6-2
Employment requisition.

Outline the content of the interview A large part of the initial discussion during the interview should be oriented toward gaining information from candidates to assess their ability to match the job requirements. Thus, supervisors should have prepared a list of questions (at least mentally) which will elicit the needed information. The basis for these questions must be taken from a list of bona fide occupational qualifications, as mentioned earlier. Supervisors are particularly vulnerable to charges of discrimination during this phase unless they are very careful. Table 6-2 provides some specific guidelines that should help supervisors avoid legal difficulties. Many supervisors complain that the laws are unnecessarily restrictive. A

TABLE 6-2
GUIDELINES FOR PREEMPLOYMENT INQUIRIES*

	Lawful Inquiries	Unlawful Inquiries
Name	"Have you worked for this organization under a different name? Is any additional information relative to change of name, use of an assumed name, or nickname necessary to enable a check on your work and educational record? If yes, explain."	Inquiries about the name which would indicate applicant's lineage, ancestry, national origin, or descent. Inquiries into previous name of applicant where it has been changed by court order, marriage, or otherwise.
Marital and Family Status	Whether applicant can meet specified work schedules or has activities, commitments, or responsibilities that may hinder the meeting of work attendance requirements. Inquiries as to a duration of stay on the job or anticipated absences which are made to males and females alike.	Any inquiries indicating whether an applicant is married, single, divorced, engaged, etc. Number and age of children. Any questions concerning pregnancy. Any such question which directly or indirectly results in limitation of job opportunity in any way.
Age	If a minor, require proof of age in form of a work permit or a certificate of age. Require proof of age by birth certificate after being hired. Inquiry as to whether or not the applicant meets the minimum age requirements as set by law and requirements that upon hire, proof of age must be submitted. If age is a legal requirement: "If hired, can you furnish proof of age?"/ or statement that hire is subject to verification of age.	Requirement that applicant produce proof of age in the form of a birth certificate or baptismal record.

*These are only *guidelines*. The courts, EEOC, and state and local fair employment practices agencies may make different interpretations.

148

TABLE 6-2 continued

Handicaps	Whether applicant has any handicaps or health problems either sensory, mental, or physical which may affect work performance or which the employer should consider in determining job placement.	General inquiries (i.e., "Do you have any handicaps?") which would tend to divulge handicaps or health conditions which do not relate reasonably to fitness to perform the job.
Sex	Inquiry or restriction of employment is permissible only where a bona fide occupational qualification exists. (This BFOQ exception is interpreted very narrowly by the courts and EEOC.) The burden or proof rests on the employer to prove that the BFOQ does exist and that all members of the affected class are incapable of performing the job.	Sex of the applicant. Any other inquiry which would indicate sex. Sex is not a BFOQ because a job involves physical labor (such as heavy lifting) beyond the capacity of some women nor can sex be used as a factor for determining whether or not an applicant will be satisfied in a particular job.
Race or Color	General distinguishing physical characteristics such as scars, etc.	Applicant's race. Color of applicant's skin, eyes, hair, etc. or other questions directly or indirectly indicating race or color. Applicant's height or weight where it is not relevant to job.
Address or Duration of Residence	Applicant's address. Inquiry into place and length of current and previous addresses. "How long a resident of this state or city?"	Specific inquiry into foreign addresses which would indicate national origin. Names or relationship of persons with whom applicant resides. Whether applicant owns or rents home.

TABLE 6-2 continued

Birthplace	"Can you after employment submit a birth certificate or other proof of U.S. citizenship?"	Birthplace of applicant. Birthplace of applicant's parents, spouse, or other relatives. Requirement that applicant submit a birth certificate, naturalization or baptismal record before employment. Any other inquiry to indicate or identify denomination or customs.
Military Record	Type of education and experience in service as it relates to a particular job.	Type of discharge.
Photograph	May be required after hiring for identification.	Request photograph before hiring. Requirement that applicant affix a photograph to his application. Request that applicant, at his option, submit photograph. Requirement of photograph after interview but before hiring.
Citizenship	"Are you a citizen of the U.S.?" If you are not a U.S. citizen, have you the legal right to remain permanently in the U.S.? Do you intend to remain permanently in the U.S.? Statement that if hired, applicant may be required to submit proof of citizenship. If not a citizen, are you prevented from lawfully becoming employed because of visa or immigration status?	"Of what country are you a citizen?" Whether applicant or his parents or spouse are naturalized or native-born U.S. citizens. Date when applicant or parents or spouse acquired U.S. citizenship. Requirement that applicant produce his naturalization papers or first papers. Whether applicant's parents are citizens of the U.S.
Ancestry or National Origin	Languages applicant reads, speaks, or writes fluently.	Inquiries into applicant's lineage, ancestry, national origin, descent, birthplace, or mother tongue. National origin of applicant's parents or spouse.

TABLE 6-2 continued

Education	Applicant's academic, vocational, or professional education; school attended. Inquiry into language skills such as reading, speaking, and writing foreign languages.	Inquiry asking specifically the nationality, racial or religious affiliation of a school. Inquiry as to what is mother tongue or how foreign language ability was acquired.
Experience	Applicant's work experience. Other countries visited.	
Conviction, Arrest and Court Record	Inquiry into actual convictions which relate reasonably to fitness to perform a particular job. (A conviction is a court ruling where the party is found guilty as charged. An arrest is merely the apprehending or detaining of the person to answer the alleged crime.)	Any inquiry relating to arrests. To ask or check into a person's arrest, court, or conviction record if not substantially related to functions and responsibilities of the prospective employment.
Relatives	Names of applicant's relatives already employed by this company. Names and addresses of parents or guardian of minor applicant.	Name or address of any relative of adult applicant.
Notice in Case of Emergency	Names of persons to be notified.	Name and address of relative to be notified in case of accident or emergency.
Organizations	Inquiry into the organization of which an applicant is a member providing the name or character of the organization does not reveal the race, religion, color, or ancestry of the membership. What offices are held, if any?	"List all organizations, clubs, societies and lodges to which you belong." The names of organizations to which the applicant belongs if such information would indicate through character or name the race, religion, color, or ancestry of the membership.
Credit Rating	None	Any questions concerning credit rating, charge accounts, etc.

TABLE 6-2 continued

References	By whom were you referred for a position here? Names of persons willing to provide professional and/or character references for applicant. Who suggested that applicant apply for a position here?	Require the submission of a religious reference. Request reference from applicant's pastor.
Miscellaneous	Notice to applicants that any misstatement or omissions of material facts in the application may be cause for dismissal.	

Source: Compiled by Clifford Coen, December 1976 newsletter of the American Association of Affirmative Action.

common joke among them is that "the only legal piece of information that can be requested is the candidate's name, and even that may be questionable."

In actuality, it is possible to get all the needed information (and then some) without asking discriminatory questions. One technique that helps do this is called nondirective interviewing. In this approach, the interviewer asks broad, open-ended questions and encourages the applicant to elaborate on areas of particular interest. Examples of open-ended questions that might be used are provided in Table 6-3.

The most common problem most supervisors have in conducting an effective interview is that they do not exercise enough self-restraint and talk too much themselves. Supervisors who are able to regulate their own talking will usually find that even the quietest applicant will open up when given the opportunity. (To prove the point, try looking anyone in the eye for thirty seconds without talking.) After the applicant does begin to open up, brief questions such as "Can you elaborate on that?" or statements such as "I don't think I quite understood what you meant" should keep the conversation going. Of course, all the questions should be aimed at gaining more information about the applicant's legitimate qualifications.

If the applicant's qualifications are a fair match with the job, the next part of the interview should be devoted to describing the major

TABLE 6-3

SOME OPEN-ENDED QUESTIONS FOR NONDIRECTIVE INTERVIEWING

1. Can you give me a brief history of yourself?
2. What do you believe are your particular strengths with respect to this job?
3. What are some possible weaknesses that you may have with respect to this job?
4. What did you like about your last job?
5. What did you dislike about your last job?
6. Why did you leave your last job?
7. What educational experiences do you have that are relevant to the present job?
8. What previous job experience do you have that is relevant to the present job?
9. Do you anticipate any difficulties in working overtime or meeting any other requirements of the job?
10. How do you get along with other people?

responsibilities and duties of the job. The major objective here is to give prospective employees as much knowledge about the job as possible so that applicants can make a rational choice as to whether or not they desire the job. Included would be the major advantages and disadvantages of working for the organization. Although candidates may be more likely to accept the job if the negative aspects are not mentioned, they are also less likely to be satisfied or to remain on the job if they do not know about them beforehand. The wasted time, expense, and turnover that results from giving candidates inaccurate information makes this practice much more costly than it would be to provide an accurate picture of the job from the beginning.

Although supervisors do most of the talking in this phase of the interview, they should also listen carefully for any additional information the interviewee has to offer. Interviewees are often able to do a better job of providing useful information if they are first given a clear picture of the job requirements.

At the conclusion of the interview, the supervisor should inform the candidate of the specific date when the position will be filled. Importantly, supervisors should let candidates know where they stand and have the proper approvals made in order to make any commitments. Nothing turns potential employees off more than not knowing where they are in the employment process or finding that the terms and conditions of an offer are not as the supervisor stated them at the end of the selection interview.

AFFIRMATIVE ACTION

Nondiscrimination and affirmative action have already been mentioned in this chapter and in Chapter 2 (on the environment). However, the laws regarding equal opportunity in employment have a particularly important impact on the staffing function today; they therefore deserve some special attention. Title VII of the Civil Rights Act, passed in 1964 and slightly amended in 1972, applies to all employers with fifteen or more employees; it includes private and public employers, unions, educational institutions, state and local governments, joint labor and management committees, and employment agencies. The act makes it unlawful to discriminate on the basis of race, color, religion, sex, national origin, or age in any aspect of employment (hiring, firing, promotion, compensation, and other terms, privileges, and conditions of employment). Obviously, this act has a tremendous impact on the role of minorities, women, and older employees in staffing the organization. Other rulings have also focused a great deal of attention on women as employees. These include the 1963 Equal Pay Act and court decisions asserting that jobs need not be identical (just substantially equal) for the law regarding equal pay to apply. The push for the ERA (Equal Rights Amendment to the U.S. Constitution) is, of course, another notable development.

The EEOC (Equal Employment Opportunity Commission), which was set up to administer these acts, has been very active. Once again, supervisors find themselves to be key people in EEOC enforcement. When the EEOC chooses to charge an employer with discrimination, it bases its decision largely on personnel records and on the treatment supervisors have given to minorities and women. Supervisors must be able to justify their actions and actually go a step further. They must take affirmative action with regard to minorities and women.

The EEOC recommends that the following steps be taken to live up to the spirit as well as the letter of the nondiscrimination laws:

Backed by legislation and
enforcement, women are rightfully
demanding equal opportunity in
employment and are beginning to
assume traditionally male-dominated
work roles (Abigail Heyman/Magnum
Photos).

1 Management should publicly issue, in writing, commitment to a policy of equal opportunity employment and affirmative action.

2 A specific individual with responsibility and authority should be designated to develop and implement an affirmative action plan.

3 The organization should widely publicize and promote its affirmative action program.

4 Minority and women employees should be surveyed and analyzed by department and job classification.

5 Specific long- and short-range goals should be established and causes of underutilization of minorities and women should be identified and eliminated.

6 Specific programs to ensure that no discrimination exists in any employment area should be developed and implemented.

7 An information system which monitors and evaluates the nondiscrimination program should be established.

8 Supportive organizational and community-based programs should be encouraged and helped.

The supervisor can be particularly helpful in steps 4, 5, 6, and 7 above. A major goal from both pragmatic and moral standpoints is to have nondiscrimination in all aspects of staffing. Equal opportunity for all employees is an important goal for all supervisors.

THE ORIENTATION PROCESS

After an employee has been selected in a nondiscriminatory manner, the next step in the staffing process is orientation. The goal here is to relieve immediate anxiety and apprehension about the job and give the new employee the basic information needed to get started properly. In most larger organizations, the personnel department provides a brief, formal orientation program for new employees. Usually this program includes things like a brief synopsis of the organization's history, an overview of the formal structure, a review of the type of product or service produced, and a summary of employee benefits such as vacations and health and life insurance. Unfortunately, very few of these standard orientation programs provide any information about the specific jobs the employees will be filling. Thus, supervisors should never feel that their employees are completely oriented before they arrive on the job. Moreover, what little research has been conducted on standard orientation programs indicates that they are of questionable value.

In any case, there is little question that supervisors play a major role in the orientation of their new employees. The following sections suggest some ways to make this orientation more effective. Although the orientation activities are discussed in a logical sequence, the supervisor can combine some of them or change their order to meet changing needs for an efficient orientation.

Schedule Initial Time with the New Employee

It is very frustrating for a new employee to have to spend the first few hours of the first day on the job sitting in the supervisor's office, waiting, while he or she completes the daily time slips, talks on the phone, assigns tasks, socializes with coworkers, and so on. If at all possible, supervisors should schedule their time so that they can devote the first few hours of the day to new employees. If they cannot do this, it may be wise to ask the new employee to come in a couple of hours late. The supervisor should then plan to spend a good part of the first day with this individual.

Relieve the New Employee's Anxiety

A major objective of the supervisor's orientation should be to relieve new employees of immediate anxieties. This can begin by spelling out in detail the first day's activities. An effective way to orient the new employee on the first day is to make a schedule similar to the one shown in Figure 6-3. The initial things on the schedule familiarize the new employee with the basic essentials and are designed to reduce the anxieties of a person who is about to enter a new environment.

Make the New Employee Feel at Ease with Coworkers

A very important aspect of the orientation process is introducing new employees to coworkers and other people with whom they will have frequent contact. Before introducing the new employee to these other individuals, the supervisor might briefly describe their functions and give the new employee some idea of each person's particular abilities and characteristics. A supervisor might say, for example:

Time	Activity
8:30–9:30	Survival rudiments: Location of the bathroom, lunchroom, locker room, and time clock; who to call when late; summary of important policies, procedures, and rules; and some informal observations about the "ins" and "outs" of the organization.
9:00–10:00	Introduction to fellow workers and other supervisors.
10:00–10:15	Coffee break/informal discussion.
10:15–11:00	Basic job information.
11:00–12:00	Lunch/informal discussion.
1:00–3:30	Place on job with a model, experienced employee.
3:30–4:00	Summary of day. Answer any important questions.

FIGURE 6-3
A typical first day of orientation
schedule.

I'm going to introduce you to Frank now. He's usually considered the technical specialist here, and people go to him when they have equipment problems. At times he can be rather short and critical with people. He'll probably have a tendency to ride you a little at first because you are new. By and large, though, he's a hell of a good guy and can really help you out of some problems if you get on his good side.

It should be noted, however, that there are some obvious drawbacks to giving "off-the-cuff" opinions of people. There is a fine line between giving the employee needed information about people and plain old gossiping. In general, new employees should be given the opportunity to make their own judgments about their fellow employees, but they should not have to walk into situations of potential conflict without at least some advance warning and information that is known to everyone else.

Familiarize the New Employee with the Job to Be Performed

In this part of the orientation, the supervisor shows the new employee where his or her job will be performed and, if possible, they observe someone else, preferably a good employee, at work on the job. The intent here is not to provide detailed job instruction but rather to relieve some of the new employee's initial apprehensions by giving him or her an initial feeling of familiarity with the job. A partial list of considerations that might be included in this part of the orientation is provided in Figure 6-4. The supervisor should be warned against trying to create too favorable an impression and excessive expectations about the job. Supervisors should be as realistic as possible in explaining major challenges or problems in performing the job effectively. For example, the supervisor of a claims department in an insurance company might say something like the following:

> The job can be very rewarding when you know you've made a reasonable adjustment on a legitimate claim and the people are truly grateful. On the other hand, it can also get pretty discouraging. You'll have some people that you just know are lying, but you have to give them the benefit of the doubt. Even these people, although they've received a more than reasonable settlement, are still not happy. So there will just be some situations where you'll lose from the beginning, but it's part of the job. Fortunately, the good outweighs the bad on this job.

Make the New Employee Proud of the Organization

During the orientation there is ample opportunity to discuss with new employees the background of the organization as well as the particular jobs they will be holding. The purpose of this kind of information is to provide new employees with an appreciation and perspective of the importance of their own jobs and the organization's role in the broader scope of things. For example, a new employee in a steel mill might be told something like the following:

> This is the third-largest basic steel plant in the world. It produces almost 70 percent of all unfinished steel in the country. That would easily be enough for all the automobiles produced this year, but a large proportion of it goes into other things—such as building and construction, tools and equipment, and smaller items such as appliances, desks, and cabinets. As a matter of fact, look around your own home. Of everything that is steel, we produced about 10 percent of it. That includes your lawnmower, coffeepot, pots and pans, refrigerator, stove, plumbing, and even the kitchen sink. So you can see we have a very important impact on people's lives.

In a similar manner, a supervisor in a rehabilitation center might emphasize some of its unique characteristics this way:

> Unlike most centers, which are funded by state and local governments, our total revenues come from the contributions of previous clients and

159

1. Who to notify in case of problems	6. Job interrelationships — problems created for other people by poor performance
2. Expected standards or productivity levels	7. If the job is uncomplicated, a quick run-through of how it is performed
3. Length of time required to become proficient	
4. Specify safety hazards	8. Where to get supplies and materials
	9. Required safety equipment
5. Function of the job — who uses the product or service and its importance	10. Chain of command — formal and informal

FIGURE 6-4
Initial job-orientation considerations.

interested members of the community. It is a tremendous thing when you stop to think of it. People who came to us with very little hope or potential are now our major source of funds. It says we are damn good at what we're doing, and there's no other institution in the country like us.

Undoubtedly every supervisor's organization has unique aspects which may make new employees proud to be part of it.

Explain Employee Benefits

Especially in small organizations, supervisors spend a considerable amount of time explaining the details of employee benefits (e.g., life and health insurance). For many employees, especially those with prior work experience, these benefits are very important and detailed coverage is appropriate. However, for other employees, especially those in entry-level positions, the details are not as important. Again, on the new employees' first day, they are much more concerned with their immediate needs with respect to the job they will hold. Thus, a good strategy is to give a brief summary outline of the benefits and then ask the new employees if they are interested in additional details. If not, set a specific later date to go over the benefits in detail.

Be Sure to Follow Up

New employees cannot possibly receive all the information they need on the first day. Supervisors should make this clear to them so that they will feel comfortable about asking questions after the first day of orientation. Depending on the nature of the job, the employee may actually assume his or her full responsibilities on the second day. However, even in the most routine jobs, it is usually beneficial if the supervisor periodically checks to see whether the employee has any questions. Gradually, this follow-up process can be lengthened until the employee has become accustomed to the daily work routine. This follow-up, like the other guidelines discussed above, is just a good commonsense approach to orientation. Supervisors will, of course, have to vary the orientation process depending on the nature of the job and the particular individual. For some jobs and people, it may be possible to do a fairly thorough orientation in a few hours. For others, such as positions which are highly technical or have some supervisory duties, the orientation process may take several weeks or longer. In any case, orientation is an important function that all supervisors must perform; it can contribute greatly to their short- and long-run effectiveness.

■ KEY CONCEPTS

Employment process
Selection
Bona fide occupational qualification (BFOQ)
Employment requisition
Lawful/Unlawful inquiries in selection
Affirmative action
Nondirective interviewing
Orientation process

■ PRACTICAL EXERCISES

(These can be performed by individuals or by groups.)
1 Find and discuss a job description or employee requisition form like the one shown in this chapter. Identify the job requirements and determine whether or not they are bona fide occupational qualifications (BFOQs).
2 Using either the same or a similar type of job description or requisition as in the preceding exercise, role-play a selection interview with one person acting the part of the supervisor, another the applicant, and the rest of the group serving as the audience. Was it an effective interview? Were all inquiries lawful? You may want to do the role-play again, with the applicant being a minority and/or woman, and then analyze it again. Were the goals of affirmative action met in this latter play?

■ DISCUSSION INCIDENTS

Hazel Foster was a 62-year-old black woman. Her supervisor directed her to move a bunch of racks from one end of the building to the other. After she had moved the first one it was plain to Hazel that this work was too hard on her. She did not feel she was strong enough to push those things that far, so she went to the supervisor and said, "I'm sorry but I just can't do that moving job you asked me to do. Is there anything else I could do instead?" The supervisor replied tersely, "Well, if you recall, a complaint was filed with the Affirmative Action officer last week that I was not treating people equal. Well Hazel, now I am going to give you equal treatment. Either get back to the job I assigned to you or go up to personnel and resign. I'm only doing what you people want me to do. I can't discriminate on the basis of age, sex, or race."

1 How well do you think the supervisor handled this situation? What do you think the outcome of his action will be? How would you handle this request if you were the supervisor?

2 Under the Civil Rights Act, is the supervisor justified in his actions? If you were the Affirmative Action officer, what would you say to this supervisor? If you were Hazel, what would you do?

Beth Majors was dejected. She was just interviewed for a job as secretary for the Peters Trucking Company. During the interview, she felt that she had given poor answers to several questions. First she was upset because she had to tell Mr. Peters that she had never graduated from high school. Then she felt bad when, on being asked whether she was married or single, she had to respond that she was divorced. Also, it did not seem favorable that she was using the bus for transportation instead of her own car. Finally—and this was really none of Mr. Peters' business—she was worried because Mr. Peters seemed particularly concerned over what she would do if one of her three children got sick. Although she had told Mr. Peters that her mother would take care of the children, she did not feel that it was a favorable answer. Despite giving what she thought were poor answers to those questions, Beth knew that she could do well on the job, since she could type over 80 words per minute accurately and was excellent at shorthand and dictation.

1 Of the questions Mr. Peters asked, which were illegal? How would you have conducted the interview differently?

2 Assume Beth was hired. What steps would your orientation consist of in the light of the information given about her?

162

TRAINING AND DEVELOPING EMPLOYEES

CHAPTER 7

Jim Keller is a supervisor in the underground construction division of Southwest Utility. His division is responsible for trenching, positioning, and implanting electrical cables and transformers in the ground. Within recent years, the underground group has experienced extremely rapid growth because of public protest over the visual pollution of unsightly overhead towers and poles. Despite the growth and new importance of Jim's division, it is still considered by most employees as "the pits." Very simply, the job involves difficult and dirty manual labor, and most employees make every effort to get out of the underground division as soon as they can. As a result, the underground division has high turnover, making it extremely difficult to develop and maintain experienced work groups. Two weeks ago, Jim's manager called all the supervisors together to discuss the decline in the ability and skills of the underground work crews, which was leading to a deteriorating performance record for the division. During the meeting, Jim's manager stressed the need to upgrade the skills and abilities in the division through a systematized and formalized scheme of training. At the conclusion of the meeting, the manager asked each supervisor to submit, within two weeks, a specific proposal for training their own work groups. Having never had any formal training himself and never given it any thought, Jim was not quite sure where to begin with this difficult assignment.

**Basic Elements
of Effective Supervision**

After reading this chapter, you should have:

A perspective of the supervisor's role in training and developing employees

An ability to identify and, in particular, distinguish legitimate training needs from other work-related problems

An awareness of and an ability to use the various training techniques

An appreciation of the supervisor's coaching function and how to carry it out effectively

The necessary background and perspective of organizational development (OD) and its related techniques

Training usually brings to mind a formal process conducted in a classroom with an instructor. This picture of training is much too narrow. In fact, most of today's employees receive very little, if any, formal classroom training. Instead, the bulk of training activities are carried out informally by supervisors and experienced coworkers. Thus, a realistic definition of employee training is that it is a formal or informal process designed to provide employees with either information or experiences to improve or aid job performance. Under this view, giving an employee a new job assignment would be considered training if it were part of a structured effort to provide the employee with additional experience or information to improve performance. Similarly, instructions concerning the job, departmental meetings, and even taking an employee to lunch can be considered training when these experiences are directed toward achieving a specific developmental goal. By the same token, when job assignments and other activities occur in a haphazard fashion without consideration for meeting developmental goals, they should not be considered training.

After examining the role that the supervisor plays in the training function, this chapter turns to ways to identify training needs and the modern methods and techniques that supervisors can use to train their people. Particular attention is devoted to the coaching process. Finally, the broader perspective of organizational development (OD) and its techniques are presented. Supervisors are becoming increasingly involved in OD efforts and should be aware of what is involved.

THE SUPERVISOR'S ROLE IN TRAINING EMPLOYEES

The responsibility for employee training lies largely with the supervisor. The reason for this can be traced back to the discussion in Chapter 1 on the role of the supervisor. There, it was brought out that a major part of the supervisor's job is getting results through people. Supervisors are responsible for the performance of their people. It follows that supervisors must constantly be analyzing performance to identify existing or potential problems and then to develop and adopt appropriate courses of action to solve these problems. Although a solution can often be found in training, there are other possibilities—such as increased staffing, new equipment, new technical systems, and reorganization of the work group. However, regardless of the solutions adopted, supervisors are responsible for the implementation of the plan and its ultimate success.

For example, if a supervisor decided that the existing work flow was creating problems in productivity, he or she might rearrange the way work is processed in the department. To do this, the supervisor could enlist the help of a systems designer or industrial engineer, a trainer, and an equipment manufacturer. Together, under the supervisor's direction, these people might help to rearrange the work flow and communicate the new procedures and methods to the employees. Although each person helping the supervisor bears responsibility for the quality of his or her work, the supervisor is responsible for the ultimate success or failure of the project. If the project fails, the supervisor may not find an excuse in saying that the equipment salesperson provided the wrong piece of equipment. Similarly, it would not be a valid excuse for the supervisor to say that productivity was low because the systems analyst did not design a proper system or because the industrial engineer had not established appropriate standards. In these types of examples, it is clear that the responsibility lies with the supervisor. Yet for some reason, training responsibilities always seem to be much less clear. Supervisors frequently register such complaints as, "It's no wonder our productivity is so low, nobody has ever bothered to train my people."

The point is not that supervisors are responsible for doing all the training of employees themselves but that they must see to it that their people are trained. Supervisors must take the initiative in determining the types of training their people need, and they must carry out the appropriate strategies to fulfill these needs. Among the resources available to them are training units within the organization, outside consultants, and college programs. However, the supervisors themselves are the ones who must determine how, when, and whether these resources are to be utilized. If such training resources are not immediately available, which is sometimes the case, it is still the supervisor's job to make sure that the employees are trained. In many cases, supervisors are left on their own to design appropriate training. In the following sections, methods for analyzing training needs and designing training programs will be discussed.

IDENTIFYING TRAINING NEEDS

The first step in designing an employee training program is to identify specific needs for training. There are two basic ways of doing this. First is the skills analysis, whereby the supervisor determines the total capabilities of the work group and its individual members. Second is the performance analysis. This latter approach offers an in-depth examination of the causes of performance problems and helps to identify appropriate strategies for solving them.

Skills Analysis

One simple way to identify training needs is to list all tasks within a particular job classification in the order of increasing difficulty and then to check off the employees who are proficient at them. Figure 7-1 illustrates such a checklist. This method provides supervisors with an overall perspective of the capabilities within the work unit. For example, the supervisor can quickly see from Figure 7-1 that there is only one person who is competent to do a complete overhaul on an engine. This might be expected, as engine overhauls represent the most complex task this particular work group is required to perform. Surprisingly, however, there are only two people experienced in tune-up work, a relatively simple task that comes up frequently. This skills analysis shows the supervisor that some training in engine tune-ups would be highly desirable.

Another thing the skills analysis does is to point out discrepancies in the development of particular individuals. For example, Terry Kene in Figure 7-1 knows the very routine tasks but also a couple of extremely complex functions such as adjusting, replacing, and rebuilding transmissions. The supervisor can safely assume that Terry can learn some of the other complex tasks and become an important asset in the shop if given the needed training and experience.

167

FIGURE 7-1
Training needs analysis checklist—auto mechanic.

Job Duty	Jamie Voter	Duane Pisca	Dan Hanson	Jim Smith	Ken Jacob	Larry Newsome	Pat Simon	Terry Kene
1. Gas car	√	√	√	√	√	√	√	√
2. Wash car	√	√	√	√	√	√	√	√
3. Replace headlights and tail lights	√	√		√	√	√	√	√
4. Replace battery	√	√		√	√	√	√	√
5. Repair tires	√	√		√	√	√	√	√
6. Change oil	√	√		√	√	√	√	√
7. Lubricate	√	√		√	√	√	√	√
8. Replace fan belts	√	√	√	√	√	√	√	√
9. Install exhaust system	√	√			√	√	√	√
10. Replace starter	√				√	√	√	
11. Front-end alignment	√	√			√		√	
12. Replace idler arms	√	√			√		√	
13. Check alternator	√	√				√		
14. Tune up engines	√	√						
15. Overhaul breaks	√	√			√			
16. Test electrical system	√	√				√		
17. Test and replace air conditioners systems	√			√		√		
18. Paint cars	√	√			√			
19. Replace and install valves	√	√			√			
20. Replace rings in engine	√	√			√			
21. Adjust transmission	√				√	√		√
22. Replace and rebuild transmission	√				√	√		√
23. Rebuild carburetors	√	√						
24. Overhaul engines	√							

Checklists like the one in Figure 7-1 can be devised for most jobs. In addition to detailed job duties, other categories such as human relations, technical, and administrative skills may be listed, or the basis of the analysis may be experience with different types of equipment. Most important is that supervisors arrive at some rational and organized plan for assessing training needs. These methods, of course, will differ, depending on the organization and the occupation. Additional aid may be found by consulting a training specialist or supervisors in charge of similar work groups.

Performance Analysis

Unlike the skills analysis, the performance analysis starts with the assumption that there are specific performance problems. This approach is most closely associated with management consultants Robert Mager and Peter Pipe. Figure 7-2 illustrates the steps in their model. As shown, they feel that an analysis of training needs should start with the identification of observable and measurable discrepancies in employee performance. Traditionally, statements of training objectives have been very vague, mentioning nonmeasurable things such as improving morale or making employees more safety-conscious. When a training program is built on such vague objectives, it follows that it will turn out to be nonspecific and generally fail to produce any actual improvement in performance or productivity.

If supervisors expect employee training to make a direct contribution to improved performance, the objectives of the training must be spelled out in observable and measurable terms. Ideally, supervisors should have measurable performance standards to use in evaluating productivity in their areas of responsibility. To identify discrepancies, supervisors simply subtract the actual, observed performance from the standard, expected performance. For example, if a work group is expected to produce 20 units per hour and is actually producing 16, there is a performance discrepancy of 4.

Some examples of how training objectives may be stated are shown in Figure 7-3. As can be seen, these objectives are specific, measurable, and observable. When training programs begin on this basis, they are much more likely to expedite the correction of actual work-related problems and to bring about better performance.

The second step, according to Mager and Pipe's model, is simply to ask whether or not the observed performance discrepancy is important. In other words, "If the objectives of the training program are fulfilled, will there be a noticeable change in the performance of the work group?" Often, supervisors are upset by things that may not be related to performance or productivity, such as extra time for coffee breaks and lunch periods, horseplay, dress habits, critical and sarcastic remarks from employees, and small deviations from company policy such as bringing in a toaster or coffeepot for coffee breaks.

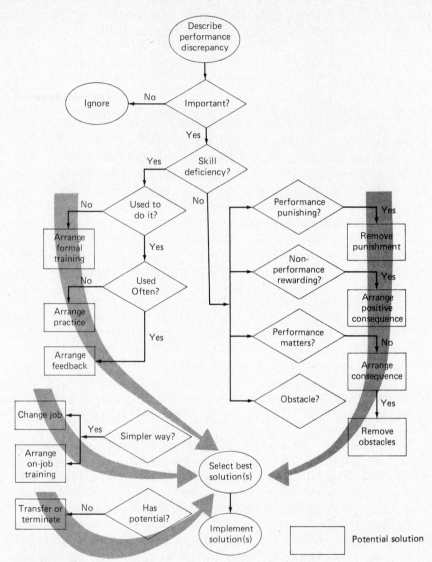

FIGURE 7-2
The Mager and Pipe problem
diagnosis model for training. (Source:
Analyzing Performance Problems, p. 3,
by Robert F. Mager and Peter Pipe, ©
1970 by Fearon-Pitman Publishers,
Inc., 6 Davis Dr., Belmont, CA 94002.
Reprinted by permission.)

170

INAPPROPRIATE TRAINING OBJECTIVE	APPROPRIATE TRAINING OBJECTIVE
1. Improve productivity	1a. Increase sales by 8 percent
	1b. Increase production on line from one to twenty units per person
	1c. Post all accounts by the end of the day
2. Make employees safety-conscious	2a. Post proper signs and always have warning lights in operation
	2b. Always have employees wear protective glasses and hats
	2c. Have area 5 completely free of grease on the floor all of the time
3. Create better attitudes	3a. Reduce customer complaints by 30 percent
	3b. Reduce the number of grievances reaching the second stage by 25 percent
	3c. Increase the activity of the employee suggestion system by 25 percent.

FIGURE 7-3
Examples of specific training objectives.

Since it is not always certain whether or not these things affect productivity, a record should be made which shows the relationship between these undesirable behaviors and productivity. It may be found, for example, that the employee who takes an extra fifteen minutes to clean up at the end of the day has invariably met the organization's production goals. Similarly, the employees with the worst "attitudes" may be the best performers. If training is going to help improve the performance of the work unit, supervisors must make sure that the behaviors that change as a result of training will actually make a difference in performance.

The third step in the model is perhaps the most misunderstood. It asks whether the performance problem is created by a lack of knowledge or whether it is due to deficiencies in the work environment. To make this decision, supervisors simply ask whether the employees could do the job if their lives depended on it. If the answer is yes—that the employees can do the job if they have to—the problem is not actually a training problem. Rather, it has to do with the way the work environment is structured; for example, what is rewarding, punishing, or interfering—in short, what the consequences of performance may be. If the problem centers around these consequences, then solutions to performance problems have to do with making changes in the work environment, not with formal instruction or training. It may be that supervisors need to provide additional or different rewards, punishments, or consequences to ensure appropriate performance. Although these environmental variables appear to be fairly obvious considerations, most practicing supervisors continually request classroom training courses on topics such as Customer Courtesy, Absenteeism, Wearing Safety Glasses and Protective Equipment, and Maintaining a Clean Work Area. These supervisors should be aware, for example, that almost every employee knows both how and when to wear safety glasses and protective equipment as well as how to get to work on time. These problems are mainly concerned with environmental factors and cannot be solved through classroom instruction. These difficulties and strategies for their resolution will be reviewed later in this chapter.

If a supervisor finds that the answer is no, that employees cannot perform the job even when they have to, the problem is more clearly a training problem. In these cases, supervisors need to provide their employees with the information, skills instruction, experience, or coaching required to perform the job adequately. Specific techniques for on-the-job training and coaching will also be covered in following sections.

The remainder of Mager and Pipe's model is fairly self-explanatory. Depending on whether there is a deficiency in knowledge, in the work environment, or in both, supervisors design specific strategies to improve performance. While they may not always follow through each step of the model, it does provide a framework for considering employee training needs that have been ignored in the past. Specifically, the model emphasizes the fact that a majority of the performance problems which were previously thought to be due to the lack of training are the result of deficiencies in the way the work environment is structured. The following sections will address traditional training issues such as training and coaching, but it will also emphasize specific techniques for managing the work environment.

TRAINING METHODS AND TECHNIQUES
AVAILABLE TO SUPERVISORS

As stated before, the purpose of training is to offer information, stimulate discussion, and provide experience which is all directed toward improved job performance. Depending upon the specific needs and objectives of training, supervisors may select from a variety of training techniques, such as those discussed in the following sections.

The Lecture Method

The lecture method is the most efficient way to communicate a large volume of information in a relatively short period of time. It can be defined as a one-way communication process where one individual communicates to a passive audience. Some major disadvantages of the lecture method are that it does not allow the speaker to receive feedback, it leaves open the possibility that some members of the audience will not understand the content, and it does not provide a means by which audience members may clarify their understanding on particular points. However, it is useful when a large volume of information has to be communicated to a mass of people and where it can be expected that the audience will readily understand, accept, and comply with the information or directives communicated. A question-and-answer period at the end can also overcome some of the problems.

The Use of Discussion Groups

Discussion groups are useful when the information is relatively complex and there are both favorable and unfavorable aspects of the topic to be discussed. Such groups can vary in size from three to twenty-five people, although most trainers favor smaller groups of about four to six. The major advantage of discussion is that the participants become actively involved and stimulated. Discussions are particularly helpful where the objective of training is to develop new procedures, policies, or work methods and where the participants' agreement is essential to adopting the new course of action. The major disadvantage of the discussion method is that it can be very time-consuming and may get sidetracked into nonproductive exchanges.

The Case Approach

The case approach provides participants with a specific, realistic situation wherein they are required to make decisions regarding the

173

appropriate courses of action. The cases found at the end of each of the chapters of this book are examples. Most often, cases are written out and each participant receives a copy. The best cases are simple and straightforward on the surface but involve a wide variety of controversial issues and problems that are not immediately apparent. Usually, participants are broken up into discussion groups of five or six people to analyze a given case. A spokesperson for each group then reports the group's analysis and decision to all the participants.

This type of training is particularly useful in occupations where employees encounter similar but complex interpersonal situations, such as insurance adjusting, police work, bill collecting, personnel work, auditing, or nursing. Its major advantage is that the participants become actively involved in realistic situations but do not experience the risks inherent on the actual job. As in the case of discussion groups, the major disadvantage here is the heavy cost in time and the possibility of nonproductive discussions.

The Role-Playing Method

Very similar to the case method is role playing. There are examples of role-playing exercises at the ends of Chapters 10 and 11. In role playing, the participants are given a description of a realistic situation and are asked to act out the parts of the characters. These parts may be written out in full, or the exercise may be unstructured and the dialogue left to the participants' imaginations. Most people find role playing extremely stimulating. If the situations are realistic, this method closely approximates the situations employees actually encounter on their jobs. Also, participants may gain remarkable insight and perspective if they are given a chance to act out roles that are opposed to those they usually play on the job. For example, relationships such as those between nurse and patient, police officer and lawbreaker, supervisor and subordinate, employee and customer or client, or collector and debtor. The major disadvantages are, again, the cost in time and also the reluctance and anxiety that some people feel at the prospect of acting out a situation in front of a group. Videotape equipment that allows replays for analysis is an effective and increasingly popular adjunct to the role-playing technique.

The Vestibule Method

The term "vestibule" is unfamiliar to most people. Just as the vestibule of a church is located outside the actual church, vestibule training takes place outside the actual work environment. Vestibule training was largely developed and heavily utilized during the 1940s, when the nation was gearing up for the war effort. At that time, of course, most experienced employees enlisted in the Armed Forces, and it was necessary to train large numbers of people who had little or no previous work experience. To accommodate this large influx of new workers, most organizations established training facilities that were separate from but very similar to the actual workplace. In this "sheltered" environment, workers were trained en masse for their future jobs. There were full-time trainers, opportunities for immediate feedback on performance, specified stages of progression, and—in some cases—even graduations.

After the war, the use of vestibule training diminished rapidly. It was no longer necessary to train large numbers of employees at a time. Moreover, companies found the method to be extremely expensive, as it required paying a full-time staff, duplicating costly facilities, transferring the training to the actual job, and distributing wages to workers who were not directly contributing to the organization.

Today, vestibule training has been revitalized and is used primarily for training workers who are disadvantaged educationally, economically, or physically. Supervisors of people who have received vestibule training before accepting their full-time positions should make a special effort to visit the training centers. Often, the trainers at these centers can offer information and advice that will facilitate the employee's transition from training to productive work.

On-the-Job Training

The bulk of training for most work groups is on-the-job training. The term is descriptive of the process. On-the-job training is instruction, information, and experience that is provided to employees on the work site. Most often, job-instruction training is oriented toward teaching an employee a particular skill, such as how to read a blueprint, operate a lathe, install an air conditioner, position an x-ray machine, fill out a counseling form, or make an arrest.

Along with vestibule training, the techniques and steps for job-

175

instruction training were developed during World War II after considerable research. The process is fairly simple and can be broken down into some basic steps. Yet many supervisors still fail to follow these steps.

The process of job-instruction training can be summarized as follows:

1 *Prepare the trainee.* The first step is designed to prepare the person to receive instruction. Initially, the trainer will want to relieve any anxiety or apprehensions which the employee may have. As in interviewing, this may be done by asking about any item of common interest to stimulate conversation. Supervisors should also try to relieve any doubts trainees may have by answering their questions and providing realistic encouragement such as: "The job may look difficult at first, and it will take you a few days to get used to it. After about a week, though, you'll be able to do it with your eyes closed."

2 *Present the big picture.* The main objective of this step is to give the trainee an overall perspective on the job. This includes telling the employee what the product or service is, who uses it or depends on it, what its critical features are, etc. For example, a supervisor of a new draftsperson who will be responsible for making blueprints might say: "A blueprint is a detailed picture of the entire job. After you become familiar with blueprints, you will almost be able to see the structures they represent. These prints are extremely important for our field people because they are the only record they have for building a structure. If something is wrong in the print and is not corrected, the building will be constructed according to the wrong specifications. Of course, corrections at that time are extremely costly. So you can see how important it is for these prints to be accurate and correct."

3 *Find the appropriate starting place.* This step is actually a small-scale needs analysis. Here the supervisor's job is to find the employee's present level of knowledge or skill. This ensures that time will not be wasted and the trainee does not become bored by instruction in aspects of the job with which he or she is already familiar. The supervisor can usually ascertain the employee's present knowledge and skill level through questions. In the example used above, the supervisor might ask questions such as: "Have you ever drawn a blueprint before?" "What types of prints are you familiar with?" "Are you familiar with these standard symbols for blueprints (pointing to a list of symbols)?" Supervisors should be particularly careful in this step not to assume knowledge that the employee does not have. At times, employees may not answer the questions quite honestly for

176

fear of appearing stupid. Nonverbal facial cues may tell more than the answer to the question: "Do you understand?" If possible, the supervisor might ask the employee to perform a portion of the task in order to assess his or her competence.

4 *Provide job instruction.* In this phase, the supervisor provides the actual job instruction. Initially, the supervisor should explain the job in detail, pointing out any part of it that is particularly difficult or challenging. If possible, the trainer should then demonstrate how the job is done, explaining each step in the process. If warranted, the supervisor should repeat the process again, pointing out key points.

5 *Encourage practice.* Up to this point, the trainee has been a relatively passive learner. Now the employee should be given the opportunity to actually perform the job. If necessary, the supervisor can instruct the employee in each step of the process. The trainee should be allowed to repeat the process several times, with the supervisor making sure that the critical points of the job are well understood.

6 *Follow up.* People learn by doing. If possible, the employee should be allowed to work independently on the job and gain some proficiency. The supervisor should check back periodically to make sure that the work is being performed correctly and in the most efficient manner. Here the supervisor must walk a fine line between being too critical and being too lenient. Poor work habits are generally easier to correct when they are detected early, but an undue amount of criticism can also be detrimental to new employees. An important challenge for the supervisor is to find the proper balance.

 Selecting Training Techniques

Actually, most training programs involve a combination of methods. For example, a formal training program might begin with a lecture; proceed to a discussion; include some vestibule training, role-playing, or case discussion; and end with on-the-job training with intermittent coaching and instructions concerning the new skills. In other instances, it may not be necessary or possible to conduct an intensive program with so many methods of training. For example, supervisors may communicate, through the lecture method, instructions on how to operate a new piece of equipment. If supervisors can expect the employee to readily accept these instructions and they are simple enough, no additional training may be needed. Thus, the purpose and the nature of instruction will dictate the appropriate

177

method(s). Table 7-1 summarizes the major attributes of the different training techniques available to achieve the goals of improved performance.

THE COACHING FUNCTION OF SUPERVISORS

Coaching can be defined as the daily interactions supervisors have with employees concerning their job performance. It includes all the instructions, suggestions, criticisms, praise, comments, and questions supervisors use to develop and motivate their employees. Although coaching is closely related to overall training, it is usually differentiated by being much less formal and more personal. In addition, it usually occurs after formal training has been completed.

Coaching can be viewed as a communication and feedback process. Figure 7-4 depicts the coaching relationship between supervisors and employees with respect to employee job performance. This model makes the point that both employees and supervisors have imperfect knowledge of employee performance. Feedback and information must flow both ways between employees and supervisors in order to correct deficiencies in performance and to provide for employee development and growth.

More specifically, in the upper left-hand corner of the model is the *public performer.* In this case, both the supervisor and the employee are aware of the employee's progress. They know where the employee is doing well and where some additional work is needed. Both supervisors and employees communicate very easily at this level. Employees will both accept and ask for instructions, criticism, and whatever else is necessary for them to do a better job.

The upper right-hand corner illustrates the *blind performer.* Here the employee/is unaware of his or her own performance, but the supervisor is aware. Unless the employee gains knowledge of these shortcomings and assets, his or her development and growth will be retarded. Employees must have a realistic view of both their assets and deficiencies in order to set realistic goals for improving their performance. When they do not, supervisors have the obligation to provide this information. This is perhaps the most difficult but rewarding part of the supervisory process. At times, employees will reject supervisors' attempts to provide feedback and coaching, even though the suggestions are sincere and constructive. Although there

THE MAJOR TRAINING TECHNIQUES

Method	Purpose	Description	Major advantages	Major disadvantages
Lecture	To convey information.	One-way communication process for large groups.	Ability to convey large amounts of information in a short time.	No opportunity for questions or clarification of difficult areas.
Discussion	To consider application of new information to problem solving.	Open-channel communication with 5 to 25 participants.	Evokes participant interest and involvement. Participants can weigh and evaluate advantages and disadvantages of specific issues.	Audience is passive and may be bored. Time-consuming. Leaders' objectives may not be accomplished.
Role playing	To provide simulated experience in interpersonal situations.	Participants act out the interpersonal relations in hypothetical situations.	Close approximation to reality. Can easily be critiqued and analyzed to provide immediate feedback.	Time-consuming. Possibly threatening and embarrassing.
Case situation	To give participants the opportunity to make decisions about situations that may be encountered on the job.	Groups of 5 to 25 read descriptions of real-life situations and provide solutions to the problems.	Opportunity to carefully weigh and consider decisions in a nonthreatening environment. Group input helps to temper irrational decisions.	Time-consuming. Nonproductive discussions.
Vestibule training	To provide realistic job experience off the job.	Participants perform work-related duties in a sheltered environment under the direction of a qualified trainer.	Provides a sheltered and nonthreatening atmosphere for learning.	Costly. Time-consuming. Transfer of training may be difficult.
On-the-job training	To provide instruction and training under actual working conditions.	Six-stage process including: 1. Preparation 2. Overview of job 3. Needs analysis 4. Job instruction 5. Practice 6. Follow-up	Comprehensive method which can incorporate other methods. Inexpensive. Trainees learn by both instruction and experience.	Costly mistakes. Possibly threatening to inexperienced employee.

	Known by employee	Not known by employee
Known by supervisor	**1** Public performer	**2** Blind performer
Not known by supervisor	**3** Private performer	**4** Unknown performer

FIGURE 7-4
A model for analyzing
supervisor-employee relationships.
(Source: Adapted from Joseph Luft,
"The Johari Window," *Human Relations
Training News,* vol. 5, no. 1, 1961,
pp. 6–7.)

is no sure-fire method of providing appropriate feedback to employees, the following may help in giving feedback and should provide guidelines for effective coaching:

1 *Intention.* Good feedback is directed toward improving job performance and making the employee a more valuable asset. It is not a personal attack and should not imply that the individual's self-worth or image is compromised. Rather, it is directed toward aspects of the job.

2 *Specificity.* Good feedback is designed to provide recipients with specific information so that they know what must be done to correct the situation. Poor feedback is general and leaves questions in the recipients' minds. For example, telling an employee that he or she is doing a poor job is too general and will leave the recipient frustrated in seeking ways to correct the problem. An example of specific feedback for a wire maker would be: "You need to pay closer attention to your quality. Quality control rejected 20 percent of the wire from your machine last week because it was scarred. I can think of three things offhand that you might be doing that would cause it. It could be that you are not changing dies on time, that you are using the wrong die, or perhaps that you are running the wrong wire. Do you have any idea which it may be, or can I help you identify the problem?"

3 *Description.* Good feedback can also be characterized as descriptive rather than evaluative. It tells a person what he or she has done in objective terms, rather than presenting a value judgment. For example, if an employee has left a messy work area, good feedback might be something like: "Last night you left the tools scattered around the work area, failed to fill the machines, and even left your paper cups and sandwich wrappings on the desk. This meant that Frank, the guy on the second shift, had to spend almost his entire first hour putting the tools in their proper places and filling the machines, not to mention cleaning the mess off the desk." Poor feedback would be: "John, I don't know what your parents taught you, but you operate like you're in a pigpen. As a matter of fact, if you continue to act like a pig, I'm going to start treating you like one." Of course, an employee is much more likely to exhibit hostile behavior when feedback is evaluative.

4 *Usefulness.* Good feedback is information that an employee can use to improve performance. It serves no purpose to berate employees for their lack of skill if they do not have the ability or training to perform properly. Thus, the rule of thumb is that if it is not something the employee can correct, it is not worth mentioning.

5 *Timeliness.* There are also considerations in timing feedback properly. As a rule, the more immediate the feedback, the better. This way the employee has a better chance of knowing what the supervisor is talking about and can take corrective action. If faulty work habits continue uncorrected, the employee may begin to assume that an improper method is acceptable. However, there are also times when employees are well aware of the fact that they have made a serious mistake; then they will generally correct the situation themselves. In such cases, it may be better for the supervisor to refrain from comment.

6 *Readiness.* In order for feedback to be effective, employees must be ready to receive it. When feedback is imposed or forced upon people, it is much less effective. Admittedly, it is very difficult to judge when employees will be receptive. Opportunities often come during the course of informal conversations. Occasionally, employees will even ask for feedback. Supervisors must continually be aware of situations where employees are asking for feedback.

7 *Clarity.* Effective feedback must be clearly understood by the recipient. A good way of checking this is to ask the recipient to restate the major points of the discussion. Also, supervisors can observe nonverbal facial expressions as indicators of understanding and acceptance. Supervisors must make sure that the feedback corresponds with their original intent.

8 *Validity.* In order for feedback to be effective, it must be accurate and valid. Of course, when the information is incorrect, the employee will feel that the supervisor is unnecessarily biased, or the employee may take corrective action which is inappropriate and only compounds the problem. Supervisors should check all reasonable sources to make sure that the feedback they are providing is correct and valid.

These points identify characteristics of good feedback that will be helpful in filling in the missing information or correcting the blind spot. Such feedback is a key to good coaching. It may be particularly helpful to review these criteria before talking to an employee with a performance problem. They are briefly summarized in Figure 7-5.

The third cell of the model identifies the *private performer;* those aspects of performance known by the employees, but not by the supervisor. Here it is the employee's responsibility to tell the supervisor where the job poses problems and where help is needed. Supervisors must be particularly sensitive to this area since employees are sometimes reluctant to bring their own shortcomings and inadequacies to their supervisors' attention. However, employees do give subtle hints and usually want help. For example, in a conversation with a supervisor, an employee may say: "Well, I think things are going fairly well." If the supervisor is listening and watching for nonverbal facial clues, he or she may find that this is actually a question rather than a statement of fact. That is, the employee may be subtly soliciting some feedback. The supervisor can test this by saying something like, "Are there any aspects of the job that you think may be improved?" This question gives the employee the option of asking for more detailed feedback.

The last cell of the model indicates the unknown performer, where both the supervisor and the employee are unaware of job-related problems. This is probably the worst situation: complete unawareness and/or ignorance on the part of both employee and supervisor. The supervisor can help solve this problem through improved observational techniques: observing employees, checking out any fluctuations in productivity, and soliciting information from employees. Similarly, if employees are aware of the objectives and goals of their jobs, they will be better able to assess their contributions and locate areas for improvement. In other words, both supervisors and employees must work together to help locate areas for improved employee performance. This way, both will increase their awareness of the employee's development and be able to move away from cell 4 and toward cell 1 of the public performer.

Finally, the coaching process should be directed toward pointing out employees' assets as well as their deficiencies. Just as employees

EFFECTIVE FEEDBACK	INEFFECTIVE FEEDBACK
1. Intended to help	1. Intended to belittle the employee
2. Specific	2. General
3. Descriptive	3. Evaluative
4. Useful	4. Inappropriate
5. Timely	5. Untimely
6. Employee readiness	6. Makes the employee defensive
7. Clear	7. Not understandable
8. Valid	8. Inaccurate

FIGURE 7-5
Characteristics of effective and
ineffective feedback used in coaching.

and supervisors may fail to recognize deficiencies, they may also fail to recognize and capitalize on the employees' assets. Research studies consistently find that there is a lack of supervisory approval and recognition. Employees need this very badly. Moreover, there is substantial evidence that when employees' assets are not recognized and reinforced, performance may deteriorate. Chapter 15, on motivation, will consider this aspect of coaching in more detail. For now, however, we are saying that supervisors, in their coaching role, should accentuate the positive as well as point out the negative.

ORGANIZATIONAL DEVELOPMENT (OD)

Earlier in this chapter, the model of performance analysis by Mager and Pipe was presented and discussed. According to this model, there were two major causes of poor performance: (1) that employees did not have the necessary knowledge, abilities, skills, or experience to perform adequately; and (2) that the work environment supporting behavior was inadequate because it failed to reward or punish performance, provided no consequence for performance, or presented competing objectives which interfered with performance. The first cause was addressed in the sections on training and coaching. This section discusses the second cause, the work environment.

Today, many management consultants believe that almost all work-related problems are caused by deficient work environments. As a result, the largest effort of scholars and consultants is to design strategies to make the work environment more productive. The majority of these strategies can be put under the heading of organizational development, commonly called OD. Basically OD is a planned process of changing the organizational environment. The major characteristics of OD are discussed in the following sections.

The Organizational Diagnosis

OD is not one specific strategy for changing a work environment. Rather, it utilizes a number of different strategies for change, depending on the specific conditions. Accordingly, a thorough diagnosis and assessment of the environment must be made before strategies for improvement can be planned. The diagnosis might consist of a series of interviews, questionnaire surveys, examinations of work records, or educated opinions by organizational specialists. Regardless of how the diagnosis is accomplished, it is understood that the strategies for improvement are based on this objective assessment of the situation rather than the immediate biases or opinions of management, supervisors, or even the OD experts.

Participation and Involvement

OD depends heavily on a participative effort requiring the combined energy and support of the total organization. Because OD strategies deal with work-related problems, it is almost essential to have the participation of relevant supervision in order to implement the strategies and see that they are carried out. Similarly, members of the work group must be included, because they are most familiar with their immediate problems and their cooperation is necessary to correct these problems. Thus, OD becomes a total participative effort encompassing all members affected by the change.

The Role of External Consultants or Third Parties

Most OD efforts employ an external consultant or at least a third party, such as an internal management development specialist. These third parties perform two major functions in the OD process. First, because of their experience and background, these outsiders can train and educate the group in the techniques and strategies of OD. Second, and closely related, is the third party's role as a facilitator or catalyst, guiding the group through the diagnosis and planning

Team Building
The objective of team building is to build cohesive and cooperative work teams. This is usually accomplished in three ways: (1) the supervisor and the work group study and analyze their behavior in structured exercises that demonstrate the important characteristics of cohesive and efficient group functioning; (2) the group considers its own organizational problems and analyzes its behavior in the process; and (3) the group sets specific goals and designs action plans to resolve its problems.

Job Enrichment
Job enrichment entails restructuring jobs so that individuals can experience satisfaction from their work. Enriching the job usually includes designing it so that (1) workers are in direct contact with the recipients of their work; (2) job content reflects a complete job as opposed to a fragmented piece of work; (3) workers can experience the immediate results of their efforts; and (4) workers have the authority and responsibility to make decisions that have an impact on their jobs.

Feedback and Reinforcement Systems
Feedback and reinforcement systems are based on the important finding that individuals perform at higher levels when they receive information concerning their previous performance. The construction of these systems includes identifying important organizational behaviors and developing systems to provide feedback and reinforcement to the persons responsible for these behaviors. Many times, data already available within an organization may be utilized.

Conflict Resolution
Conflicts often occur which limit an organization's ability to function properly. Conflict resolution would include methods of identifying the conflict, discussing it, and developing action plans to reduce it.

Goal Setting
An important component of organizational effectiveness is an explicit statement of organizational goals. In this procedure, which is essentially the MBO process, workers define their major organizational and individual goals. Periodic review processes are arranged to ensure effective attainment of the stated goals.

Transactional Analysis
Organizational members participate in lectures and exercises that help them identify transactions which can create communication difficulties. Informal agreements are made to decrease destructive communications such as destructive games and hidden agendas.

FIGURE 7-6
Summary of popular OD interventions.

process of OD. The ultimate objective, however, is to transfer OD skills to the supervisor so that the effort can continue without the third party.

OD Interventions

A variety of OD strategies are available. Which one is used, of course, depends upon the characteristics of the work environment specified by the diagnosis. Because the various strategies are relatively complex and usually require the help of an external consultant or experienced practitioner for implementation, a detailed discussion is not within the scope of this book. Nevertheless, supervisors should

185

have a working knowledge of OD techniques; therefore a very brief summary of some of the more popular OD interventions is provided in Figure 7-6.

■ KEY CONCEPTS

Training needs
Skills analysis
Performance analysis
Lecture method
Case approach
Role-playing exercise
Vestibule method
On-the-job training (OJT)
Coaching
Organizational development

■ PRACTICAL EXERCISES

(These can be performed by individuals or by groups.)

1 Find a puzzle, application form, or other task which requires at least a minimum of instruction to perform. Before discussing OJT, ask one member of the class to study the task, and, through a lecture, to provide the class with brief instructions. Then, after discussing OJT, have another group member provide instruction to the class using the principles of OJT. Analyze and discuss the differences between the two training approaches.

2 Agree on an appropriate job where the necessary information can be readily obtained and do a skills and/or performance analysis to identify training needs. Using one or more of the techniques covered in this chapter, set up a hypothetical training program that would take care of the needs that were identified.

■ DISCUSSION INCIDENTS

Mary Taylor studied business in college and earned her degree last year. Upon graduating, she accepted a training position with the railroad which, supposedly, would lead to a full-time supervisory job in the personnel department. She spent the first four months on two-week assignments with various supervisors throughout the railroad. The idea was that this rotating schedule would help her gain experience throughout all parts of the company and provide a solid base for her supervisory career. Mary would have been in the program about eight months before she became a supervisor. But she quit after six months. Her reasoning was vague. She just said that she did not feel comfortable at the railroad and that she had not been given any real opportunity or challenge. The training director was baffled because all the supervisors that Mary had worked for had given her excellent recommendations.

1 What do you think really happened when Mary was rotated from supervisor to supervisor? Do you think a systematic analysis of her training needs was made? How would you make such an analysis?

2 Do you have any suggestions for designing better training programs for people like Mary? Be specific in your answer; set up a training program for Mary.

Jim Sims is the day-shift supervisor for Midtown Bakery. Just before quitting time, the owner of the bakery read Jim the riot act. The OSHA inspector had been by and had cited Midtown with no less than fourteen violations. Most of the violations had to do with failure to wear protective equipment such as gloves and face masks. The owner told Jim that he had better design and present some safety training for his people within two weeks or look for another job. Somehow Jim felt that safety training was not the answer, but he could not explain why.

1 Explain why Jim's feelings may be correct—that safety training will probably not reduce the OSHA violations. What other alternatives are available to reduce the OSHA violations?

2 Is Jim's boss wrong in placing the responsibility for the problem on the supervisor's shoulders? How about training in general? Is it the supervisor's responsibility?

CONTROLLING
FOR
RESULTS

CHAPTER
(8)

John Wishart has been the captain of the patrol division of the Rocky City (population 50,000) police department for seven years. During that time, the public has shown little concern for police performance and accountability. People accepted the police officers' authority and actions without question. Recently, there has been a real shift in sentiment and the public has been demanding that police officers be held accountable for their actions. Two of the most recent incidents emphasizing this shift were greatly publicized by the local newspaper. The first involved a physical confrontation between an officer and a black citizen. The black man claimed that the officer used unnecessary force in apprehending him for a misdemeanor. Upon a reporter's investigation, it was found that several other black and white citizens felt that they had been assaulted unnecessarily by this same officer without any real provocation. When the police department denied any knowledge of the officer's previous behavior, the major issue became the lack of any method or system for recording and controlling the behavior of police officers. The second incident closely followed the first, and it was equally infuriating to the public. It involved another reporter's criticisms of the accounting and record-keeping systems of the police department. Some specifics in the report included the disappearance of dangerous drugs from the evidence storage facility, warrants issued on several residents for traffic violations on which the fines had already been paid, and lucrative sums of money spent by the department for "training seminars" at plush resorts. Very soon after these incidents were publicized, both the mayor and the chief of police promised to install effective controls within the department, putting an end to these problems once and for all. John was the supervisor personally charged with the responsibility for developing and implementing this new system of controls. He felt strongly that the public was right in demanding accountability from its officials and agreed that it was about time to begin. Unfortunately, he felt poorly suited to tackle this challenging task and wished that he really understood what they meant by "control"; he felt that there was a need for more formal guidelines before he could establish specific techniques to get the job done effectively.

■ **LEARNING OBJECTIVES**
After reading this chapter, you should have:

An understanding of a comprehensive four-phase approach to the control process and a knowledge of its application

The knowledge and techniques to use feed-forward control effectively

The information and methods necessary to use in-process control effectively

An understanding of the concept and techniques of feed-back control

The ability to analyze situations so that policies can be developed and applied appropriately

The information needed to establish effective standards for control

The techniques required to measure the achievement of performance standards

The background necessary to make effective control decisions

A practical understanding of the techniques and constraints associated with commonly used control procedures such as budgeting, accounting, MBO, performance appraisal, MIS, and management by exception

Controls are an integral and unavoidable part of life in the twentieth century. Each day of our lives we are subjected to countless controls: alarm clocks, automatic toasters and coffeemakers, fuel gauges on cars, traffic signals and signs, reminders about unpaid bills, the radar-surveillance police officer asking us to pull up, and even the sermon delivered by the pastor of the local church to help people gain control over their lives. At times it seems that there is a bit more control than is needed, and "control" takes on a negative connotation. Yet without control there would be chaos. Envision a world with no alarm clocks, no rights of way on city streets, no parking ordinances, and bills being paid at people's convenience. Obviously at least a minimum of control is necessary to maintain basic order in a society.

Organizations are really minisocieties, and as such they also require control. That is, control is a necessary part of all modern organizations. Within organizations, a variety of controls are used: time clocks, budgets, schedules, audits, and inventory reports, to mention only a few. The purpose of this chapter is to analyze the effective use of control within modern organizations. Therefore it will carefully examine both the definition and philosophy of the control process. Specific techniques and methods of control are given the most attention. Throughout, the supervisor's role as a decision maker in the control process is stressed.

THE CONTROL PROCESS

Control may be defined as a process, active or passive, for regulating organizational activities to ensure that they contribute to effective performance. Inherent within this control process are four important elements: objectives, standards, activities, and decisions. Briefly, the process begins with a set of *objectives* for the effective performance of the organization. In most organizations, these objectives are incorporated into the planning activities during the initial phase of the processes described in Chapter 3 (e.g., MBO, budgets, or network plans). If the objectives of these plans are to be viable, however, they have to be further scaled down and translated into *standards* of performance. That is, there must be a specific yardstick which indicates when the plan has been achieved and, preferably, indicates progress or benchmarks toward achieving the plan. This standard is the *activity* which can be measured. The activity measurement is then compared with the standard to indicate progress. Up to this point, the control process is very closely related to the planning process covered in Chapter 3. The last step of the control process is the control *decision.* Generally, if the activity measurements meet the desired standards, the supervisor would make a passive decision not to act. However, when activities do not measure up to standards, then an active control decision is necessary.

A control decision can take three general forms. First, the supervisor may decide that the objectives of the plan are unrealistic; therefore they would have to be either modified or eliminated. Second, it may be decided that the standards are inappropriate. That is, the basic objectives and guidelines in the plan may remain intact, but it may be decided that the specific standards relating to volume of work, time allotted, or resources expended must be made more realistic. Finally, the supervisor may make a decision to change the quality or quantity of activity necessary to achieve the plan. An extra employee may be added or subtracted, additional equipment may be borrowed or purchased, or there may be a change in the supply of materials.

As stated before, the control process (at least the first three steps of it) is very closely related to the planning process. The major difference between the two is that plans are futuristic and concern an organization's intentions. Control, on the other hand, is an active and immediate process. It incorporates all the elements of planning but adds the additional ingredient of active decisions to change organizational objectives, standards, or activities to ensure that the organization is performing according to the plans that have been set out.

A Simple Example of the Control Process

Up to now, our explanation of the control process has been theoretical. As an example to illustrate the process on a practical, applied level, consider a family driving from New York to San Francisco to see their relatives for two weeks. The family's objective can be stated as driving from New York to San Francisco to see the relatives for two weeks.

This family incorporated both standards and projected activities, which are parts of most good objectives. The standard was 500 miles per day, figuring that it would take about 6 days at 10 hours per day to make the 3,000-mile trip. The projected activities incorporated into the objective were things such as departing each day by 7 A.M. and stopping at 5 P.M., changing drivers every 175 miles, maintaining a speed limit of 55 miles per hour, and stopping about 45 minutes per day for lunch. The family thought these plans were realistic and acceptable and used the odometer on the car to make sure that their daily activities were in fact matching up to the standard of 500 miles per day. However, during the course of the trip, there were several difficulties. First was rush-hour traffic. The family found that by leaving at 7 A.M., they ran into rush hours in New York, Philadelphia, and Cleveland on both the first and second days. The rush hours delayed them a total of $2\frac{1}{2}$ hours. Their control decision was to change their planned activities and to drive an extra $1\frac{1}{4}$ hours each day. Moreover, they decided to check the map for large cities and stagger their starting and ending times each day to avoid rush hours. In other words, they were able to modify their activities in order to maintain their overall objective.

A second difficulty in the course of the trip was not as easy to solve. The fuel pump malfunctioned near a small town in western Nebraska. By the time the car was towed in and a replacement was found and installed, the whole day was lost. At that time, they had completed three days of the trip and were on the fourth. Of course, they were very tired and worn around the edges. Yet in looking at the situation, they found a whole range of alternatives for the control decision: (1) modify the objective—plan to spend one less day in San Francisco; (2) modify standards—cover another 130 miles per day; or (3) modify activities—drive 15 miles per hour faster, change drivers more often, and plan to get up earlier and go to bed later. The family decided that 13 hours per day on the road was just too much and that exceeding the speed limit might actually delay the trip further if they received a ticket for speeding. Thus, they decided to modify their objective and spend one day less in San Francisco. Had their objective been

193

different (e.g., making a date for an important appointment in San Francisco), their control decision would undoubtedly have been different.

Two things should emerge from this example. First, the control process is not always cut and dried. It is sometimes difficult to distinguish between objectives, standards, and activities. One could say, for example, that maintaining the speed limit of 55 miles per hour was a standard rather than an activity. The distinction made in the example was one of practicality. The 500 miles per day was probably the best gauge or benchmark the family could use to make control decisions. Other standards simply would not have worked as well. It was a practical matter to list the other quantifiable elements under activities. Second, and most important, is that although the breakdown of objectives, standards, and activities is somewhat artificial, it helps the person who is doing the controlling to define alternatives more clearly when a choice is necessary. In this case, if the family had not set objectives and standards as well as deciding activities for achieving them, there would have been no way of determining when or how they would have arrived. Thus, in the end, the control process helped the family both to make and to modify their plans so that they could have a relatively safe and enjoyable trip.

Categories of Control

Before looking at specific techniques and methods for control, there are three general categories of control mechanisms that should be considered: feed-forward control, in-process control, and feed-back control.

Feed-forward control This category of control is a relatively new concept. The rationale behind feed-forward control is that the damage has already been done if the first control decision is made after the objectives, standards, and activities have all been completed. For example, it does little good for the nursing supervisor to decide to reorder priorities in the emergency room after a patient has died waiting on the operating table. Similarly, when a supervisor burns out a $150,000 machine and loses $60,000 in production waiting for a replacement, plans for a preventive maintenance program are just a mite late. Thus, according to the feed-forward concept of control, supervisors must work through the process beforehand and make control decisions before crises occur.

The feed-forward process can be illustrated if we use the systems variables of input, processing, and output. Figure 8-1 depicts some examples of this breakdown in a number of organizational settings. Of course, within each of these organizations, there would be many more than are shown in the figure. For example, Figure 8-2 breaks down further some of the inputs for a nursing supervisor. If this supervisor were to take a feed-forward control approach, she would carefully consider each of these inputs and project how unanticipated changes would affect both the process and the output. The nurse would ask questions such as: "What should be done in the event that a patient is in a critical state and the patient's doctor is not available?" "Should there be a backup doctor for each patient?" "What if we run short of a critical drug? Should we have an emergency inventory on the floor?" "What if the respirator breaks down with a patient in it? Do we need a backup?" "What should be done if a nurse disagrees with and refuses to follow a doctor's orders? Should she be fired? Should there be an appeal process?" The list of questions that the nursing supervisor could ask is endless, but it is an important list for feed-forward control. Supervisors who deliberately ask these questions become masters of the feed-forward process and learn to anticipate problems, not just to react to them.

Some examples of feed-forward control mechanisms are the following:

1 *Policies* which become predetermined courses of action for a given set of conditions. Policies may or may not spell out actions that have occurred before. Policies on things such as bomb threats, floods, fires, and the possession of alcohol or firearms on the premises are examples of anticipating rather than reacting to crisis situations. The use of policies as a control technique is discussed more extensively later in this chapter.

2 *Warning Signs or Signals.* These mechanisms warn people when there is an imminent threat to their lives, such as a high-voltage current or toxic chemicals.

3 *Checklists.* A predetermined checklist of a process which must be completed before the process itself begins may avoid unnecessary waste and problems later on.

4 *Prescreening.* This amounts to checking the quality of inputs to the process beforehand rather than waiting until afterward to check the quality of the finished product or the service outcome.

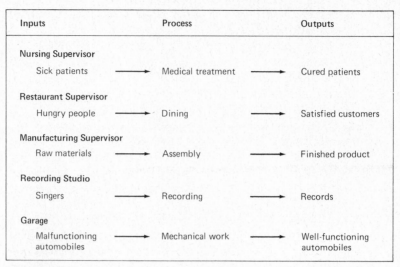

Inputs	Process	Outputs
Nursing Supervisor		
Sick patients ⟶	Medical treatment ⟶	Cured patients
Restaurant Supervisor		
Hungry people ⟶	Dining ⟶	Satisfied customers
Manufacturing Supervisor		
Raw materials ⟶	Assembly ⟶	Finished product
Recording Studio		
Singers ⟶	Recording ⟶	Records
Garage		
Malfunctioning automobiles ⟶	Mechanical work ⟶	Well-functioning automobiles

FIGURE 8-1 The input-process-output model for feed-forward control analysis.

The whole purpose of these mechanisms and the perspective of feed-forward control in general is to anticipate and prevent. If followed, this approach can eliminate many of the crises facing most supervisors in all kinds of modern organizations.

In-process control In this second category of control, the idea is that it may be possible to apply controls in a more efficient manner at the process stage rather than waiting for the outcome. A good example of in-process control is the gasoline gauge on a car. The gauge shows a continuous "real-time" (instantaneous) measure that lets the operator know beforehand when gas is needed. In recent years, gauges for oil pressure and voltage have been converted over to red warning lights. Many of the more mechanically minded have resisted this change because they feel that these new systems are not precise enough and do not provide ample warning of critical situations.

Examples of in-process control systems in today's organization include the following:

1 *Real-Time Computer Systems.* These systems can give the supervisor an up-to-the-second report on specified factors such as inventory or reservations.

```
   INPUTS
Doctors' orders
Drugs
Room Space
Sick Patients
Superior's orders
Patient's requests
Other nurses
Equipment
Supplies (bandages, sutures, etc.)
```

FIGURE 8-2
Inputs for a nursing supervisor.

2 *Numerical Counters.* These are automatic devices which record the number of completed units, whether they are finished products or services, intangibles such as the number of phone calls, entries into the computer, or listings in an accounting ledger.

3 *Automatic Switches.* These are devices which automatically shut down a system in a state of emergency. Fuses which burn out in the event of an electrical overload are a good example. These types of devices are common on sophisticated machinery and equipment.

In-process controls represent the middle ground. They do not necessarily anticipate problems, as in the case of feed-forward, but instead monitor performance while it is happening. They are necessary to effective control.

Feed-back control The final category is after-the-fact feed-back control. (Notice the use of the hyphen in the word to distinguish it from the other uses of "feedback" found in other chapters of the book.) The feed-back occurs when the process is complete. Of course, feed-back is the most common but perhaps the least desirable form of control, since it occurs after the problem has occurred. It is directed toward correcting future deviations in performance. Examples of methods of obtaining feed-back for control are the following:

1 *Accounting Reports.* These are summaries of all basic operating and financial data gathered according to the accepted principles of accounting.

2 *Performance Appraisals.* These are periodic reviews of employees' past performance and can be conducted several ways. Chapter 10 examines these in detail.

197

3 *Quality Control.* These are checks on the quality of the finished outputs or services.

4 *Monthly Reports.* These reports usually contain statistics for various organizational units.

Today the emphasis on feed-back control is changing. The movement is toward converting feed-back processes into feed-forward and/or in-process controls. This conversion process can be illustrated by using the same examples above:

1 *Accounting Reports.* There is a movement toward keeping running tallies of financial and operating data either manually or on real-time computer systems. The data are summarized either instantaneously, daily, weekly, or monthly. Cash flow and cost accounting techniques are good examples. This approach allows deviations to be detected and controlled in process rather than waiting until the end of a lengthy period of time (e.g., quarterly or annually).

2 *Performance Appraisals.* Here feed-forward control can be exercised by setting objectives with employees and providing daily or weekly coaching and assessment rather than waiting until the end of the year.

3 *Quality Control.* The approach here would be to identify key quality problems and have them checked in process rather than expanding additional materials and labor into an already deficient product or service.

4 *Monthly Reports.* As with accounting reports, where possible a running tally would be kept on the available statistics so that deviations could be corrected in process, before they get out of hand.

The second major change in the emphasis of feed-back has to do with the question of who should be receiving the feed-back information. Today's large organizations crank out literally tons of operating and financial data. Much of this data generation becomes an end in itself and the results never reach the levels where they could really be helpful. In particular, most supervisors could receive important data and information regarding their work units, which would greatly aid employee performance. Fortunately, there is now a push to provide all data and information to the individuals responsible for producing the statistics and who ultimately have the potential to improve future reports. The rationale behind this movement lies within motivational theory, which will be covered in Chapter 15. For now, it can be said that research indicates that feed-back on performance usually improves performance. When the feed-back is above expectations, employees consider it reinforcing and performance improves. When the feed-back is below expectations, it is thought to be punishing, and the employees will strive to perform at higher levels to avoid the punishment and attain the reinforcement they received for better performance. These findings point to the importance of providing employees with relevant feed-back on their performance.

Important data and information that are often withheld (not necessarily intentionally) from employees of three representative types of organizations are described below.

1 *Restaurants* often do not tell employees their profit margins for particular items on the menu. One restaurant which did break down the profits per item and informed employees found that profits quickly increased by 20 percent. In this case, employees suggested wine with meals, the item which had the highest profit margin.

2 *Manufacturing* organizations frequently do not tell employees the selling prices of their finished goods. Some companies that made this information available have realized a significant decrease in unnecessary scrap.

3 *Service* organizations frequently do not have or feed back data on profit margins for particular services. For example, it may be much less profitable to replace a valve in an air conditioner than to perform the yearly maintenance service.

Most supervisors can probably find readily available information in their organizations, which can result in significantly improved performance if it is made available to their employees.

ESTABLISHING STANDARDS FOR CONTROL

Perhaps the most difficult part of the control process is deciding on the standards for control. For the family driving to San Francisco, the standard of 500 miles per day turned out to be a pretty good gauge of their progress. Yet they could have also chosen miles per hour, time on the road, hours of driving, or even tanks of gas as their standard. The choice of standards is a complex process which is ruled by one overriding consideration: "What is the best and most efficient gauge of progress in meeting the objective?" Other relevant questions in determining standards include the following:

1 What standard will be easiest to understand and communicate?

2 What standards will be least expensive and time consuming to collect?

3 What standard will be easiest to measure and quantify?

4 Which standard is most meaningful in relation to the objective?
5 If several standards are selected, what is the least number which will give a good overall picture of progress toward the objective?

The Relationship between Objectives and Standards

An important consideration in establishing standards is identifying the areas which need to be monitored to determine progress toward the objective. This can best be illustrated by a discussion between a young engineer and an external management consultant. The engineer was complaining bitterly to the consultant. He had made several innovations which had saved his small company thousands of dollars, yet the president and owner was not happy. Moreover, the engineer had made a number of cost-saving suggestions that he was positive would save the company even more money, but they were flatly rejected. The engineer concluded his argument with: "It's unbelievable. I know he understands that this suggestion would make him thousands of dollars, and he is in business to make money, isn't he?" The consultant's answer stunned the young engineer. It was, "Probably not." The consultant went on to explain that while making money was certainly *one* of the owner's goals, there were other goals that were equally important. After discussing the situation further, they concluded that the owner actually had several different goals: (1) profitability, (2) building quality units, (3) keeping the work force steadily employed, (4) maintaining a favorable image in the surrounding community, and, not least, (5) achieving the status and recognition that go with running a one-person show. Once the engineer became aware of these multiple goals, he was able to see the owner's rationale for rejecting his suggestions.

This situation is very similar to that faced by most supervisors. It is impossible for them to locate a single goal and set a standard that will measure success. The problem becomes one of determining what the objectives—either explicit or implicit—of the organization are and designing standards and a system for combining these standards to measure progress and accomplishment. An example of a company that did this successfully is General Electric.

GE started developing areas for standards by asking the question: "Will continued failure in this area prevent the attainment of management's responsibility for advancing General Electric as a leader in a strong competitive economy, even though results in other key areas are good?" Through this method, GE was able to identify eight key

**Basic Elements
of Effective Supervision**

areas for results: profitability, product leadership, personnel development, market position, employee attitudes, public responsibility, productivity, and balance between long- and short-range goals. Once these key results areas had been identified, each operating unit was charged with developing standards to measure them.

Although GE is probably unlike the organizations where most supervisors work, the principles GE used can be applied in many types of organizations. Of course, some of the key result areas will differ depending on the organization. Some more general areas for control applicable to most supervisors would be the following:

1 *Quantity.* Most organizations find it desirable to develop some standards for the amount of output produced. Examples are the number of widgets completed, number of customer contacts, number of job placements, number of cases closed, and number of completed repairs.

2 *Quality.* Quality is also an important goal for most organizations. When physical products are being produced, there are usually some qualitative standards that can be applied. Examples would be the number of defects and the number of objects beyond a particular tolerance. In service organizations, where outputs are not as tangible, there must be an agreed upon set of quality standards which are at least observable and measurable. For a rehabilitation service, supervisors might measure job placements within particular salary ranges, the number of clients released who eventually need further rehabilitation, or the number of clients who request to change counselors. Customer/client/patient complaints can also be used to measure the quality of service in various types of organizations.

3 *Morale.* Employee morale is often a goal in organizations. Standards which may be used are grievances, employee suggestions, absenteeism, turnover, and requested transfers. Many organizations also use the results of standardized attitude surveys for year-to-year comparisons. OD diagnostic techniques (discussed in the last chapter) can also be employed.

4 *Market Position.* Often industrywide or local/regional data are available to assess an organization's share of the defined market. At times, public agencies and hospitals also have statistics that can be used as benchmarks for measuring relative position. This "share" concept is an important measure because the relevant supervisor has direct control over it, whereas he or she may not be able to influence such factors as fixed costs or external variables such as the economy.

5 *Costs.* A very common area where organizations set standards is costs. There are numerous ways to break down costs. For example, labor costs can be broken into two categories: direct labor (all persons who physically work on the product or service) and indirect or expense personnel (all support people, such as materials handlers and maintenance personnel). Ratios of direct to expense personnel, such as ten direct to one expense, are standards for control. Similar methods are used to partition and develop ratios for costs such as raw materials, machinery, and marketing expenses. Additional methods for analyzing costs will be provided in the discussion on budgets and accounting.

6 *Time.* Time is another variable which organizations traditionally have found useful in setting standards. Time standards are often closely related to quantity, and productivity may actually be a ratio of quantities produced to amount of time. In addition, time may be used as a standard for things such as the completion of a research project or the construction or renovation of a building.

MEASUREMENT TECHNIQUES FOR CONTROL

This section will explain a variety of ways in which organizational outputs can be measured. Discussing measurement in this way is, of course, an artificial division, since in most cases the techniques for measurement are inseparable from the standards themselves. Moreover, measurement sometimes actually precedes the establishment of the standards. For instance, where a specific standard cannot be derived intuitively, supervisors may measure an output over a period of time and use the average of these measures to establish the standard. Thus, although measurement is presented here as a separate part of the control process, it is very closely related to the standard-setting process. The following sections examine the specific techniques of measurement.

Personal Observation

This is probably the most widely used technique for measurement. It consists of simply observing employees or other factors in the work environment to determine whether or not the outcomes are meeting the expected standards of performance. It can be done very loosely, without any method of tallying or categorizing observations. Feedback to employees is usually very general in nature and, at times, questionable. On the other hand, personal observation can also become a very rigorous method of control.

Supervisors can establish categories for observation such as the number of absences, number of times returning late from breaks, number of times away from the work station, number of complaints, number of "heated" exchanges with customers, number of units produced, etc. Where supervisors are willing to take the extra time to tally observations in this manner, they can usually provide employees with much more precise and meaningful feedback.

Some of the major limitations of personal observation as a way to measure for control are the following:

1 *Perception.* Observers may be biased in their interpretations and be accused of seeing only what they want to see rather than what is really happening.

2 *Agreement.* Employees may not agree with the observations of the supervisor or may object to the way the standards were set and how they are interpreted.

3 *Timing.* It may not be possible to observe important activities at the critical times.

4 *Sensitivity.* Employees may resent the feeling of "being watched" and in some cases the observation may approach the invasion of the person's privacy.

5 *Spontaneous Perfection.* This means that employees may perform up to standards while being observed but will perform poorly when observations are not being made. In other words, everyone makes it a point to look busy when the boss is around (as when the members of a construction crew fight for a pick or a shovel when the supervisor comes around).

Regardless of its limitations, personal observation remains the most used method of measuring and can be effective. It is the only method available in some areas of performance, and it can compensate for some of the gaps and inequities that exist with even the best performance standards.

Engineering Approaches to Measurement

Industrial engineers over the years have developed a number of methods for measuring performance and establishing standards. One of the more popular methods is the time-and-motion study. Here the engineer observes employees over a period of time. A stopwatch is used to time precise movements that contribute to efficient job performance. At the conclusion of this analysis, the engineer may average the various times, add them up, and develop a time standard for efficiently completing the job. By adding in time for lunch, coffee breaks, setting up, and cleanup times, the engineers can derive a standard for output in an eight-hour day. In addition, there are even some methods for establishing time standards that do not require direct observation by the engineer. Here the engineers have charts and published materials which contain standardized ratings, developed over the years, for components of the jobs. Using these standards, the engineers can come very close to the standards for a specified job without ever having directly observed the employees in their own organization. Of course, this latter approach is only applicable to highly repetitive, specialized jobs.

Most large organizations, especially those in manufacturing, employ a staff of industrial engineers to perform these job-standards studies. The line supervisors in these organizations should familiarize themselves with the particular methods used by the engineers and should learn what goes into a given job standard. A supervisor who works in a smaller organization or one that does not use an engineering staff might suggest contacting a professional engineer to do a job analysis. Although engineering types of standards are particularly adapted to wage-incentive programs, they are also helpful in providing supervisors with feedback where their workers are not on wage-incentive programs.

It should be noted, however, that—as with other standards—workers may offer resistance to time standards. This resistance goes back to the abuses of old efficiency engineering, which was used as an excuse for job speedups. This problem can be avoided if the supervisors completely explain the measurement system and its impact on the individual employee. One way of doing this is to allow the employee to participate fully in setting and implementing the standards.

Self-Reporting Techniques

When direct observation of employees is not possible, self-reports, either verbal or written, may be used to measure performance. Among the ways in which self-reports may be made are the following:

1 Sales personnel call in to the home office giving pertinent data

such as the number of sales, dollar volume of sales, number of customers contacted, and number of miles traveled.

2 A nurse reports back to the supervisor about the types of treatment dispensed to patients as well as any particular problems.

3 A retail distributor calls in to the home office detailing sales and registering orders for new products.

4 A taxicab driver calls the dispatcher to verify that a customer has been picked up and to ask for or provide the next destination.

5 A customer-relations representative tallies the number of calls received per day, the number of irate customers, and the number of satisfied customers.

6 An assembly-line worker turns in a "bogey sheet" at the end of the day, indicating the number of units produced.

In general, it has been found that self-reports can be very effective, accurate, and timely ways of measuring. This is particularly true when statistical reports accompany and can be used to verify self-reports. Where self-reports are not validated by other reporting mechanisms, supervisors should use spot checks to determine their accuracy. For example, the owner of a television repair shop may make occasional field visits to ensure that employees' reports are accurate. There are research findings indicating that employees can be trusted to report accurately, even when the results are not favorable to them and they know the supervisor cannot check their reports. In these studies, it was found that the most important variable for accurate reports was the supervisor's behavior. Where supervisors reprimanded or punished employees with undesirable reports, employees began to alter them to make themselves look better. However, supervisors who rewarded employees for *accurate* reports (not necessarily favorable ones) and helped the employees work through job-related problems found that the integrity of self-reports was maintained. In other words, employees will be honest if they are rewarded for honesty.

Statistical Reporting Techniques

Another common measurement method involves the collection and numerical summary of vital operating information. In larger organizations, there is often a staff of people called "operations analysts" whose primary function is to collect and analyze statistical information. The information may be data relevant to the internal performance of the organization (for example, the performance of personnel, machines and equipment, or financial indexes). Very often, however, data may also be collected from outside the organization— from competitors, associations, or government agencies. The external sources of data are very valuable for comparative purposes of the total organization. In addition, data from one part of the organization may be compared with data from other parts to ensure that everyone is making a reasonable contribution. Finally, data from the current year may be compared with historical data to see if there are any significant changes or trends which need attention.

Although smaller organizations do not usually retain operations analysts on their staffs, they can still use statistical measurements and analyses to make control decisions. For example, all organizations can keep their accounting statements and compare them from year to year for any radical changes in the different categories. Another example would be a small sales or service organization which could keep records of the number of transactions at particular times of the day or year to determine the best business hours and staffing levels. Finally, while statistical reports may be necessary to keep track of deviations in large organizations, supervisors in smaller organizations are usually so familiar with changes in the operating statistics that they are able to anticipate trends far in advance of any formal statistical analyses. Thus, statistical approaches to control can be extremely valuable in large organizations, where supervisors cannot be familiar with all aspects of the organization. In smaller organizations, the personal observations of supervision may actually be much more sensitive to important deviations in performance.

COMPREHENSIVE CONTROL TECHNIQUES

The purpose of this section is to review some of the more comprehensive control techniques used by organizations. These techniques usually take into consideration the setting of standards and the measurements of performance which have been discussed so far in this chapter as well as some of the specific techniques such as MBO and PERT, which were covered in Chapter 3, on planning. Also, performance appraisal—an extremely important control technique for employee performance—is the major topic of Chapter 10. These aspects of control, which again point out the interrelationships of the various supervisory functions and techniques, are only given brief coverage in this section. Major attention is devoted to accounting and budgeting techniques and newer methods such as computerized information techniques.

Accounting for Financial Control

Probably the most commonly thought of approach to control is accounting. While accounting processes can be extremely complex, the conceptual idea behind them is relatively simple. Basically, accounting can be defined as a system for recording, balancing, and reconciling financial transactions; it takes several forms.

Cost accounting In cost accounting, each financial transaction is carefully recorded and placed into a category by assigning it an account number. Typical categories of transactions which are assigned account numbers include sales, purchases, wages, and insurance. After the transactions have been recorded, accountants collect the information from the various units of the organization and sort the transactions according to the account numbers. This gives the accountants a fairly accurate picture of the organization's financial activities within particular cost categories. If one category—for example, wages—is inconsistent in proportion to other categories or previous historical information, it is a "red flag" to look into the matter and, of course, helps to control costs.

Balance-sheet accounting Another important accounting technique is the balance sheet. Here the accountants sort all financial transactions into one of two general categories: assets and liabilities. Assets are everything the organization owns which can be considered a credit to the organization. This includes things such as the physical facilities, accounts receivable, raw materials, inventories, and machinery and equipment. Liabilities are everything which the organization owes; included would be items such as accounts payable, taxes, and long-term debt. Theoretically, both the assets and liabilities should balance out to equal zero. When they do not, the accountants are charged with finding the missing capital. These types of accounting sheets are typically called balance sheets; they show an organization's financial status at particular points in time, such as December 31.

Profit-and-loss accounting Another accounting mechanism is the income statement. Here the accountants tally all the costs of doing business, such as raw materials, wages, rent, and interest costs. These costs are then compared with the sales revenues and other earnings. The difference between the costs and revenues indicates the organization's profits (or losses) over a specified period of time (usually a month or a year).

Supervisors' involvement in accounting Most supervisors will become involved in these accounting processes to varying degrees. For example, supervisors are commonly assigned several different account numbers to which they must charge all financial transactions. At the ends of specified periods of time, they are required to balance their books. That is, just as the accountants balance the overall organization's assets and liabilities at specific times, most supervisors will have ledgers that categorize all incoming and outgoing monies, which must balance to zero. Of course, if these books do not balance, the accountants will want to know why and will try to help reconcile the differences. At times, it can become very frustrating trying to account for one missing dollar on a budget that amounts to thousands. However, it must be remembered that this is an important responsibility and that, in many cases, there may be legal difficulties for the organization if all the money cannot be accounted for. Thus, from an accountant's point of view, it is absolutely necessary that supervisors carefully categorize and keep accurate records of all their financial transactions. Most organizations will provide at least on-the-job training and in some cases formal classroom training regarding the specifics of their particular accounting systems.

Besides the responsibilities for keeping accurate records for the balance sheet, supervisors may also become involved directly or indirectly with both cost accounting and income statements. As previously explained, cost accounting is a method of categorizing financial transactions to see whether or not assets are being expended in the appropriate categories. Some organizations will require supervisors to do their own cost accounting, while others will tally the information from the records supervisors submit. Regardless of the approach, when top management gets into a belt-tightening posture, among the first things they look at are the cost accounting data. Supervisors should be prepared to respond to these pressures to cut costs. They should be able to demonstrate their efficiency and should have considered their cost data beforehand, so that they will be ready with suggestions or programs for cutting costs in categories which may be out of line.

In addition to the balance sheet and cost accounting involvement, there may be mini-income statements or profit centers for the various parts of the organization. Supervisors should be aware of the contribution their units make to the overall financial performance of the organization. When the profit ratios for their units are high, they can often use this as a justification for asking and obtaining additional assets. If their profitability is low, they should be ready to explain their reasons and suggest ways of improving their units' contribution to the financial success of the organization.

The Budgeting Process

Closely related to accounting control of financial resources is the budgeting process. A budget can be simply described as a projected accounting statement. Budgets can become extremely complex, depending upon the organization, but conceptually they are simply control mechanisms.

Budgeting involves three major phases:

1 *Projection.* In this initial phase of budgeting, an estimate is made of the required financial resources for a specified period of time, usually the fiscal year. The basis for these projections may be previous budgetary information, projected sales or business, or some set of specific plans. "Zero-based budgeting," which became popular in the federal government with the Carter administration, simply means that previous budgetary information does not serve as the basis for future budgets. Instead, all budgets must begin from scratch or "zero," and the use of each projected dollar must be explained in the proposed budget.

2 *Use.* Assuming that the budget is approved, the supervisor now has a specific allocation of money to use. Every dollar spent must be recorded and posted against the various categories of the budget. It is in this phase that in-process control can and should occur.

3 *Feedback.* In this third phase of the budgeting process, feedback control takes place. The supervisor compares the amount budgeted with the number of dollars actually spent. Most supervisors set up comparison periods of about one month for a year-long budget. This way the supervisor can get periodic feedback to make sure that the amount spent will not exceed the amount budgeted for the fiscal year.

Despite the fact that the budgeting process is easily understood and budgets are commonly used as a control technique, they have a very negative connotation and are associated with conflict and other internal organizational problems. One noted researcher and organizational behavior expert, Chris Argyris, has summarized some of the major human problems associated with budgets as follows:

1 Budget pressure tends to unite the employees against management and tends to place the factory supervisor under tension. This tension may lead to inefficiency, aggression, and perhaps a complete breakdown on the part of the supervisor.

2 The finance staff can obtain feelings of success only by finding fault with factory people. These feelings of failure among factory supervisors lead to many human relations problems.

3 The use of budgets as "needlers" by top management tends to make each factory supervisor see only the problems of his own department.

4 Supervisors use budgets as a way of expressing their own patterns of leadership. When this results in people getting hurt, the budget, in itself a neutral thing, often gets blamed.[1]

Of course, the problems Argyris identified for factory supervisors also apply to supervisors working under the constraints of budgets in all modern, large organizations.

Despite the negative side effects, budgets can and should be viewed as very potent tools for documenting and controlling organizational performance. The following suggestions should help supervisors use budgets most effectively:

1 *Do your research, your "homework," before the budget is submitted.* Supervisors who can demonstrate the necessity for each dollar in their budgets have a much greater chance of having their budgets approved and effectively used.

2 *Be prepared to "sell" your budget.* Although it may sometimes seem like a game, supervisors should be prepared to give a full explanation of their budgets to their superiors. Often historical data may be useful in justifying the budget. Similarly, supervisors should be prepared to explain the importance of their units' functions and its contribution to overall goals of the organization as a whole.

---

[1]Chris Argyris, "Human Problems with Budgets," *Harvard Business Review*, January–February 1953, p. 108.

3 *Expect that there will be pressures.* Supervisors should expect pressures to reduce their budgets. Budgets are easily measurable in terms of dollars and are a direct reflection of the organization's financial health. It is a rare organization that does not exert continual pressure to reduce budgets.

4 *Try not to take budget cuts as personal defeats.* In most organizations budget cuts are as inevitable as death and taxes. Supervisors who take these cuts personally are usually doing themselves an injustice and cause themselves unnecessary worry and guilt.

5 *Communicate budget information to the relevant personnel.* The only people who can really help supervisors keep their budgets in line and make them work are their employees. Yet, too few supervisors let employees see budgeting information. Making this information available and explaining its rationale can help employees stay within budget limitations and help achieve cost-reduction goals.

6 *Manage the budget.* The budget is a valuable control mechanism for supervisors who use it properly. Supervisors should study their budgets carefully and set interim objectives or "milestones" for achieving their budgets. Often supervisors have some discretion regarding the different accounts to which they may charge expenditures. If they know the present status of such accounts, they can make decisions that will aid them in the long run.

These suggestions can make the budget an effective control technique for better supervision instead of a "straitjacket" and barrier that supervisors have to put up with and try to overcome.

Management by Objectives

MBO was outlined in Chapter 3. Besides being a major technique for planning, it also encompasses both elements of the control process: (1) setting goals and standards and (2) appraising by results. The second half of MBO, appraising by results, is most closely associated with control. However, another important control aspect of MBO, often ignored, is the follow-up that occurs in an effective system. That is, in order to make MBO an effective approach for both planning and control, there must be constant follow-up and adjustment through control decisions. When the periodic appraisals indicate that objectives are not being met, the following types of control decisions could be made: (1) the objectives may be changed; (2) the methods of measurement may be reconsidered; or (3) activities and/or resources allocated toward the achievement of objectives may be adjusted. In

211

other words, MBO becomes an effective system when supervisors actively manage the process through a series of control decisions.

Network Planning

The control aspects of network planning are very similar to MBO. PERT and other network approaches covered in Chapter 3 are both planning and control techniques. When dates of the network model do not appear feasible, several alternative control decisions are available to the supervisor: (1) change the objective in terms of the completion date; (2) adjust the measuring techniques that are being used; or (3) reallocate personnel and/or resources needed to achieve activities. Again, as with MBO, network techniques can become more effective when supervisors are making active control decisions.

Policies as a Control Technique

An often overlooked technique for control involves the various policies that exist at all levels of a modern organization. A policy can be simply defined as a guideline or, more narrowly, a rule which is designed to be applied under a given set of circumstances. Policies are one of the best methods of feed-forward control in that they are designed to give guidelines for appropriate behavior and to prevent problems. Some policies, of course, deal with very mundane things like dress codes, smoking, travel, and ways to handle expenditures. However, policies can also pertain to very important strategic issues such as organizational structure, product or service offered, and relationships with government, unions, and competitors. In general, however, the purpose of the policies remains the same. They tell both supervisors and employees what is expected of them and forewarn them of consequences that can be anticipated when they do not meet expectations. In this sense policies can be a very potent feed-forward control mechanism.

When policies are violated, they become a feed-back approach that requires control decisions by supervisors. In the case of policy violations, supervisors should use as a guideline the elements of the control process in making their decisions. First, they should examine the objective of the policy and determine if that objective will be served by applying the policy in that particular case. Next, they need to consider whether or not the standards for the policy have been violated. This is usually more difficult than it appears, because many policies are poorly written and do not contain relevant, measurable standards. Often, the best indication of the standard is a check to see how the policy has been applied in the past. The final step is determining what activity is required to meet the standard. For serious deviations from policy, offenders may have to be seriously disciplined. The next chapter covers ways in which this can be done. In other cases there may be some alternative corrective actions that will help violators correct the problem and conform to policy. In either case, however, policies are more effective in the feed-forward sense than in the feed-back.

Often policies are only thought of as formal written documents which are formulated and issued from top-level management. Fortunately this is not true. Most supervisors can greatly benefit from establishing their own informal policies to serve as feed-forward controls for their areas of responsibility. Some examples of informal policies supervisors may establish are: (1) personnel rotations for lunch and coffee breaks; (2) systems for ordering supplies and materials; (3) procedures for reporting injuries, illnesses, and absences; and (4) procedures for requesting maintenance or repairs on equipment. In many cases, supervisors can greatly increase efficiency in these areas by posting a written policy.

If the supervisor formulates a policy that represents a radical departure from present practices, the employees should usually be consulted and be kept informed. The supervisor should explain the situation and why there is a need for the new policy. The supervisor should solicit suggestions and/or alternative solutions. Finally, the supervisor should formulate the policy which represents the most workable solution leading to effective performance. Throughout this process, the supervisor should stress the elements of the control process: the objective or reason for the policy, standards for measuring the policy, and what actions will be taken if the policy is violated. Even if the policy is unpopular, employees are much more likely to accept it and respond favorably if they have some input and know the reason for it. This participative approach is given further attention in the last part of the book.

Management Information Systems

Management information systems (commonly called MIS) are computerized systems which provide supervisors with important data on

213

all aspects of their operations. Usually the MIS is grouped into subparts. For example, there might be a separate system for personnel information that provides things such as seniority lists, wage rates, retirement dates, accrued vacation and/or sick-leave time, educational and/or training progress, and job grades. Other subgroupings of information might include operating data on quantity and quality, financial data, inventories, and sales information. Ultimately, a supervisor who knows how to use the system should be able to request needed data from a remote computer terminal in order to make better control decisions.

To date, most organizations do not have a fully operational MIS. By the same token, almost all organizations of any size are moving more and more into computerized MIS and already have at least some information which is computerized and can help the supervisor make control decisions. Where needed information is not available on the computer, there is usually some type of manual system for tabulating and filing data. Supervisors who know their organizations well can usually obtain this information to help them make control decisions. Where information is not available, supervisors should carefully consider the kinds of information that will aid their decision processes. If the information is valuable enough, they may decide to collect it themselves or assign the responsibility to members of their units.

Theoretically, a supervisor should be able to make all control decisions on the basis of a complete MIS. Although this is far from a reality today, supervisors should be constantly aware of, searching for, and developing information which can help them make better control decisions.

Performance Appraisals

Appraising employee performance is an integral part of the control system of most modern organizations. Since this process will be reviewed in detail in Chapter 10, only a few brief comments about the control aspects of appraisal are discussed here. First of all, supervisors should view employee appraisals in light of the entire control process: objectives, standards, activities, and decisions. Too often, supervisors do not take this comprehensive approach to appraisal and automatically assume that employees are deficient in performance. Like any control decision, performance appraisals should encompass a hard look at the objectives, standards, and activities for employee performance. Very frequently faults in performance can be traced back to the lack of appropriate objectives, standards, and activities. In other words, supervisors must often bear partial responsibility when employees do not perform adequately.

A second point for emphasis on the role that performance appraisals have in control is the feed-forward perspective. Performance appraisals should be used for setting objectives, determining standards for measurement, and designating appropriate activities for employee behavior; these are just as important as the evaluation of past performance. In a feed-forward perspective, performance appraisal sessions would be viewed as proactive, designed to help employees improve their performance.

Finally, it should be emphasized that supervisors *must* make control decisions in performance appraisals. Too often the appraisal process is viewed as just another example of bureaucratic red tape which is never given any attention by top management. The appraisal process can become a valuable mechanism for control only when supervisors become actively involved in making control decisions and communicating them to their employees. Chapter 10 will provide more specific details on how to conduct effective employee performance appraisals.

Management by Exception

Very simply, management by exception (MBE) recognizes that there are a multitude of decisions that must be made within each organization on a daily basis. If supervisors gave a great deal of attention to all these decisions, there would not be enough time in the day. Chapter 4, "Time Management and Delegation," pointed out that MBE can help alleviate this problem.

Some of the methods for highlighting key decisions for MBE have already been discussed. Chapter 4 emphasized setting up reporting relationships that would flag the supervisor's attention when exceptional problems arose. Similarly, discussions concerning MBO, PERT, and MIS systems pointed out that control decisions were necessary only when there were radical departures from standards. When minor deviations are detected, most effective control systems provide for the activation of appropriate alternatives. For example, the average supervisor has already identified the person who will take charge in the event that he or she becomes sick. Thus, there is no disruption in the normal work procedures and people do not spend unnecessary time or divert important organizational resources to handle such problems.

It should be noted again that MBE is distinctly different from management by crisis. When managing by crisis, supervisors move frantically through the day from one crisis to another. Usually this is because a supervisor does not have appropriate feed-forward controls. Management by exception, rather, is the idea that the supervisor's day is relatively free so that exceptional, important critical events can be dealt with. When these exceptions occur, the supervisor can devote the necessary time and energy to make effective decisions. After dealing with the immediate crisis, the supervisor analyzes the objectives, standards, and activities carefully and develops either procedures or alternative courses of action so that a crisis is even less likely to occur in the future.

As described above, MBE is a carefully considered control technique which sifts out low priorities and allows supervisors to spend their time making important control decisions and planning ways to avoid future crises. Supervisors who use MBE—combined with the other methods and techniques discussed in this chapter—will find that they can develop very effective ways to control for improved results.

■ KEY CONCEPTS

Objectives

Standards

Activities

Feed-forward control

Policies

In-process control

Feed-back control

Personal observation

Accounting controls

Budgeting

Management information systems

Performance appraisal

Management by exception

■ PRACTICAL EXERCISES

(These can be performed by individuals or by groups.)

1 Examine your school's (or company's) process for controlling student and teacher (or employee) performance or payment of tuition and fees (or costs). Can the process be specified in terms of objectives, standards, activities, and control decisions?

2 Locate a policy handbook for your school or relevant work organization. Discuss how these policies can be implemented into all phases of the control process (i.e., objectives, standards, activities, and decisions).

3 Work through a simple balance-sheet accounting problem (use either real or made-up items and numbers) and discuss its implications for organizational control.

■ DISCUSSION INCIDENTS

Art Arnold was normally a soft-spoken, peaceful person, but he was about to lose his patience. Mr. Finkwinkle, the accountant from the seventh floor, had just requested another appointment. Art had just spent three hours with Finkwinkle on Monday trying to track down $45.30 which he had somehow failed to record on his accounting sheet. Art was fully aware of the fact that he had made the mistake and he even told the accountant that he would take care of the $45.30 out of his own pocket. Finkwinkle would not hear of it. He just kept insisting that he had to retabulate the records in the hope of finding the error. Art was beginning to feel that the entire process was ridiculous, especially in light of the fact that his total operating budget was over $180,000. At this point, he would gladly give Finkwinkle the $45.30 if he would just go away. Art felt his time was worth more than this.

1 Is it so important that the $45.30 mistake be found and corrected? Why or why not?

2 What type of accounting control is being used in this incident? What are some other techniques that Art could use to control his department?

Lake Enterprises was having some serious attendance problems. Some employees had as many as thirty to forty absences per year. The reasons for the absences varied. Some were obviously caused by illness. However, some definitely resulted from relaxed supervision. Many supervisors were liberal in granting employees requests for days off as long as the employees asked in advance. But there were employees who simply stayed home if they were tired or had something better to do. Several days ago the problem came to a head when so many workers were absent from the fabricating operation that it had to shut down. Top management was furious. They called an emergency meeting with all supervisors.

1 From a control standpoint, what do you think top management would say in this meeting? What do you think they should say? Why?

2 If you were asked at this meeting to suggest a control process for employee attendance, what would you propose? Be specific in your answer.

Helen Dilger is the floor supervisor of Orthopedics in Community Hospital. Recently, a top-rated consulting firm set up a system of measurements and standards for her work group. Her group was supposedly going to be a model for the rest of the hospital. The standards for her group applied to most of the relevant areas of medical care and included things such as time ratings for bathing patients, making rounds, acquiring and administering medication, keeping records accurately, preparing for and recovering from surgery, and doing physical therapy. Helen felt that, on the whole, the standards were pretty much on target. Yet, several of her nurses had publicly stated that they would quit the organization if these standards were used in appraising their performance. Their argument was that the standards were arbitrary. They pointed out, for example, that surgery preparation could vary greatly depending on the type of surgery being done. Helen did not quite know how to reply, since she knew that such times would vary greatly. The nurses stress that the standards might control quantity of medical care but not quality.

1 Discuss and develop an argument that would help Helen support the case for control standards.

2 Is the quantity versus quality argument a valid one? Can quality controls be established in services such as health care? How?

DISCIPLINING EMPLOYEES

9CHAPTER

Betty Parkins, the new supervisor of building services, is confused and unsure about what to do with Neva. When Betty accepted her promotion, Neva was one of the people she inherited. Neva has not progressed beyond her present job as mail carrier and messenger, even though she has been with the company almost ten years. During that ten-year period she has averaged almost thirty days absent per year, mostly on Mondays, Fridays, and the days before and after holidays. Despite Neva's poor attendance record, Betty is hesitant about discharging her because there are still other employees with worse attendance records. However, there are additional performance problems with Neva. For example, last week Neva refused to pick up a parcel at the south location because it was raining and freezing outside. When told to pick up the package or go home, Neva went home. Just today Betty realized that Neva had taken the morning off to attend a friend's funeral even though she had been told that she could not have the time off. Betty was genuinely concerned because she knew that Neva was the sole source of support for an ailing mother. She wished that she had had more training in discipline and counseling so that she could deal with problems of this sort in a positive, constructive manner and turn employees like Neva around into acceptable, productive members of the department.

■ LEARNING OBJECTIVES

After reading this chapter, you should have:

The ability to discriminate between and effectively use positive and negative approaches to discipline

An understanding of and caution about the possible negative side effects that may accompany punitive approaches to discipline

The information necessary to apply the "red hot stove" approach to discipline

A grasp of the steps through which a system of progressive discipline is implemented

The information needed to develop skills and techniques to counsel problem employees effectively

An understanding of the personal problems of employees and the ability to cope with them

In the last chapter, emphasis was placed on controlling for results in areas such as finance and productivity. This chapter and the next also deal with control, but in a much more personal sense. Specifically, this chapter is devoted to how supervisors can effectively discipline employees. Both positive and negative approaches are given attention, and specific techniques are offered to deal with this difficult problem.

WHAT IS MEANT BY DISCIPLINE

The word "discipline" is used in many different ways and has many different connotations. One example is "the *disciplined* athlete." The athlete carefully watches diet, completes a specific regimen of exercises daily, refrains from smoking or drinking, and is careful to get enough rest. Nowhere in this use of the word "discipline" is the idea of punishment implied. Rather, in the case of the athlete, the "discipline" refers to a carefully controlled regimen to attain a desired objective. The regimen and control are usually self-imposed rather than exerted from the outside.

A second use of the term "discipline" describes an academic area of study. For instance, there are the *disciplines* of the arts and the sciences. In this usage, "discipline" implies using specific techniques and methods for inquiry. Those in a particular academic discipline are expected to act in a particular way. For example, chemists spend their time in laboratories and professors of English

Ballet dancers are certainly disciplined. But for supervisors, discipline is controlling employee behavior to accomplish organizational objectives (Vinnie Fish/Photo Researchers, Inc.).

read and write. Thus, there are prescribed activities for academic disciplines in order to meet predetermined objectives.

In a third usage, *discipline* is imposed on the person by outsiders to reach prescribed objectives. A football coach, for example, imposes a disciplined routine for the team to follow. Although punishment may be involved in this use of discipline, most often—as in the case of the football team—those who are disciplined comply voluntarily with the directives and suggestions they are given. Thus, in this sense, discipline can be thought of as a program of activities controlled by an external source to achieve goals.

Finally, discipline can be interpreted as being the same as punishment. When small children disobey their parents, they are disciplined with a whack on the bottom. Similarly, when employees' attendance records are poor, they may be disciplined with layoffs. In both of these cases, punishment is intended to channel behavior so that the individual involved can achieve either the parents' or the organization's objectives. Thus, in this sense, discipline can be viewed as punishment designed to eliminate behavior which is detrimental to the achievement of objectives.

The common thread in all the uses of the word "discipline" is that people are being controlled to ensure the achievement of objectives. In some cases, the control is self-imposed. In others, control is imposed by an outsider. In most cases, however, the control is voluntary and does not involve punishment. Taking all the commonalities and differences of the usage of this word, we can arrive at a workable definition of it for the work environment. "Discipline" can be defined as a technique of controlling employee behavior through either positive or punitive approaches which are imposed by the self or others and are designed to aid in the accomplishment of organizational objectives.

WHY DISCIPLINE IS NECESSARY

Discipline is necessary for the effective functioning of an organization. The actual process of discipline is very similar to the overall control process discussed in the last chapter (i.e., objectives, standards, activities, and decisions). The objectives are the employees' work-related responsibilities; standards are the indexes which supervisors have established to indicate employees' progress in meeting objectives. The activities are the behaviors employees engage in to meet standards and objectives; and, finally, the control decision can involve discipline.

The control decision becomes *positive discipline* when supervisors recognize employees' progress in meeting objectives and standards and help them to develop more efficient work methods. The control decision becomes *negative discipline* when supervisors punish employees for deviations from standards and make no attempt to help employees correct the problem.

Because discipline sometimes involves punitive control, it has a very negative connotation. This is not always justified. In fact, most employees want and respect discipline from their supervisors. This is particularly true when employees view their jobs as being important. Just as the members of a football team will not respect a coach who lets the star athlete drink and stay out late, employees expect their supervisors to enforce work rules and to discipline those who break them. The great majority of employees do not violate work rules. Most employees recognize the importance of control and authority in the workplace and act accordingly. However, there are always a few who do not feel this way and are constant offenders. When these offenders are allowed to maintain their undisciplined behavior, most conscientious employees will object. They feel that they are not being rewarded for the work they do well if the offenders are paid the same and allowed to turn in sloppy performances. Moreover, the good employees also realize that, in the long run, the effectiveness of their own work—as well as the overall organization—suffers because of these chronic offenders. All this leads to strong pressures from the employees themselves for supervisors to use and respect discipline as a necessary part of an effective organization.

POSITIVE AND NEGATIVE DISCIPLINE

Positive discipline was said to be any control action by supervisors which results in employees' increased efficiency in attaining objectives or standards. Most often, positive discipline is associated with the "goody-goody" approach, where the supervisor walks around smiling and patting people on the back. While this kind of supervisory behavior *may* be appropriate, positive discipline places much greater emphasis on providing employees with feedback information or experiences that will help them attain their objectives and standards. An important part of this is rewards and recognition, but another aspect involves on-the-job training and experiences which help employees improve their effectiveness. In addition, it should be emphasized that, although it may seem contradictory, positive discipline can also involve punishment, as long as that punishment facilitates the attainment of work objectives and standards. For example, a positive disciplinary approach would be to require a machine operator to clean the work area, even though it is a laborer's job, *if,* after *repeated warnings,* the operator continues to leave the work area in miserable condition. In this way, the operator can experience at first hand the punishing task that would otherwise be left for others. Even though the discipline is punitive, it is very directly related to helping the machine operator develop a more accurate picture of job-related objectives. While punitive control such as this is not always advocated, it is considered to be positive discipline if handled in this way. The distinction between positive and negative discipline is not whether it is punitive or rewarding. Rather, positive discipline is anything which helps employees achieve work-related objectives, while negative discipline does not have this effect.

Negative discipline involves control by supervisors which does not aid employees in achieving their work-related objectives and standards. Both the rewarding and punishment of employee behaviors by supervisors can result in negative discipline. For example, if an employee asks a supervisor for an assessment of his or her work and the supervisor tells the employee that it was a good job when it was actually not, this is negative discipline. The supervisor is rewarding the employee for poor work and can therefore expect more poor work. Similarly, when supervisors administer punitive controls without consideration for their effect on the employee's performance, this is also a form of negative discipline. For example, supervisors who resort to disciplinary layoffs for absenteeism are usually using negative control. They are working against themselves, because the employees get three more days of rest and relaxation in which to wonder how it can be so important to be on the job when the supervisor can lay them off for three days without worry. In summary, discipline is only functional when it helps employees attain work-related objectives and standards.

The Case against Punitive Discipline

Although it is recognized that punitive control can serve as positive discipline, some difficulties with its use must be aired. First is the fact that, even when supervisors direct punishment toward achieving work objectives, employees may react emotionally. In other words, when someone gets kicked, he or she is likely to kick back, even when there was a good reason for the first kick. For each way supervisors have of punishing employees, the employees have as many different ways of getting back. Employees can slow down work, sabotage the work process, create disturbances in the work group, and even turn the work group against the supervisor. This possibility of employee retaliation is one good reason not to use punitive control.

Another argument against the use of punitive control is that it limits supervisors' abilities to use positive control. It is inconsistent to punish people one minute and reward them the next. It is difficult for the supervisor to wear both hats: both that of the punisher and that of the rewarder. When supervisors make a habit of using punishment, their very appearance becomes punishing and their ability to reward employees is severely limited.

A third argument against punishment as a disciplinary technique is that it is often nonspecific. Employees frequently fail to comprehend or agree with the supervisors' reasons for imposing punishment. An example is the secretary who is asked to type a rush report or letter. The secretary hurries through the job, doing as well as possible within the time constraints. When it is finished, the boss comes back and angrily demands that a misplaced punctuation mark or misspelled word be corrected immediately but fails to comment on the excellent job that has actually been done. At this point, of course, the secretary is, in effect, being punished for having done the report quickly. Even though the boss says that the problem is the misspelled word or punctuation mark, it makes no difference. This example points out a very real danger of using punishment: that it may be misinterpreted by employees.

Another and perhaps the biggest limitation of punishment is that its effects are only temporary. If a supervisor punishes an employee for not wearing safety glasses, for not returning on time from a coffee break, or for making personal phone calls at work, the employee will usually obey—until the supervisor is absent or not looking. After the supervisor is gone, the punished employee will revert to old behavior patterns, but this time he or she will be more careful not to get caught.

Guidelines for Administering Punitive Discipline

Although the preceding discussion of the case against punishment is convincing enough, it is recognized that punishment is sometimes necessary. Perhaps the best approach to the use of punitive discipline is the "red hot stove" principle. According to this approach, punishment is analogous to being burned by a red hot stove. Because it is red, everyone has fair warning that the stove is extremely hot. The stove does not discriminate; it burns everyone who is foolish enough to touch it. Furthermore, the burn is automatic and immediate, and its severity depends on the degree of the person's offense. Using the red hot stove as a point of departure, the following guidelines are offered for the effective administration of punitive discipline in the workplace:

1 *It should be expected.* People need to know the rules of the game. Just as individuals know what happens when they touch a red hot stove, employees should be fully aware of the consequences of either following or not following the prescribed rules. These rules should be thoroughly communicated to employees, and they should fully expect the consequences that follow violations.

2 *There should be a clear warning.* Just as those approaching the hot stove are warned by its red cover, employees should always receive a warning that they will be disciplined for inappropriate behavior. This warning should be consistent for everyone and should be issued a prescribed number of times. Often a warning is sufficient to change behavior, so that punishment, with all of its negative side effects, may not be necessary. It is like the parent who says "one," "two," "three" before punishing the child. If punishment always follows "three," the child will change the behavior before punishment is required.

3 *It should be consistent.* Just as the stove burns everyone who touches it, supervisors should always be consistent in administering discipline. Such consistency, however, is often difficult to attain. In one real case, a supervisor discovered two employees fighting. One was fired and the other was not. The one who was fired had been involved in a similar incident two weeks before, had a poor attendance and work record, and had been with the company only a short time. The other employee had never been involved in a similar incident during a successful seventeen-year tenure with the company. Obviously, it takes two to make an all-out fight, but one person was fired and the other was not. This appears inconsistent, but in this case the supervisor said that the decision was fully justified by the employees' work records. Thus, the supervisor had defined standards for the decision and was consistent in the application of these standards even though the results for the two employees were different. In other words, consistency does not always mean equal treatment. But—as the next guideline points out—the supervisor should strive for consistency and equality.

4 *It should be objective.* Effective discipline does not depend on the whims and biases of the supervisor. Like the stove, it is automatic and nondiscriminatory. Supervisors should have set standards for behavior and performance. When employee behavior fluctuates beyond these standards, discipline naturally follows. However, because supervisors are not always available to observe employee behavior directly, it is difficult to avoid bias. When employees are disciplined, a common reaction is to accuse the supervisor of being biased and discriminatory because the disciplined employee has seen other employees behave similarly without being disciplined. This problem is difficult to resolve. However, if the supervisor makes a conscientious effort to avoid bias, most employees will respect the supervisor's judgment over the long run.

5 *It should be immediate.* Effective discipline closely follows the infraction. This immediacy helps clarify the reason for the discipline because the employee still vividly remembers the behavior. When supervisors delay their comments or remarks for a time, they are much more likely to be accused of picking on employees or of being biased. Furthermore, over a period of time, employees may develop rationalizations for their behavior or may even forget it completely. Once again, however, there can be exceptions to the rule. Occasionally, employees make mistakes which they themselves consider extremely serious. If they are upset over such mistakes, immediate comment from the supervisor may not be helpful. It may be better to sit down with the employee at a later time, when things have calmed down, and to discipline the employee positively in a more rational way.

6 *It should be impersonal.* Effective discipline does not become a personal attack on employees. Discipline should be administered so that employees know that *it is their behavior* with which their supervisors find fault, not themselves as persons. The characteristics of feedback listed in Chapter 7—particularly those emphasizing specificity, intention, and descriptiveness—should help supervisors to avoid criticism that may be interpreted as a personal attack. Both the supervisor and the organization lose when discipline becomes a personal vendetta against certain individuals.

7 *It should be fair.* Finally, employees must feel that they have been treated fairly, that "the punishment fits the crime." That is, the intensity of the discipline should closely match the infraction that has occurred. This is somewhat different from consistency, because a supervisor may be very consistent in punishing all infractions far too harshly.

It should be emphasized that these guidelines apply to supervisors who are administering both negative or positive discipline as well as to those who are using the reward system. Just as supervisors need to make sure that punishment will be expected when certain inappropriate behaviors occur—and that it will be consistent, nondiscriminatory, immediate, and impersonal—so must they also use these guidelines to reward appropriate behaviors. In this way, employees clearly understand what behaviors lead to both rewards and punishments. Provided that the behaviors upon which rewards and punishments depend have been carefully identified by supervisors, movement toward a system of positive control of employee behavior can begin. Chapter 15, on motivation, will discuss in detail how positive control works and specific ways of accomplishing it.

TECHNIQUES FOR ADMINISTERING DISCIPLINE

Effective discipline is an important function of supervision. As previously noted, discipline takes in all aspects of the control process. For example, planning can be considered as an approach to discipline in that it helps set objectives and standards for appropriate employee behavior. Training, organizing—in fact, each of the topics covered in this book—are or could be related to developing employee discipline. In other words, it is beyond the scope of this chapter to explain fully all the techniques that supervisors could utilize to establish effective discipline. However, there are three specific disciplinary areas which warrant particular attention. They are: (1) deciding on appropriate disciplinary actions, (2) developing progressive discipline, and (3) conducting a counseling interview.

Deciding on Appropriate Discipline

One of the most delicate and difficult jobs in supervision is deciding on the appropriate action to take when employees seriously violate work rules or standards. Some examples of serious violations in most organizations would be having and/or consuming alcohol or drugs on the premises, chronic absenteeism, and serious, sustained failures to meet performance standards. In these cases, supervisors are impelled to take some form of disciplinary action, which is frequently punitive. Below are some things that a supervisor should take into consideration before deciding what disciplinary action to take:

1 *Don't lose your temper.* When violations are extremely flagrant, there is a strong chance that supervisors may lose their tempers and not be able to make rational decisions. It is, in fact, unwise even to try to exercise judgment when one is feeling anger or other strong emotions. There are two ways to gain needed time. First, if the violation is serious enough, the supervisor can give the individual a temporary suspension. In such an instance, the employee should be told to go home and that the employer will be in touch with him or her within a specific period of time regarding any possible punitive action. This can save supervisors the embarrassment and possible long-run damage of having a decision to terminate an individual overturned by higher management. Another way of handling such a situation is to summon the employee to the supervisor's office for a cooling-off period. The supervisor will then have time to become composed and begin to do some research on the facts in the case before confronting the employee. It should be emphasized that these techniques are only recommended in certain cases, and it must be remembered that the advantages of immediacy are sacrificed while the supervisor is cooling off. During this period also, the employee may be building a case against any possible disciplinary action.

2 *Find the objective facts.* Before rendering a decision, supervisors should be fully familiar with all the information relevant to the case at hand. If the offense is a serious one, the supervisor should have concrete facts to support his or her decision. All the whos, whys, wheres, hows, and whens of the situation should be known. Importantly, this information should be gathered before the decision is made. When the decision is to dismiss an employee and the employee appeals the decision through the grievance procedure, the information gathered at this stage is particularly important. In such cases, supervisors are called upon to provide concrete facts and information to support their decisions.

3 *Consider the employee's history.* Another important basis on which a disciplinary decision may be rendered is the employee's work record. If there is a record of previous, similar offenses, the supervisor is generally on safer ground in deciding on dismissal. Things such as length of service, job position, absenteeism record, and records of other disciplinary actions are all important in making a disciplinary decision. Generally, a good work record and seniority warrant more lenient treatment than does a long history of problems.

4 *Make a comparative analysis.* Before making a decision, supervisors should be familiar with disciplinary decisions made previously in similar situations. If the supervisor's disciplinary actions are consistent with previous actions, they will generally be supported by both management and the union. When disciplinary actions are more harsh than they have been for similar situations, it is more probable that these actions will be overturned by management or contested by the union through the grievance procedure.

5 *Develop alternatives.* This step in the disciplinary process involves developing alternative methods. Throughout this process, the consideration should be whether or not the discipline will help the employee to achieve expected, appropriate behaviors in the future. That is, short-run punishment applied only to inconvenience the employee is usually not effective. Often, other supervisors or the personnel manager can offer some realistic and effective alternatives.

6 *Evaluate alternatives.* Each alternative should be evaluated in order to select the one which will be most helpful in correcting the employee's future behavior. Again, advice from the personnel manager or other experienced supervisors can be extremely helpful. If the supervisor sits down and discusses the situation with the employee, this input may also help the supervisor decide on the most appropriate course of action.

7 *Implement the decision.* The final step is communicating the disciplinary decision to the employee. During this discussion, the supervisor should review with the employee the basic steps through which the final decision has been arrived at. In other words, the supervisor should reiterate the information relevant to the decision, the employee's work record, and the effort that has been made to ensure that the decision is consistent with past practices.

8 *Follow up.* Discipline, of course, is only effective when it is carried out. If the discipline calls on supervisors to take certain actions, then supervisors should make sure that these actions are, in fact, carried out. Supervisors should conduct periodic observation and counseling sessions with employees who have been disciplined to make sure that the discipline is having a positive effect in terms of helping them.

9 *Defend your stand.* When disciplinary actions are severe or felt to be unjust, more and more employees will try to overturn these decisions by appealing to higher management or the union. Provided that the supervisor has followed and documented the previous steps, this should not present a problem. Yet even when there is adequate documentation and the decision appears to be necessary and rational, supervisors' disciplinary actions may be overturned. This has tended to occur more often in recent years. It is becoming extremely important for supervisors to get commitment from management and/or the labor relations staff prior to making a discipline decision if they wish to prevent unnecessary embarrassment and hassles later on. In some situations, the supervisor may want to notify union officials of disciplinary actions and may even request their presence during disciplinary interviews to help avoid misunderstandings and later problems.

These considerations for taking disciplinary action are briefly summarized in Figure 9-1. By following these ten guidelines, supervisors can effectively decide on the most appropriate disciplinary action to take.

Progressive Discipline

Besides following the guidelines suggested in the previous section, another effective approach is that of progressive discipline. The idea here is that discipline should be less severe at first, giving the employees a chance to improve on their own. Once the employees have been made aware of their inappropriate behaviors though repeated and successively more severe warnings, harsher forms of discipline, including termination, are appropriate. Generally, progressive discipline can be broken down into four major stages:

1 *Verbal Warning.* At the time of an employee's first offense, especially a minor one, a verbal reprimand is usually enough. The employee may not be aware of the infraction or its severity and the verbal warning may be sufficient to motivate the employee to correct the problem. An important thing to remember, however, is that even though the warning is verbal, the supervisor should make a written record of the conversation and place it in the employee's file. This record will be important in the event that the employee has future problems and additional discipline is required.

2 *Formal, Written Warning.* If, after a verbal warning, the inappropriate behavior continues, a formal, written warning is recommended. This warning should describe in detail the policy or work rule which has been violated. It should also briefly summarize and describe the employee's previous and present offenses. A short statement of the purpose of the policy or rule is also wise to help the employee better understand the importance of the violation. When this written reprimand is complete, it should be given to the employee and its meaning for future disciplinary actions should be outlined. Many organizations also suggest sending a copy of the warning to the appropriate union officials, the supervisor's immediate boss, and/or the personnel director.

3 *Disciplinary Layoff.* The third step in progressive discipline, provided that it is warranted by the offense and/or by previous offenses, is a disciplinary layoff without pay. The purpose of this layoff is to warn the employee of the severity of the offense. Again, the layoff should be accompanied by a detailed verbal and written explanation, and the supervisor should keep this information on file. Also, the employee

1. Do you need to cool off before making the decision?

2. Do you have all the pertinent information and facts? Who? What? How? Why? When? Where?

3. What is the employee's record of similar previous offenses?

4. What is the employee's work record and history in terms of productivity, attendance, and seniority?

5. In the past, what type of disciplinary action has been taken for similar offenses?

6. What are the alternate forms that discipline may take?

7. Will your own management support the disciplinary decision?

8. Have union officials been notified to limit the possiblities of later misunderstandings?

9. Could your decision be supported by management, accepted by the union, and, if necessary, upheld by an arbitrator in the grievance process?

10. Will the disciplinary action result in improving the behavior of the employee?

FIGURE 9-1
Ten guidelines supervisors can use to administer discipline effectively.

should understand that this is the third step in the disciplinary process and that he or she will be subject to dismissal when the next infraction occurs.

4 *Termination.* The last step is dismissing or firing the employee. Although this is the most severe form of discipline, the employee has been given ample warning and opportunity to improve through the progressive disciplinary process. This step is considered a last resort. Most large organizations are very reluctant to fire experienced people not only from a humane standpoint but also because of the costs involved in hiring and training new employees. Moreover, dismissing even an incompetent worker can cause feelings of insecurity and low morale among the others, and that can be costly in the long run. In addition, supervisors can most often expect unions to fight dismissal decisions through the grievance and arbitration process. Unless supervisors have closely followed and documented the stages of progressive discipline, they will be more and more likely to find themselves overruled.

As outlined above, this progressive procedure is generally recognized by management, unions, and employees as a just way of administering discipline. Often the exact progression is specifically spelled out in organizational policies. Only in very rare instances, such as threatening a person with a firearm on the premises or possessing and using a dangerous drug, will severe disciplinary decisions such as termination be upheld without recourse to the policy of progressive discipline.

The Counseling Interview

The counseling interview goes hand in hand with progressive discipline and helps supervisors gather facts and information to help make disciplinary decisions. Its basic purpose is to work with the employee to establish positive discipline *before* severe disciplinary actions are needed. Very simply, the counseling interview can be defined as a discussion between a supervisor and an employee concerning a specific aspect of the employee's behavior. Unlike the performance appraisal interview, which covers the entire range of the employee's performance over a period of time, the disciplinary counseling interview is aimed at a more specific problem. Most often, the reason for the interview is a problem such as a flagrant violation of a work rule, repeated failure to meet performance standards, or chronic absenteeism. However, it should be noted that a counseling interview can also be used for other purposes, such as career counseling or to help out with a personal problem. This discussion will be limited to the use of a counseling interview for corrective discipline, but the same general principles apply to its other uses.

Supervisors have a wide range of choices regarding the manner in which they conduct a counseling interview. They can be very brief and authoritative with employees and control the entire interview. Some supervisors even recommend giving an employee a "good dressing down." Perhaps there is some merit in such an approach for some supervisors and employees under certain conditions. Yet most experienced supervisors and counseling experts recommend a more nondirective, participative approach. This latter approach is the one that is recommended and discussed below. Nevertheless, from the contingency perspective, each supervisor should adapt the guidelines for a nondirective, participative interview to his or her own specific style and circumstances.

The initial steps of a counseling interview The supervisor takes initial steps of an effective counseling interview by gathering all facts and information relevant to the discussion. These will include the details of the problem that is under discussion as well as information about the employee, such as length of service and work record. In addition, a site for the interview should be selected. The major consideration in site selection is finding a place where the employee will feel comfortable and distractions will be at a minimum.

At the start of the interview, the employee should be put at ease and the purpose of the interview fully explained. Next, the supervisor should review the facts and information gathered up to this point. The employee should then be encouraged to express his or her opinion and viewpoint on this information. By careful questioning, the supervisor should be able to resolve matters that appear uncertain. At this point, however, supervisors should take a relatively passive role, allowing the employee to speak as freely as possible.

Next, the supervisor should summarize the information brought into the interview along with anything added or modified by the employee. The objective here is for both the supervisor and the employee to reach a mutual understanding on whether or not the employee's behavior must change. On the other hand, if they mutually agree that the employee's behavior is appropriate, the interview ends on a positive note. If they agree there is a problem, then the actual counseling takes place.

Counseling the employee Counseling is markedly different from other disciplinary procedures. The central theme of nondirective, participative counseling is that, if the employees' behavior is going to improve, then the employees themselves can provide the best analysis and insights for corrective actions. Therefore, having reached agreement that there is in fact a problem, the supervisor *asks the employee* for his or her analysis of the situation and specific methods for improving future behavior. This is done through open-ended questions such as the following:

> Can you explain to me more specifically some of the areas where you are having difficulty?
> What do you think would be most helpful to you in solving the problem?
> Can you give me any suggestions on what we can do to correct this situation?

In cases where the root of the problem lies within the individual (e.g., feelings of personal inadequacy) open-ended questioning can be particularly helpful. The purpose of such questions is to help the employee examine his or her own behavior and thus to develop constructive insights. Examples of such questions are:

You say you don't feel comfortable with that aspect of the job—can you explain?

You mentioned Sally gives you a hard time—does this always happen or does it occur only at specific times?

You noted that giving you decision power on quality would help you out—can you explain this further?

As these questions indicate, the supervisor acts much like a mirror, causing the employee to reflect back upon his or her own thoughts.

This nondirective interviewing technique is widely used by professional counselors in working with people who have psychological problems. In encouraging them to use the same technique, there is no implication that supervisors should take on the responsibility of counseling employees with severe mental or emotional problems. Applied to discipline, the counseling interview's objective is to help the employee analyze work-related problems and develop some viable solutions.

If the interview goes well, the employee should have selected and agreed to a workable course of action for the future by the close of the session. This is the ideal, of course, because people are much more likely to work on and implement solutions which they have arrived at themselves. Realistically, however, the supervisor must continue to observe the employee's behavior to make sure that the suggested course of action is, in fact, being carried out. Similarly, if the supervisor has made a commitment to helping the employee, it is important actually to provide this help. If the solution is not working out as intended, the supervisor may schedule additional counseling interviews with the employee to straighten out the difficulties.

PERSONAL PROBLEMS OF EMPLOYEES

So far in this chapter, general disciplinary problems and methods have been discussed. This section deals with more specialized personal problems that supervisors will undoubtedly encounter. In particular, problems such as alcoholism, drug addiction, mental illness, and chronic absenteeism are discussed. A generation or two ago, such problems were not of great concern to most supervisors. In recent times, however, they have grown in both number and severity. The managers of most modern organizations are now aware of their seriousness and are committed to doing something about them.

There are two major reasons for the new, enlightened attitude of responsibility toward the personal problems of employees. First is the new emphasis on the quality of work life in America. In the late sixties and early seventies, organizations of all types were being highly criticized by intellectuals as well as the general public for their ignorance of human needs. Today, almost everyone agrees that organizations in which people spend more than half their waking lives have an obligation to adapt themselves to human needs and help improve the quality of working life.

The second reason for the new emphasis on personal problems is basic dollars and cents. Before, employees with personal problems were generally fired and replaced. This may have been appropriate in the past, when the economy was growing and there was a large pool of qualified employees to draw from. Today, however, in a technological society needing highly skilled and trained employees, the same practices may be economically unsound. In simple cost-benefit terms, it may be much more expensive to dismiss employees with personal problems than to support their rehabilitation. Thus, today, many organizations have both a humanistic and an economic interest in the personal well-being and health, both physical and mental, of their employees.

How to Deal with Personal Problems

Because the formal recognition of personal problems is relatively new to organizations, most have not developed policies or procedures. The following discussion is offered to provide guidelines for dealing with the personal problems of employees.

The first thing the supervisor should take into consideration is the right to become involved. That is, personal problems such as alcoholism and marital difficulties are extremely touchy and private. Supervisors cannot and should not become involved in them without careful consideration of the individual's personal privacy, rights, and freedoms. One guideline for helping the supervisor determine whether to become involved or not is the definition of a problem employee: one whose problems are affecting or may affect *work-related* performance. According to this definition, the supervisor's involvement begins when the employee's work performance suffers as a result of personal problems. The words "may affect" in the definition mean, more specifically, that on at least two separate occasions the supervisor has noted decreased productivity related to personal problems. Where this criterion of a problem employee is met, the supervisor should probably get involved. If the employee has a problem but his or her performance is not affected, then the supervisor should probably not get involved.

Up to this point, the supervisor has done nothing except observe personal problems which appear to be related to performance difficulties. The second step is making the employee aware of the problem and its effect on performance. Again, the idea is that supervisors have a legitimate right to discuss an employee's performanace. A primary objective of the discussion is to give employees the opportunity to realize the fact that a personal problem is affecting their work. This discussion should follow the counseling interview format discussed in the last section. If the employee identifies and admits the problem, the supervisor can then help the employee seek qualified help. If the employee does not admit the problem, the supervisor will not have created difficulties, since the basis of the discussion was the employee's performance. In no case should the supervisor attempt to diagnose and treat the employee's personal problem. This is the job of a qualified counselor or psychologist.

If the employee admits that a personal problem is the basis of the difficulty, the supervisor can offer help in identifying an appropriate counseling agency. A growing number of large organizations have special counselors whose duty it is to help employees with personal problems. Where this position exists, the supervisor should refer the employee to the counselor, who will, in turn, recommend an appropriate treatment agency. If the organization does not have special provision for such counseling, supervisors might take it upon themselves to help employees find appropriate treatment in the community. Most cities of any size today have a counseling assistance line, free of charge, which can help locate appropriate treatment agencies. In some cases, the services of the treatment agency may cost little or nothing. In addition, the supervisor should check out the organization's policies regarding funds for the treatment of personal problems. A growing number of fringe benefit packages cover such costs.

If the employee accepts treatment from the appropriate agency, the supervisor can be expected to be contacted. Professional counselors will often make specific recommendations to supervisors on how to handle a particular employee. Sometimes these suggestions for helping the employee with a personal problem may be contrary to the supervisor's own inclinations. In some instances the counselor from the agency may actually recommend more of a hard-line approach than the supervisors themselves would consider. The counselor may also ask for some special consideration for the problem employee. In keeping with the aim of doing everything possible to help the employee with a problem, supervisors should generally try to follow the recommendations of a professional counselor.

The discussion of personal problems so far has assumed that the employee in question admits there is a problem. There is always the possibility that the employee will not admit a problem or accept help. In this situation, it is particularly difficult for supervisors to avoid diagnosing the problem and getting personally involved, but the wise course is always to stay out of it. A basic prerequisite to the resolution of most personal problems is recognition of the problem by the person who is most immediately affected by it.

While supervisors can stimulate discussion and create an environment in which employees feel that they can disclose their problems openly, a supervisor cannot force the fact of the problem on the employee and expect effective results. Basic ingredients of successful treatment are personal recognition of the problem and self-motivation to solve it. In addition—even in the case of alcoholism, where the symptoms are fairly obvious—supervisors can create legal difficulties for themselves if they make accusations that the employee denies. A proper diagnosis can only be made by a qualified professional in the health field.

Once again, the supervisor should deal with personal problems only in relation to performance. If, however, an employee comes to work seemingly under the influence of alcohol or drugs, the supervisor can send the employee to a doctor for diagnosis. Supervisors should check with the policies of their organizations to determine whether this is the appropriate course of action to take.

If the employee's performance continues to decline after continuous counseling efforts, the employee may be dismissed for performance-related reasons. Written statements, documents, and warnings should not contain the supervisor's opinion of an employee's personal problem. Rather, they should document performance problems only. It is legitimate to document that the employee was incoherent, staggering, and using foul language, but it is not acceptable to say that this employee was an alcoholic. Again, this last statement is a diagnosis that only a professional person in the health field can make, not the supervisor.

Finally, it should be emphasized that all interactions with the employee in question should be fully documented and kept on file. If the employee is eventually fired, the sequence leading up to this action should follow the guidelines suggested in the previous section on progressive discipline. Although termination is not a very desirable alternative, in some cases it is the only realistic way to handle the problem.

■ KEY CONCEPTS

Positive discipline
Negative discipline
Punitive discipline
"Red-hot-stove" principle
Progressive discipline
Counseling interview
Problem employee
Personal problems

■ PRACTICAL EXERCISES

(These can be performed by individuals or by groups.)

1 Many policies on absenteeism use a progressive disciplinary procedure which requires a mandatory layoff of three days after repeated violations. Discuss the pros and cons of this policy. Can you suggest any alternatives?

2 An exchange between two employees occurs where one gives the other a large sum of money in return for several cellophane bags filled with what appears to be marijuana. Discuss the implications of this incident and propose a policy for dealing with it. How would you react to this situation if you were the supervisor?

■ DISCUSSION INCIDENTS

Jack Gray supervises eight people for a small heating and air-conditioning service company. One of his employees, Al Day, appears to be an alcoholic. At times, Al's breath smells of alcohol, his speech is slurred, and his dress and appearance are sloppy. Yet Al is an excellent employee and completes an average of 10 percent more calls than other employees. More importantly, Al is an experienced and capable person who is able to solve many of the more complex problems that other employees cannot handle. The only signs of decline in Al's performance are an occasional day when he misses several calls and occasional complaints that he has been rude to a customer. Other than that, Al is a model employee.

1 What is the supervisor's right and responsibility to become involved in Al's "problem?"
2 Describe how the supervisor might approach Al about his potential problem.
3 Select one member of the group to play Al and another to play Jack. Role-play a counseling interview between Al and Jack.

Brian Stern was an experienced supervisor at the physical plant of the university. A newly appointed supervisor, Jake Haskell, went to Brian for advice. "Brian, as you know, I have been a supervisor for only a couple of months. I really like it except for one aspect. I really feel uncomfortable about disciplining my employees. By nature I just hate to chew people out. Even my wife chides me for never disciplining the kids enough. You've been at this game a long time, can you give me some pointers?" Brian replied, "Sure, Jake. The thing you've got to remember, whether it's kids or employees, is that they don't respect you unless you really punish them once in a while. I would go so far as to say that you should give them a good chewing out every once in a while, whether they deserve it or not. That's how I handle discipline."
1 What do you think of Brian's advice? Does either supervisor understand discipline?
2 What type of advice would you give Jake?

APPRAISING EMPLOYEE PERFORMANCE

10 CHAPTER

Jim Kettering was the supervisor of outreach services for a Department of Labor job-service agency in a city of 265,000. Jim's people were responsible for locating and contacting hard-core unemployed workers, establishing training and development services for them, and placing them in suitable jobs. Recently, an investigative reporter published an article on the job service which severely criticized its effectiveness. Jim's boss, Ella Wilkins, responded to the reporter's criticisms very graciously in a letter to the editor. Unfortunately, she was not nearly as gracious with her staff of six supervisors, one of whom was Jim. In a group meeting, she severely (and rightfully) criticized the ability of her own agency to discipline itself. After suggestions for improving agency performance were taken, it was argued that at least one positive measure would be to conduct periodic appraisals of employee performance that would be used for all personnel actions such as promotions, transfers, and salary increases. Each supervisor was given the responsibility for designing an appraisal report form and conducting appraisals in the way he or she saw fit. Jim was in total agreement with this new policy, but he was also concerned about some of the personnel problems the appraisal might create if it were done improperly. Jim had previously seen and collected a number of different kinds of appraisal forms. Some were mostly narrative. Some had little boxes for rating the employees. Others had places for employee responses and participation. Jim wondered what style of appraisal would be most appropriate and effective.

LEARNING OBJECTIVES

After reading this chapter you should be able to:

Understand the purposes and functions that performance appraisal serves in effective supervision

Know why timing is so important to the appraisal process

Grasp and apply the various approaches to appraisal and evaluation of employee performance

Obtain the necessary information and skills to conduct an effective appraisal interview

Identify and overcome the possible problems in doing effective appraisals

Besides discipline, which was covered in the last chapter, another critical element in the control of human resources is performance appraisal. The appraisal process can be defined as a series of formalized discussions with an employee about performance over a specified period of time. It is more than just coaching, because it is a summary process as opposed to a day-to-day occurrence. Unlike discipline, appraisal covers the whole range of performance-related behaviors. After explaining the purpose and functions that appraisal can serve in an organizational unit, this chapter looks at the timing and ways to measure performance of employees. A detailed discussion of how to conduct effective appraisal interviews ends the chapter.

THE FUNCTIONS OF PERFORMANCE APPRAISAL

Like the other functions discussed in this part of the book, performance appraisals make an important contribution to the effective supervision of today's employees. The functions and purposes of the appraisal system can be summarized as follows:

1 *Feedback.* Performance appraisals provide employees with needed information about their performance—how they are progressing on the job.

2 *Recognition.* In well-executed appraisal systems, employees who are performing well receive formal recognition for their performance.

3 *Performance Improvement.* The feedback and recognition provides a point of departure for improving employee performance.

4 *Records.* Performance appraisals serve as a written record of employee performance that can be used for personnel actions such as promotions, transfers, terminations, or wage increases.

5 *Planning.* Performance appraisals are an important input into the planning process. Appraisals summarize employee achievements and help supervisors gauge the effectiveness of their plans. Supervisors often set interim goals with employees during performance appraisals, which become tied into their overall plans.

6 *Development.* Appraisal systems summarize not only employee achievements but also plans for employees' future development and growth.

7 *Expectations.* Through the appraisal process, supervisors can clearly communicate their standards and expectations for employee performance.

8 *Legal Obligations.* Indirectly at least, the equal opportunity laws require that employees be kept informed of the quality of their performance. Organizations that do not have formal appraisal systems run the risk of violating federal or state equal opportunity laws.

These eight points are not the only reasons for having appraisals, but they do indicate a wide variety of purposes. The following sections examine ways of improving the effectiveness of appraisals and suggest some specific ways to conduct them.

TIMING OF THE APPRAISAL

An important aspect of effective appraisals is timing. When should appraisals be conducted? The answer to this question, like most questions about supervision, is that it depends. In this case, it depends on who is being reviewed as well as his or her experience, job grade, and past performance. Generally, most organizations find that annual or perhaps biannual reviews work best for experienced employees. New employees, however, are usually reviewed every three to six months for the first year or two. In addition, upper-level managers generally require less frequent reviews, and employees paid hourly, in the lower job grades, require more frequent reviews.

Another consideration in timing the appraisal is the performance itself. If an employee has done an exceptionally good job in previous months, it may be beneficial to accelerate the review date so that this performance may be recognized and rewarded. Similarly, review dates may be accelerated for poor performance in order to suggest ways to correct problems before they get out of hand. Finally, many organizations recommend that appraisals be given prior to important personnel actions such as promotions, salary/wage raises, transfers, or terminations. Thus, one year or six months is the general guideline, but special consideration should be given to experience, performance, and personnel actions.

Recently, many personnel experts and researchers have pushed for more frequent appraisals, even to the extent of one-month intervals. More frequent appraisals become very important where discipline, on-the-job training, rewards, planning, control, and communication are not working well. However, supervisors should be careful not to let appraisals become substitutes for these important aspects of effective personnel management. The appraisal is a summary statement that pulls together these other areas, so that both the supervisor and employee can evaluate and document their progress. Instead of being used in place of other supervisory techniques, the performance appraisal should serve simply to provide immediate and timely feedback.

MEASUREMENT OF PERFORMANCE IN THE APPRAISAL PROCESS

Another important dimension of the appraisal process is the measurement of employee performance. Performance appraisal rating systems have at least four important objectives. First, the system must be easy to use and understand. If the appraisal system is a hassle, supervisors will be less likely to use it efficiently and will find it difficult to explain to employees. Second, the system must be as objective as possible. If traits and standards are seen as being unrelated or unimportant to the job, there is a greater chance that employees will object to being evaluated. Third, the system must be equitable. Employees must feel some assurance that the ratings given by their supervisor are similar to those that other employees would receive from other supervisors for similar performance. Finally, the rating system should be based strictly on job performance—it should not reflect the worker's personal qualities. Appraisals that depend on personality characteristics are often, justifiably, seen as biased and unrelated to job performance.

Rating Techniques for Appraising Employees

Several rating techniques that attempt to meet the above criteria have been developed. Briefly summarized, the various rating techniques used in performance appraisals are as follows:

247

1 *The Trait Method.* This is perhaps the most commonly used method of rating employees. Here, the form is designed around a list of traits or categories which are thought to be critical for job performance. Examples of traits that frequently appear on such forms are neatness, ingenuity, motivation, initiative, ability to follow instructions, promptness, and ability to get along with coworkers. Categories which are commonly included for rating are productivity, quality, dependability, attendance, safety, and attitude. Usually these traits are measured on some scale of one to five or one to seven.

2 *Forced Choice.* This is perhaps the most popular rating mechanism. With it, the supervisor evaluates an employee's performance on the basis of the categories or traits listed above, but the supervisor is forced to make a simple yes-or-no judgment. Examples of the forced-choice technique are shown in Figure 10-1.

3 *Scaling.* Another method of measuring employees is scaling. Here the supervisor places a check mark on a continuum to indicate the employee's performance with respect to the trait or category. Figure 10-2 shows this approach. The advantage of scaling is that there is more flexibility and supervisors are not forced into an either-or, black-or-white choice.

4 *Critical-Incident Technique.* This technique can be used in combination with a forced choice or scaling method of measurement. Here the supervisor recalls and writes down specific incidents that indicate the employee's performance. Supervisors who use this technique generally keep a running file on each employee's behavior. If the supervisor tries to depend on memory at the time of an annual appraisal session, then this technique becomes less effective, because the most recent incidents will be remembered most clearly. The appraisal should be a summary of critical incidents over the entire period being rated. An example of the critical incident-technique combined with the forced-choice method is shown in Figure 10-3.

5 *Ranking.* Another method of appraisal is to rank all employees in a given unit with respect to categories or traits. Usually each employee is assigned a number, depending on performance with respect to a category or trait. Although this method can create healthy competition among members of the work group, it can also lead to personal jealousies between employees. Figure 10-4 illustrates the ranking method.

These five methods are the most commonly used ways of measuring and rating employee performance. Each of them may be used by itself or in combination with the others. Recently, there has been

Example 1

	Poor	Fair	Average	Good	Excellent
1. Honesty			✓		
2. Effort				✓	
3. Appearance					✓
4.					
5.					

Example 2

Category	Comments	Poor	Fair	Average	Good	Excellent
1. Productivity	Produces in excess of 10 units of standard on an average day.				✓	
2. Quality	No complaints from quality control			✓		
3.						

Example 3

	Poor	Fair	Average	Good	Excellent
1. Job output	0	0	0	●	0
2. Job knowledge	0	0	0	0	●
3. Motivation to do job	0	0	0	●	0
4. Work habits	0	0	●	0	0
5.					

FIGURE 10-1
Forced-choice rating.

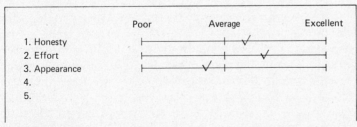

FIGURE 10-2
The scaling technique for rating.

PERFORMANCE	CRITICAL INCIDENTS OF STRENGTHS AND WEAKNESSES	Poor	Needs Improvement	Average	Very Good	Out-standing
1. Productivity (Amount of work produced)	During week of Jan. 20, processed in excess of 200 claims. Processed 80 in week of Feb. 21. Averages 120 per week.				√	
2. Quality (Accuracy, neatness, and customer satisfaction)	Work is always neat. Incident on Jan. 28 caused significant loss of time because of error. Several letters received were complimentary of employee's courtesy.			√		
3.						

FIGURE 10-3
The critical incident technique.

Category	Joe D.	Andy S.	Sally S.	Allen R.	Joe P.	Cathy M.	Frank D.	Ken F.	Allen D.	Dan M.
1. Productivity	7	3	8	4	1	9	2	10	6	5
2. Job knowledge	6	4	10	2	1	9	5	8	7	3
3. Quality	6	2	9	1	3	10	4	5	7	8
4. Attendance	1	6	9	7	4	5	2	10	3	8
5.										

FIGURE 10-4
Appraisal by ranking.

justified criticism of appraisals which are based on lists of categories or traits. On the humorous side, Table 10-1 indicates some of the problems associated with the traditional approach to appraisal. No one could possibly exemplify all the traits that are traditionally given attention (or could want to do so). More importantly, even if one did, there are still serious doubts that such a person would be a productive employee! In other words, there is no proved relationship between the traits and employee performance. The list of traits and categories are not solidly anchored to behaviors that characterize

TABLE 10-1
HUMOROUS APPRAISAL FORM USING PERSONAL TRAITS

Personal traits	Far exceeds job requirements	Exceeds job requirements	Meets job requirements	Needs some improvement	Does not meet minimum requirements
Quality	Leaps tall buildings with a single bound	Must take running start to leap over tall buildings	Can only leap over a short building or medium one with no spires	Crashes into buildings when attempting to jump over them	Cannot recognize buildings at all, much less jump over one
Timeliness	Is faster than a speeding bullet	Is as fast as a speeding bullet	Not quite as fast as a speeding bullet	Would you believe a slow bullet?	Wounds self with bullets when attempting to shoot gun
Initiative	Is stronger than a locomotive	Is stronger than a bull elephant	Is stronger than a bull	Shoots the bull	Smells like a bull
Adaptability	Walks on water consistently	Walks on water in emergencies	Washes with water	Drinks water	Passes water in emergencies
Communication	Talks with God	Talks with the angels	Talks to himself	Argues with himself	Loses those arguments

Appraising Employee Performance

productive employees. One way of getting around this problem is to appraise the results themselves rather than the traits that presumably lead to the results.

Appraisal by Results

Tied into the management by objectives (MBO) process discussed in Chapters 3 and 8 is the technique of appraisal by results. It can best be explained by referring to the sample form illustrated in Table 10-2. As shown, the supervisor lists the employees' major duties and responsibilities. Then, the appraisal centers around the results actually achieved in each of these areas. Standards are reviewed and the employees' performance with respect to these standards is analyzed. Importantly, a separate column is provided for training and development needs, so that there may be planned improvement.

There are, of course, many alternatives to the form illustrated in Table 10-2. Using the control model, the categories could be objectives, standards, performance, and corrective actions. Regardless of the type of form used, the major thrust is appraisal based on performance. Where supervisors are not using an MBO system, they will frequently find that available job descriptions can be used to derive the list of the major responsibilities that form the basis for a results-oriented appraisal. If standards are not available, supervisors should, after conferring with their employees, set at least some guidelines for achievement. While this may seem to be a most time-consuming chore, it is usually worth the effort. The benefits that are derived in terms of more objective appraisals and improved performance far outweigh the time spent in establishing these guidelines and analyzing the results.

Finally, although some supervisors may favor the appraisal-by-results approach, they may feel that their hands are tied because their organizations use the trait approach. Before the appraisal-by-results approach is discarded, it should be remembered that the traits usually do provide a general description of the person's performance; the problem is that it is not specific enough to be meaningful. Using appraisal by results, supervisors can tie these traits to specific objectives. For example, if the form says "dependability," a supervisor can define that in terms of a job result, such as having not more than an average of one absence per month. Similarly, "productivity" may be defined as producing x number of units per day. Thus, the key

TABLE 10-2
AN EXAMPLE OF APPRAISAL BY RESULTS

Job duties	Applicable standards	Results	Analysis	Development or training needed
1. Wire making	1. One hundred spools per day within 1/1,000 of specifications.	1. Averages 105 per day with 7 per day rejected for not meeting specifications.	1. Output is excellent. Quality needs work, particularly in maintenance and changing of dies.	1. Supervisor will help follow up on quality problems and establish guidelines for changing dies.
2. Maintenance of machine	2. Less than 5 hours downtime per week.	2. Averages 4 hours downtime per week.	2. Excellent performance.	2. None.
3. Maintenance of clean work area	3. Area is free from loose wire that may be a safety hazard.	3. Area is neat and clean at all times.	3. None.	3. None.
4. Attendance and promptness	4. One day per month or less absence or lateness.	4. Average 6 days absent per year, with 4 lates.	4. None.	4. None.
5. Recording of product produced	5. Record available for each machine run.	5. Ten instances of records unavailable in 6-month period.	5. Serious deficiency which leads to considerable expenditure of time in the office, tracking down product.	5. Supervisor will check records once per week. Will also purchase notebook and ledger forms to simplify record keeping.

to using trait forms is to define the traits in terms of expected job results and then to appraise accordingly.

THE APPRAISAL INTERVIEW

Just as the counseling interview is an important aspect of discipline, so is the evaluation interview a vital part of the appraisal process. During this appraisal interview, both the supervisor and the employee communicate their perceptions of the employee's performance.

The first decision a supervisor has to make in the appraisal interview is whether to be participative or directive. In any interview, the participative style encourages the employee to take part. In the appraisal interview, therefore, the employee may critique his or her own performance and offer suggestions for improvement and development. The supervisor acts mainly as counselor and adviser. Of course, the supervisor can agree or disagree with the employee. In general, the participative interview technique has proved more effective than the directive technique in increasing the employee's motivation and improving performance.

During a directive type of interview, the supervisor tries to tell the employee about his or her performance. Numerous studies have pointed out, however, that the more directive the appraisal, the less effective it is in improving performance or motivation levels. Therefore, it is recommended that the participative style be used in most circumstances.

General Guidelines for an Effective Appraisal Interview

There are four general guidelines that can help supervisors conduct an effective appraisal interview. Briefly, these are:

1 *Listening.* One of the primary purposes of the appraisal interview is to determine methods of increasing employee performance. Both the supervisor and the employee have ideas that must be exchanged if this goal is to be accomplished. Therefore, the employee must be given the opportunity to communicate. So that employees are not inhibited from contributing, it is suggested that they be given the opportunity to provide input *before* the supervisor makes any suggestions.

2 *Maintaining an Open Mind.* Although the supervisor will have prepared backup data, final judgment regarding performance should

Appropriate interviewing procedures
are vital to an effective appraisal (René Burri/Magnum Photos).

be reserved until the employee has had the opportunity to provide input. It may be, for example, that a major objective has not been achieved, but this may have been due to circumstances beyond the employee's control. In such cases, the supervisor should modify the appraisal and either set a more reasonable objective for the next appraisal or modify the circumstances so that the employee can gain control.

3 *Being Honest.* Too often we interpret the participative process as a prescription for being the "good guy." It is not that. Where performance is not acceptable, the employee must be told and the statement must be backed up with observable incidents of the employee's performance. On the other hand, when an employee's performance is commendable, he or she should be told, and the supervisor should fully recognize commendable incidents of the employee's performance. Thus, the interview should serve as a vehicle for communicating accurate feedback regarding performance.

4 *Being Prepared for Feedback.* Since the supervisor plays a crucial role in helping the employee to achieve objectives, it is entirely possible that the supervisor may be identified as a roadblock to achievement. The supervisor must recognize and prepare for this possibility. If the interference is obvious, it should be pinpointed in terms of specific incidents so that action to relieve the problem may be planned. With respect to accepting criticism, there is also the possibility that this criticism may not be justified. If a supervisor suspects this—and no one else will be able to make this determination—the employee may be asked for additional feedback so that the objective may be more precisely determined. In any case, it will probably do no harm to let employees get what they have to say off their chests. Likewise, it will probably not aid the effectiveness of the interview if the supervisor disagrees with the employee and escalates the performance interview into an argument. Thus, it is probably most beneficial for all parties if the supervisor accepts the employee's feedback without a point-by-point rebuttal.

Preparing and Planning the Appraisal Interview

Like the other activities discussed in this book, appraisal interviews require careful preparation and planning by supervisors. The following are some specific items which should be given attention before the appraisal interview takes place:

1 *Review instructions.* If a formal appraisal is going to occur, the instructions and method recommended for carrying out the interview should be gone over carefully. Nothing can be more embarrassing for a supervisor—and belittling to an employee—than for a supervisor to misunderstand the purpose and mechanics of the appraisal system.

2 *Explain.* If possible, the employee should be given a copy of the interview agenda several days before it actually takes place. The supervisor should fully explain the purpose of the interview and the method that will be used to conduct it (i.e., participative or directive). This approach, by providing a general idea of what to expect, will help to reduce the employee's anxiety.

3 *Choose the location for the interview.* The interview should be conducted in a quiet place where there will be no interruptions. When possible, have all telephone calls canceled. Employees should be made to feel that they have the top priority during the interview.

4 *Anticipate emotional reactions.* Where the feedback may be negative, the supervisor should try to develop a manner of presentation that will not come across as a personal attack on the employee. The interview may be canceled and rescheduled if it becomes overly emotional.

5 *Prepare a draft.* A preliminary draft, not the final appraisal, should be taken into the appraisal interview. This draft should be the basis for the discussion with the employee. It should contain specific instances of the employee's performance in relation to standards, both favorable and unfavorable, which both the supervisor and the employee can recall and agree upon.

The Conduct of the Appraisal Interview

The purpose of the introductory portion of the interview is to relieve any anxiety that the employee may feel. The supervisor can begin with any friendly and casual conversation. After the employee appears to be relatively at ease, the supervisor reviews the purpose of the interview and briefly describes the process that will follow.

Some organizations prefer to have supervisors discuss the employees' job descriptions. Others do not. In either case, it is advisable in the first part of the interview to discuss the overall description of the employee's job and its major objectives. It is logical to begin a performance review with agreement on the employee's major responsibilities and objectives for attaining performance. If the employee is genuinely encouraged to talk at this stage, this may become a major portion of the overall interview, so that the discussion regarding the appraisal of performance then serves as a summary statement of this discussion of objectives and responsibilities.

Having discussed the employee's general duties and responsibilities, the supervisor next undertakes a thorough discussion and analysis of the employee's performance in these areas. This part of the appraisal interview can be broken down into several specific steps.

Discuss the measures of performance Once agreement has been reached on an employee's objectives and responsibilities, this part of the interview should center on the criteria that are relevant for judging performance. If a standard such as number of sales, quantity of units produced, or number of clients served is available, this is where it would fit into the appraisal interview. Similarly, if the supervisor is using a formal MBO system, the goals and objectives set at a previous meeting will serve as the standard for evaluating

257

performance. Where neither goals nor standards are available, supervisors must try to work with employees to define, as objectively as possible, what constitutes acceptable performance in each area of responsibility.

Discuss the actual performance Having agreed upon an employee's responsibilities and standards on which performance will be judged, it follows that this part of the interview should center on the employee's actual performance. If records of employee performance are available, they should serve as a basis for the discussion. Where records of performance are not available, the supervisor should be able to refer to clear-cut examples of employee performance which demonstrate meeting, exceeding, or falling short of standards.

It is particularly important, at this point, to give employees the opportunity to provide input. When the employee offers a contribution, the supervisors should support the employee by providing similar information that may have been observed or recorded. However, supervisors also have the obligation to comment on performance which is less than satisfactory. These comments should be based on employees' actual and observable behavior rather than their attitudes or personalities. For example, it is not enough to tell an employee that he or she lacks motivation. Specific examples must be provided, such as: "Your coffee breaks average almost a half hour—Tuesday it was 35 minutes;" "You were asked to revise this report form two months ago, and even with repeated requests, it has still not been revised;" or "Your plan for this project took almost three weeks, although you have completed similar plans in three days."

Provide feedback During the discussion of actual performance, feedback should be provided to help employees analyze their effectiveness and plan for improvement. As indicated in earlier discussions in this book, two important characteristics of effective feedback are specificity and immediacy. Effective feedback should be related to performance which employees can specifically recall, analyze, and act upon. It deals with a description of what the employee did rather than judgments of the employee's attitude, personality, or individual traits. Provided that both supervisors and employees can communicate specific feedback regarding each area of accountability, the appraisal can become an important tool for improving employee performance.

Rate the performance The actual rating is probably the most delicate part of the interview for both supervisors and employees.

Studies have indicated that employees have a tendency to feel that their performance is better than the supervisor's rating would indicate. Where supervisors must make a forced-choice rating of performance, they may well encounter opposition or even hostility. Moreover, this problem cannot be solved by giving employees higher ratings than they deserve. First, it would defeat the entire purpose of the appraisal. Second, where the appraisal is used for personnel actions, supervisors may be forced to promote an undesirable employee if that employee has more seniority and is rated as high as other candidates for the position. These problems suggest the importance of giving accurate and honest ratings.

Perhaps the best alternative to methods such as forced-choice or scaling is a written narrative of the supervisor's evaluation. Examples of narrative ratings are as follows: "Frank is doing a pretty good job for a relatively new employee. Performance levels are almost up to standards in each of his areas of responsibility. However, his quality record needs improvement and his absenteeism record is higher than desired," or "John is doing an excellent job. In productivity areas he meets or exceeds *all* standards. He is particularly adept in his work with customers and has received several letters of commendation from clients. His absenteeism record is exceptionally good."

As indicated in the examples, there is clearly a difference in the performance of these two employees. This is the purpose of the supervisor's rating. Supervisors should be particularly careful to make sure that they do not become stuck in a rut and make all narrations similar. Only when the ratings accurately discriminate between different levels of employee performance do they fulfill their purpose. Throughout this evaluation process, both the supervisor and the employee must carefully consider the contribution and/or responsibility which the employee assumes.

Achievement or failure regarding a particular area may generally be attributed to three sources: (1) the employee, (2) the supervisor, and (3) external conditions and circumstances. Both the supervisor and the employee should consider and discuss these three factors before establishing a judgment of the employee's performance. Obviously, the employee assumes less responsibility when achievement is highly dependent upon external circumstances or the supervisor's own performance. If the supervisor and the employee still disagree after a thorough discussion and analysis of performance, it is best to close the discussion with a statement that recognizes the employee's opinion but does not compromise the supervisor's judgment. For example, a supervisor might say, "I understand what you are saying, but since I don't assign the same priorities to these factors as you do, I can't change my rating."

Give suggestions for improvement and/or organizational change This stage of the interview is reserved for suggestions to improve the employee's performance. Here again, the employee should initiate the conversation regarding self-improvement. Provided that the previous discussion was fairly specific, the employee should be able to pinpoint those areas which need improvement. Likewise, supervisors should be prepared to offer suggestions for changes in the operation of the organization, relationships, and/or resources which will aid the employee. Conducting this last phase of the discussion in a participative manner is extremely advantageous, since the employee is most likely to engage in constructive change when it is perceived to be self-initiated.

Make overall appraisal When all major areas of the job have been discussed and appraised, a final rating may be appropriate. The employee should be allowed to initiate this process also. The rating and its explanation should consider the performance in each area of responsibility, with heavier emphasis on those responsibilities which are most crucial to the business of the organization. Supervisors should consider the employee's self-rating and then provide their own with explanatory comments. These comments should focus on the relative importance of the employee's performance in each area of responsibility.

When possible, supervisors should focus on specific examples of performance to support their judgment. If the supervisor and the employee disagree with regard to the overall rating, the supervisor should listen without interruption to the employee's argument. If a change is not warranted, the decision should be repeated and explained again, emphasizing the relative weights of the various accountabilities and performance-related examples.

Outline development plan This final stage of the performance interview involves allowing the employee to set future objectives and making a commitment to provide the required activities or resources to attain these objectives. Both the supervisor and the employee should carefully consider the alternatives for development because they will be committed to the fulfillment of these objectives. Supervisors must therefore make sure that they are able to provide the time or resources that the employee needs before making a full commitment. Likewise, the employee must carefully consider the objectives to ensure that they are realistic and obtainable.

Activities and resources that might be directed toward achieving responsibilities or long-range goals could be job assignments, task assignments, training programs, improved attendance, and improved interpersonal relationships. When the resources and activities have been determined, both parties should agree on a method for evaluating their accomplishment at the next appraisal session. For example, improved interpersonal relationships could be evaluated by frequency of arguments. Participation in training programs could be measured by whether the employee attended or was absent, and attendance improvement would be evaluated by the relative improvement in the number of days absent.

Close the discussion The interview should end with a short summary of the content of the performance discussion. This summary should include the employee's major responsibilities, incidents of both desirable and undesirable performance, the overall rating, and development plans.

Appraisal Interview Checklist

Although it is hoped that the supervisor will be able to follow all the suggestions discussed so far, it may be beneficial to go through the following list of precautions one more time:

1 Do not make promises on which you cannot deliver.

2 Do not discuss salary during a performance appraisal interview.

3 Avoid comparing one employee to another. Provide feedback on the basis of observable incidents of the employee's performance.

4 Avoid making judgments of personality characteristics (e.g., lazy, discontented, irresponsible). Provide feedback on the basis of observable incidents of the employee's performance.

5 Use the same system for all employees whom you directly supervise. Major modifications of the system within your area could be labeled discriminatory by the courts.

6 Do not hide behind the form. The most important component of the appraisal process is *you.* You cannot rely on the form or the system to do your work. Only *you* can provide the participation necessary to make the process work.

7 Do not expect miracles. The first few appraisal interviews you conduct will be learning experiences and may not go as smoothly as you would hope.

OVERCOMING PROBLEMS IN APPRAISALS

Whenever one person rates another, there are some built-in problems and biases. The five biggest rating errors that supervisors must recognize and attempt to overcome are the following:

1 *Distribution Errors.* Distribution errors are the result of underrating, overrating, or simply failing to discriminate between employees. These errors are illustrated by the graphs of supervisors' appraisal ratings presented in Figure 10-5. As can be seen in the example of overrating, supervisor A rated fifteen employees excellent, ten very good, two average, and one poor. Obviously, the appraisal serves very little purpose for the supervisor, because it does not adequately discriminate between good and poor performers. Similarly, supervisor B rated almost all employees poor or very poor and supervisor C rated almost everyone average. The best way to avoid these kinds of problems is for a supervisor to graph an entire group's ratings before completing the appraisals to make sure that ratings are being distributed as evenly as possible.

2 *Recency Errors.* Another kind of error is called recency. Here a supervisor rates an employee on the basis of the most recent performance rather than the performance over the time period for the appraisal. To avoid this error, supervisors should carefully keep and review records and files on employee performance for the entire appraisal period and not be unduly influenced by the most recent incident.

3 *Primacy Errors.* This is the opposite of a recency error. Here supervisors rate an employee because of the way the employee was previously rated. Again, supervisors should carefully review employees' records but try to eliminate from consideration the performance of the previous appraisal period.

4 *Job Errors.* Occasionally, supervisors fall into the habit of rating the job rather than the person's performance. For example, a supervisor might rate all maintenance and cleanup personnel low but all office workers high. If the supervisor focuses on job responsibilities and employees' performance of these responsibilities, this error can be avoided.

5 *Halo Effects.* This is the error of basing a rating on one or a very few

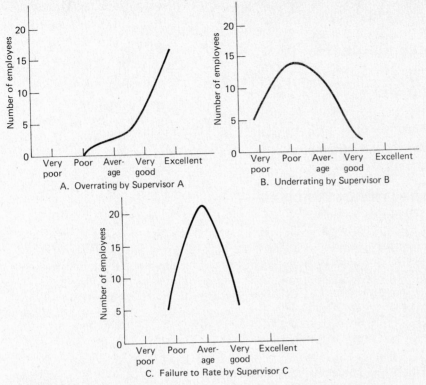

FIGURE 10-5
Examples of distribution errors in
rating.

desirable traits or characteristics that are not necessarily related to
job performance. Because of this halo effect, an employee may
receive a rating higher than is deserved because he or she graduated
from a prestigious school, keeps an ideally clean work area, dresses
sharply, is good looking, or is related to the boss. Again, the key to
avoiding this type of error is concentrating on employee performance
and not on irrelevant traits.

6 *Stereotyping.* Like the halo effect, a stereotype is the result of a
particular trait or characteristic, but the results are usually negative
for the employee. Here the supervisor places an employee in an
undesirable category because of a trait such as age, race, or body
build. One of these characteristics generalizes to the whole individual.

Supervisors must be particularly careful to avoid these errors and, again, will do so if the only important characteristics they consider are job- and performance-related.

■ KEY CONCEPTS

Appraisal functions
Timing of appraisal
Performance rating
Appraisal by results
Appraisal interview
Appraisal errors

■ PRACTICAL EXERCISES

(These can be performed by individuals or by groups.)

1 Obtain an appraisal form from your employer and/or some other source. Examine and critique the form(s). What are some of the strong and weak aspects? How could it (they) be improved?

2 Role-play a performance appraisal interview using the following situational descriptions for the participants. No participant should read another's part. The rest of the group—the observers—may read both parts.

The Role for John the Supervisor:

You supervise twenty meter readers for a utility district. In the residential areas, which are all quite similar, most of your readers finish about seventy-five houses per day. On the average, the readers report that they cannot gain entry into approximately 10 percent of these dwellings per day. Pete has been working for you about two years. In the past, he has always reported that he could not gain entry into the houses about 8 percent of the time and has averaged ninety houses per day.

You have recently noticed a change in Pete's performance. Several weeks ago, he averaged ninety houses per day but reported that he could not gain entry in 25 percent of them. This pattern continued as follows:

	Houses/Day	Inaccessible
4 weeks ago	90	24%
3 weeks ago	89	26%
2 weeks ago	84	18%
last week	95	27%

On one occasion, two weeks ago, you referred the problem to Pete in a friendly manner by asking, "Hey Pete, what in the world happened last week? Was everybody on vacation?" Pete responded, "Well, I'm sorry, that's life. You know how it is." He then walked away quite abruptly.

Pete usually doesn't act like this, so you were quite surprised and decided to leave him alone. Also, you recalled that about three weeks ago Pete had requested a leave of absence for two days. He said something about his son participating in a debating tournament and asked permission for time off. But since your section was short-handed and the billing date was approaching, you told Pete you could not let him go. When he protested, you responded with exactly the same words that Pete later used in answering you.

Instructions: Set up and conduct a performance interview with Pete.

The Role for Pete the Subordinate:

Several weeks ago your son, who is now attending college, came home to participate in a debating tournament. You asked John, your supervisor, if you could take two days off to attend. John said no, he couldn't spare you at the time. When you protested, he cut you short by saying, "Well, I'm sorry, that's life. You know how it is."

You've really never gotten along well with John. He's the kind of guy who doesn't spend much time with the employee. All he cares about is whether or not you get your work done so that he doesn't look bad. This never really bothered you too much until the incident over the debating tournament. At that time, you decided that you were going to shake John up and make him realize that you're not his dummy.

The next week you decided on a plan of action. You would read as many meters as possible (so that you could not get into performance trouble) but report that the meters were inaccessible as often as possible. Your performance over the past month has been as follows:

	Houses/Day	Inaccessible
4 weeks ago	90	24%
3 weeks ago	89	26%
2 weeks ago	84	18%
last week	95	27%

John said something once—two weeks ago. You just ignored it and told him exactly what he had told you—"Well, I'm sorry, that's life. You know how it is." You walked away immediately and chuckled to yourself—John got his own medicine straight back. Ever since then, he's been avoiding you. If he'd just act like a human being for once, instead of a stopwatch, you might come around.

At the completion of the appraisal interview, the participants and observers should discuss the following questions:

1 What did John do, if anything, to set Pete at ease?
2 Did John use a directive or a nondirective approach?
3 Did John rely on facts and information?
4 How did John end the interview (summary, statements of goals, etc.)?
5 How could the interview have been improved? Be specific in your answer.

■ DISCUSSION INCIDENTS

Mary Schaefer has been a secretary for Webber Air Freight for one year. On the average, she is about ten minutes late for work each day. Her typing leaves something to be desired, with an average of four or five errors per page. Whenever she tries to improve on her accuracy, she becomes so slow and deliberate that her output is too low. As a result, much of her work has to be shifted to the others in the office. Because Mary has a very congenial attitude and disposition, her coworkers do not seem upset over her failure to carry her own weight.

1 Using the role-play technique, act out the dialogue you think should occur between this employee and her supervisor in an appraisal interview.
2 Seriously discuss and consider whether or not an appraisal would be helpful in this case. What should the nature and objective of the appraisal be? What technique(s) could be used?

Gary Ebers was upset and worried. He had just received a phone call directly from the head of personnel which instructed him to reduce at least two of the employees he had rated as "outstanding" to "very good." In addition, he was asked to shift at least four employees rated as "very good" to "average." In total, he had rated five employees as "outstanding," eight as "very good," and five as "average." It just didn't seem fair to Gary. He felt that all his workers had done an excellent job in the previous year. He simply did not agree with management's idea of "forcing" the rating distribution.

1 What type of rating error did Gary make? In all probability, what type of appraisal and appraisal technique led to these high ratings? Is this an effective way to appraise employees?

2 Provide and discuss at least three advantages and three disadvantages of management "forcing distributions" on supervisors.

LABOR RELATIONS AND THE GRIEVANCE PROCEDURE

CHAPTER

11

The NLRB-sanctioned election was now over and the union had won a clear majority of the votes. Helen Graves, the head of the "severely handicapped" section of the Vocational Rehabilitation Office, could not believe it. That night she said to her husband, a dispatcher at a local truck firm, "Honey, this union election really has thrown me for a loop. I can't for the life of me imagine why all those counselors voted to unionize. I thought they were supposed to be professionals. Now I will have to learn all about unions because the director said I would be vitally involved with something called the grievance procedure. You've dealt with unions all your life. Can you explain to me what's going on?" Mr. Graves shook his head and said, "Good luck! I think you had better take a crash course on the background of the union movement and what's involved in administering a contract. From the sound of things, I think you're going to need all the help you can get."

■ LEARNING OBJECTIVES

After reading this chapter, you should have:

A working knowledge of the major pieces of legislation affecting labor relations

An appreciation of both the positive and negative attitudes toward unions

An understanding of the internal structure of unions at all levels

Knowledge of how a union gets started and what can be said or done

A detailed understanding of the grievance procedure and the necessary skills to operate effectively within it

So far in Part II, we have discussed the basic functions of supervision. In this last chapter of Part II, the emphasis shifts to the supervisor's role in the important function of labor relations and the grievance procedure. The term "labor relations" means different things to different people, but most would agree that it essentially involves the relationship between the employer (management) and the employee (labor). Since the beginning of the factory system of work, this relationship between management and labor has been of critical importance to the industrialization of this country and to the effectiveness of individual organizations.

Supervisors occupy a unique position in labor relations. As Chapter 1, "The Role of the Modern Supervisor," pointed out, they are caught in the middle. Supervisors are the important link (or sometimes the bottleneck) between management on the one hand and the rank-and-file employees on the other. As such, supervisors have a very political role to play in labor relations. Like elected officials in public life, supervisors must use their wit, charm, and perseverance to pacify and get the often warlike parties together for a healthy, productive relationship. Supervisors are more severely challenged in their labor-relations activities when the employees band together to form a union. After the employees are unionized, the supervisor's job is drastically affected. No longer can supervisors deal directly with employees over hours, wages, and working conditions. Instead, they must deal with the union on these matters.

The purpose of this chapter is to give the present or potential supervisor the necessary background on unions and the collective bargaining process so that the labor-relations function can be handled in a positive, efficient manner. Supervisors in industrial and construction types of operations have always dealt with unions. Almost half of all workers in manufacturing are unionized. Although the percentage of the unionized work force has declined slightly over the years (i.e., in 1955, about a third of all employees were unionized, while today only about a fourth are), the absolute number of unionized employees has been growing. Union growth is occurring especially in nonmanufacturing areas. In recent years, unionization has been making dramatic inroads into government agencies, hospitals, educational institutions, and police and fire departments; even the military and farmers are beginning to organize. Over half of all government employees at the federal level and about a third of state and local government employees are unionized. Today, many teachers, nurses, and members of the police and fire departments are either already organized or about to become so. Most labor-relations experts predict that this trend will continue. When it is realized that the percentage of professional, service, and white-collar employees is dramatically increasing and that they are the ones who are becoming unionized, it makes sense that present and future supervisors should fully understand all aspects of unions. In particular, they should know how collective bargaining works and is effectively administered through the grievance procedure.

IMPORTANT LEGISLATION AFFECTING LABOR RELATIONS

Unions have been in existence in this country almost from the beginning. The Philadelphia Cordwainers (shoemakers) Union was founded in 1792; after attempting to bargain with their employers, they were found guilty of criminal conspiracy in 1806. Since this less than auspicious beginning, the labor movement has had its ups and downs through the years. The best way of tracing this background and at the same time making supervisors aware of the legalities is to highlight the landmark legislation.

The Wagner Act

Initially, the legal environment for labor relations consisted of a number of court cases that usually went against the union. The 1890 Sherman Anti-Trust Act was usually the basis for upholding free competition and preventing unions from representing employees in collective bargaining and the use of strikes in a dispute. This climate existed up to the time of the Great Depression and the advent of very liberal New Deal legislation.

In 1935, the highly significant, prolabor National Labor Relations Act, more commonly known as the Wagner Act, was passed. Specifically, section 7 of this act gave employees the following rights:

1 *To organize*—to form, join, or assist a labor union

2 *To bargain collectively*—to allow a union to represent them in bargaining over hours, wages, and conditions of employment

3 *To strike*—to engage in concerted activities of all types

After the passage of the Wagner Act, if a majority of the employees of a defined unit wanted a union to represent them, the employer had to recognize the union and bargain in good faith. The act also went one step further. In section 8, it spelled out some specific unfair practices of employers. Briefly summarized, it became illegal for employers to do any of the following:

1 Coerce or in any way interfere with the employees' right to form a union and have it represent them in collective bargaining

2 Threaten to close or move to another location or spy on union meetings

3 Create their own unions or contribute financial support to the union

4 Discriminate in any way in the employment of individuals because of their union affiliation or activities

5 Discharge or discriminate in any way against employees because they filed charges or gave testimony under this act

The National Labor Relations Board (NLRB) was set up by the act to conduct the employee elections for union representation and investigate and judge charges of unfair labor practices by employers and, by later legislation, to police unfair practices by unions and make judgments on them.

As the provisions of the act outlined above show, the legal pendulum had swung very much in favor of labor. As a result, union membership soared and unions became very powerful. Management and its political forces were naturally upset with this turn of events. These voices were largely unheard, however, until the unions went too far. In 1946, there were a record number of strikes, and the war-weary public demanded that something be done to curb the power of unions. The result was the Taft-Hartley Act, passed in 1947.

The Taft-Hartley Act

The Labor-Management Relations Act, more commonly called the Taft-Hartley Act, essentially amended the Wagner Act of a dozen years earlier. Because of the growing public disenchantment with the labor movement, Congress, over President Truman's veto, attempted to restore a balance of power to labor relations with the passage of the Taft-Hartley Act.

Rather than eliminating the provisions of the Wagner Act, the Taft-Hartley Act simply identified and made illegal certain unfair practices of unions. Specifically, the act makes it unlawful for unions to do the following:

1 Restrain, coerce, or threaten nonstrikers from crossing picket lines during a strike

2 Attempt to cause the employer to discriminate against an employee in order to encourage or discourage union membership

3 Force an employer or self-employed person to join a union

4 Force the employer to bargain with one union when another was already the elected representative

5 Engage in *secondary boycotts,* which involve forcing an employer to cease doing business with or handling the products of another employer

6 Engage in *jurisdictional strikes,* which involve forcing an employer to assign work to employees belonging to one union rather than another

7 Charge excessive or discriminatory initiation fees

8 Engage in *featherbedding,* which means making the employer pay for services that were not actually performed

With the above provisions from Taft-Hartley, it becomes mandatory for both management and labor to bargain in good faith. Another relevant provision from the act aimed at supervisors is that it considers them part of management rather than just employees. Supervisors must be aware of and follow the provisions of both the Wagner and Taft-Hartley acts. If they do not, they can get their employers into serious trouble.

The Landrum-Griffin Act

The third major piece of labor legislation is considered to be the Labor Management Reporting and Disclosure Act, or Landrum-Griffin Act, passed in 1959. This act was the direct result of a Senate investigation that uncovered some blatant racketeering, violence, and collusion in the internal affairs of certain powerful national unions.

The provisions of this act gave the government more direct power over labor relations. For example, the financial interests of union officials, employers, and consultants must be reported, and union officials entrusted with union funds must be insured. Experience with this act has shown that it is very difficult to legislate honesty and integrity. There are still many abuses. But what the Landrum-Griffin Act did do was to set an important precedent for increased government interference in the private sector. The debate of whether this is good or bad continues, but there is little question that unless both labor and management take a positive, responsible stance in collective bargaining, there will inevitably be more government regulation in the future.

UNDERSTANDING UNIONS

So far we have discovered that there have always been unions in this country and that, since 1935, they have legal backing. In order to understand unions better, the supervisor should be aware of the pro and con arguments surrounding them, have some idea of their internal structure, and know how the organizing process takes place.

Positive Attributes of Unions

Unions are here to stay. Despite this reality, most people still have very strong feelings about them. Supervisors are once more caught in the middle of the controversy; they should be aware of the issues on both sides, starting with the positive. Obviously unions have many different advantages and there are various reasons for belonging to them. Some of the more widely held, important reasons are the following:

1 *For Strength in Numbers.* Ever since the beginning of the factory system, the management side of labor relations has been unified and strong. Employees, on the other hand, have often operated as isolated individuals. Obviously, a strong, unified employer versus a single employee is no match. Management can dictate terms of employment to powerless employees and let them quit if they do not like the arrangement. However, if the employees band together into a union and present a united front to management, then they have considerable power and can make serious demands to improve their welfare. If their demands are not met, they can go on strike, which involves serious consequences for the organization. As many unionized employees in the public sector have found out in recent years, a great deal of their power depends on their ability to strike. It is just not a matter of forming a union but of doing something about an organization's failure to meet union demands.

2 *For Job Security and Fair Treatment.* The union and the resulting written contract prevent the supervisor from treating employees arbitrarily. Union members know that they are not at the mercy of an unfair supervisor. The contract eliminates favoritism and spells out a systematic approach to wages, hours, discipline, promotions, layoffs, benefits, working conditions, and terminations. Having this contract, and knowing that the union has full backing in any legitimate dispute with management over these matters, gives the employee a feeling of security and well-being.

3 *For Self-Respect and Social Relations.* An employee who has an interesting, challenging job with good potential for growth and promotion sees little need for a union. Most supervisors find themselves in this position. On the other hand, most rank-and-file employees do not. As previous chapters have pointed out and chapters in the next part will emphasize, most employees today find themselves in boring, dead-end jobs with little hope for the future. They feel they are underpaid and are resentful of their lot in life. A union is very appealing to these people. It gives them a chance to achieve some self-respect and offers a means of alleviating their frustrations. Social psychologists have found the old adage that misery loves company to be true. By joining together into a union with others in the same miserable situation, employees can gain a measure of self-respect and strike back (literally and figuratively) at management, which is viewed as the major source of all their problems.

4 *For Better Wages, Benefits, and Job Conditions.* This is the most obvious but may be one of the least important reasons for joining a union. There is probably little argument that unions have secured a bigger piece of the pie for their members. Higher wages, many benefits (including more vacation days, better insurance coverage, pensions, severance pay, and the move toward a guaranteed annual wage), and improved working conditions can be attributed to unions. Even those organizations that have remained nonunion have been greatly influenced in these areas by the union movement. In the latter organizations, it is a matter of keeping up with the unions or becoming unionized themselves. Yet these gains, though undeniable victories for the unions, do not necessarily represent basic motives. The feelings of power, security, and self-respect the unions can provide probably have more to do with leading people to join and

With public sector agencies becoming increasingly organized, the union movement is broadening in scope and power (United Press International Photo).

support them than does the chance to make a few more cents an hour, to obtain a better medical plan, or to have the rest rooms made more attractive.

5 *In Order to Secure Employment.* Although the Taft-Hartley Act makes it illegal to coerce or intimidate an employee in order to encourage union membership, the fact is that many unions have secured closed or union shops. A *closed shop* is one in which only union members may be hired and employed. Although about 40 percent of the states have "right to work" laws which prohibit closed shops, in reality closed shops may still exist even in the right-to-work states. The union shop is a step backward (or forward, depending on your perspective) from the closed shop. In a *union shop* the employer can hire a nonunion person, but it is understood that this person will join the union within a stated period of time. It is generally estimated that about two-thirds of the collective agreements in force today contain provisions for a union shop. In other words, many employees join a union because they have no other choice; it is a condition of their employment.

The above advantages make a convincing argument for unionization. The fact remains, however, that about three-fourths of the work force are not union members. Examining the reasons why people reject union membership is equally important to the supervisor.

Negative Attitudes toward Unions

Unions do have advantages for employees. Yet many people, including the majority of managers, wish that they would go away and vigorously fight to keep unions out. Unions, like many of the major collegiate football powers around the country, stir up strong feelings of either love or hate among the people. As with religion and politics, it is difficult to argue the pros and cons of unions because people are so emotionally charged about the subject. Those who hate unions accuse them of being a major contributor to the problems facing contemporary society (e.g., inflation, unemployment, and continued interruptions in vital services caused by strikes). Many managers also blame unions for rising costs, poor quality of work, and declining morale. Is this criticism of unions justified? Even more important is why three-fourths of the work force have resisted joining. Obviously, there are no simple answers to these questions, but supervisors should at least think about them so they can better analyze the issues involved.

Probably the biggest reason why some people are so antiunion is because, in both principle and practice, unions run counter to the widely held values of individualism and free enterprise. These values are especially prevalent among middle-upper-class people who hold professional, managerial, or white-collar jobs. They associate unions with collectivism, socialism, and a welfare state. With the increased unionization of professionals (e.g., teachers, nurses, members of police and fire departments) and white-collar employees in all types of organizations in both the public and private sectors in recent years, some of these attitudes toward unionism seem to be changing.

On the other hand, more and more people are being inconvenienced by strikes in vital services (education, transportation, medical service, and even police and fire protection), and this—in terms of public opinion—does not favor the unions' cause. Another source of antiunion feeling is the economy. When costs are rising and unemployment is increasing as they have been in recent years, the public in general, and cost-conscious management in particular, do not see how unions can justify their seemingly outrageous demands.

In a more pragmatic sense, individual employees may not join a union because they see no reason to. They may like their jobs, feel that they are being treated fairly, and think the pay and benefits are good. Why pay union dues and fatten some far-removed union treasury? Along these same lines, many employees reason that if they form a union, it will antagonize management to such an extent that the workers will be much worse off than they were before the union existed.

How supervisors weigh the pros and cons of unions will depend on their own values and experiences. Regardless of personal feelings, however, supervisors must remember that, in labor relations and in dealing with unions, they are representatives of management and should always think in terms of what is best for their employees and the objectives of the organization.

The Internal Structure of Unions

There are three levels in the internal structure of unions. At the top is the federation; next comes the national or international unions; and finally there are the local unions.

The federation During the Civil War, the number of unions in the industrialized North grew tremendously (i.e., in 1863, there were only eighty local unions in the twenty Northern states; by the end of the war, this number had grown to three hundred). At that time, the leaders of the union movement reasoned that the philosophy of strength in numbers, then being applied in the organization of employees, could also be applied in organizing the various unions. Therefore, in 1869, the first major federation of unions, the Knights of Labor, was formed. This federation grew rapidly for the next couple of decades; at its peak, it had almost three-quarters of a million members. Then a series of unsuccessful strikes and lack of unity led to its demise.

In 1886, several craft unions got together to form the American Federation of Labor (AFL), with about 138,000 members. By 1920, the AFL had over 4 million members, which represented about 75 percent of all union workers. The members in the AFL were formed on the basis of their craft and not on the basis of the company or industry that employed them. However, as the number of unskilled and semiskilled employees grew in number and strength relative to craft or skilled workers, many union leaders felt that the federation should also permit unions to be formed along industry lines. The internal politics came to a head in the 1930s, when ten unions were suspended from the AFL. Under the direction of mining union leader John L. Lewis, a Committee for Industrial Organization was formed. This group severed all ties with the AFL and in 1938 held a constitutional convention that created a new federation, the Congress of Industrial Organizations (CIO).

The CIO member unions organized workers by industry (e.g., the United Mine Workers and the United Steel Workers) and were very successful. By World War II, there were about 6 million members affiliated with the CIO, which was generally recognized to be more aggressive than the AFL. At the same time carpenters, electricians, plumbers, sheet-metal workers, and bricklayers who were members of craft unions remained affiliated with the older AFL. Then, in 1955, the strength-in-numbers philosophy prevailed again and the two federations merged into one, the AFL-CIO. George Meany has been head of the huge AFL-CIO for a number of years. Of the 21 million plus who belong to unions today, over 80 percent are affiliated with the AFL-CIO.

The nationals and locals The national (or international if they have members outside the United States) unions make up the national level of organization. The largest nationals are the Teamsters

(2 million), Auto Workers (1.6 million), Steelworkers (1.3 million), Electrical Workers (1 million), Machinists (1 million), and Carpenters (900,000). The fastest growing white-collar unions include the State, County, and Municipal Employees, which have about three-quarters of a million members, an increase of about 200 percent over 1964. Others in this category include the Postal Workers, Teachers, Federal Employees, and Firefighters.

The two largest nationals (the Teamsters and the Auto Workers) are no longer members of AFL-CIO. The withdrawal of these and a few others indicate that the real source of power in the American labor movement is at the national, not the federation level. The nationals set and enforce policies on wages, hours, union security, and benefits for their respective locals. They also provide a whole range of services and assistance for locals and are beginning to assume a larger role in collective bargaining.

The local, of course, is where supervisors will have the most contact. A local union must be authorized by the national and follow its constitution and bylaws. The organization of the local is very basic and usually has the following personnel:

1 *President.* Like the elected president of most organizations, this person presides at union meetings, represents the union at official functions, and participates in collective bargaining.

2 *Secretary-Treasurer.* This is the person in charge of the purse strings of the local. If the union is big enough, this may be a full-time job.

3 *Business Agent.* Sometimes appointed, this person conducts the day-to-day business of the union and is almost always employed full-time. The business agent is usually a professional with a great deal of training and experience in running a union, negotiating contracts, and administering the contract through the grievance procedure.

4 *Steward.* This is the supervisor's counterpart on the union side of labor relations. The supervisor will have the most interaction with this union representative, who is sometimes called the committee person. The steward plays a major role in day-to-day labor relations and is especially important in the grievance procedure, which is given detailed attention later in this chapter.

Supervisors should remember that these union officials with whom they will be in contact are elected by the membership and, as such, often take political rather than objectively rational actions. Nevertheless, if the supervisor respects them and genuinely attempts to deal with them on a positive, fair basis, they can help rather than hinder those who are working toward effective labor relations.

The Unionization Process

Besides understanding the background, legal foundation, and internal structure of unions, supervisors should be aware of the process of becoming unionized. While most manufacturing firms have already been unionized through the years, supervisors in the service industries and in the public sector may be facing union organizing drives in the near future. Knowledge of this process can be very critical to the supervisor.

The impetus for a union can come from either the employees or a union. In some cases, the union may be already entrenched in some other part of the organization or in similar types of organizations. An organizer takes over to generate interest in the union and attempts to get the number of signatures required (normally 50 percent of the members of the identified bargaining unit) to have an NLRB-supervised election. A secret-ballot election is then conducted. If the union wins (by a simple majority of those who vote), it becomes certified by the NLRB as the exclusive bargaining representative for all those in the identified unit.

Besides following the provisions of the Wagner Act which forbid unfair labor practices, the guidelines below may also be helpful. The supervisor can:

1 Attempt to correct any obvious untruths or misleading statements made by the union
2 Avoid asking employees to talk in private about the union
3 Talk publicly to employees about the union except for the twenty-four-hour silence period before the election
4 Talk to the employees about the disadvantages of a union (e.g., dues, meetings, strikes etc.) *without* in any way posing a threat of reprisal
5 Avoid spying on employees' union activities
6 Insist that if organizing activities clearly affect the job, they must take place during nonworking hours

These suggestions are meant to serve as guidelines only, since matters of this sort can become very messy. As a rule, supervisors should say and do nothing during an organizing campaign. The unfortunate part is that if management and supervisors had been doing an effective job of labor relations all along, a union campaign might never have gotten off the ground in the first place.

Collective Bargaining

After the union is established, the parties enter into the collective bargaining process. There is much more involved in this process than management and union officials sitting in a smoke-filled room, making demands and counterdemands. This is the negotiations phase of collective bargaining during which, except for providing some important informational inputs to the management negotiating team, the supervisor plays a minor role.

The other phase of collective bargaining, the interpretation and day-to-day administration of the written agreement, falls largely on the shoulders of supervisors. Once again, the supervisors become the important link. They represent management in the day-to-day relationships with the union and must know and be able to implement the contractual policies and procedures that have been agreed upon. The most important aspect of administering the collective bargaining agreement that is relevant to supervisors is the grievance procedure. The remainder of this chapter will be devoted to this aspect of administering the collective bargaining agreement.

THE GRIEVANCE PROCEDURE

The grievance procedure is a formal appeals process through which employees can have their complaints expressed and fairly resolved. The term "grievance" in this instance means more than an expression of dissatisfaction or irritation; rather, it refers to a formally registered complaint stemming from a real or imagined injustice. Supervisors must recognize, however, that what starts off as mere dissatisfaction or irritation may end up as a formal grievance.

As an example, let us say that an employee makes a request to the supervisor for the day off to attend his daughter's college graduation exercises. At this stage, there is no anger, and the situation is under the supervisor's control. Let us further assume that, after very little thought, the supervisor denies the request. Now the employee becomes upset and has a complaint. Even though the employee is frustrated and angry, the situation at this point is still under the control of the supervisor. The supervisor can carefully explain why the request was denied and thus resolve the complaint. However, suppose that the supervisor simply blurts out: "Charlie, if I let people off for stuff like that, we wouldn't have anybody around here to do the work. Request denied!" Charlie walks away very unhappy and angry. After all, he had sacrificed many years to put his only daughter through college, and her graduation was one of the most important occasions of his life. He vents his anger with some coworkers and one of them says, "Gee, I heard when Harry Paulson's kid graduated from medical school they gave him the day off with full pay." After hearing this, Charlie feels that he has been unjustly treated and promptly goes to the union steward to file a formal grievance.

There are a couple of important points to be made concerning this hypothetical situation. First, if the supervisor had been doing his job more effectively, he would not now be faced with a very disgruntled, angry employee who is filing a formal grievance. This does not mean that the supervisor should necessarily have granted Charlie's request for a day off. Good supervisors can and do have to say no some of the time. It does mean that the supervisor in this case probably handled the request very badly. He should have been more sensitive to Charlie's feelings about the importance of this event and should have known the established procedures and reasons for granting time off.

The way things were handled, Charlie felt that he had been treated in an arbitrary, unjust manner. Whether his treatment really was or was not unfair is not as important in this instance as the fact that he felt, probably rightfully, that his supervisor had behaved improperly. In this and many other cases, the formal grievance probably could have been avoided if the supervisor had taken the appropriate action.

The Grievance Procedure in Nonunionized Organizations

Most large organizations have a grievance system, whether they are unionized or not. In nonunionized organizations, there may be a spelled-out procedure that employees can follow if they have a grievance. They are assured that this is their right and that there will be no repercussions. Unfortunately, except in some rare instances, this generally does not turn out to be true. Most employees of nonunion organizations who file formal grievances soon find out that "rocking the boat" in this manner does not lead to a good result. There are many indirect ways in which supervisors can "get even" with such employees. The person who files a grievance may be passed over for a promotion, be labeled a troublemaker and get low ratings for merit pay increases, or be assigned the most undesirable jobs.

If nonunion organizations truly want effective grievance procedures, they should make sure that these are clearly spelled out in writing and that there is some forum for expressing grievances that is either confidential and/or anonymous or so open as to guarantee free expression and discussion. The latter may be accomplished by a representative committee with members from both management and labor and/or by neutral, external third parties who have the power to resolve the grievance in question. Unionized organizations, of course, have grievance procedures spelled out in their contracts.

The First Step in the Grievance Procedure

The exact nature of the grievance procedure and the number of steps it involves may vary somewhat from place to place. Most contracts specify from three to five steps. The first one, however, is of greatest impact and concern to supervisors. If—as in the previous example concerning Charlie, who wanted a day off—employees cannot get satisfaction from the supervisor and decide to file a formal grievance, they will go to their union steward. If the steward agrees that there is a case for a grievance, he or she will then take the issue to the supervisor. After careful review, the grievance is then either granted or denied by the supervisor.

This first step in the grievance procedure greatly depends on the supervisor's relationships with the union steward. It must be remembered that stewards are first of all employees. However, of undoubtedly greater importance to them is the fact that they have been elected by their friends and coworkers to represent them. Supervisors have many functions (as described so far in this book) and may look upon the grievance process as an extra burden. Union stewards, on the other hand, regard the grievance procedure as their major function. They are usually thoroughly trained by the union in the handling of grievances.

Unless supervisors have a good, personal working relationship with stewards, they are headed for trouble. Therefore, if this first step is to be handled effectively, *both* the supervisor and the union steward should:

1 Know and enforce the contract
2 Be genuinely concerned with the best interests of all employees

3 Be fair and avoid becoming emotional or angry
4 Keep each other informed and maintain a good working relationship

Whereas these rules apply to both supervisors and stewards, supervisors should always remember that they represent management rights and that stewards speak for the union and its constituents. If there is a positive relationship between the supervisor and the steward, only legitimate, realistic complaints will ever reach the point of a formal grievance. If there is an antagonistic, combative relationship between the two, the supervisor can count on being continually plagued by petty, unrealistic grievances.

Supervisors should strive to maintain a positive relationship with the steward and resolve grievances in a win-win rather than win-lose or lose-lose manner. If both management and employees can benefit from the supervisor's way of resolving grievances, then this is the ideal. However, if one party wins and the other loses—even worse—if both parties lose, then there are bound to be labor-relations problems now and in the future.

Subsequent Steps in the Grievance Procedure

If the grievance is not satisfactorily resolved at the first, supervisor-steward level, then the contract spells out a second step in the procedure. This usually involves the supervisor's superior (the superintendent or a department head) and/or a representative from the labor-relations department (the director of labor relations or the personnel manager) on the management side and a union grievance committee consisting of stewards and an official from the local union (the business agent).

The supervisor should have been keeping his or her superior fully advised of all the events and feelings involved when the grievance first came up. Now the supervisor must be very careful to present a full briefing of what has transpired so far and why the grievance was denied. Supervisors, of course, want their superiors to back them up in this second step, but supervisors must also realize that matters are now out of their hands and that they must accept whatever decisions are made.

At the second and third levels (top management and union grievance committee, usually consisting of the chief steward, business agent, president of the local, and a representative from the national), a more legal approach is taken. Broader-based experience and precedent with similar grievances will, it is hoped, focus in on the grievance at hand. At these second and third levels, the whole organization and union are involved. The costs and time spent are beginning to mount. Top management's case rests largely on the supervisor's original actions and documentation of those actions. So even at this level of the procedure, the supervisor still plays a pivotal role in determining how the grievance will be processed and acted upon.

Arbitration as the Terminal Step of the Grievance Procedure

If the grievance is still not resolved after going through the prescribed levels, almost all contracts call for arbitration as the terminal step. Whereas an impasse during the negotiation of contractual terms may end in a strike or lockout, neither management nor the union is willing to take such drastic action if a grievance cannot be resolved. Instead, they will submit to the binding decision of an arbitrator.

Arbitration is sometimes confused with conciliation and mediation. As applied to labor relations, each is different. In *conciliation,* a neutral, disinterested outside person attempts to get the parties together and help them explore ways of settling the dispute. The conciliator does not give specific recommendations or make a decision. In *mediation,* the neutral third party also gets management and labor together to discuss and analyze the issues in the dispute. In this process, however, unlike conciliation, the mediator does make specific recommendations and does render a decision. The decision of the mediator, however, is not binding; neither party is forced to accept it. Only under arbitration do the parties agree that the decision of the arbitrator will be final and binding.

The arbitrator (usually a lawyer, professor, or public official) is selected by mutual agreement. Sometimes a *tripartite board* consisting of a management representative, a union representative, and an agreed-upon, neutral third party is specified in the contract to arbitrate grievances.

The tripartite approach has the advantages of keeping the neutral arbitrator better informed of both sides of the dispute. Its decision also meets with better acceptance because each side participated fully and had an opportunity to present its case.

In large organizations, the arbitrator may be named during negotiations to serve the length of the contract. Such a permanent arrange-

287

ment provides the distinct advantages of (1) consistency, (2) time and cost efficiency, and (3) expertise and full knowledge of the contract terms. Unfortunately, most organizations name the arbitrator on an ad hoc basis and thus lose these advantages.

Whatever form arbitration may take, the process is vital to the success of healthy, positive labor relations. It guarantees that there will not be a work stoppage or slowdown over a grievance. Both management and the union may have tried their best to settle the grievance fairly, but the problem is still largely a political one. Therefore unfortunate things like face-saving and previous bad experiences enter the picture, and a mechanism such as arbitration is needed to prevent a serious blowup in which everyone would lose. In addition, arbitration helps to clarify some of the vague areas of the contract in a fair, quasijudicial manner. During negotiations, the pressures to compromise often make it difficult to apply many provisions of the contract. The arbitration process is probably the best way to iron out these difficulties, so that the contract can be realistically administered on a day-to-day basis. A final advantage is that an outside, analytical look at the labor relations of an organization is probably good for both parties. That is, they may have become so partisan that an outsider is needed to put things back into the proper perspective.

Practical Hints for the Supervisor in Handling Grievances

Before we end our discussion of the labor-relations function, it is important to supply some helpful hints on how to handle requests, complaints, and grievances. As in the medical field, prevention is much better and more effective than treatment if a healthy state of affairs is to be maintained. As the coming chapter on communications will point out, no news is not necessarily good news for the supervisor. It is wrong to suggest that effective supervisors will not be faced with grievances from their people. Even the best-supervised departments will have some grievances; if there are none, this may be because the people are afraid to speak up for fear of reprisals. Grievances can actually be a form of needed upward communication. On the other hand, from a labor-relations perspective, it should be clear by now that supervisors must attempt to settle grievances at the lowest possible level.

As a rule, grievances are settled at the first level about three-fourths of the time. Very few reach arbitration. To keep and even improve upon this record, supervisors can use the following guidelines:

1 *Be a good listener.* Never treat a request or complaint lightly. Always hear the employee out. By listening carefully, the supervisor shows respect for the employee. Even if the supervisor's initial reaction is that the request or complaint is not justified or even silly, it is important to remember the employee does not feel this way. It took considerable courage for the employee even to bring the complaint to the supervisor. If the supervisor brushes it aside or laughs it off, ill feelings and a formal grievance will surely follow.

2 *Remain calm and rational.* One of the surest but easiest ways to escalate a simple request or complaint into a formal grievance is for a supervisor to "fly off the handle." The employee usually is in an unhappy, antagonistic mood. The complainer may even be rude and challenge the supervisor's authority. It is very easy for the supervisor, under these conditions, to become angry and allow the interchange to degenerate into a shouting match. However, the supervisor must remain cool and rational. After having made sure that all the facts have been gathered, the supervisor must carefully identify what the problem really is and explore alternative solutions with the employee. One major input in developing alternative solutions is the employee's suggestions. This rational process can occur only when the supervisor remains calm and collected.

3 *Be fair and explain the decision fully.* After going through a rational problem-solving process, be sure that the decision is fair. Remember, a grievance comes about when the employee feels an injustice. The supervisor must fully explain whatever decision is made. A "yes" decision is easy. A "no" is much more difficult and must be fully justified to the employee. If supervisors cannot explain decisions to their own satisfaction, they had better rethink them. They must be positive and confident and appeal to the employee's sense of fairness and spirit of cooperation. One guideline supervisors can use to gain this type of acceptance is to "sell" rather than "tell" their decision.

4 *Follow up.* Effective supervisors never just drop the matter after they render a decision. They should allow the employee a chance to appeal the decision if he or she is not satisfied and should explain how this can be done. If the employee seemingly accepts the decision, the supervisor should periodically check out whether this is in fact the case. Asking coworkers can help in this regard.

By following these guidelines, supervisors can go a long way toward promoting better labor relations.

■ KEY CONCEPTS

Wagner Act
Taft-Hartley Act
Landrum-Griffin Act
Prounion attitudes
Antiunion attitudes
Union federation
Union steward
Unionization process
Collective bargaining
Grievance procedure
Arbitration

■ PRACTICAL EXERCISES

(These can be performed by individuals or by groups.)
1 Briefly summarize the major pieces of labor legislation. Do you think both parties are getting an even break in terms of this legislation? Why or why not? What do you think the future of labor law will be?
2 Role-play the following situation between a supervisor and a union steward. The person who plays each role should not read the other's script, but the observers should read both.

Supervisor's Role

Tom takes pride in the fact that every grievance decision that he has made has been upheld when the union appealed to the next level. Lately, there has been growing animosity between Tom and the union steward, Sam White. Tom feels that he is genuinely fair with the workers in the department, but deep down he thinks that unions are not good for the country, the company, or the individual employee.

Union Steward's Role

Sam is going on his third year as union steward. He really enjoys the position and would like to move up in the union hierarchy in the future. A small but very vocal group of members is dissatisfied with the way Sam always seems to come out second best in any encounter with Tom Barron, the supervisor. Sam is determined that Tom is not going to "soft soap" or intimidate him any more.

290

Situation

Mary Lane's father was very ill and her mother had been letting things pile up at home while she was visiting him at the hospital. One day, Mary completed all her assigned work for the day, looked at her watch, and thought to herself: "I have a couple of hours to go till quitting time, but I think I'll slip on home and help Mom out." When Tom Barron realized she had left, he became upset and docked her pay for the whole day. When Mary learned of this action, she went to Sam White and said: "Hey, I did enough work for the whole day. I needed to get home early so I left. The way I read the contract, it says we must maintain minimum standards of performance. I did that. I don't think I should have my pay docked at all, but at the very most it should only be for the two hours I was gone, not the whole day. I have medical bills to pay and I can't afford this. Sam, I want you to back me up on this!"

Act out the dialogue that would now take place between Tom and Sam. After this role-play takes place, the observers should answer questions such as these:

1 Did the supervisor follow the guidelines for handling a potential grievance? Where did he violate them?

2 Do you think the situation was decided in the right way?

3 Do you think that the supervisor's action would hold up in the upper levels of the grievance procedure? Why?

4 What do you predict for the future of labor relations in this department? Why?

■ DISCUSSION INCIDENTS

You are the desk sergeant for the downtown police precinct. The other day in the locker room, you overheard a couple of patrolmen discussing their recent meeting at the bowling alley lounge with a union organizer. The patrolmen sounded very enthusiastic about the prospects of becoming unionized. One of them said, "My uncle is a cop in Capitol City, and when they went union, everybody got a big jump in pay. I don't know about you guys, but I can't make ends meet with what the city fathers are paying me to put my life on the line every day. I'm going to persuade every guy I know on the force to go union."

1 What would you do after hearing this? Would you tell the captain? Would you try to talk them out of going union? Would you pull rank and tell them never to talk about this at the station again?

2 Do you think the patrolman is right in wanting to unionize? Why or why not?

Your elderly uncle has been a bricklayer all his working life. He says to you, "You young guys are all alike. I've worked with my hands all my life and been a good union man. Nowadays you guys want to get a soft desk job and put down the union as being old-fashioned. Well, I'm here to tell you that I have gotten a lot of satisfaction from my craft, and if it wasn't for the union, I would have been exploited and paid very little. Mark my words, I don't think things will be any different for you."

1 Do you agree or disagree with the old bricklayer? Do you think things are different today than they were in his time? How?

2 Argue the pros and cons of unionization for the old bricklayer and for yourself in your present or future job.

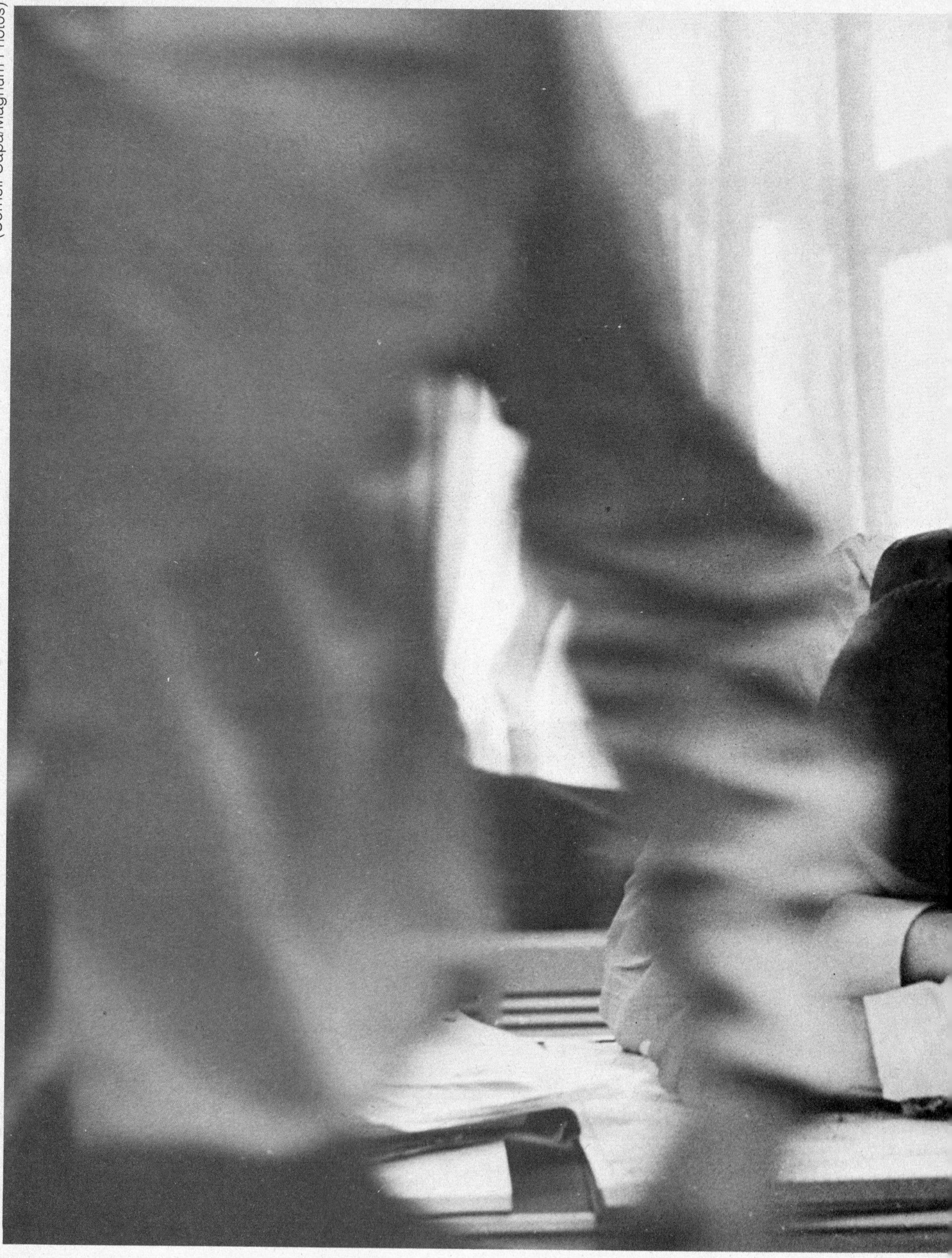

(Cornell Capa/Magnum Photos)

PART 3
HUMAN RELATIONS
FOR EFFECTIVE SUPERVISION

UNDERSTANDING EMPLOYEE BEHAVIOR

CHAPTER 12

Carlos Manta was being considered for a supervisor's position in Section A. He had worked for the company for thirteen years and had earned an associate of arts degree through night school at the local community college. His boss called him in and said, "Carlos, what do you think about being made supervisor of Section A when Ann retires next month? What do you think being a supervisor is all about?" Carlos knew he was being considered for the job and had given this question some prior thought. He replied, "Well, as you know, I have several years of experience in the department so I can handle the technical side of the section. What I would concentrate on as supervisor would be planning, organizing, and controlling the activities of the section to improve the performance of the department." The boss replied, "That is a good answer, but where would people fit into the picture?" Carlos replied, "Well, I have dealt with people all my life. I can handle that aspect of the job with ease." The boss replied, "I agree you have dealt with people all your life, but do you really think you understand why they behave the way they do, and does it make any difference in the way you would supervise the section?" Carlos had a puzzled look on his face and answered, "Gee, I really hadn't given that much thought. I assumed I knew all about people and didn't think it had anything to do with how I would run the section."

After reading this chapter, you should be able to:

Know the reasons why the study of employee behavior is so important to effective supervision

Understand how personalities develop

Know the basic principles of perception, learning, and motivation

Use the frustration model in order to explain certain behaviors such as aggression, withdrawal, fixation, and compromise

Part II of this book was concerned mainly with the basic supervisory functions. As was brought out, people play an important role in supervisory functions such as planning, organizing, training, delegating, controlling, disciplining, appraising, and labor relations. However, the human side of supervision is becoming so much more important that these last chapters are specifically devoted to human relations for effective supervision. In this chapter, a basic discussion of employee behavior is presented. It will serve as the foundation for the subsequent chapters on groups, communication, motivation, and leadership.

WHY WE STUDY EMPLOYEE BEHAVIOR

Some supervisors may feel that they are already experts when it comes to understanding people. After all, they have dealt with people all their lives, and that experience alone should lead to adequate understanding. There is no doubt that the experience factor does count, but—unfortunately—it has also proved to be a big barrier to the more effective supervision of people.

Because supervisors, and people in general, feel they are experts on human behavior, they do not attempt to study and learn about it, as they do with the other aspects of their jobs. Yet, this is where the major problems facing today's supervisor lie—in the "people" part of the job. Commonsense and experienced-based approaches to supervising employees have just not worked out.

The record speaks for itself. Tardiness, absenteeism, and turnover are very big problems with most organizations; even more disturbing are the surveys reporting that today's employees are working at only about 50 to 75 percent of capacity on their jobs. For example, in a recent Gallup poll, half the wage earners admitted they could accomplish more each day, and three in five said they could increase their

299

performance by as much as 20 percent or more. In other words, even those organizations that do not have absenteeism problems may still be getting only eight hours a day out of their employees. They are not getting anything near what the employees are capable of giving to the job. As one supervisor recently remarked, "Most of my employees have retired, but they have anywhere from ten to forty years to go until they draw their pensions."

Besides the people problems facing modern supervision, it must be realized that by far the largest percentage of a supervisor's operating budget is devoted to people. In manufacturing concerns, labor represents the biggest single cost; in the rapidly expanding service and public sector organizations, people typically account for 75 to 90 percent of the costs. Thus, from either a priority problem perspective or just plain dollars and cents, supervisors, to be effective, must be able to understand their employees' behavior better.

EMPLOYEES ARE CHANGING

A good starting point in understanding today's employees is to realize that their values are undergoing drastic change. The simple fact is that employees of previous generations had different expectations about work, authority, what one might expect from a job, the meaning of the dollar, and so on, than do today's employees. One extensive survey of supervisors across the country found that their employees over the last several years had less pride in their work (little concern for quality, waste, and housekeeping) and less loyalty to the organization, were less responsible to authority, had less interest in working overtime, and, in general, were more eager to control their own destinies.[1] The issue is not whether the supervisor agrees or disagrees with these values—they are here, like it or not. Instead, the supervisor must understand how these values arose and, through better understanding, learn to deal with and manage their people more effectively.

HOW PERSONALITIES DEVELOP

Personality represents the entire person psychologically. The parts of the personality are made up of such psychological dimensions as

[1]See Leslie E. This, *A Guide to Effective Management*, Addison-Wesley Publishing Company, Inc., Reading, Mass., 1974, pp. 19–22.

perception, learning, and motivation. These will be considered later in our discussion. For now, the question to be answered is how personality develops.

Although the specifics differ widely, psychologists are pretty much in agreement that, for the most part, an individual's personality develops (learned) over the years. Most behavioral scientists would agree that a person is not born with fixed personality characteristics or attitudes toward work. These are acquired primarily in the so-called developmental years—the early years of life. This does not entirely rule out the possibility that some traits such as intelligence are partly the result of heredity, but it does suggest that a study of the developmental process plays the biggest role in understanding personality. Very briefly, this developmental process can be broken down into what psychologists call modeling, identification, and socialization.

The Modeling Process

The modeling process takes place very early (roughly between ages 2 and 5). The very young child simply imitates a model (usually the parent). For example, when small boys are asked what they want to be when they grow up (apart from the usual cowboy and fireman), they will often say they want to be like Dad. If pressed to explain what "being like Dad" means, they will usually respond with things such as: "The guy who gets to mow the grass." (Most fathers will gladly grant their boys this wish as soon as their little arms can reach up to the mower!) Or they may respond with: "The guy who gets to drive the car." In other words, the child going through the modeling process is only imitating—he or she is only looking at the most superficial, often the apparently enjoyable things (e.g., mowing grass, driving a car, etc.) that the model does. It is not until the child grows a little older that the more deeply held values and enduring personality characteristics begin to develop.

The Identification Process

Somewhere between age 5 and about 8 or 9, the child begins what psychologists call the identification process of development. At this point, the child actually starts to identify (rather than just imitate, as in the case of modeling) with the model. Usually the parent of the same sex serves as the model for identification unless, of course, that parent is off the scene or not around very much. With the increasing divorce rate, more and more jobs that keep parents away from home, and the growing trend for mothers to hold full-time jobs, the traditional parental model may no longer be serving the purpose it once did. Teachers, baby-sitters, friends, and especially television characters may be replacing parents as models for identification. In any case, the child will identify with someone during this phase and actually take on the personality traits and values of the model. Obviously, this identification process becomes very critical to a person's subsequent personality.

The Socialization Process

"Socialization" simply refers to the process whereby others shape an individual's personality and values. The parents and other family members play a role in socialization, but friends and the social group become especially important to the socialization process of older children and adults throughout their lives.

At about age 9 or 10 (there is nothing hard and fast about any of these ages for the various developmental processes), the child lets go of the apron strings and becomes a member of the social community outside the home. At about this age the child usually does not have to come home right after school but instead spends time with friends and begins to be influenced by them. This influence becomes stronger as the child grows older—as any parent of teenagers today would verify. Even in adults, the socialization process continues and, of course, an employee's work group has a great influence on the way he or she behaves. The next chapter will get into the specifics of groups and their impact on individual employees.

Why Understanding Personality Development Helps Us Understand Employees

At this point, the reader might say, "Well the discussion so far is interesting, but what does the developmental process have to do with understanding my employees?" The answer is that by understanding the developmental process, supervisors can begin to see why their people have the values and characteristics they have and why they act the way they do. For example, take the older employee versus the younger one. The employee in his sixties went through the developmental process (modeling, identification, and socialization) over fifty years ago—during the 1920s. What was it like to grow up in the 1920s? This era, often nicknamed the roaring twenties, must surely have had a much different impact on the children growing up than did succeeding decades. For instance, during the twenties, a daring young man might ride a Model-T Ford down a cowpath at 19 miles per hour while taking an occasional nip of bootleg gin. Today, on the other hand, his counterpart might be riding a Corvette at 119 miles per hour down an interstate highway while smoking a joint.

There is some similarity in these two examples, but they also point to some drastic differences between then and now. We are living in a much faster-paced, technologically advanced period of social upheaval. This rapidly accelerating change that is occurring has been called "future shock" by the author/lecturer Alvin Toffler. Because their growing-up experiences have been so different, those in their sixties have different values and personality characteristics than employees in their twenties. The same analysis can be made of other employees by age. For example, those raised during the Depression (now in their fifties) would place a much higher value on job security than those (now in their thirties) brought up during the affluent 1950s.

This type of discussion should help supervisors begin to understand their employees better. They do not necessarily have to agree or disagree with the young long-haired guy or the old gray-haired guy. Instead, this type of analysis may help head off a polarization between the young and old and through better understanding of the developmental processes, begin to bridge the generation gap.

PEOPLE AS PSYCHOLOGICAL SYSTEMS

A discussion of personality development and value formation serves as a point of departure for understanding more specific employee behavior. It was stated that the personality represents the whole person. Another way of looking at and studying employee behavior is to use the systems concept. In particular, an individual can be thought of as a system made up of interacting and interrelated elements. Two of the major subsystems would be the physiological and the psychological. The physiological subsystem (e.g., muscles, blood, nerves, brain, and skeletal framework) is not as important to the understanding of employee behavior as is the psychological subsystem. Three of the most important elements in the psychological subsystem, from our point of view, are perception, learning, and motivation.

The Perceptual Process

One of the basic building blocks in human behavior is perception. This psychological process involves the way people select, organize, and interpret the many things around them. There are literally hundreds of different things affecting a person's senses (sight, smell, taste, sound, and touch) at any one time. The person, however, selects out and attends to only one or a few of these. Once something is selected, it is then organized into a meaningful whole and interpreted by the individual. It is this interpretation that is most closely associated with perception. No two people make exactly the same interpretations; therefore everyone has a unique perception of the world. This latter point suggests how difficult and complex human beings really are and why it is not a simple matter for supervisors to understand them.

An example of how the perceptual process works may be provided by the typical office in any type of organization. There are numerous things going on in this situation: people talking, typewriters tapping, phones ringing, people walking around, the odor of cigarette smoke, a light flashing on the intercom, the air conditioner humming, a car honking in the street outside, a person touching another as they discuss something, the taste of a cough drop, and so forth. A particular individual will select out only one or a few of these possible perceptions. Let us say that the secretary attends to the flashing red light on the intercom. She is, of course, aware of the light's message—that the boss wants something and she had better respond. She may interpret this message in several ways, such as: "Well what does the old boy want this time" or "Gee the boss needs my help on something, I had better get in there right away." In summary, the perceptual process involves:

1 *Selecting* out one or a few stimuli from the hundreds that impinge on a person's senses at any given moment
2 *Organizing* the incoming stimuli into a meaningful event
3 *Interpreting* the event in a unique manner

Knowledge of this perceptual process helps supervisors to realize that everyone perceives the world in a different way. The salesperson may perceive the sales quota much differently than the sales supervisor does. The production worker may perceive the quality problem much differently than does the production supervisor. The police sergeant may perceive the new regulation much differently than does the cop on the beat. In other words, a grasp of what is involved in perception helps explain the individual differences among employees and the reason why supervisors may not "see" a particular situation or event in the same way as their people do.

Figure 12-1 demonstrates a common perceptual phenomenon. You can probably see either an old lady or a young lady. In order to see both, you must look very carefully for the profile of an old lady with a large nose and her chin buried down into the fur. The young lady is also a profile but has a very dainty little nose and her ear is the old woman's eye. Can you now see both women?

The old woman–young woman picture demonstrates that two people can look at the *same* thing and interpret it completely differently (young and beautiful or old and ugly). When a memo from top management spells out a new organizational policy, the supervisor's perception may be: "This is beautiful; it is about time we had this policy." But the employees may perceive the same memo very differently, interpreting: "This is ugly; we just can't live with this policy."

Once again, if supervisors realize that they may not perceive things the same way that their bosses and subordinates do, they can be a bit more tolerant and understanding of the divergent interpretations of what (to them) is "obvious" and begin to improve their communication both upward and downward. Chapter 14 will examine more closely the role that perception plays in communication.

The Learning Process

The perceptual element is very important to a person's psychological system. However, as in any system, the parts do not operate in isolation. Perception interacts with and is dependent upon the other psychological processes. One of the most important of these is learning. Almost *everything* that *everyone* does is based on learning.

Simply defined, learning is a change in behavior that is based on reinforced practice or experience. Thus, from this definition, learning can be summarized as involving (1) changed or modified behavior and (2) reinforcement. However, it should be noted that psychologists do not agree on whether these are the only elements of learning.

FIGURE 12-1
Ambiguous picture of a young woman and an old woman. (*Source:* Edwin G. Boring, "A New Ambiguous Figure," *American Journal of Psychology,* July, 1930, p. 444. Also see Robert Leeper, "A Study of a Neglected Portion of the Field of Learning—The Development of Sensory Organization," *Journal of Genetic Psychology,* March 1935, p. 62. Originally drawn by cartoonist W. E. Hill and published in *Puck,* November 6, 1915.)

Some would argue that learning takes place within one's head. Most of the others (and this book as well) deal only with the impact that learning has on observable behaviors. In other words, our approach is to look at behaviors and those of their consequences (reinforcement) that can be observed and measured. Accordingly, we shall not concentrate on the elusive mind, which cannot be observed and measured. This does not imply that the mind is not important, but it does emphasize that the most profitable way to achieve a better understanding of behavior and then to do something about it is to take a behavioral approach to learning.

Classical conditioning The basic building block for understanding learning comes from the classical conditioning framework. Probably the most famous experiment conducted in the behavioral sciences was done by the Russian Ivan Pavlov at the turn of this century. He found that when a bell was rung in the presence of his dogs (the subjects in his experiments), they did nothing. When meat was presented to them, they began to salivate. However, if the ringing of the bell was closely followed by the presentation of the meat over a few trials, the animals would begin to salivate to the ringing of the bell *alone,* even when no meat was presented. The dogs had, in other words, been *conditioned* to salivate to a bell. This type of classical conditioning (i.e., pairing a neutral stimulus such as the bell with a meaningful stimulus such as the meat, which will naturally lead to a response) is an elementary form of learning. The dogs in Pavlov's experiment learned to respond to the bell.

It is useful to know about classical conditioning not because it helps to explain much of human learning but because it shows how the basic elements of learning can be broken down and analyzed. Classical conditioning, for the most part, explains only reflexive behaviors and possibly emotional behaviors in human beings. For example, when a snake is presented to a very young child, the child's reaction is to either ignore it or to reach out and try to touch it or hold it. However, after a screaming mother has been paired with the snake several times (as might easily happen in real life), the child quickly becomes conditioned to fear the snake. Some emotional behaviors on the part of employees and some aspects of training in new procedures and skills involve such classical conditioning. However, of much more importance to the understanding of employee behavior is operant conditioning.

Operant conditioning Whereas classical conditioning is attributed to Ivan Pavlov, operant conditioning is based on the work of the famous Harvard psychologist B. F. Skinner. He was the first to make the important distinction between respondent or reflexive conditioning and operant conditioning. From extensive research, Skinner was convinced that, except for reflexive behaviors (involuntary behaviors, such as crying when an onion is peeled), human behavior depended upon its consequences. The person *operates* (thus the term "operant conditioning") on the environment in order to produce a desired consequence. If the consequence of a particular behavior is pleasurable (rewarding or reinforcing), then the behavior will tend to be repeated. On the other hand, if the consequence of the behavior is undesirable (punishing), then the behavior will tend not to be repeated.

Obviously, the consequent environment under operant conditioning is very important to understanding employee behavior. In a nutshell, operant conditioning suggests that *employee behavior depends on its consequences.* This is a very significant statement for supervisors to understand. If a supervisor wants to modify or change an employee's behavior (the first dimension of learning), then he or she has to give attention to the consequences (reinforcement to increase it or punishment to decrease it). Under this operant approach, the supervisor would give more attention to the environment of employees than to the employees themselves. This represents a significant departure from the traditional approach to managing human resources. Chapter 15, "Motivating Employees," will describe in detail some of the specific ways in which supervisors can use this behavioral management approach.

The Motivation Process

"Motivation" means different things to different people, but most would associate it—more closely than any of the other psychological processes—with overall employee behavior. Motivation is the driving force, the energizer behind human behavior. The exact nature of this force is open to many different explanations, but—like perception and learning—it is a psychological process.

The motivation process begins with a need. A motivational need is a felt deficiency or want. These needs can be physiologically based (e.g., bodily needs for food, water, sex, or sleep) or psychologically based (e.g., learned needs for power, achievement, or affiliation). It is important to note that these needs are largely, if not always, unobservable. A supervisor cannot observe an employee's needs for water or for achievement. What the supervisor *can* see is the behavioral outcome of the need. This observable behavior is the second part of the motivation process and is called the drive. Thus, the need for food is expressed as the hunger drive and the need for power is expressed as the power drive. Specifically, a drive can be defined as a deficiency with direction. The drive is directed toward a goal—the third and last major dimension in the motivational process. A goal (in the motivational sense) is anything which alleviates or satisfies the need and reduces the intensity of the drive. The actual food or water would be the goal of the hunger or thirst drive, and being accepted by a particular group may be the goal of the affiliation drive.

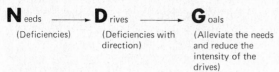

N eeds ⟶ **D** rives ⟶ **G** oals

(Deficiencies)　(Deficiencies with　(Alleviate the needs
　　　　　　　　direction)　　　and reduce the
　　　　　　　　　　　　　　　intensity of the
　　　　　　　　　　　　　　　drives)

FIGURE 12-2
The motivational process.

Figure 12-2 depicts the motivational process. As shown, the needs will invariably (with the possible exception of the need for oxygen) set up drives which are aimed at appropriate goals. Therefore, since needs always lead to drives, the two terms can be used interchangeably, as they will be in this book.

The physiological needs/drives are necessary to the very survival of the individual. People must have food, water, and sleep to survive—and, of course, sex (especially according to the founder of psychoanalysis, Sigmund Freud) plays an important role in much of human behavior. But these unlearned physiological needs are not very important to the understanding of employee behavior. Most of today's employees have their basic needs satisfied. Of much more importance are the learned psychological needs. Although there are a great number of such needs, we know the most about power, achievement, and affiliation, and these are the most important to an understanding of employee behavior.

The need for power Often abreviated as n-Pow, this need refers to the desire to "be in charge" or to "manipulate others." This need generally has a negative connotation in our society; that is, being "power hungry" is regarded as an undesirable trait. But as Harvard psychologist David McClelland points out, there are actually two faces of power—personal power and social power. Personal power is the striving for power for selfish reasons and often has dangerous outcomes for those affected by it. Social power, on the other hand, is more concerned with the means to attain desired group goals (not individual goals, as in the case of personal power). There is research evidence accumulating to indicate that supervisors who use social power are more effective than those who depend on personal power only. In general, supervisors will have a much higher need for power (personal and social) than will rank-and-file employees. This is important for supervisors to remember. They do not have the same needs as their subordinates.

Employees as well as athletes have
needs that motivate them to
accomplish goals (G. Cranham from
Rapho/Photo Researchers, Inc.).

The need for achievement We know more about the need for achievement than any other. Commonly labeled n-Ach, this need has been thoroughly researched by psychologists, and they have been able to determine the characteristics of high achievers fairly accurately. A high achiever tends to:

1 *Take moderate risks.* This characteristic may be counter to common belief. Most people would probably guess that high achievers take high risks. There is substantial evidence that the low achiever either takes high risks or low risks, but the high achiever takes moderate risks. The simple child's ring-toss game can be used to demonstrate this characteristic. If you ask a group of people to stand anywhere they want to toss the rings on the peg, high achievers will behave much differently than low achievers. The low achievers will either stand very close and almost drop the rings on the peg (low risk) or they will stand ridiculously far away and wildly toss the rings at the peg (high risk). The high achiever, on the other hand, will carefully calculate the exact distance that will test his or her abilities and will then challenge anyone else to perform as well at that distance. This same characteristic of taking moderate risks would carry over to the decision-making behavior of supervisors.

2 *Want immediate feedback.* High achievers need immediate, objective feedback on how they are doing. It is because of this characteristic that high achievers usually have hobbies such as woodworking instead of a stamp collection and gravitate into careers like sales instead of research and development or teaching. In woodwork and sales, the person gets immediate, objective feedback of how he or she is progressing. High achievers need this information.

3 *Be a loner.* This third characteristic also may take people by surprise. Because our dominant middle class cultural values involve upward striving and getting ahead in the world, most of us somehow hope we are high achievers. This third characteristic may dampen our enthusiasm for being high achievers. Research shows that high achievers do not depend upon nor form close relationships with others. They do not need others and act independently. High achievers are certainly not shy and can most often handle themselves very well in a social setting, but they do not tend to empathize with others and generally will have few if any close friends. This characteristic brings out a common mistake that is often made. The best producer or salesperson may, for example, be promoted to supervisor. A high need for achievement may have been the major factor behind this individual's success. But now, after being made supervisor, the high achiever (who is also a loner) may become ineffective in his or her job. If, as a supervisor, this individual does not like people or cannot get along well with them, it is very unlikely that he or she will be a good supervisor. Yet this fact is commonly overlooked when promotion decisions are made.

These characteristics are usually but not always found in the high achiever. In general, supervisors will have a greater need for achievement than their subordinates. On the other hand, some individual employees, like those in sales or perhaps the union steward, may have very high n-Ach.

The need for affiliation This need, sometimes called n-Aff, refers to the intense desire most people have to belong to a group and be accepted by others. Autobiographical accounts of people who have been stranded on desert islands or lost in the wilderness and stories of prisoners who have experienced solitary confinement attest to the almost unbearable pain that is associated with being cut off from other people. As far back as the Hawthorne studies, which were discussed in Chapter 1, it has been shown that this need for affiliation is very intense among employees.

Whereas both the power and achievement needs were said to be relatively more intense in supervisors than in their subordinates, the reverse is true in the case of affiliation. Rank-and-file employees are generally more motivated by the chance to become accepted members of their work group and to abide by its norms than they are by opportunities for promotion into positions of power or the opportunity to achieve. This is hard for supervisors to understand. They think of and treat their subordinates as if they were motivated the same way the supervisors themselves are. Obviously this is not the case. Employees have various motives and, as this chapter has repeatedly shown, these motives are very complex. The next chapter uses the need for affiliation as a point of departure for the discussion of employees in groups, and Chapter 15 looks at the details of work motivation and some of the actual approaches that can be used by supervisors to motivate their employees.

THE FRUSTRATION MODEL

An extension and refinement of the motivation process is the use of the frustration model to provide insight into employee behavior. Frustration results when a motivated drive is blocked before the intended goal is reached. Figure 12-3 depicts the frustration model.

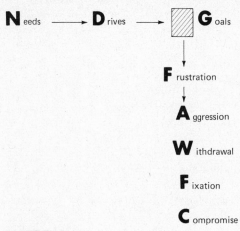

FIGURE 12-3
The frustration model.

As shown, there are four major categories of behavior that result from frustration: aggression, withdrawal, fixation, and compromise.

The Aggressive Reaction

The aggressive reaction to frustration arises when a person tries to remove by violence, either physical or symbolic, whatever is standing in the way of a desired goal. For a long time, psychologists believed that frustration always led to aggression and that all aggression could be traced to frustration. This "frustration-aggression hypothesis" is no longer generally accepted. Instead, aggression is now felt to be just one of the major reactions to frustration.

A very simple example of aggression would be that of a thirsty person who is driven to seek water—the goal in this case. Let us say that a barrier—a stuck door—stands between the thirsty person and the goal. Since this barrier prevents the person from attaining the goal, the person becomes frustrated and reacts aggressively by kicking the door or swearing at it.

A more complex example might involve a member of a minority race who has strong needs for power and achievement. These needs are aimed at a goal of a high-level job in a large organization. The drive in this case would be to search for such a job by applying and interviewing. If this person encounters barriers in the form of prejudice and discrimination, which prevent him from obtaining the desired job, he might react (aggressively) by throwing a Molotov cocktail through the window of one of the firms that rejected him. Or, after having been rejected, he might taunt the personnel manager, calling him or her a "bigoted, redneck honkey."

These examples show that the frustration model can explain very simple aggressive behaviors such as kicking or swearing at stuck doors or more complex antisocial behaviors such as violent race riots and hatred. But what about employee behavior? As has been pointed out in this chapter, employees have a wide variety of needs. Motivating these employees would be easy if the paths to their goals were free of any obstacles. Unfortunately, this is not the case. There are numerous barriers (e.g., job design, bureaucratic rules, and supervisors themselves) that prevent employees from attaining their goals. Some employees react to these barriers in an aggressive manner. When frustrated, they may lash back by hitting the supervisor in the mouth or swearing at him or her. More likely, they will displace their aggression by stealing from the organization or deliberately sabotaging the operation. Stealing and destructive sabotage are tremendous problems in organizations of all kinds across the country. The frustration model helps to provide insight into this type of undesirable behavior among employees.

The Withdrawal Reaction

Another form of reaction to frustration is to back off or withdraw from the barrier that prevents one from attaining a goal. In the case of the frustrated thirsty person, this reaction would consist of simply backing away from the stuck door or perhaps saying something like: "The doors around here never work." The latter example is a variation of withdrawal called regression, where the individual reverts to a less mature, childlike way of behaving. Withdrawal in the case of the minority person who met a barrier of prejudice and discrimination would involve an acceptance of defeat. He would stop looking for a good job and stay at home, sit on his doorstep, or hang around the street corner, drawing his welfare check. He would become a dropout from society.

In the work setting, withdrawal is a more socially acceptable reaction to frustration than is aggression. When an employee is prevented from attaining motivated goals, he or she is much more likely to withdraw than to react aggressively. Such withdrawal may, for example, take the form of apathy or daydreaming. All one has to do is look in on or briefly spend some time at a modern office or factory to see that many employees show the symptoms of withdrawal. The case of these "blue-collar blues" or "white-collar woes" is most often said to be a "motivation problem." Most supervisors will look at an apathetic, daydreaming employee and conclude that this person has "no motivation." But supervisors should remember that there is no such thing as a person with no motivation. People are motivated all the time (unless they are dead). The key to effective supervision is finding a way to channel that motivation toward rather than away from organizational goals. The apathetic daydreamer may well be a highly motivated individual who has been frustrated on the job.

The Fixation Reaction

In the fixation reaction, a person simply pretends that the barrier does not exist. The thirsty person, for example, might simply keep trying the door over and over again, finally getting to the point of knocking her head against it. The frustrated minority member would continue to knock on employers' doors, pretending that prejudice and discrimination did not exist. He would then be reacting the way many in our society expect him to react—ignoring the prejudice and discrimination and "pulling himself up by his own bootstraps." Unfortunately, this type of fixation reaction seldom brings down the barrier in question.

On jobs, the fixation reaction is typified by the plodder or the bureaucrat who pretends that the barriers are not there or simply puts up with them. This type of employee is frustrated but reacts by "knocking his head against the wall." This reaction is somewhat pathetic, but it may not cause any problems for the supervisor. Therefore it is often not noticed or considered to be a problem and no attempt is made to correct it. The supervisor should realize, however, that fixation is just as useless for achieving goals as are the other reactions to frustration.

The Compromise Reaction

The last major type of reaction to frustration is compromise. If the motivated individual is blocked from attaining the desired goal,

315

another goal with a clear path to it may be substituted or another path to the original goal may be taken. On the surface, this appears to be a logical and acceptable solution to the problem of frustration. Unfortunately, the substitute goal is invariably less desirable and the alternative path much more difficult to follow.

The thirsty person who is prevented from reaching the water fountain (the goal) out in the hall may, instead, drink a half-empty cup of coffee she finds in the room, or she may try to climb out the window and go in the front door in order to reach the water fountain. The minority job-seeker, having failed to obtain a good job, might join a radical nationalist group, which serves him as a substitute means of expressing his needs for power and achievement. Another possibility is that he may attempt to reach his goal by going back to night school and becoming overqualified for the type of position he is seeking (that is, he will take another route to the goal).

Employees very commonly react to frustration through compromise. They are prevented from obtaining need fulfillment on the job, so they compromise and "live outside the job." They express their needs through community activities or perhaps a hobby. They may find an alternative path to their goals through extra schooling or perhaps through an unauthorized strike. This is a sad commentary on modern organizational life. There are so many barriers preventing people from attaining goals that they are forced to channel their motivation outside the job or into undesirable reactions such as aggression, withdrawal, or fixation.

The solution to the problem of frustrated employees is relatively simple. The barriers that are preventing people from attaining goals must be removed. To be sure, some of these barriers lie beyond the direct control of the individual supervisor. The technological environment (e.g., the assembly line) and many of the bureaucratic rules that are causing employees to feel frustrated cannot be eliminated by supervisors alone. But many of the other barriers can. The previous chapters and those that remain all indicate ways in which supervisors can eliminate employee frustrations and channel the tremendous, largely uptapped motivation of today's employees *toward* instead of away from organizational goals.

■ KEY CONCEPTS

Personality
Modeling

Identification

Socialization

Perception

Learning

Motivation

Frustration

■ PRACTICAL EXERCISES

(These can be performed by individuals or by groups.)

1 One of the sections in this chapter is titled "Why Understanding Personality Development Helps Us Understand Employees." In your own words, describe and give examples of the processes of personality and explain why some knowledge of them can help a supervisor understand his or her employees better.

2 What are the major psychological processes? Take a particular job behavior that you have observed recently and attempt to analyze and explain it in terms of these processes.

3 List specific examples of the four reactions to frustration that you have observed.

■ DISCUSSION INCIDENTS

Jimmy Jones, age 20, has been on the job for two months. This is his first full-time job after his graduation from trade school. He has long hair and is very bright. His supervisor, Charlene Aims, has been with the company twenty-one years. Charlene has never married and expects to stay on as supervisor until she retires. Almost immediately, Jimmy and Charlene started to have differences, and now it is getting to the point where something has to give. Charlene called Jimmy into her office and said, "You young long-haired guys are all alike. You think the world owes you a living. What do you want? I am at my wits end trying to find out what makes you tick. I don't have any real quarrel with your performance, but you sure rub me wrong. What do you have to say for yourself?"

1 How would you answer Charlene's question if you were Jimmy? How can you explain the personality clash in this incident?

2 What is going on here in terms of Charlene's perception of Jimmy? What are some of Charlene's motives? Jimmy's motives?

While growing up, Jake O'Brien had developed very high needs for achievement and power. However, when he got into high school, he could not abide by the rules and he finally dropped out. As a high school dropout, the best job he could get was pushing a broom. One day his supervisor remarked, "Boy, is that Jake O'Brien ever lazy. He seems like he is in another world. He is always daydreaming and is really a motivation problem."

1 If Jake had such high needs for achievement and power, how do you explain his dropping out of high school and his present problem of motivation?

2 What do you think the probabilities are that Jake might become a union organizer? How would you explain this?

GROUP DYNAMICS, DECISION MAKING, AND MEETINGS

CHAPTER 13

John was an excellent auto mechanic. He worked hard for fifteen years for an auto dealer, saved his money, and last year opened his own shop. The shop was a new concept. Its only function was to balance, align, and service front ends. At first, business was slow and John was on the brink of bankruptcy. Then, after about six months, business picked up. After some advertising in the local newspaper, both individual car owners and auto dealers caught on to the idea that front-end work was specialized and that John's place could do the best job at the lowest price.

Now, after suffering through the growing pains of establishing a new business, John is experiencing a new problem. When he first started, he had one part-time and two full-time employees. Now, he has ten full-time people and, he says, he also has all the problems that ten people could possibly have. When asked to describe the situation, John is very discouraged: "Sometimes I think I'm running a zoo, not a garage." He then goes on to describe the following recent events:

Well, there's just a lot of crazy things happening. Sometimes they're downright bizarre. Take last week. Fred took the grease gun and completely filled Harry's tool box. Everybody thought it was pretty funny, but now Harry won't even talk to Fred. To make it worse, Harry used to be our best producer, servicing as many as a dozen cars per day. Now he's lucky if he does six or eight. The horseplay has just gotten out of hand. One of the favorite tricks is to sneak up and hide a guy's tools when he's got his head under the hood. There's just a lot of that type of junk going on. I wouldn't mind so much except that I really think it is beginning to hurt our productivity. And it always seems that they pick on my best workers. In fact, Bart, who is my best man and has been with me from the beginning, quit about a month ago. He just got fed up with all the horsing around. I really don't know what to do. I can take care of the technical and financial problems and all the other things it takes to build a sound business like this, but this kind of stuff . . . I really wonder if it's worth it sometimes.

Human Relations for
Effective Supervision

■ LEARNING OBJECTIVES

After reading this chapter, you should be able to have:

An understanding of the characteristics and dynamics of groups

The information needed to help structure and develop strong, cohesive, and productive work groups

The ability to analyze group processes and potential problems

An appreciation and understanding of informal groups

An understanding of the decision-making process

Knowledge that will aid in the selection and use of specific techniques for effective decision making

Guidelines and pointers to help conduct effective meetings

While not all groups are as troublesome and difficult to deal with as those working in John's garage, it is nevertheless important to understand the behavior of employees in groups if one expects to supervise people effectively. The purpose of this chapter is to provide a basic understanding of the nature and dynamics of groups and to suggest specific techniques and guidelines for generating group support and managing groups effectively in decision making and during meetings.

GROUP DYNAMICS

A group can be defined as two or more people who come together to pursue a common purpose. The word "dynamics" implies power and change. The study of group dynamics, therefore, is the study of the power of groups and how they change. A group tends to be dynamic. It contains sources of power and change. "Group dynamics" suggests that a group is something more than the sum of the individual members. Thus, a unique and important characteristic of groups is the way individuals change when they become members of a group. That is, groups tend to highlight, magnify, and bring out characteristics of individuals that were not formerly apparent. In other words, groups are not merely collections of individuals. Something unique happens when people come together in a group.

Two examples will serve to illustrate group dynamics. First is a recent news story reporting an auto accident in which a man was pinned under a car. His wife (who weighed 138 pounds) and his 7-year-old son lifted the 4,200-pound car off the man. It seems impossible that they should have been able to do this, but somehow

321

they did. Another example is the well-known story of the New York Mets, who were the world's champions in 1960. Preseason predictions by the experts clearly illustrated, through position-by-position and man-for-man comparisons, that the Mets did not have a chance of coming out on top that season, let alone winning the world championship. But the Mets did win the World Series. In both examples, the group seemed to have more strength than the combined power of its individual members. The unique combination of the individuals' needs, abilities, and common goals produced a totally new dimension in the behavior and performance of the group. Just as two deadly chemicals, like sodium and chloride, can combine to make a life-sustaining substance like salt, the combination and interaction of individuals in groups can result in totally new dimensions of behavior.

The remainder of this chapter will focus on the unique characteristics of groups. Careful descriptions will be provided of the formation of groups and their unique methods for controlling members' behavior. In addition, special emphasis will be given to the techniques supervisors can use when working with groups. However, a word of caution is in order at this point. Despite the information provided here, in the final analysis, supervisors themselves must develop a unique style in working with their groups. The example of the master chef and the apprentice can illustrate the point. The master can teach the apprentice about recipes, temperatures, and the techniques of gourmet cooking. Yet even with this knowledge and instruction, the apprentice may never become a gourmet cook. This is because the style or approach that separates an ordinary cook from the gourmet cook cannot be communicated in a recipe or in technical instructions. Rather, something like a sixth sense seems to develop through understanding and experience. Similarly, the study of group dynamics in this chapter does not guarantee a supervisor's ability to become an effective group leader. On the other hand, knowledge of group characteristics and the techniques for working with groups will greatly improve a supervisor's chances of leading work groups effectively.

The Power of Groups

The sheer power of groups is often underestimated. To provide some idea of the power and potential locked into group dynamics, the following sections briefly summarize three of the best-known studies of group dynamics.

The bank wiring room at Hawthorne The first scientific study of work groups was part of the famous Hawthorne studies conducted more than forty years ago. The "bank-wiring-room phase" was planned after a series of interviews with workers had suggested the power of informal groups. For example, workers were more interested in following the informal group norms (rules of behavior) than they were in following the formal organization's norms. In order to learn about these dynamics more directly, a study was set up in which one of the researchers became a member of the bank wiring group. This group's major responsibility was to connect and solder wires onto large pieces of electrical equipment called banks. Estimates based on time studies showed that each worker should make about 7,000 connections per day, which would mean 2½ banks per day. In fact, the workers in this group were averaging less than 6,000 connections or 2 banks per day.

The researchers found that despite the company's scientifically determined standards and the assumption of economic motivation (the more the group produced, the more money they made), the group established their own standards and enforced them rigorously. The informal group norm was 2 banks per day, as opposed to the official standard of 2½ banks. They enforced this norm through powerful social sanctions such as name-calling, ridicule, exclusion from the group, and even physical punishment through a game called "binging." The rules for the binging game were that a worker could punch another worker in the arm as hard as possible as long as the other worker had the right to return the punch. In order to enforce the informal norm, workers (called "rate busters") who produced above the agreed-upon amount were forced to play the game much more often than the other workers. Sometimes a worker would miss the rate busters' arm and hit other places. Thus, this study demonstrated for the first time that work groups not only set their own informal rules and standards but also had some highly effective and sometimes punitive means of enforcement.

Today, when supervisors like John (in the opening example) observe outlandish incidents such as one worker filling another's tool box with grease, nailing a worker's office door closed, or gluing somebody's coffee cup to the desk, it may be an instance of the application of sanctions against a violator of group norms.

The Asch conformity study Another famous study demonstrating the power of groups over individuals was reported by social psychologist Solomon Asch over twenty years ago. In his study, he asked individuals to judge the length of lines. The person was shown a card with several lines on it and was asked to pick the one that was equal in length to the one on the left. This task was very clear-cut and seemingly simple. The catch, however, was that all except one of the people in the experiment had prearranged with Asch to give clearly wrong answers on two-thirds of the line-judgment trials. Importantly, the unknowing subject went last. The results were very interesting. Almost 40 percent of the unknowing subjects gave in to the group pressure and gave clearly wrong answers.

Asch's findings are important to the study of work groups because they emphasize the great power that the group has over individuals. If the group can have such dramatic influence over individual judgment in a black-and-white situation like Asch's experiment, it is not difficult to imagine how groups influence individuals in situations where the correct answers are less obvious, such as questions involving union-management disputes, the effectiveness of new work methods, or the dismissal of a worker.

Decision-making studies Besides the famous Hawthorne and Asch studies, there have also been a number of widely recognized studies demonstrating the impact of group dynamics on individual decision making. Perhaps the most famous was conducted during World War II by the recognized father of group dynamics, Kurt Lewin. At that time there was a severe meat shortage and housewives were encouraged to buy less expensive cuts of meat, such as liver and beef tongue, to help alleviate the shortage. Lewin tried several methods to get the women to purchase the less desirable cuts. First he tried the traditional lecture method, where the women listened to a speaker who provided information and rational arguments for buying the less expensive cuts. At the conclusion of the meeting, the women freely voted to begin following this advice. Yet, after a follow-up study, it was found that their purchasing patterns had not changed. In another group, a discussion method was used. Here, the women openly discussed the problem and exchanged their own ideas and information as a group. Then, together, they decided to begin purchasing the less expensive cuts. Follow-up research showed that the purchasing patterns of these women changed dramatically. The change, for the most part, was attributed to the opportunity that the women had to freely present, discuss, and analyze their *own* feelings with other members of the group. As the individuals found that other members of the group had similar feelings and apprehensions, they became much more ready to actually go out and buy the less costly cuts of meat. On the other hand, the women in the lecture groups had little or no opportunity to discuss and analyze their feelings with each other. Thus, they really did not accept the reasons given by the lecturer, and they did not have the opportunity to receive social support from the other members of the group.

Since Lewin's study, numerous other researchers have demonstrated the importance of group dynamics in the decision process. Today, it is widely recognized that the dynamics of group participation are indispensable in situations where leaders expect to produce changes in group behavior. That is, rather than relying on supervisory edict to change behavior, it is often far more productive to make use of group discussions and group decisions, which greatly increase the probability that the behavior will change. A good example of how this group interaction might be used is the safety meeting. Traditionally, workers are lectured on the need to wear protective equipment and to follow safe work practices. Lewin's research suggests that promoting a free and open discussion on safety procedures would produce much more actual safety behaviors on the job.

How Groups Form

Over the years, there have been many explanations for group formation. Most of these cite some specific needs which groups are able to fulfill for individual members. For example, one common explanation for the formation of labor unions is that they fulfill workers' social, economic, and security needs. Similarly, the needs for affiliation and self-esteem appear to be related to the formation of professional groups. Other needs which have been cited as important in group formation include the needs for identification, safety, self-actualization, and social support. In addition, several experts on group dynamics have suggested that people with common backgrounds, those living or working in close proximity, and those with common goals are most likely to form groups.

The ideas and theories of group formation are best summarized in terms of a simple exchange theory. As applied to groups, this theory says that people contribute their time and energy to groups in exchange for the fulfillment of their individual needs through group participation. Provided that the fulfillment of individual needs is more

Groups are very complex and potentially can be very powerful and have a big impact on organizational effectiveness (René Burri/Magnum Photos).

valued than the energies expended, individuals feel that they profit by the relationship and continue to participate in the group. This theory is summarized in Figure 13-1. It simply says that there must be a positive exchange—that the rewards must be greater than the costs—for individuals to become part of a group.

Factors Contributing to Group Strength

Very closely related to group formation and membership are the factors contributing to group strength or cohesiveness. Although research in this area is still being accumulated, the following factors have been identified as contributing to group strength and cohesion:
1 *Isolation.* One suggestion is that groups which are physically or socially isolated from other groups have more strength and cohesion

| Fulfillment of Individual Needs | − | Individual Time and Energies | = | Profit and Group Formation |

FIGURE 13-1
Exchange theory of group participation.

than those which are not. For example, the "group back on the shipping dock," isolated from the rest of the organization, often has members who are intensely loyal to the group.

2 *Size.* The viewpoints on how size affects group strength vary. Extremely small groups, although cohesive, may have little impact on the larger organization. They do not have the numbers to be powerful. On the other hand, extremely large groups are often ineffective because of communication problems and differences between group members. Groups of moderate size, say five to twenty members, are generally thought to be strongest.

3 *Face-to-Face Contact.* On the whole, it appears that groups with the greatest opportunities for face-to-face contact and interaction—other factors being equal—are more cohesive than those in which the members do not have this opportunity.

4 *Similarity or Homogeneity.* There are two opposing camps regarding the impact that the similarity of members has on group cohesiveness. On one side, there are those who say that the more similar the individuals within the group, the greater the likelihood of group strength. This viewpoint can be demonstrated in organizations where the "old-timers" often band together and exclude newer employees. The other viewpoint says that groups that contain individuals with widely differing abilities and characteristics are likely to be more cohesive. This view would especially apply to groups like research teams, where the different abilities of the members might prove complementary, each providing a different function. Thus, a cohesive research unit might include people specially qualified in the roles of organizer, technical specialist, social coordinator, and spokesperson for the group. This diversity would tend to strengthen the group.

5 *External Pressure.* The common view is that outside pressures and forces exerted on a group can often produce greater cohesion and strength. Thus fringe groups such as homosexuals, political radicals, and prisoners are often viewed as gaining increased cohesiveness as a result of societal pressures. Similarly, small, isolated groups in work organizations (e.g., computer technologists, accountants, industrial engineers, or highly skilled operating personnel) may gain cohesive-

327

ness if they perceive conflict from the larger organization. The same could be said for the nurses in a hospital or the laboratory technicians in a police department.

Supervisors with knowledge of these factors can better understand why some groups seem very close and others do not. Armed with this understanding, supervisors can also promote or discourage group strength and cohesiveness.

How Groups Control Their Members

One aspect of group behavior that is particularly important to supervisors is the way in which groups control their members. Supervisors who are aware of these mechanisms of control can better interpret and explain the behaviors of their work groups.

Norms or standards Norms were mentioned earlier and were said to be standards, guidelines, or expectations for behavior. Norms ensure consistent and predictable behavior within groups. Some common examples of group norms found in organizational life include rules about the following:

1 *Dress.* There are usually implicit expectations regarding dress for different groups in organizations. Male managers are usually expected to wear coats and ties and female managers are expected to wear dresses or pantsuits. Supervisors are expected to dress differently than their staff. Sometimes these differences are very subtle, but they are usually rigorously enforced by the group.

2 *Titles.* Very often, people at the same level in an organization are expected to address each other on a first-name basis. However, people of lower organizational status are usually expected to address those with greater status by such titles as Mr., Mrs., Ms., Sir, or Dr. However, like styles of dress, this norm is changing in some organizations where all employees, regardless of level, are expected to address each other by their first-names.

3 *Flexibility of Time.* Although many organizations set specific times for arriving at and leaving work, for coffee breaks, and for lunch periods, there is usually an informal group norm regarding the degree of flexibility allowed. Thus, it may be acceptable to take ten minutes extra at coffee break and fifteen minutes at lunch. Similarly, workers may expect fifteen minutes of cleanup time at the end of a shift. Supervisors who attempt to counteract these time norms may encounter extreme resistance from work groups, including turnover, sabotage, and work slowdowns.

4 *Productivity.* As was brought out in the discussion of the Hawthorne studies, groups often set up their own productivity norms. Just as students who raise their hands too often in class or volunteer to do extra work are frequently ostracized by their classmates, employees who work above the group norm or suggest more effective work methods are often ridiculed as "rate busters," "company men," "scabs," or "brownnosers." The restrictive group norms for productivity are by no means found only in industrial settings. University professors, for example, often become jealous of and criticize their most productive colleagues. Similarly, athletes, both professional and amateur, frequently find personality flaws in the superstars and are very critical of them.

These are but a few examples of group norms found in modern organizations. Although many seem very petty, they do exist and all supervisors must recognize and face up to this fact. Moreover, such norms can serve some very important functions for groups. First, they stabilize the relationships and behaviors in the work environment. For example, it is important for employees to know that they can take an extra fifteen minutes for lunch without harassment. Because the employees know that the supervisor does not have to allow this practice, they may be more likely to be cooperative when the supervisor needs a little extra effort or time. Second, norms help to set apart the different groups in an organization. Thus, within almost all organizations, there will be noticeable differences in the norms for various groups such as computer programmers, doctors, accountants, machinists, hourly workers, salaried employees, executives, and secretaries. The differences between these various groups suggests a third characteristic of identification. That is, just by the very fact that there are different expectations for different groups, each group has its own individual identity. Thus, each group can claim an individual identity and derive from this a feeling of satisfaction and a unity of purpose. The challenge for the supervisor is to get these groups moving toward the deaprtment's and overall organization's goals rather than at cross purposes with them.

Role expectations A role consists of the behavior that is expected of a person in a given position. It is like the role an actor has in a play. Supervision involves certain role expectations. Chapter 1 was devoted to these roles of the modern supervisor.

Besides supervisory roles, there are prescribed roles for every type of position in the organization and in the various formal and informal groups. Most members of organizations play more than one role. For example, a male employee may have the roles of machine operator, husband, father, son of elderly parents, bowling-team member, and church member. Similarly, a female employee may have roles of supervisor, mother, daughter of elderly parents, wife, homemaker, and Girl Scout leader.

Supervisors should realize that, many times, these multiple roles conflict with one another. For example, there may be a conflict between the organizational role and a personal role such as that of parent. Another conflict may occur when a supervisor is promoted from within his or her own work group. Such a supervisor's new role of directing people who were once coworkers often conflicts with the group's expectations. It is hard for the group to realize that this individual is now the boss, where before he or she was simply "one of the gang."

There are several things supervisors can do to minimize or reduce role conflicts. First, whenever a person within the work group is given new responsibilities, these responsibilities should be clearly communicated to *both* the individual and the work group. Second, the supervisor who is caught in a conflicting role situation should carefully consider exactly which expectations are creating the conflict. Then the supervisor's role should be clarified with both superiors and the work group through mutual discussions regarding the conflicts. Also, supervisors should make a determined effort to clarify their roles through their behaviors. Finally, supervisors can minimize role conflicts within their groups by making sure that each employee has a full understanding of his or her job description and responsibilities.

The implications of status Besides norms and roles, another mechanism of group control is status. Status is the relative position one holds in the group. Status indicates the relative amounts of power, authority, and prestige held by individuals within the group. Although, in the final analysis, an individual's power, authority, and prestige are determined by other people's attitudes, status is commonly communicated through various symbols. Some examples of status symbols found in today's organizations include the following:

Work Areas. In many organizations, characteristics of offices and work areas indicate status. The floor the office is located on and its windows, carpeting, furniture, walls, and bathroom facilities confer status. In operating areas, similarly, the equipment, tools, locker rooms, and amount of physical space can communicate status.

Titles. A person's title confers status. The functional designation of a supervisor (for example, production supervisor, office supervisor, floor supervisor, or desk sergeant) has definite status implications. But again, it should be remembered that status is relative and the ranking of functional titles depends on the situation. Thus, in a manufacturing plant, operations personnel generally have high status, but in a hospital they do not. Because titles are so important to most people, fancy titles have proliferated in recent years (e.g., janitors become maintenance engineers), sometimes taking the place of a raise. But because status is relative, a title loses its meaning as a status symbol if everyone has an impressive one.

Telephones. In some organizations, telephones indicate status. First of all, having your own phone implies status. But a step beyond that is the type of phone one has. Black telephones with manual dials are lowest on the status totem pole. Colored push-button phones with several extensions, colored lights, and a speaker for conference calls are at the top of the status ladder.

Dress. Dress also indicates status. For example, it may be acceptable only for managers to wear formal attire such as coats and ties or pantsuits. Similarly, hourly workers may wear yellow hats while supervisors wear white hats. The medical personnel in hospitals wear different uniforms, according to their status; and in military organizations, arm patches, decorations, hats, and uniforms represent different status levels.

Other Status Symbols. Other symbols of status in organizations include automobiles, nameplates, expense accounts, size of staff, diplomas, stationery, access to office supplies, size of budget, selection for training programs, invitations to organizational social functions, use of organizational facilities, and paid memberships in civic, professional, recreational, or social organizations—to mention only a few.

The need for status symbols In many respects, concern with status seems silly or petty. Yet status symbols do communicate important information regarding the relative authority, power, and ranking of individuals. Without status symbols, employee behavior can become very confusing and inappropriate. An example of the

331

need for status symbols comes from an organization that tried to get rid of all status symbols. The result was chaos. Managers and supervisors who had authority and power had extreme difficulties in directing and controlling their employees. The employees were confused and simply did not know who to respond to and in what manner. Within a few days after the experiment began, informal symbols of status began to appear, and shortly thereafter the organization reverted back to the formal status system.

Supervisors can be more effective by understanding the status system. First, petty arguments between employees about things like use of cars, equipment, and location of their offices or work stations are often more deep-rooted than they appear on the surface. Most often, the monetary costs involved in these disputes are minimal, but supervisors should understand that the real stake in winning or losing status disputes lies in self-esteem. Thus, status arguments must be resolved very carefully, with an understanding of the underlying psychological aspects of the dispute. Second, supervisors themselves need to be constantly aware of the status messages they are sending whenever they interact with employees. Failure to accept or utilize the recognized symbols of their position may diminish their authority and influence. Similarly, taking on the symbols of status before he or she has achieved the corresponding power and authority may create problems between the supervisor and cosupervisors or bosses. Finally, supervisors must be extremely careful of the way they allocate their resources, so that they do not unknowingly create status conflicts among members of their work groups. Thus, consideration should be given to dispensing work supplies, making work assignments, assigning work areas, and other matters which could be considered symbolic of status. In other words, supervisors must be very careful in the handling of status in the work group. If it is handled haphazardly or badly, there can be serious repercussions for the long-run effectiveness of the group.

The use of sanctions Sanctions are applied to enforce group norms. Some common sanctions, already mentioned, include name-calling, ridicule, ostracism (not speaking or including a person in the group), and physical or psychological harassment. As in the case of status, supervisors should not simply react to sanctions at face value.

What often appear to be isolated disputes among employees are really part of a total pattern of group behavior. Thus, when one worker fills another's tool box with grease, or hides another's equipment, or engages a colleague in a verbal or physical dispute, there generally are two sides to the story. The antagonist usually feels that the victim is seriously disrupting group norms and that sanctions are necessary, while the victim may be guilty of violating the group norms without even knowing it. A discussion with both parties, emphasizing the underlying causes of the behavior and pointing out both sides, can sometimes solve the problem. Similarly, supervisors who carefully observe such disruptive behavior may be able to influence group norms so that these disruptions will cease. In addition, discussions with the victims of sanctions may be helpful in aiding them to adjust to the work group and become accepted members of it.

Finally, it should be emphasized that not all sanctions are negative. There are also positive sanctions. For example, a supervisor who carries on a bull session with employees fifteen minutes after the official lunch period has ended is giving a positive sanction to the extended lunch period. Similarly, a supervisor who observes rude treatment of customers without commenting may be viewed as supporting this kind of behavior. Thus, supervisors must be particularly careful of their own behavior to make sure that they are not responsible for sanctioning counterproductive behavior. Some supervisors, for example, make themselves scarce during lunch breaks. In this way, the employees can take their extra fifteen minutes but never feel that it is officially sanctioned. If the group needs to be disciplined for productivity, the supervisor can then enforce the established lunch period without seeming to violate an informal agreement with the group.

Informal Groups/Organizations

A formal group is one in which the roles and relationships of individuals are designated by a recognized source of authority. Formal groups in organizations are specified by organization charts, committee assignments, and sometimes elections. An informal group, on the other hand, is one that does not have the official sanction of recognized officials. Most often, informal groups or organizations form through the personal preferences of the group members; they would include coffee-break groups, lunch groups, golf groups, and so on.

Traditionally, managers and supervisors have viewed informal groups as a source of irritation and disruption and have felt that they should be stamped out. Informal groups were commonly associated with such counterproductive behaviors as establishing productivity norms that were lower than organizational standards, encouraging unnecessary socialization that detracted from productive work, and creating unnecessary squabbles and friction among group members. Today, we know that this view of informal groups is not entirely justified. It is now recognized that there are deficiencies in the formal organization that can be corrected only by the informal group. For example, supervisors cannot tell employees through formal channels that they disagree with specific company policies. Yet as members of an informal group within the organization, they can and often do express discontent with upper-level management. In many cases, such behavior helps supervisors win the confidence of their employees. Second, the informal organization can help give employees a sense of meaningfulness, identity, and recognition where the formal organization does not. Informal leaders, social directors, and authorities emerge and are given recognition and status by the informal group. Finally, the informal organization can provide functions for the formal organization where it is deficient or has failed. Where a supervisor is particularly incompetent in functions such as planning and organizing, an informal leader usually emerges to help the work group out in these areas. The informal organization can also supplement the formal communications channels. In total, there is little question that informal groups can provide some very constructive functions for both individuals and groups within the formal organization.

Another important point that supervisors should realize is that informal groups emerge regardless of efforts to retard or eliminate them. Informal groups are a fact of organizational life. Supervisors really have little choice regarding the emergence of an informal organization within their formal work organizations. The issue then becomes how supervisors view and utilize these informal groups. Supervisors should try to use the informal organization to their own advantage, rather than fighting it or trying to eliminate it. They should make use of informal systems of leadership, recognition, communication, and work behavior. As in the case of the formal system, it is much easier and more effective for supervisors to work within the informal system than to try to work around it.

Before we leave informal groups, a special word must be said about informal leaders. Just as informal groups are inevitable, informal leaders are sure to emerge out of any group. These informal leaders can provide many functions such as planning, organizing, and even delegating work among the members of the work group.

When supervisors cannot be present then, to a large extent, informal leaders determine both the quality and quantity of the work accomplished by group members. If supervisors encourage these informal leaders, learn to work with them, and get them on their side, they will often find that their own effectiveness is greatly enhanced. On the other hand, if informal leaders are viewed as encroaching on a supervisor's power and authority and efforts are made to undermine or embarrass them, supervisors run the risk of undermining their own positions by turning the informal organization against themselves. Thus, as with other aspects of the informal organization, supervisors should generally attempt to work with rather than against informal leaders.

THE DECISION-MAKING PROCESS

One of the primary determinants of an effective supervisor is the ability to make good decisions. Most often supervisors do not make decisions in isolation. They interact with superiors, cosupervisors, and subordinates in this process; therefore decision making is covered in this chapter. After we review the basic decision-making process in this section, we shall focus, in the remainder of the chapter, on the contributions of groups and the specific techniques which can be used to make effective group decisions.

Steps in the Decision-Making Process

There is no universal agreement on the exact steps of the decision-making process. It must be remembered that any listing of steps such as this does not give a true picture of the way in which decisions are actually arrived at. They are not made in independent steps; in fact, all phases of decision making are interdependent and interrelated. That is, decision making involves a process designed to isolate an appropriate alternative. The particular sequence of events leading up to the decision is not so critical as long as the process enables the supervisor to make the appropriate choice.

While recognizing the limitations involved in defining steps for decision making, the following list helps structure the discussion and can give supervisors some helpful guidelines for making effective decisions:

1 *Identify the problem.* The first step in decision making is identifying the problem. Often, this step is viewed in a negative context, where supervisors are simply reacting to situations which are causing disruptions in the work group. Actually, supervisors should constantly be searching their environment for potential problems or opportunities to make significant improvements. The supervisor, by making careful observations of group dynamics and using his or her listening skills, can make the group a valuable source for identifying problems.

2 *Define the relevant variables.* Once the problem has been identified, it is important to assess the situation fully. This involves defining all factors contributing to the situation, potential factors which can influence the problem, and a list of all factors, human and work-related, which the problem affects.

3 *Develop alternatives.* The third step is gathering all information relevant to the problem and developing some possible alternatives. Here the task is to experiment with different combinations of relevant factors and to try to determine the outcomes of the various alternatives. Again, ideas and suggestions from the work group can help the supervisor to develop new and creative alternatives for solving the problem.

4 *Evaluate alternatives.* Having outlined as many courses of action as are feasible, the supervisor should consider the relative merits of each. Most often, no single alternative is clearly better than all the others. Each alternative has its own relative advantages and disadvantages. Moreover, there is often no way of quantifying the values of each alternative. Yet in most situations, choices can at least be narrowed or ranked.

5 *Make a choice.* Finally, the supervisor must make a choice. Usually there are a number of feasible alternatives, with the advantages and disadvantages of each balancing out. But one alternative must be selected; therefore the supervisor's chief aim is, normally, simply to arrive at a satisfactory decision. The choice problem can be illustrated by the problems of a cafeteria manager. The manager is asked to select the best food possible, considering taste, cost, ease of preparation, and nutritional value. Because people's preferences and their willingness to pay for food differ, the manager can probably never make a decision that will make all customers happy. Most situations faced by supervisors are similar. Supervisors generally have to consider many factors; when evaluating their decisions, they may value these various factors differently. Thus, only satisfactory decisions are viable. Group support and understanding of the decision is critical at this point, since resistance to the decision could arise from any one of the various considerations. Even though the supervisor has made the best choice, it will not be carried out unless it is accepted by the group, and a decision that cannot be executed is worthless.

6 *Implement the choice.* Once the choice has been made, it must be implemented into actual practice. Importantly, either delaying implementation or failing to make a choice also constitutes a decision. The supervisor should be careful to involve the group in this implementation phase.

7 *Provide for feedback and evaluation.* This final phase of the process is often ignored on the assumption that once a decision is made, it is final. Supervisors are often wrongly advised to consider their decisions as final, so that they stick to their guns regardless of the consequences. Such advice appears to be ill-considered. While it is true that many decisions must go through a trial period before they are accepted, none are irreversible. Throughout the process of implementation and for the duration of the decision, supervisors should constantly analyze the effectiveness of the course of action they have selected. When the basic nature of the situation changes or new alternatives are found which would lead to a more effective solution, a new decision should be implemented. This does not, however, suggest that supervisors should be constantly changing their minds and be inconsistent. In fact, unless the alternative is noticeably superior, it is probably better to stick with the original decision. Most groups will resist frequent, ill-considered, and inconsistent changes but will agree to accept changes if they can understand their purpose and can see their advantages.

These steps summarize the decision process. Once again, however, it should be remembered that decision making is a dynamic process in which these steps frequently overlap or blend together. For example, an employee may suggest a solution before the supervisor is even aware that a problem exists. Similarly, through lack of activity in an area, a supervisor may actually have made a decision unknowingly. In such cases, it is often helpful to trace through the steps in the decision process so that similar errors can be avoided or more favorable alternatives can be generated.

The Group's Role in Decision Making

Most decisions that supervisors make affect a number of people in the organization. For example, a supervisor's decision to purchase new equipment usually affects personnel in the financial area, higher

337

levels of management, and the employees who will be using the new equipment. Similarly, a decision by a supervisor in the wage and salary area of a personnel department to deposit employee paychecks directly into bank accounts affects each and every one of the employees. Even top-level managers who make financial decisions affect many employees' jobs because of the impact these decisions have on the health and solvency of the organization.

Because of the importance of getting decisions accepted, it has been falsely assumed that all employees affected by the decision should participate. Although, like other techniques and approaches presented throughout this book, such participation can be very helpful, a contingency approach to participative decision making must be used. Participative decision making will be more effective in some conditions than in others. Supervisors should take into consideration the following kinds of variables when trying to determine how much group involvement there should be in decision making:

1 *Complexity.* A great deal of evidence from research and practice indicates that when decisions are extremely complex, group involvement is very beneficial. The group provides specialized inputs in defining variables and suggests alternatives that the supervisor acting alone would be unlikely to come up with. At least for very complex decisions, a group, according to research, makes better decisions than an individual.

2 *Time.* There is little question that group decisions take much more time than individual decisions. If time is critical, therefore, group inputs may not be practical. However, there is evidence that, over a period of time, groups working together do become more efficient in their use of time.

3 *Participation.* There are conflicting views regarding the participation in decision making of the group members who will be directly affected by the decision. One position is that involvement is highly motivational and will lead to acceptance and commitment. Another is that the group participants may be extremely biased if the personal gains and losses resulting from the decision are likely to be great. Adopting the latter view, almost all organizations discourage employee participation in decisions affecting wage increases, promotions, and transfers. A compromise is to allow employee input in the steps of defining and developing the alternatives of the decision but excluding the employee from the choice process itself.

4 *Knowledge.* Another criterion for member participation is knowledge. If the supervisor has all relevant information, group participation may not appreciably affect the quality of the decision. However, if group members can provide additional information, their contributions are likely to result in a better decision.

5 *Importance.* Supervisors make literally hundreds of decisions each day: who will perform a particular task, whether the boss should be told about a particular problem, when to order materials and supplies, whether to send a package air mail or first class, etc. Obviously, many of these decisions do not affect the work group and many more are the kind that will be accepted without question. In other words, the majority of decisions should be made independently by the supervisor. Only important decisions and particularly decisions which directly affect the group as a whole should be made on a group basis. Expanding the group decision process beyond these boundaries can be an unnecessary drain on the time and talents of both the supervisor and the group.

6 *Probable Outcome.* Although they base their attitude largely on intuition, many practicing supervisors feel that the likelihood that an acceptable decision will come from the group is an important consideration. That is, if it is highly likely that the decision of the group will *not* be acceptable to either the supervisor or management, it would be pointless to pretend that the group had decision-making authority. In such a case, its decisions would only be overturned, and this would be detrimental to all concerned. That is, if the decision of the group will probably not be acceptable, group decisions should be avoided. On the other hand, if group input is critical, the group may be involved in the initial stages of the decision process but excluded from the choice process. In most cases, members of the group will accept their exclusion from the choice process if they are told of this arrangement beforehand.

It must be emphasized that these considerations—and particularly the recommendations—are tentative. Neither research nor practice has developed to the point where absolute rules or guidelines for group decision making can be provided. Each supervisor must carefully weigh considerations such as these in terms of simple common sense and personal experience in order to determine the best approach.

GROUP DECISION TECHNIQUES

Apart from the general implications of groups for decision making in general, there are a number of specific techniques which have been developed to help supervisors make better group decisions and manage their groups more effectively. These techniques include brainstorming, Delphi, nominal group processes, and meetings.

Brainstorming

The technique of brainstorming was originally developed by Alex F. Osborn to help advertisers be more creative. Today, it is a widely accepted way in which supervisors can use groups to come up with creative solutions for a whole range of problems. The term "brainstorming" describes what the technique is all about. Essentially, it means attacking a problem like a storm trooper, firing out ideas as fast as possible until one hits the target.

Most brainstorming sessions are relatively short, ranging anywhere from five minutes to a couple of hours. The group generally consists of anyone who may have a creative idea or insight on the topic to be discussed. At the beginning of the session, the leader introduces a topic or problem and the group begins throwing out ideas and solutions. The leader records these ideas on a blackboard or in some other way easily visible to the whole group. Even poor ideas are encouraged, since they may trigger a more productive idea in another group member. Throughout the session, members are urged to combine ideas or expand on the ideas of others. Criticism of ideas is strictly prohibited, since the purpose is to increase the number of ideas rather than to evaluate them. Humor, joking, laughing, and what Osborn called "freewheeling" are encouraged, since it is thought that such freedom will facilitate creativity. Throughout the session, the leader's main function is to record the group's ideas. Directive action by the leader occurs only when it is necessary to discourage evaluative remarks. Finally, after the group's energies are exhausted and a large number of ideas have been generated, the session begins to wind down. Figure 13-2 summarizes these steps.

The major contribution of brainstorming is in the early stages of the decision-making process. Brainstorming helps people and groups to expand their thinking, so that the decision maker has a more complete and diverse range of alternatives than with more traditional techniques. Only rarely, however, are decisions actually made during a brainstorming session. More often, the original group is disbanded and a second group is then picked to evaluate and discuss the ideas generated. Eventually, this group narrows the choices and the decision is made.

Brainstorming techniques can be used by supervisors to solicit

1. Generating Alternatives (15 minutes)
   a. All persons capable of contributing suggestions are invited to a meeting. The more varied the group, the better.
   b. The leader defines the problem.
   c. The craziest, wildest, and most ridiculous ideas are encouraged and criticism is outlawed.
   d. Quantity rather than quality of decisions are encouraged.
   e. The leader functions primarily as a recorder and moderator, ensuring that participants refrain from criticism and elaboration at this stage.
   f. The mood in this phase most closely approximates horseplay rather than serious, deliberative decision making.

2. Refining Alternatives (45 minutes)
   a. Ideas are elaborated upon, combined, and synthesized.
   b. Additional suggestions are included.
   c. Absolutely impossible or implausible alternatives are eliminated.
   d. The four or five best alternatives are identified.
   e. The leader serves primarily as a catalyst, stimulating conversation and participation from group members.

3. Choosing an Action Plan (unlimited time)
   a. The size of the group may be reduced, leaving only members with direct responsibility for the solution.
   b. Ideas are compared and evaluated by pointing out the advantages and disadvantages of each.
   c. The most advantageous course of action is selected.
   d. The leader plays a much more active role, making the selection of the final alternative where he or she is responsible.

FIGURE 13-2
The steps in brainstorming.

group ideas in a wide variety of areas. Formal sessions might be held to generate alternative ways of solving problems concerning such matters as quality control, productivity, absenteeism, work-group recognition, and behavior problems among employees. Figure 13-3 shows an example of a disciplinary problem on a more informal basis. The ideas and concepts behind brainstorming encourage supervisors to be less evaluative of group inputs when they are exploring alternative decision routes with both individuals and groups. Often, very brief sessions with small groups or even with an individual can help develop insights into problems.

The Delphi Technique

Another group decision technique designed to help supervisors in decision making is Delphi. This technique was developed by N. C. Dalkey and members of the Rand Corporation's "think tank." It can be briefly described as a method that uses anonymous input from group members and generates composite feedback on which predic-

Fire him	Reward him every time he does not do it
Promote him	Punish him every time it happens
Give him a new title without a change in responsibilities	Buy him lunch, dinner, or coffee and talk to him about it
Give him a written reprimand	Call a psychiatrist
Tell his wife and children	Send him to a doctor
Tell his coworkers	Put him on a different job
Have the general manager talk to him	Put a dunce cap on him
Put him on the night shift	
Lay him off	

FIGURE 13-3
Brainstorming alternatives for a
disciplinary personnel action.

tions or solutions may be based. The name comes from the oracle of Delphi, a shrine at which the ancient Greeks prayed for information about the future.

More specifically, Delphi involves the following types of steps:

1 *Panel Selection.* A panel of experts in the selected fields relating to the problem is usually selected. The more diversified the expertise on the panel, the better.

2 *First Round.* Members of the panel may be mailed brief questionnaires asking them to state, anonymously, their predictions on a specific issue and the corresponding reasoning.

3 *Compilation.* The predictions and the reasoning behind them are summarized into a composite format.

4 *Feedback and Second Round.* All members of the panel receive a summary of the estimates and reasoning and are asked to make a second prediction on the basis of this composite feedback.

5 *Convergence.* The process of compiling the information, feedback, and further predictions continues until there is convergence or the participants are no longer shifting their predictions and changing their rationale.

6 *Results.* The predictions of the final round are combined to yield the final estimate.

The key to the Delphi process is the anonymous input. Because of the requirement of anonymity, members of the panel are not intimidated by the games that are often played between members of traditional face-to-face decision-making groups. The anonymous input tends to eliminate the counterproductive effects that status, intimidation, emotion, face-saving, and argumentation can have in traditional face-to-face group decision-making procedures.

Delphi has been traditionally applied to making predictions where future conditions are complex and uncertain. For example, Delphi has been used to predict such things as the date at which the unit price of gas will equal that of electricity, the date at which gasoline prices will rise to $1 per gallon, or the length of a union strike. But Delphi can also be applied to more commonly encountered problems. For example, relevant supervisors could form a Delphi panel to predict such things as the date for moving to a new building, how long a particular piece of equipment will last, or the length (in time) of a particular product line.

In addition to these types of applications, Delphi, like other techniques of supervision, can be modified to meet supervisors' particular needs. One supervisor, for example, used the Delphi process to predict whether or not the new board of directors in his company would cancel an important project his work group was undertaking. Each member of the group was asked to record, anonymously, his or her best guess, together with the corresponding reasoning. The supervisor then summarized this anonymous input and held a group meeting to give the feedback information and predictions. The group, as it turned out, predicted that the new board would cancel the project. Later, much to their disappointment, they found that their prediction had been correct. But at least with Delphi, they were able to anticipate the problem instead of just reacting to it. Besides being used to make predictions, Delphi can also be applied to almost any problem faced by supervisors. It does take more time and effort than other group processes, but studies have shown that it can definitely be more effective than normal face-to-face interchanges.

The Nominal Group Technique

The nominal group technique (NGT) is a modification of Delphi. NGT tries to take advantage of both individual and group decision making. A nominal group is a "paper group"; it consists of a number of individuals acting independently whose actions are then added together. Briefly summarized, the steps of NGT are as follows:

343

1 *Problem Presentation.* The problem is presented to the group by the group leader.

2 *Individual Idea Generation.* Each member independently writes down his or her particular solution or approach to the problem. There is no interaction with other members. This is the nominal grouping phase.

3 *Round-Robin Recording.* Each member, in round-robin fashion, submits one idea or solution at a time, and these are visually summarized (on a blackboard or flip chart). However, the member's name is not necessarily associated with a given solution.

4 *Discussion and Analysis.* Each of the ideas/solutions is fully discussed, clarified, and evaluated by the group members. This is where the group interaction comes into play.

5 *Choice Activity.* The final choice of the group can be made by each of the group members rank-ordering the alternatives on a private ballot. Then the mathematical sum of the rank determines the choice. The choice can also be made on the basis of group consensus, or the supervisor can make the decision on the basis of what transpired in the other phases.

NGT can be applied by any supervisor. It can even be an approach to use on a supervisor-subordinate relationship. For example, the supervisor may approach a subordinate and work through a problem as follows: "Here is a problem I am faced with. Take a few minutes to think through how you would solve it. Okay, what do you think? Let's analyze and discuss those possibilities. Based on this, I think this would be the best solution. Do you agree?" In addition to this approach to problem solving with individual subordinates, the steps of NGT can be successfully applied to any group decision-making effort, such as the numerous committee or staff meetings held by supervisors. NGT has proved to lead to better decisions than the usual decision-making procedures of groups.

Like the Delphi technique, NGT avoids many of the dysfunctions of face-to-face decision making in groups (the first three steps avoid this). On the other hand, in step 4 of NGT, the advantages of face-to-face decision-making techniques come into play. There is accumulating evidence that NGT is more effective than normal group interactions; with simpler, nonpredictive types of problems, it is superior to the Delphi technique. Supervisors can use NGT for a wide range of problems, such as deciding what type of new equipment is needed, determining the best procedure for scheduling vacations, and deciding on new or improved safety or work procedures. Who will make up the group will depend on the type of decision to be made.

MEETINGS AS A FORM OF GROUP PROCESS

One of the most common ways work groups get together is in meetings. A meeting can be defined as any group of persons called together to interact for a specific reason for a specific time period. Besides providing a framework for decision making, meetings are also typically used to gather and disseminate information. Because so much time and effort goes into meetings, it is important for supervisors to be familiar with some guidelines that make them more effective.

Problems with Typical Meetings

One way of trying to make meetings more effective is to look at some of the major problems encountered in them. The following comments, which anyone who has spent any time in meetings may have made or heard, are representative of the problems involved:

1 *One-Person Domination.* "Wow! That was the worst one yet. I spent the whole afternoon listening to Frank harp on how his people never get any breaks . . . and that stupid Harry just doesn't have enough guts to tell him to shut up so we can get on with the purpose of the meeting."

2 *Wasted Time.* "When I was hired, I thought most of my time would be spent with patients, working out their treatment programs. Instead, I'll bet I spend over half of my time in meetings that are a big waste of time."

3 *No Purpose.* "I don't really know what purpose these meetings serve. All I know is that every other Friday I spend two hours listening to Margaret babble on and on about one irrelevant, insane thing after another. If there were a purpose for the meetings, I could see it. But if there isn't anything to talk about, why have a meeting?"

4 *No Follow-Through.* "Don't get me wrong; not all meetings are bad. But even when it seems that we've got a problem solved, most often, nothing ever comes of it. You know what I mean . . . we come up with solutions and still nobody ever does anything about them."

5 *Wrong Persons Attending.* "That really ticks me off! I asked John if I had to go to that meeting and he kept on saying how he needed my valuable input. Well, I sat there 2½ hours and the one time I did try to say something, John was the one who cut me off."

6 *No Agenda.* "If I could just plan a little bit, these meetings wouldn't be so bad. As it is now, you've got no idea what's going to be discussed. Like yesterday, I had to go all the way downtown in the middle of the meeting to get the records for the east section because Mel wanted to talk about it. If I'd known that beforehand, all those people wouldn't have had to wait for me."

7 *No Time Limits.* "They'd be OK if they'd just end sooner. The last half always turns into a bull session. I just don't have time for that stuff."

8 *No Priorities.* "We always seem to get hung up on the darndest things. You know what I mean . . . little unimportant trivia. Then there's no time left for the important issues."

9 *Hidden Agendas.* "It seems like somebody's always got an ax to grind. Like last Friday, Alice made a good proposal, but this other guy, Tim, was trying to get back at her for taking one of his best employees. He just kept on Alice until she dropped the whole thing."

These comments indicate that meetings can be very distressing for the participants and may lead to very poor results. Careful consideration of these criticisms, however, indicates that none of them is an inherent problem of meetings themselves. Instead, the problems are caused by both poor organization and ineffective leadership. The following section will discuss some practical suggestions and guidelines for conducting more effective meetings.

Guidelines for More Effective Meetings

The first area of consideration in conducting more effective meetings involves design, organization, and planning. Listed below are some guidelines that can help improve these aspects of meetings:

1 *Purpose.* The first step is determining the purpose of the meeting. If a specific purpose and objective for the meeting cannot be specified, it is probably unnecessary.

2 *Group Role.* After determining the purpose, the supervisor should carefully consider the role the group is to play in the meeting. For example, if the members of a group are informed that they are going to be asked to suggest decision alternatives but that the supervisor will make the final decision, they will usually be very cooperative. On the other hand, if the group members are given the impression that they will make the final decision and are then not permitted to do so, they will undoubtedly be uncooperative in future meetings. Both the group as a whole and the individuals in it should be fully advised of their roles so that their expectations will be realistic.

3 *Size.* The size of the group is an important consideration in planning meetings. Generally, groups of about five or six are about the right size for decision-making purposes. In larger groups, communications become difficult. In smaller groups, factions frequently develop, to the detriment of the purposes of the meeting. On the whole, however, the single most important consideration is the number of persons who can provide valuable inputs to the purpose of the meeting. Although there are some general rules of thumb, supervisors must use their own best judgment and common sense in determining group size.

4 *Participants.* Closely related to the above guideline is the selection of the participants. Generally, only those participants with a particular interest or expertise in the areas to be discussed should be invited to attend the meeting. If only a particular portion of the meeting is relevant for a particular person, he or she should be allowed to enter and leave the meeting while it is in progress.

5 *Agenda.* Once the previous guidelines have been implemented, an agenda will evolve naturally. It should include the purpose of the meeting, time limitations, major topics to be discussed, and a list of the decisions and actions which are expected to result from the meeting. The agenda is an important communication device which allows each member to prepare accordingly. If a written agenda is not possible, the leader should, when inviting people to the meeting, provide at least a verbal summary of the information.

6 *Time.* Meetings should have a stated beginning and end. Importantly, leaders should not wait for late arrivals, since this only punishes those who have arrived on time. The meeting should begin even if key personnel are absent. After initiating these practices, most supervisors find that, within reason, all personnel begin showing up on time. Moreover, it is also important to end meetings on time. Interestingly, it seems that the time required to make a decision is in direct proportion to the time allotted. If meetings *always* end on time, supervisors will find that the majority of the decisions are made within the scheduled time period.

7 *Use of Time.* A good rule of thumb is never to do anything in a meeting that could be done outside of it. Thus, the reading of printed material or discussions between the leader and individual members should take place either before or after the meeting.

8 *Process.* If the meeting has been called for the purpose of making a decision, the general outline of the decision process as presented above should be followed. During the meeting, the leader should be constantly appraising the group's progress and giving feedback on this to the group. For example, a leader might say, "OK, we've suggested five options, now let's take about five minutes to discuss each before we make our decision."

9 *Decision.* Finally, if a decision is needed, the supervisor should be prepared to give the final push that is sometimes needed to make the decision. Failure to do this can frequently negate all the preceding work and frustrate the group members.

The Role of the Leader in Effective Meetings

The meeting leader's role also plays a part in making meetings more effective. In meetings designed to communicate or disseminate information, the group leader usually assumes a fairly strong and authoritative role. However, during a problem-solving or decision-making meeting (i.e., meetings designed to maximize group input), the leader assumes a much different role. In this latter role, the leader is more like a referee at a football or basketball game. The referee lets the group know when the game begins and ends, clarifies rules and disputes, and makes sure the game proceeds in an orderly fashion. The final outcome of the game, however, depends upon the participants. Thus, the referee can be viewed as a person who helps groups to have a contest which is both orderly and fair and that ends in a positive fashion. Similarly, the leader of a meeting designed to solve a problem or make a decision can be viewed as a facilitator who makes sure that the group proceeds in an orderly fashion, allowing everyone to contribute to a good solution or decision.

Supervisors may find the following guidelines useful in conducting a meeting:

1 *Enforce the rules.* The leader of an effective meeting makes sure that the group meets its time deadlines and follows the agenda. When members stray too far from the agenda, the leader may make an appropriate remark such as: "John, what you're saying is interesting, but I think we're getting off the track. Let's try to stick to the agenda, and maybe we can include that issue in next week's meeting."

2 *Solicit inputs.* It is the leader's duty to make sure that everyone gets a fair opportunity to provide input, a chance to speak. A leader might encourage a nonparticipant with a question such as: "Hal, we've heard from everyone else, what do you think?"

3 *Clarify inputs.* A leader can help the group greatly by clarifying suggestions and summarizing inputs at the various stages of the meeting. In this way, the leader can be assured that all members are on track and trying to come up with the best solution or decision.

4 *Keep cool.* It is very important for the leader to remain calm throughout the meeting so that he or she can assess the group's progress accurately. The leader should be particularly careful not to be defensive when an opposite or unpopular viewpoint is presented. Both defensiveness and/or criticism of group inputs will retard creativity and stifle the effectiveness of the group.

5 *Resolve conflict.* Occasionally, members of the group will become engaged in arguments. The leader can usually terminate these by pointing out that such controversies will not help to resolve the problem at hand.

6 *Monitor hidden agendas.* As was discussed previously, there are often hidden and surface agendas in meetings. Surface agendas are the group members' apparent reasons for saying something. Hidden agendas are the real, underlying reasons for saying something. Leaders must be particularly aware of hidden agendas, since they can often retard the meeting's progress and frustrate the members. For example, one person may have an ax to grind with another member of the group and make this the hidden agenda of the meeting. In such a case, the leader must bring the group back on track with a comment such as: "Tim, I'm still not sure whether you're against Alice or her idea. I'd appreciate it if you'd stick to criticizing the idea instead of Alice." This technique is called leveling, and it simply lets the group know that the leader is aware of the underlying purposes of these comments. Generally, this leveling approach should be used only in extreme situations. Most often, leaders should remain aware of hidden agendas but purposefully and tactfully steer meetings through them.

7 *Assign action steps.* Finally, the leader has the job of assigning action steps at the conclusion of the meeting to make sure that what is agreed upon is actually implemented. This is usually a difficult task and sometimes a painful one, but it must be accomplished if the meeting is to achieve its goals.

These suggestions should serve supervisors as useful and practical guidelines in conducting effective meetings. Once again, however, suggestions should be interpreted in light of a participative group decision process. That is, the guidelines should be modified to fit the style of the individual supervisor and the type of meeting that is being conducted.

■ KEY CONCEPTS

Group dynamics and power
Group formation
Group cohesiveness
Norms
Roles
Status
Sanctions
Informal groups
The Decision-making process
Brainstorming
Delphi
Nominal group techniques (NGT)
Meetings

■ PRACTICAL EXERCISES

(These can be performed by individuals or by groups.)

1 Identify and list the specific factors which determine the norms and status in a classroom or other relevant organizational setting. You should also identify and discuss some of the sanctions used to control group behavior.

2 Estimate something such as the exact number of people in your school or other relevant organization by each of these methods: *(a)* average of the individual guesses, *(b)* the result of the nominal group technique used by one group, and *(c)* the results of the Delphi technique used by another group. Make sure the steps of Delphi and NGT are used as described in this chapter. After completing the exercises (other estimates or problems can also be used), answer the following questions:

Which of the three approaches seemed to be the most effective? Why?

What are some of the problems or limitations of the techniques that were used?

Would you use this technique in the future? How and where?

■ DISCUSSION INCIDENTS

Harry Haskins is the supervisor of a new department at a local television station. He has eight people under him, and—for the most part—they work well together. His "problem" is Betty Newcomb, his first and only female reporter. At first, Harry thought Betty would work out. But now, after a two-month trial period, Harry is doubtful. To him, Betty appears to be extremely nervous and increasingly more antagonistic toward him and the organization. Yesterday was the topper. Betty and Harry became involved in a bitter argument which ended with her calling Harry a male-chauvinist pig. She had three major complaints that Harry all but refused to consider. The complaints were:

1 That she was the only reporter without an office and was forced to share desk space with the women on the secretarial staff

2 That she was paid 10 cents an hour less than the president's secretary and almost $1 an hour less than her supposedly equal (male) coworkers

3 That she was the only reporter who did not have a company car

Harry agreed that Betty's observations were correct, but he said that these inequities were unintentional. He told her that she was getting upset over nothing and that eventually everything would work out.

1 Discuss this case in terms of role conflicts between *(a)* males and females and *(b)* the female role and that of a reporter.

2 Suggest a solution for Harry. Will this solution be acceptable to all members of the reporting staff? Why or why not?

Kevin Bradley, the construction supervisor, was really impressed with Sidney Ganes, his new employee. Sidney had more initiative than anyone he had ever seen before. He was always on the job at 8 A.M. sharp and ready to go. Sidney could keep at least seven bricklayers supplied while the other laborers could handle only about four. If asked to work overtime, Sidney was always ready and willing. At the end of the day, he would keep going right up to 5 P.M., whereas the other workers usually took fifteen to twenty minutes to wash up before quitting time. Although Sidney is a model employee, Kevin, the supervisor, is starting to worry about him. The other workers are beginning to exclude Sidney from their daily activities. For example, Al, one of the older guys, has gotten into the habit of sending Sidney off on some kind of bogus errand every time a coffee break comes near. Kevin has also noticed some strange behavior at lunchtime. The men eat at picnic tables, and in order to exclude Sidney, they put their lunch pails on the bench. If anyone comes along, they move a pail, but not for Sidney. The incident that was the real cruncher, however, happened yesterday when Kevin was away for the afternoon. Hank, a coworker with more seniority, told Sidney to move a pile of dirt from one side of the street to the other. Then, just when Sidney had finished the job, Al came over with the backhoe and moved the pile back across the street. Shortly afterward, Kevin returned to the job and Sidney dejectedly told him of the incident.

1 Explain and analyze the actions of the work group toward Sidney in terms of group sanctions. Does Sidney deserve this type of treatment from the group?

2 What can the supervisor do, if anything, to help Sidney become part of the work group? Is it inevitable that Sidney's productivity must suffer before he becomes part of the work group? Do you know of any similar incidents that have happened to you or that you have observed in the course of your work?

COMMUNICATING WITH EMPLOYEES

⑭ CHAPTER

"I don't know what to do about Bud and his 'rumor mongering,'" said Chuck Stacy, line supervisor for Collins Manufacturing. Bill Wolf, manager of production, asked Bud to be a little more specific. "Well, it wouldn't be so bad if Bud worked off in a corner someplace," he said, "but as you know, Bud is a materials handler, providing work materials to all our work stations to make sure the assembly line can continue without stopping. Because of his job, he has personal contact with everyone in our department. Thus, whenever Bud gets a spicy piece of information, you can bet that everybody else in the place gets it too. Last week, for example, everybody was excited about layoffs and slowing work down because there was a rumor about shutting down line number 10. I'm sure that Bud had a lot to do with that rumor and I just wish there was something I could do to stop him. Bill, do you have any idea on what I might do?" Bill just shook his head and said, "Sounds like a rough one, Chuck. You know we never fire anybody around here unless it's really something serious, and Bud's got a good work record. You're going to have to find a way to work around this one." Chuck was disappointed with Bill's reply. He felt that if he just knew a little bit more about communication, he could solve his problem with Bud and his boss. It just seemed like communication was breaking down in all directions on both organizational and interpersonal levels.

■ LEARNING OBJECTIVES

After reading this chapter, you should have:

An understanding of the organizational and interpersonal communication process

A grasp of methods for top-down, upward, and horizontal communication and how they can be effectively applied

Information that can help you better understand and utilize the grapevine (informal communication) in a positive manner

An awareness of ways in which information is inadvertently distorted and how this can be corrected

The ability to identify and interpret nonverbal communications

Knowledge of transactional analysis and how it can lead to more effective interpersonal communication

Communication is a personal process; it involves the transfer of ideas and information from one person to another. It is at the very heart of supervisory and overall organizational effectiveness. Communication is the primary method of providing employees with information and instructions about their jobs, the organization they work for, their job performance, rules, regulations, and everything else that is necessary for effective performance. Similarly, supervisors need to use the communication process in order to coordinate tasks and jobs in their work groups and gather the information they need to identify and solve problems or conflicts within their organizational units. In other words, effective communication is almost synonymous with effective supervision.

The importance of the communication process is also brought out by the tremendous amount of time supervisors spend communicating while on the job. Although the estimates vary, it is generally concluded that supervisors spend about two-thirds of their time communicating. Some estimates go as high as 90 percent. With this amount of time spent in communication, there should be little question of its importance to supervision.

By recognizing the importance of communication, the supervisor should not fall into the trap of considering all problems as being communication problems. Communications should not become a "crutch" for all the problems of supervision. It should be remembered that communication is a vital part of most of the other supervisory functions such as planning, organizing, and controlling. When communication problems do occur, they should often be interpreted in the context of the organizational process or activity in which they are occurring.

The purpose of this chapter is to provide supervisors with the techniques and skills necessary to communicate effectively. Two major perspectives of communication are provided. At first, an organizational communications perspective will be used, with specific emphasis on the description of communication and methods for communicating up, down, and across organizational units. The second and probably most important part of the chapter to the supervisor is communication viewed as an interpersonal process. This perspective emphasizes that boxes on an organization chart do not communicate with one another. Rather, communication is a personal process, and the key to better communications is a better understanding of people and how they relate to one another. The last part of the chapter uses the popular transactional analysis (TA) approach to provide insight into and improve interpersonal communication.

ORGANIZATIONAL COMMUNICATION

In an organizational communications perspective, each line on the formal organizational chart is considered to be a formal communications channel. Using the simplified organizational chart shown in Figure 14-1, the following channels (routes and patterns) of communications can be identified:

1 *All-Channel.* This communications network can be defined as an arrangement where all members may talk freely with each other. This network is represented by the board of directors in Figure 14-1 and the diagram in Figure 14-2. Besides boards of directors, all-channel networks are usually found in most committees and in areas like union contract negotiating teams. Research on all-channel networks generally indicates that they are very effective at solving complex problems and that individual members express high satisfaction with this arrangement. On the other hand, these all-channel networks generally take a great deal of time to arrive at a decision.

2 *Wheel.* The wheel network is where one member has two-way communications with all other members but where none of the other members are permitted to communicate directly with each other. The term "wheel" represents this network because the center has two-way communication with all members, but the other members can communicate only with the center. In Figure 14-1, this network is

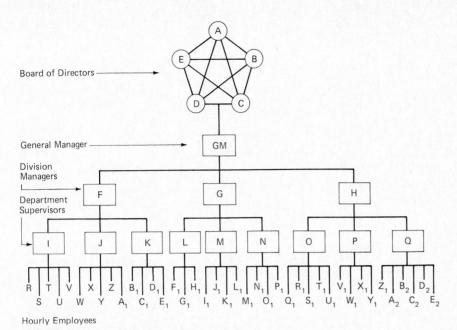

Board of Directors ⟶

General Manager ⟶

Division
Managers

Department
Supervisors

Hourly Employees

FIGURE 14-1
A simplified organization chart.

represented by the supervisory group in which the letter I designates the hub and R, S, T, U, and V are noncentral members. Figure 14-2 also shows this network. Research on wheel networks generally indicates that they make simple decisions efficiently. On the other hand, they are less effective in solving complex problems (mainly because the central member cannot process all the information), and the noncentral members often express discontent with their minor, uninteresting role.

3 *Chain.* The chain can be defined as a linear communications arrangement. This network closely follows the idea of the chain of command. In Figure 14-1, a simple chain is shown from GM to F, from F to J, and from J down to Z. Another chain arrangement occurs when V communicates to R_1: V to I, I to F, F to GM, GM to H, H to O, and O to R_1. Diagrams of chains are also included in Figure 14-2. The following conclusions are drawn from the research conducted on chains: *(a)* communication can be rapid if each member is diligent in relaying information; *(b)* distortion usually increases as the number of links in the chain increases; *(c)* satisfaction varies, with persons on the ends

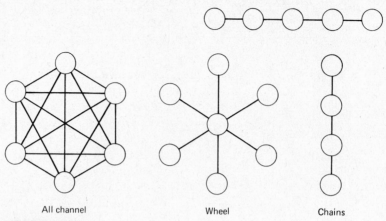

All channel   Wheel   Chains

FIGURE 14-2
Communications networks.

generally being less satisfied than persons in the middle; and *(d)* difficulty is usually experienced when the chain is used for problem solving. Chain arrangements are commonly used to issue orders or directions in organizations and to communicate across departmental or divisional lines.

These observations summarize some of the major communications networks which are typically found in today's organizations. Another way of looking at organizational communication is according to the directions in which communications can flow in an organization: from the top down, from the bottom up, and horizontally.

Top-Down Communication

Top-down communication involves the flow of information from policies, directives, memos, instructions, and decisions from the apex of the organization to the lower levels. The various networks discussed in the last section have some implications for top-down communication. First, because decisions at the top of organizations frequently make use of all-channel networks such as boards and executive committees, responsiveness and action at the top often appear to be quite slow. Thus, for example, a top-management committee may take a long time to decide a relatively minor issue such as whether or not to allow smoking privileges at employee work stations. Second, because chains of command from the upper to the lower levels may be relatively long, information is often lost or distorted by the time it reaches the lower levels. One study, for example, found that rank-and-file employees received only a small percentage of the information initiated by the board of directors that was intended to be fully communicated. Supervisors, of course, are vital linking pins in the top-down process. They are the critical link between management and the employees. Thus, the success or failure of top-down communication is largely due to supervisors. Once again, this observation points out the important role that supervisors play in the effectiveness of organizations.

Finally, because of the generally long chains of command involved in top-down communication, it frequently happens that persons at the top of organizations are unaware of the needs for information and communication at the lower levels. Several studies have demonstrated this by asking both managers and employees to rate employee needs. The general findings are that managers at the upper levels of organizations are very unaware of and have misconceptions about their employees' needs. For example, one study found that the three needs rated at the top by employees were rated at the bottom by management.

Somehow information gets distorted or even lost as it goes from top to bottom. One way to overcome this problem is to use more than one medium. The idea here is that if employees receive the information in several different ways on several different occasions, they are more likely to receive what is intended. Using this approach, supervisors are encouraged to make full use of traditional communication techniques such as speeches, meetings, bulletin boards, letters, newsletters, posters, public address systems, reports, handbooks, and magazines. Today, additional emphasis is being given to newly developed and specialized mass-media techniques such as conference telephones, closed-circuit television, and computerized information systems. Yet, despite the potential these mass-media techniques have for improving downward communication, they are not the complete answer. With a mass-communication system that is very sophisticated technologically and by which employees are continually bombarded with information from above, it is still possible to have ineffective downward communication.

Because of dissatisfaction with the mass-media approach to downward communication, efforts have been made to understand people's needs for information more thoroughly. The key to this

359

approach is not more information from the top down but, rather, more communication from the bottom up, so that the needs of the people receiving the information can be more fully understood. This perspective leads us to the upward communication process.

Upward Communication

Upward communication is assuming increased importance in organizational communication. Supervisors can become aware of the important problems, concerns, and needs of their workers through the upward system. Moreover, employees can often provide input to supervisors in helping solve technical and organizational problems.

Because upward communication has traditionally been ignored, techniques are just starting to be developed. The following sections briefly summarize the major techniques for upward communication.

The grievance procedure The grievance procedure has been around for a long time but has been ignored as a possible channel of upward communication. It has been ignored because of its negative connotation. Supervisors often feel that whenever a grievance is filed, it is a black mark against them. As a result, they do everything possible to squelch or discourage grievances. Similarly, employees often feel that grievances are an affront to their supervisors and therefore file only when they are extremely upset.

However, supervisors can view the grievance procedure as an upward communication device and a way of measuring potential problems before they arise. For example, the specific reason for the grievance may be unimportant, but it can become an important indicator of employee dissatisfaction. The grievance becomes a way for the supervisor to hear out employee complaints.

As was brought out in Chapter 11, the first step of the grievance procedure is listening, not arguing. Although apparently contrary to good employee relations, it may actually be beneficial to encourage employees to file more rather than fewer grievances. If this is encouraged, however, then employees must understand that the grievance process is a method of working out differences constructively. The same goes for top management. They must also realize what the grievance process is being used for and not penalize supervisors who are getting a lot of grievances. Some organizations are currently taking this approach and are finding upward communication significantly improved as a result.

Team development Besides the grievance procedure, a more recent approach to generating upward communication is team development. In a team-building approach, surveys, interviews, and meetings are used to identify potential problems and enhance cooperation. This, of course, promotes upward communication. Although the specific steps differ, the following represents a typical approach to team building:

1 *Data Collection.* First, a survey, interview, or meeting is conducted to collect data that will help identify problem areas. The questions that are asked are directed at planning, work-unit goals, quality and quantity standards, cooperation, and supervisory competence in areas such as providing employees with feedback on performance, discipline, and training.

2 *Problem Identification.* The second step in team development usually involves a meeting. During the meeting, the team is given a summary of all of the information collected in the first step. The team thoroughly discusses all aspects of the data so that most of the major problems are identified by the end of the session.

3 *Setting Priorities.* The next step involves arranging the items to be worked on in order of priority. The relative importance of the various problems is discussed, but the team refrains from coming up with solutions at this point.

4 *Problem Solving.* At this stage, attempts to solve the problems are made by following guidelines such as the following: *(a)* discussing the problem and its impact on people and the organization; *(b)* identifying alternatives to solving the problem; *(c)* selecting the appropriate alternative through a process of consensus and agreement; *(d)* assigning specific action plans and responsibilities to the person or persons who are going to work on the problem; and *(e)* establishing target dates for reviewing progress. Other group problem-solving techniques—such as the nominal grouping technique (NGT) discussed in the last chapter—can also be applied by the team.

Some disadvantages are associated with the team building process. First is the fact that developing a team in the manner described above takes time. It can also be risky to the extent that a problem will arise that cannot be adequately resolved and may therefore become a bigger problem than it was before. It is difficult to be an effective team leader. Supervisors who use this approach must make sure that the group feels free to participate and provides input, but they must also be fairly directive to ensure that the steps outlined above are followed. Because this is so difficult to accomplish, it is recommended that team development be conducted by professional third-parties, i.e., outside consultants. However, supervisors who understand the process and feel comfortable with it can be effective team builders.

Meetings as a form of upward communication The last chapter discussed in detail all aspects of meetings. It is obvious but seldom pointed out that meetings can be used to generate upward communication. Specifically, if the supervisor remembers to play the role of the facilitator and listener rather than the director, meetings can serve this purpose very effectively. Moreover, by utilizing some of the previously discussed team-development techniques during meetings, most supervisors will find that their meetings can effectively serve to identify and solve problems.

Open-door policies Some supervisors maintain at least an unofficial open-door policy. The idea behind this is that whenever an employee has a problem or grievance, he or she should feel free to discuss the situation openly with the supervisor. Some organizations go a step further and encourage employees, if they are not satisfied with the response and follow-up given by the supervisor, to go to the next level in management.

Unfortunately, the open-door policy often turns out to be "open" in name only. The door is open, but woe to the person who registers a complaint. To improve upward communication, supervisors should reward the employee who is willing to explain a problem to them, even if they disagree. The supervisor might say something like: "John, I want to thank you for letting me know how you feel about this. As you are aware, I don't agree with you, but I do want to emphasize that I'm glad that you told me how you feel." In this manner, employees will feel more free to communicate with supervisors, even when the supervisor disagrees. In other words, the open-door policy can become an effective method of upward communication if it is a reality, but it can backfire if supervisors are not sincere about it.

In addition to the ways discussed so far, supervisors can also use such methods as suggestion systems, group discussions, recreational activities, and organizational functions like banquets or picnics to promote more and better upward communication. But in the final analysis, the technique that is used is not as important as the supervisor's overall perspective and approach. Regardless of the specific technique that is used, the most important thing supervisors can do to improve upward communication is to create a climate of openness and trust, where employees feel free to communicate their true feelings and suggestions for accomplishing goals more effectively.

Horizontal Communication

According to the formal communication network in organizations, all communications to various parts of the organization must follow the chain of command—the formal lines of authority and responsibility. Referring back to Figure 14-1, if U wished to talk with U_1, the following sequence of events would have to occur: U to I, I to F, F to GM, GM to H, H to O, and O to U_1. Obviously, this chain pattern becomes very frustrating and time-consuming. In addition, there is a good chance that the communication will become lost or distorted when it finally arrives at its destination. To get around this lengthy chain, people work out informal arrangements so that they may communicate horizontally across organizational lines.

There are many reasons why horizontal communication is so important to effective supervision. The most obvious is coordination of work efforts. For example, production must be in constant communication with engineering, purchasing, and labor relations in a manufacturing plant, and the nurses have to be in constant communication with the dietary, medical, and housekeeping services in a hospital. Another reason for horizontal communication is the need for information and social relations throughout the organization. People have an interest in other people and what is going on in the organization at large. Personnel naturally seek out and establish informal lines of communication to various parts of the organization. This informal communication is commonly called "the grapevine."

The Grapevine as a Form of Organizational Communication

The grapevine has been the subject of considerable debate and controversy over the years. One argument is that it can be beneficial and is necessary to supplement formal channels, while others argue that it is nothing but trouble and should be eliminated altogether. The leading researcher on the grapevine as a form of organizational communication is Professor Keith Davis of Arizona State University. His findings have shed much light on both the pros and cons of the

The informal group plays a big role in communication. The grapevine is useful in supplementing the formal channels of communication and in getting things done, but it can also lead to false rumors (Chester Higgins from Rapho/Photo Researchers, Inc.).

grapevine. Perhaps his most interesting finding is that participation in the grapevine is more a function of position than personality. That is, people are active in the grapevine because their jobs put them in frequent contact with others in various parts of the organization. Thus, people like receptionists, mail and message carriers, delivery persons, maintenance personnel, and materials handlers are likely to be vital elements of the grapevine. Their own personalities and interests in "juicy" pieces of information appear to have less of a bearing on their participation in the grapevine. An important implica-

Human Relations for
Effective Supervision

tion of this finding is that supervisors cannot squelch the grapevine by firing the "rumor mongers." The next person who steps into the position, regardless of personality, seems to pick up where the previous person left off.

Another interesting finding is that the grapevine has many positive aspects. By keeping an ear turned to the rumor mill, supervisors can identify important problems and concerns among their employees. Even when the information is inaccurate, the grapevine indicates that there is at least a need for the type of information being transmitted. Another benefit is that supervisors can use the grapevine to test employees' reactions to potential changes and to let employees know, on an informal basis, when he or she does not agree with organizational policy. The grapevine also serves an important social function for people. Without the informal communication and friendships derived from participating in the grapevine, organizational life would be extremely dull. In addition, the grapevine can serve as an informal method of coordinating work. People learn to do reciprocal favors for one another and, in many cases, these favors help rather than hinder the work. Finally, Davis found that the information in the grapevine is surprisingly accurate. After analyzing the information bit by bit, he found that the accuracy was as high as 85 percent. However, even though the grapevine is largely accurate, the few rumors that are not true can be very damaging. One such case was a rumor that an employee was arrested on a morals charge. As it turned out, all the details were correct except for the fact that the guilty person was someone else in town with the same name.

Finally, although our discussion here generally favors grapevine communication, it should be emphasized that the formal channels are also important to effective organizational communication. An unwritten law of most organizations is that an employee never goes over his or her superior's head. Yet this is what happens when employees in two different work units arrive at an informal agreement to cooperate in their work. In effect, both may be obligating their unknowing supervisors to an agreement that the supervisors disapprove of. Similarly, when an employee discusses his or her supervisor's plans with other supervisors or work groups, the supervisor may suffer embarrassment. It is therefore suggested that supervisors establish some very clear guidelines with their people regarding the kinds of information and work arrangements that can be exchanged informally with other groups. Employees must keep their supervisors informed whenever they have discussed information or agreed upon arrangements that will affect their unit. As was pointed out earlier, it is imperative for employees and supervisors to establish a free, open climate of communication.

Hints on How Supervisors Can Keep Informed

One method supervisors can use to keep informed is to insist on getting copies of all memos that subordinates send or receive to other parts of the organization. For example, when a grievance is discussed with a staff member in the industrial relations department, this should be summarized in a memo and a copy forwarded to the relevant supervisor. In this way, supervisors are kept informed of any matters that may affect their organizational units.

Such documentation of organizational activities is not always needed where there is healthy, open communication. In other words, when organizations have an atmosphere of openness there are frequent upward and horizontal communications, and there is little need for documenting communications and sending copies of memos to supervisors. On the other hand, when organizations are undergoing stressful situations and conflicts are prevalent, there is a tendency to play a game called CYA (cover your posterior). In CYA, all communications to other parts of the organization are thoroughly documented. Then, if there is a misunderstanding, one is always covered and repercussions are minimized. Neither the person's boss nor people in other parts of the organization can claim that they were uninformed, because they have a copy of the transaction. Thus, although many people view the practice of sending multiple memos as tedious, there are, under certain circumstances, good reasons for it.

In conclusion, all aspects of organizational communication (downward, upward, and horizontal) are highly dependent upon the interpersonal trust and relationships among the organization's members. The last part of this chapter will give specific emphasis to this interpersonal dimension of communication.

INTERPERSONAL COMMUNICATION

The interpersonal perspective emphasizes that communication is a personal process between a sender and a receiver. This section will look at some of the variables and implications of this sender-receiver interaction.

Ways in Which the Supervisor Influences Communication

The catty remark "Consider the source" does point out the important role that the supervisor can play in communication. In other words, if the supervisor is the point of origin, then he or she becomes the first critical link in the communication process. Specifically, there are three major ways in which the supervisor can influence communication:

1 *Idea Formulation.* The first requirement of effective communication is that it be clear. Supervisors must spend considerable time and effort getting their own thoughts straight before they attempt to communicate them to others. Too often, supervisors protest that they have been misunderstood when, in reality, their own thoughts were not clear at the beginning.

2 *Assumptions.* A second critical area involves supervisors' assumptions about themselves and other people. Some assumptions which are critical to effective communication are summarized in Figure 14-3.

3 *Authority.* Another important consideration in effective communication is the authority of the supervisor. Messages take on meaning and importance depending upon the authority of the source. Thus, a handwritten message from a top manager will usually be considered more important by employees than a message from the supervisor. When messages are extremely important and the recipients' compliance is essential, it is often an effective supervisory strategy to ask a top manager to sign the memorandum or conduct the meeting.

How Supervisors Distort/Organize Information

Supervisors can use many techniques to organize information. For example, computerized information systems or filing systems can be used. But there are supervisors who typically distort information in the course of the communication process. The following sections highlight the major problems supervisors have in organizing information.

The parable approach Many supervisors avoid giving employees negative feedback. Instead, they try to relate the employee's problem to a story or illustration while hoping that the employee will get the message. The supervisor using this approach might, for example, tell an employee who is chronically absent the story of "John Smith," who was fired for absenteeism—all the while failing to mention the

ABOUT OTHERS

The other person has the same knowledge of the subject that I do.

The other person knows nothing about the subject.

The other person feels the same way that I do.

The other person either does or does not feel strongly about the situation.

The other person's ability to understand the situation is identical to mine.

The other person understands me and my motivations.

ABOUT SELF

My own interests and biases do not influence what I am trying to communicate.

I am completely rational and objective in what I say and how I am saying it.

I have a complete understanding and command of the situation I am discussing.

FIGURE 14-3
Assumptions supervisors make when they communicate.

employee's own problem. Similarly, an employee who is doing poor work might be told about the fine job another employee is doing, the hope being that the poorly performing employee will take the hint and emulate the more competent one. Again, the supervisor may never even mention the employee's own poor performance. All this time, the supervisor hopes the employee will "get the message" and believes that he or she is being tactful. Unfortunately, however, the employees on the receiving end of these parables often walk away shaking their heads, wondering what the supervisor was trying to say. The implication is clear: The most direct route to effective communications is the direct route. When supervisors say what they mean, there is much less chance of a misunderstanding or misinterpretation.

The good-times approach Closely related to the use of the parable is the "good-times" approach. Again, supervisors wish to avoid negative feedback or disappointing information, so they lace their communications with humor, stories, and jokes. Many supervisors feel that they are practicing good human relations with this approach, yet it can be ineffective. Few employees appreciate jokes on serious occasions like performance appraisals or at other times when they are being given vital information. Sometimes humorous tangents can disrupt the logical flow of communication and create misunderstandings. In addition, employees can lose important information in the midst of the jokes and stories. Rather than illustrating a point, humor has the potential for wiping the point away completely and creating some very ill feelings. This is not to suggest that humor should be eliminated. In fact, humor can promote human relations and communication very effectively. What is called for here is good judgment in using humor so that it does not detract from the supervisor's message.

The shotgun approach Although a shotgun can do well at short range, it is ineffective at long ranges because its power lacks concentration and focus. The communicator who sends out bits and pieces of information can be compared to a shotgun. Each day the supervisor who uses this approach gives the employee a new tidbit of information. Then, at the end of the month, the supervisor asks the employee how the new project is going. The employee replies: "What project?" The supervisor becomes frazzled, knowing that the employee has been given all the information needed to complete the project. And the supervisor is right. The employee, however, is confused, protesting that neither the project nor the relevant information have been communicated. And the employee is right. Both are right from their own perspectives. The supervisor is right because the relevant information has been delivered, and the employee is right because the supervisor never took the time to organize the information and integrate it into a meaningful whole that the employee would be able to perceive as an identifiable project.

This kind of problem can be corrected in three ways. First, the supervisor must take time to organize and integrate information so that it is meaningful. Second, when new information becomes available, the supervisor should communicate not only the new information but also the relationship of this new information to that which was given previously. Finally, both parties need to provide more and better feedback to one another. The supervisor must solicit and use feedback from the employee to make sure that the information is being understood. In addition, the employee has to let the supervisor know when the purpose of the information is unclear.

Information overload At the other extreme from the shotgun approach is the problem of information overload. The idea here is that too much information can be as bad as too little. It is said that some branches of the federal government actually capitalize on this problem. When they are required to disclose information which they do not particularly want distributed, they bury it in thousands of pages of irrelevant documents. Sometimes it seems that supervisors, at least unconsciously, do the same thing. That is, they overwhelm their employees, particularly the new ones, with so much information that they cannot possibly tell what is important. Thus, when large amounts of information must be communicated, supervisors have to take particular care in organizing, arranging, and summarizing this information. Often, summarizing at the beginning, during, and at the ends of conversations can help overcome this problem.

The top-secret syndrome Some supervisors use an approach that could be labeled the "top-secret syndrome." Such a supervisor feels that there is information that is too important or confidential to share with employees. The underlying theme here is the supervisor's misplaced sense of self-importance, leading him or her to believe that the control of privileged information adds to one's prestige. In order to become important, some supervisors bog down the communication process by insisting that even some very commonplace information is top secret. Communication suffers because necessary job information is withheld. Importantly, supervisors must carefully consider and determine whether information is really confidential or not. The supervisor should never violate true confidentiality, but this seldom happens in most organizations.

Needling This approach is characterized by the person who tries to needle people into doing a better job rather than attacking the problem in terms of the poor work itself. An example would be the supervisor who tells the young employee about the high quality of work back in "the old days." Another example is the supervisor who tells the employee that his five-year-old kid could do a better job. This approach usually communicates nothing except the supervisor's displeasure. Most often, it gets nothing in return except the personal disdain of the employee. Instead, supervisors should take time to examine employee problems and provide specific information that can help them solve work-related problems. General caustic comments and irrelevant information serve little purpose. Moreover, they frequently cause disagreement and bitterness. Supervisors should take the time to analyze employee problems, organize their own thoughts, and provide employees with specific job information that can help them solve problems and become more effective.

Steps Supervisors Can Take to
Overcome the Distortion of Information

Supervisors should carefully analyze the way in which they organize information so as to try to overcome some of the real or potential problems discussed above. The following four questions can help the supervisor do a better job of structuring information:

1 Do I have the information clear in my own mind before I try to communicate it?

2 Do I need more time to collect and organize my thoughts before communicating?

3 Do I withhold important information?

4 Am I direct and considerate in my approach or do I try to tell stories and jokes while hoping that the person gets the message? Should I be more direct?

5 Do I needle people or do I analyze the situation carefully so that I can provide organized, job-specific information that helps employees solve problems and be more effective?

Ways in Which the Supervisor Can Transmit Information

Besides considering the source of the information and the way in which it is organized, another important aspect of the supervisor's role in interpersonal communication is the way the information is transmitted. There are many possibilities; the major techniques and problems associated with them are discussed in the following sections.

Written communications One of the most common ways of transmitting information is through memos, letters, and other forms of written communication. There are several important characteristics of information that make written communication preferable to oral communication. Specifically, written communication is preferable when:

1 Information is very complex and its oral transmission may result in confusion

2 The communication must be documented, as in cases of contractual obligations or for personnel selection or discipline

3 Time is critical and a meeting or travel is out of the question

4 Employees are to be rewarded and they value physical evidence of the reward.

While complete coverage of effective writing skills is not within the scope of this book, supervisors should be able to benefit greatly from the following helpful hints:

1 *The first sentence* should communicate the purpose for the letter or memo (e.g., "I am writing to you because I need your help . . .").

2 *The last sentence* should summarize any action that the reader is required to take (e.g., "Please tell me whether or not to go ahead with the plan before next Friday, Nov. 12.").

3 *Use simple language.* The purpose of written communication is to communicate. Therefore, complicated phrases and difficult or uncommon words should not be used. Omit words like "henceforth," "herewith," "heretofore," and other archaic phrases. Also omit trite phrases like "upon further consideration" and "it has come to my attention." If you do not use the word or phrase in everyday language, it should not appear.

4 *Keep it short.* Very few people appreciate long, "windy" letters or memos. Many do not even bother to read them. A key to effective written communication is brevity.

5 *Use a logical progression.* The letter or memo should be carefully thought out and organized before it is written. Thoughts and ideas should flow in a logical sequence rather than being scattered in bits and pieces throughout the letter or memo.

Oral communication Although oral communication is the most common way to transmit information, it is also the most neglected. People take speaking for granted and fail to organize their thoughts. In reality, preparation is required to hold an effective conversation just as it is to write letters and memos or to conduct effective meetings. The following hints can help supervisors become better oral communicators:

1 *Prepare* for speaking just as if you were going to write a letter or a memo. Determine the purpose of the conversation, what is to be said, how you are going to say it, and the reaction you want from the other person.

2 *Clarify delicate issues* in your own mind first. Nothing can be more frustrating and ineffective for you and the other person than to start stumbling and hesitating over your own words. Think these issues through in your own mind and determine what you will say and how you will say it.

3 *Clarify difficult or complex issues.* Again, like the delicate issues, the difficult and complex issues should be thought through before the conversation so that they can be stated clearly and confidently during the exchange.

4 *Anticipate the listener's reactions.* Here again, the supervisor should think through the conversation and be able to clarify or explain any real or potential issues that may be particularly disturbing to the other person.

5 *End with a summary* of the conversation. If future action is going to be required from either party, this should be stated or reemphasized at the end of the conversation.

Nonverbal communication A third major method of transmitting information is by nonverbal means (i.e., through body movements or position, facial expression, voice inflection, and tone). People in general and supervisors in particular often ignore this very important part of the transmission process. Yet, communications experts generally agree that actual words communicate only a very small percentage of the information transmitted in face-to-face conversation. The bulk of the information is transmitted by voice tone and inflection as well as physical posture and facial expressions. Figure 14-4 summarizes some of the common forms and meanings of nonverbal communication.

Naturally, there is room for interpretations other than those given in Figure 14-4, and this is why one should not depend too much on nonverbal means to communicate. Yet because so much information in the communication process is transmitted in this way, supervisors should never ignore it. They should develop an awareness of their own use of nonverbal signals and consciously try to interpret and clarify it.

Unintended ways in which supervisors affect the communication process Often the supervisor will unintentionally distort information or otherwise cause a communication problem. Listed below are some examples of how these distortions occur:

1 *Paper Shuffling and Telephones.* Incidental activities that take place during important conversations with employees often distort communication. Two types of activities that supervisors should try to avoid are paper shuffling and telephone interruptions. For example, even though you may be extremely sincere, it is not helpful to be shuffling through an employee's records or to be jotting down comments during a serious conversation. This distracts attention on both sides and may distort the communication badly. The employee may react to such behavior by thinking: "The boss really doesn't give a damn about me and is only interested in filling out that stupid little form." Similarly, supervisors who interrupt important conversations

373

Nods: I agree.

Nods and smirks: I heard you but still don't believe you.

Points finger at you: You better listen to me.

Cloudy and blinking eyes during a meeting: What you say doesn't interest me in the least, and you aren't very important anyway.

Laughing: I am pleased with what you said.

Furrowed eyebrow: I don't think you should have done that.

Folded arms: I'll handle this.

Disheveled appearance: I'm depressed and this situation depresses me.

Immaculate appearance: I'm important, and I can be picky at times.

Deep voice intonation: I'm the person with the authority here.

Erratic, high-pitched, uneven voice: I'm frightened and uncomfortable.

Red-flushed face: I'm either awfully mad or awfully shy.

Sits apart from the group: I'm uncomfortable in this situation.

Raises hand: Wishes to speak or be recognized.

Raises eyebrows: What a surprise!

Frowns: I dissapprove.

Winks: I'm with you on that one.

FIGURE 14-4
Nonverbal communication language.

to answer the telephone and work out the details of an after-hours appointment distort communication. The employee's reaction may be: "You'd think that telephone was the most important thing in the boss's life. I take time to come in personally and half the time goes into talking with other people on the telephone."

2 *Status Messages.* Another common way in which supervisors unintentionally distort communication is through status messages. Each time a supervisor assigns a job, a location in the office or other work area, or tools and equipment, there are subtle messages involved, such as: "I am giving you the best tools (or office) because you are my best worker." Importantly, these messages are communicated to employees and may distort what is going on regardless of what the supervisors' intention may have been. Supervisors need to ask themselves: "What kinds of things do I tell my people by the way I assign jobs, locations, and equipment?"

3 *Informal Associations.* Another way supervisors can transmit distorted information is through their informal associations. The last chapter pointed out that informal groups have particular characteristics that transmit information about the participants. For example, consider the lunch-table arrangements in the organization. One can probably make a pretty good guess of a person's salary, attitudes toward the organization, status within the organization, and attitudes toward other people on the basis of the table at which he or she sits. Similarly, throughout the workday, participation in informal work groups or cliques transmits a great deal of information to other people. Supervisors should be aware of the information they transmit through their associations with others. Supervisors need to analyze the messages they are sending by asking themselves questions such as: "Who do I sit with at coffee and lunch? Are my close friends in the organization below my organizational level, at the same level, or above my level? Who from the organization do I associate with during outside social activities? What does each of these relationships tell other people? Are these the messages I wish to convey?"

4 *Credibility Gaps.* A gap in credibility occurs when there is a difference between what people say and what they do. The supervisor who admonishes employees for the loss of tools and then openly takes pens, paper, and pencils home for the kids is creating a credibility gap. Similarly, supervisors who lecture employees on the need for protective safety equipment but do not wear it themselves generate credibility problems. Obviously, these gaps in credibility distort communications, so that employees will not respond in a consistent manner. Supervisors must be particularly aware of these inconsistencies.

COMMUNICATION AS A TRANSACTIONAL PROCESS

So far we have presented and analyzed communication from an organizational and interpersonal perspective. Figure 14-5 shows a commonly used model of the various elements in this complex communication process. Some aspects of the model have been discussed in detail and others have not. In any case, present or future supervisors can trace through the steps of the model to get an idea of what is involved and improve their communication effectiveness.

The theme of our entire discussion of organizational and interpersonal communication—and of the summary model in Figure 14-5 as well—is the importance of the psychological dimension of communication. A currently popular and effective way of analyzing the psychological aspects of communication is through transactional analysis, or simply TA.

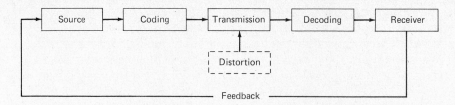

I. **The Source**

1. Has the source been clearly identified?

2. Was the idea clear in the sender's mind prior to transmission?

3. What assumptions did the sender make about himself or herself or about other people in sending the message? Were they appropriate?

II. **Coding**

1. Was the method clearly and carefully organized?

2. Did irrelevant humor, jokes, or stories wreck the organization of information or obscure the important points? Should you be more direct?

3. Did the person receive an integrated message or was a shotgun approach used, scattering and disorganizing the information.

4. Does the receiver suffer from information overload, having received too much information?

5. Did the receiver get all relevant information or does the sender suffer from a top-secret syndrome, withholding important information?

6. Was the person actually told what to do or how to correct a problem or instead was he or she just needled for doing a poor job?

III. **Transmission**

1. Did I carefully select the transmission process and consider letters, personal conversations, telephone conversations, bulletin boards, closed circuit TV, etc.?

2. If a letter was used, consider the following: length, language level, statement of purpose, logical organization, and clarity of the actions requested from the receiver.

3. If a personal conversation was used, consider: preparation, presentation of disturbing or difficult topics, anticipation of listeners' reactions, and the presence or absence of a statement requiring a specific reaction from the receiver.

4. Check your body language. Does it contradict or change the meaning of your verbal communications?

IV. **Distortion**

1. Do you shuffle papers or answer telephones during important personal conversations?

2. Do your actions, or body language, contradict your verbal messages to employees?

3. Is there a credibility gap between what you say and do?

4. Does physical noise cause information loss? Could a better place for communicating be selected?

FIGURE 14-5
A comprehensive
communication model.

5. Is there psychological noise? Have important communications been transmitted under psychologically stressful conditions, thereby losing information?

6. Is timing causing interference? Would it be be better to schedule important communications so that they do not conflict with coffee break, lunch, or quitting times?

7. Is the listener talking back, thereby causing disorganization and loss of information?

V. Decoding

1. Is jargon or specialized technical terms confusing the listener? Consider new employees or personnel unfamiliar with your operations.

2. Are there possible double meanings for words or expressions you are using?

3. Are experience, knowledge, and abilities factors in limiting the receiver's understanding?

VI. The Receiver

1. Are the receivers' assumptions or expectations of the communication distorting the information they receive?

2. Is the communication consistent with the receivers' needs, or are these needs creating misinterpretations?

3. Is there a possibility that a psychological block in the receiver is causing a misinterpretation?

4. Could the receiver's previous learning or experience lend a different interpretation to the message? Could the lack of experience or knowledge cause misunderstanding?

VII. Feedback

1. Did the receiver acknowledge an understanding of the communication?

2. Did the sender allow the receiver an opportunity to ask questions and clarify the communication?

FIGURE 14-5 (continued)

Background of TA

Eric Berne, the founder of TA, was a clinical psychologist who developed this technique as a means of helping his patients diagnose and analyze their personal problems. Although it began as a clinical diagnostic device, the theory was quickly recognized by Berne and others as a very effective tool for analyzing interpersonal communications. TA was popularized and presented to the public through Berne's book *Games People Play* and a later book by Thomas Harris called *I'm OK—You're OK*. The following sections will summarize the important concepts developed by Berne and Harris and will apply TA to the communication process.

The Ego States in TA

TA is built around the various ego states, which are defined in terms of early memories, experiences, and feelings stored in three basic

Communication is a complex, interpersonal process (Burk Uzzle/ Magnum Photos).

areas of the personality. These three personality dimensions or ego states are labeled the *Parent,* the *Adult,* and the *Child.* The beauty of TA is that everyone can relate to and understand its terminology. In this case the three ego states are closely related to the common use of the term "parent," "child," and "adult," but they are defined more specifically as follows:

1 *The Parent.* The parent is viewed as the source of both critical and/or supportive behavior. It develops from early interactions with the person's own parents and significant adult figures. During these early interactions, the parents are viewed as extremely powerful by the helpless infant. As a result, the child learns to accept without question the behaviors of these powerful adult figures. As one grows older, the impressions of these early experiences remain and are reflected in the way one communicates. Of course, some people do modify or alter their behavior—that is, they may reject certain traits they have seen in their parents. Yet many people remain relatively unchanged. Examples of parental ego states that are seen in supervisory situations are provided in Table 14-1. As can be seen from these examples, the Parent ego state is very important since it is from this source that employee behavior is both rewarded and punished.

2 *The Adult.* The adult is the rational, mature side of the personality. It develops slowly, as the individual learns to adapt to and test reality. It is objective and unemotional and is the source of decision-making and problem-solving skills. It asks questions, analyzes information, and solves problems. Examples of adult behaviors and statements are provided in Table 14-1. In addition to its function as the "brain trust" of the personality, the Adult ego state is also regarded as the control mechanism for the Child and Parent ego states. That is, the Adult analyzes the situation and determines when Parent or Child ego behaviors are appropriate. When they are not, it keeps them in check.

3 *The Child.* The Child ego state is viewed as the source of emotion and feeling. The person in this state may react very positively or negatively to a situation, but almost always the reaction is filled with emotion and feeling. From the Child originate a wide variety of emotional, immature statements, from "I adore you!" to "Go to hell!" In addition, the Child is seen as the source of creativity and curiosity. A sample of Child ego behaviors and statements is shown in Table 14-1. Although some view the Child ego state as detrimental to effective interpersonal relations and communication, it can also be extremely beneficial. It can be a source of creative problem solving and humor, both of which are necessary to the healthy functioning of people and organizations.

In summary, the ego states are components of the personality. Everyone's personality includes all three and each is essential to the functioning of normal, healthy individuals. The next section examines what happens when these ego states interact with one another in interpersonal communication.

Types of Transactions

The types of transactions are the second major cornerstone of TA. A transaction can be defined as any exchange or interaction between

TABLE 14-1

EXAMPLES OF SUPERVISORY EGO STATES IN TA

The Parent: Critical and supportive behavior or communications

	Critical	*Supportive*
Does:	Paces work area with frown on face.	Gives fellow worker an approving smile.
	Points finger at employees while giving directions.	Sends flowers to a sick employee.
		Pats employee on the shoulder or back.
	Folds arms before making an important point.	Sends the employee's spouse a birthday card.
Says:	That's the last time you'll pull that on me.	Keep up the good work!
	My 2-year-old kid could do a better job!	Excellent, you're doing a great job.
	You're absolutely impossible.	You're the best employee we have.
		I think of you as my son (daughter).

The Adult: Rational, objective, mature and unemotional

Does:	Gathers facts and information.	Avoids displays of anger.
	Determines priorities.	Promotes a participative, trustful atmosphere.
	Seeks opinions of others.	Asks numerous questions.
Says:	What are the facts?	When did it happen?
	What is your opinion?	How did it happen?
	The facts demonstrate that . . .	It's our only logical choice.

The Child: Emotional, uninhibited, immature, carefree, and can be either fun-loving or unhappy

Does:	Plays practical jokes.	Occasionally tips a few at lunch.
	Plots and schemes to get back at someone.	Refuses to work with fellow workers.
	Has temper tantrums.	Is a constant complainer.
Says:	Wow! Come look at my new office!	Wow! We blew it that time!
	Fantastic! We've got the best operation here.	Nothing ever goes right for me.
	Dammit. It's just not worth it.	I'm never going to speak to you again.

the ego states of the communicating parties. There are three general types of transactions:

1 *Complementary or Parallel Transactions.* Parallel transactions occur when the sender receives an expected, complementary response. When this occurs, the lines of communication are open and individuals can have effective communication. Examples of parallel transactions are illustrated in Figure 14-6.

2 *Crossed Transactions.* Transactions are crossed when the sender receives an incompatible, crossed response. When this occurs the lines of communication are crossed and there is a communication

COMPLEMENTARY TRANSACTIONS

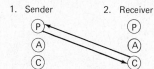

1. Sender   2. Receiver

1. You have to do better than that or you're going to be in trouble.

2. You're right, I promise I'll do better.

1. Sender   2. Receiver

1. This is an important report. Can you get it to me by next week?

2. I will reorder my priorities and make sure you get it.

CROSSED TRANSACTIONS

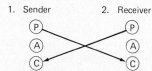

1. Sender   2. Receiver

1. You have to do better than that or you're going to be in trouble.

2. And just who the heck do you think you are telling me that?

1. Sender   2. Receiver

1. This is an important report. Can you get it to me by next week?

2. Why should I rearrange my whole schedule to accommodate you?

ULTERIOR TRANSACTIONS

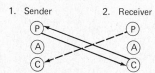

1. Sender   2. Receiver

1. You have to do better than that or you're going to be in trouble.

2. You're right. I'll bet I can get almost as good as you (meaning: you don't do much better).

1. Sender   2. Receiver

1. This is an important report. Can you get it to me by next week?

2. I don't see why not with all the help you give me (meaning: sure, you don't do anything anyway).

FIGURE 14-6
Types of transactions in TA.

breakdown. Examples of crossed transactions are found in Figure 14-6.

3 *Ulterior Transactions.* Ulterior transactions have dual messages. On the one hand, there is an obvious message carried by the superficial meaning of the words. On the other hand, a hidden but real message, often critical, is communicated by the manner in which the sentence is expressed. For example, a person reasonably skilled in voice inflection can say "Good job" in several different ways, each with a completely different meaning. Examples of ulterior transactions are provided in Figure 14-6.

The use of complementary transactions In general, complementary adult-to-adult transactions are recommended for supervisory-employee relations and communications. In these transactions, both parties are in mature, rational, problem-solving ego states and are communicating freely with one another. Parent-to-child interactions can work *if* the employee accepts the role of the obedient subordinate. Yet such transactions are generally not very healthy for effective human relations and communication and can backfire if, for example, an employee responds to a parentlike supervisor in a rebellious, childlike manner. An example would be the subordinate who is severely criticized for poor work habits by a parentlike supervisor and reacts like a rebellious child stomping his feet and telling the supervisor that he or she is being grossly unfair. Although there is a complementary transaction in this example and the lines of communication are open, the result is a very "free-flowing" argument and nothing progresses.

The use of crossed transactions These transactions are generally not recommended unless the supervisor intends to cut off communication. An example is shown in Figure 14-7. Here the constant complainer attempts to engage the supervisor in an argument. Instead of arguing back, as a parental ego state would dictate, the supervisor crosses the transaction with an adult question, putting the pressure for an adult response back on the employee. As a general rule, however, crossed transactions are undesirable, because supervisors want to encourage free-flowing job-oriented communications with their people.

Listed below are three strategies for avoiding or uncrossing incompatible transactions:

1 *Adult Strategy.* The first recommendation for avoiding crossed transactions is to avoid communications to employees which originate from either the parent or child ego state. This is particularly important when the transaction is potentially threatening to the employee. In the example in Figure 14-8, the supervisor could have avoided the crossed transaction by a careful and considerately worded adult question such as: "John, can you tell me what hap-

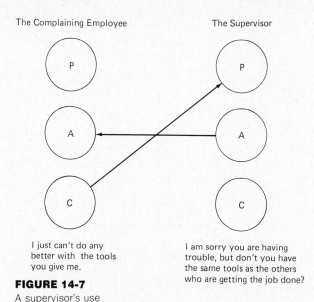

The Complaining Employee   The Supervisor

I just can't do any
better with the tools
you give me.

I am sorry you are having
trouble, but don't you have
the same tools as the others
who are getting the job done?

FIGURE 14-7
A supervisor's use
of a crossed transaction.

pened on that last job?'' The supervisor should always consciously try to remain in the adult state under this strategy.

2 *Crossing with the Adult.* Despite consciously trying to avoid it, all people eventually find themselves involved in crossed transactions. The simplest way to return the situation to a complementary transaction is to cross the transaction with an adult question. In the example illustrated in Figure 14-8, the supervisor could salvage the transaction by responding: ''How can I help so that we can avoid these situations in the future?'' This latter response should stimulate an adult reaction from the employee and force him or her to analyze the reasons for the poor performance.

3 *Cool Off.* Finally, there is the possibility that either the supervisor or the employee becomes so emotionally involved that crossed transactions become almost unavoidable. In these situations, the best strategy may be to discontinue the conversation until a later date. For example, the supervisor might say something such as: ''Mary, this is an important issue, but I don't think either of us is in the proper frame of mind to discuss it further. Why don't we both think on it and get together a little later?''

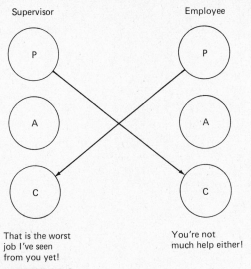

Supervisor   Employee

That is the worst
job I've seen
from you yet!

You're not
much help either!

FIGURE 14-8
An example of a crossed transaction.

The use of ulterior transactions Like complementary and crossed transactions, there are appropriate and inappropriate uses of the ulterior transaction. On the positive side, ulterior transactions can be an important part of humor. The classic example from this point of view is the "double entendre," where a seemingly innocent statement is made with a humorous hidden meaning that sometimes has sexual overtones. Ulterior transactions can be used to help employees set challenging goals and expectations for themselves. For example, a supervisor might challenge an employee who is bragging about an accomplishment by replying: "That is fantastic. The only other employee who could consistently pull off something like that was Harry. He's the supervisor of the night shift now." The hidden meaning in this example is, "I'm very pleased with your performance on that project, but can you do it on a daily basis? If you can, you may be considered for a supervisory position someday."

Most often, however, ulterior transactions are very destructive; they are detrimental to employee-supervisor relations and lead to communication breakdowns. Listed below are some tips for avoiding and reacting to destructive ulterior transactions:

1 *Ignore it.* Employees, coworkers, and supervisors frequently and sometimes unknowingly communicate messages such as: "It's all your fault," "You're stupid," and "I'm better than you are." Most often, the persons sending these messages have their own feelings of inadequacy or uncertainty, which form the bases of these communications. Responding to these ulterior transactions in a negative way often serves only to intensify these feelings of inadequacy and makes the situation worse. These unpleasant situations can often be avoided by responding only to the surface meaning of the statement and ignoring the hidden meanings.

2 *Discontinue the conversation.* Despite efforts to ignore destructive hidden agendas, there will be times when the other party persists. The best strategy under these circumstances may be to discontinue the conversation completely until another time.

3 *Level.* In this strategy, a conscious attempt is made to bring the hidden meanings to the surface. It is the most risky strategy but can be very effective. For example, after a string of transactions where one person implies that the other is incompetent, the hidden meaning might be brought into the open with the remark: "You seem to be saying that the problem is all my fault. Is that what you mean to say?" At this point, the hidden meaning surfaces and the real issue can be openly discussed. Of course, there is no guarantee that this leveling strategy will resolve the problem, but at least it will be out in the open and there will be a better, more effective chance of solving it.

Games People Play in Organizations

A third major aspect of TA deals with games people play. Games can be analyzed in terms of the transactions that take place. Most games start with a series of complementary transactions. That is, the parties are engaged in transactions where both usually feel they are being honest and open. But underlying the seemingly compatible transactions are ulterior transactions such as: "You are incompetent," "I feel inadequate," "I am better than you are," and "You goofed up." Throughout the game, subtle ulterior transactions communicate these real meanings. At the conclusion of the game, the ulterior meanings or hidden agenda surfaces and one or the other party is made to feel superior or inferior.

Examples of typical games people play in organizations are described in Table 14-2. Of course, there are many other games, and each organization has its favorites.

Importantly, games are usually very destructive to good human relations and effective communication because they waste time and

TABLE 14-2

GAMES PEOPLE PLAY IN ORGANIZATIONS

Name of Game	Brief Description of Game
1. Now I've Got You, You S.O.B. (N.I.G.Y.S.O.B.)	One person gets back at another by luring her into what appears to be a natural work relationship. Actually the situation is rigged so that the other will fail. When the inevitable mistake is made, the game player pounces on the associate and publicly embarrasses her.
2. Poor Me	The person depicts himself to the supervisor as helpless. Criticisms for inadequate performance are avoided because the supervisor truly feels sorry for the individual, and he may actually begin to feel sorry for himself.
3. Blemish	The supervisor appears to be objectively evaluating an employee's total performance. In reality, the supervisor is looking for some minor error. When the error is found, the employee is berated for the poor performance, the inference being that the whole project/task/report is inadequate.
4. Hero	The supervisor consistently sets up situations where employees fail. At some point, the supervisor steps in to save the day miraculously.
5. King of the Hill	The supervisor sets up situations where employ-

someone always gets hurt. The suggestions for stopping games are largely the same as the suggestions for uncrossing transactions and responding to ulterior transactions.

Other TA Concepts and Applications

Besides ego states, transactions, and games, there are several other TA principles which can help one understand and improve human relations and communications. Some of the more important TA concepts for the practice of supervision include the following:

1 *Stroking.* Stroking is very similar to the reinforcement concept which was introduced in Chapter 12 and given more detailed discussion in the next chapter. Stroking goes back to a mother cuddling and giving warmth and comfort to her child. People learn to depend

**Human Relations for
Effective Supervision**

TABLE 14-2 (continued)

	ees end up in direct competition with her. At the end, she steps in and demonstrates her competence and superiority while publicly embarrassing her employees.
6. Cops and Robbers	An employee continuously walks a fine line between acceptable and unacceptable behavior. The supervisor wastes unnecessary time desperately trying to catch the employee, while the employee stays one step ahead and laughs to himself through the day.
7. Prosecutor	The employee carefully carries a copy of the union contract or organization regulations and investigates supervisory practices. This employee dares the supervisor to act in an arbitrary manner. Once he does, the employee files a grievance and attempts to embarrass the supervisor.
8. If It Weren't for You	The employee discusses her problems openly but carefully works the conversation around so that she can rationalize her failure by blaming the supervisor for everything that goes wrong.

on this stroking; for adult employees, it is expressed as attention and recognition. Effective supervisors recognize this need and stroke desirable behavior that leads to performance improvement. Ineffective supervisors recognize and give attention to poor performance, thereby reinforcing poor performance. People give and receive strokes every time they enter into a transaction or play games. Positive strokes would include simple recognition, such as "Nice job" or even "Good morning."

2 *Stamps.* This TA concept says that there are feelings that people save up (like trading stamps) until they feel justified in "cashing them in." The concept of stamps is captured in the phrase "the straw that broke the camel's back." For example, people collect red stamps when they have angry feelings and criticisms and cash them in after a while by "blowing their stack." Importantly, many arguments are the culmination of a series of previous transactions and indicate an ongoing problem rather than a single incident. In addition to red

	Supervisor feels "OK" about self	Supervisor does not feel "OK" about self
Supervisor feels OK about the employee	Winner supervisor	Martyr supervisor
Supervisor does not feel OK about the employee	Prosecutor supervisor	Loser supervisor

FIGURE 14-9
Life positions for supervisors.

stamps for anger, people can also collect stamps for feelings of inadequacy or depression and even for "good deeds." Each stamp has a color and a method of cashing it in. For example, good feelings are labeled gold stamps in TA, and they can be cashed in by taking the afternoon off.

3 *Life Positions.* Their life position may, for example, indicate how supervisors feel about themselves in relation to their employees. The basic life positions are illustrated in Figure 14-9. In the winner position, the supervisor conducts mostly adult-to-adult complementary transactions, gets involved in few destructive games, gives and receives positive strokes, and does not collect or cash in destructive stamps. In the other positions, of course, the supervisor enters into many crossed and ulterior transactions, plays destructive games, gives or receives negative strokes, and cashes in stamps. Through better understanding of themselves and those with whom they interact, supervisors should be able to move toward being winners.

■ KEY CONCEPTS

Organizational communications networks
Top-down communication
Horizontal communication
Upward communication
Team development
Open-door policy
Grapevine or informal communication

Distorted information
Nonverbal communication
Transactional analysis

■ PRACTICAL EXERCISES

(These can be performed by individuals or by groups.)

1 Provide a brief verbal description of any interesting incident (e.g., something that recently happened to you on a job, in twenty-five words or less) to one member of the group. Ask that member to relay the description to a second member who did not hear your words. Repeat until the message has been relayed through several people. Have the first and last people in the chain write their descriptions down. Now compare the two descriptions and discuss the implications for communications in organizations. Do you have any actual examples where this sort of distortion has affected you or someone you know? Explain.

2 Take four or five simple geometric shapes—such as squares, rectangles, and triangles—and connect them at end points or midpoints. Select one group member as an experimental subject. Show the configuration of geometric shapes to the class but not to the subject. Then have the group attempt to give verbal instructions to the subject on how to draw the configuration without using the words "square," "rectangle," or "triangle" or allowing the subject to face the class or ask questions. Next, allow the subject to face the class and ask questions. Analyze the importance and implications that the feedback and absence of feedback had for interpersonal communication.

3 Make up a role-playing situation that takes place between a supervisor who is coming from a Parent ego state and a subordinate who is coming from a Child ego state. After this transaction has been acted out, take the same situation but have both the boss and the subordinate come from an Adult ego state. Contrast the two role-plays and analyze the implications this has for interpersonal relations and communications.

■ DISCUSSION INCIDENTS

"The trouble with this place is that we just don't have a good system of communicating with the employees," said Jack Blair, the head teller of State Bank and Trust. "We now have plans to rectify that situation. We are hiring two communications experts. They will be responsible for both a monthly newsletter and videotaped presentations of special events or information that is of interest to our employees." "Jack," interrupted Jim Zorn, "I wonder if that's really going to solve our problem. Is it possible that our employees' complaints and attitudes are down because of some other reason besides our formal system of communication?" "Come on now, Jim," said Jack, "You know that our competitor, Central Bank, installed this same system a year ago. We've got to get off our duffs and get this moving if we're going to remain the leading bank in town."

1 Is formal communication technology this bank's real problem? What do you think the real problem is?

2 From which TA ego states are the communications of the people in the above example coming? What are the implications for the organization if the head teller constantly speaks from the ego state at which he was in this incident?

Tom Cullen was confused. He had just finished talking with Teresa, his supervisor. Teresa had told him a long story about an aspiring young employee who was once invited to the general manager's Christmas party. In the story, the young man overindulged in the refreshments and told some rather off-color jokes to some of the other guests. To top off this behavior, the employee became sick and was picked up for drunk driving on the way home. Eventually, Teresa told him that the young man was fired. Tom was concerned and confused because, on the previous night, he had visited a bar after work with Tony Pinardo, the assistant to the general manager. Everybody stayed for a few hours but nobody's behavior was particularly notable. Tom did not know what his supervisor was trying to tell him. He was not even sure his supervisor knew he had been out the night before. He wondered whether he should abstain from drinking, avoid drinking with top management, or not tell off-color stories.

1 In terms of TA, what ego state was the supervisor speaking from and what type of transaction could this communication be called? What specific TA technique is suggested to stop this type of transaction?

2 Identify some of the assumptions the supervisor made about Tom during their conversation. Provide and discuss some suggestions that will help supervisors avoid distorting their information.

MOTIVATING EMPLOYEES

15 CHAPTER

Jack Hansen had only a few years left before retirement. He had come up through the ranks of Huge Corporation. The company was committed to training and development, and Jack had attended all the courses offered through the years. Now he received a memo that he was to attend a training session titled "Motivating Your Workers: Internal and External Approaches." Jack chuckled to himself when he read the title. He said to himself, "What will these training guys think of next? First it was 'Be nice to your people,' then it was 'Be sensitive to your people,' then it was 'Respect your people.' Now they pour the same old wine in a new bottle and call it internal and external motivation. I've been around long enough to know the score. We sure need something in this company to motivate our people, but they have never given us anything useful yet in these seminars and I really doubt if this is going to be any different. What we need is something beyond paying them more, giving them better working conditions, and being nice to them. I sure hope they have some answers because I think these younger supervisors are going to have an even tougher time motivating people in the future than I have had."

0

After reading this chapter, you should be able to:

Examine the way in which motivation has traditionally been handled

Understand the internal approaches to motivation, such as Maslow's hierarchy of needs and Herzberg's two-factor theory

Apply job enrichment to motivate employees

Understand the external environmental approach to motivation

Apply the five-step organizational behavior modification (O.B. Mod.) approach to change employee behavior for performance improvement

Motivation is more closely associated with the human relations aspects of supervision than any other single topic. Chapter 12 said that motivation was a driving force, the energizer behind human behavior. It was presented as a process consisting of a need that sets up a drive to accomplish a goal. The three most important needs for understanding employee behavior (power, achievement, and affiliation) were given attention. The discussion in Chapter 12 serves as the point of departure for one approach to employee motivation, the internal approach. The equally important, but often overlooked, alternative approach to employee motivation, simply labeled here "the external approach," is based on the discussion of learning in Chapter 12. The principles of classical and, especially, operant conditioning serve as the point of departure for the external approach to motivation.

This chapter is broken down into three major parts. The first part examines the traditional approaches to work motivation. These were initially dominated by the scientific-management concern for economic motivation and later evolved into a simplistic, prescriptive approach that if you paid people well while also giving them good working conditions and fringe benefits, they would be motivated and productive. The second major part of the chapter takes an internal perspective. After explaining what is meant by this, the Maslow and Herzberg theories and applications are used to represent the internal approach to employee motivation. The final part of the chapter takes an external perspective. After explaining what is meant by this, the specific steps of organizational behavior modification are discussed in detail.

TRADITIONAL APPROACHES TO EMPLOYEE MOTIVATION

The overriding theme behind early work motivation schemes was that people were mainly, if not solely, economically driven. The scientific-management movement at the beginning of this century is often falsely accused of ignoring the human element. Scientific-management pioneers such as Frederick W. Taylor and Henry L. Gantt did, in fact, give specific recognition and even emphasis to the importance of human beings in the workplace. They devised elaborate incentive systems to motivate employees. Basically, these were piecework plans that paid workers a high rate for production above a scientifically derived standard of performance and a low rate for below-standard work. Most modern piecework incentive plans are patterned after these scientific-management approaches to motivation.

While the scientific-management pioneers are unjustly accused of ignoring the human element, they can be legitimately accused of oversimplifying human motivation. Their approach was based almost solely upon the economic motive; they failed to recognize the complexity of human motivation. They felt that workers were interested in only one thing—more money. And the way to motivate them was to devise ways of tying their productivity into the way they were paid. The logic was: The more you produce, the more money you will make. Let us admit from the outset that there is nothing wrong with this logic. Money *is* important to people. But it is not the end-all of motivation. People are also motivated by other things, some of which money provides and some of which it does not.

Especially during Taylor's and Gantt's times, economic motivation undoubtedly had a much greater appeal than it has had more recently. In the early days of American industrialization, employees were barely making enough to provide the basic necessities of food, clothing, and shelter for themselves and their families. But as things got better over time (for example, Henry Ford paid his workers a very high wage of $5 a day in the early part of this century), economic motivation began to give way to other, higher-level motives such as opportunities to achieve and grow in one's work. Yet as these other motives began to become more important to employees, the human relations prescription for motiviating employees remained the same. Up to about a decade or so ago, the approach to motivating employees was relatively simple:

1 Pay people well and possibly give them good working conditions and extensive fringe benefits;

2 This will make them motivated and satisfied with their work;

3 Happy, satisfied employees are productive; they will perform well. This formula of

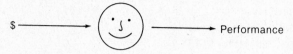

dominated the traditional approach to human relations. Today, we know that this is much too simplistic. First of all, we know that there is much more to motivation than simply money or even working conditions and fringe benefits. Human motivation is extremely complex and involves much more than money. We cannot equate money and motivation. Once again, this does not imply that money is no longer a factor in employee motivation—an unrealistic and downright foolish suggestion. As this chapter unfolds, the importance of money as a motivator is repeatedly emphasized, but there are many other things that are also important to employee motivation.

A second aspect of the simple human relations prescription is the relationship between motivation and satisfaction. We now know that the two are not necessarily the same. Motivation is a much more complex concept than is satisfaction. And the relationship between satisfaction and performance is not as clear-cut as was once assumed. Research is beginning to show that the direction of causality may be that performance leads to satisfaction as much as satisfaction leads to performance. In any case, it is becoming very evident that the traditional approach is at least much too simplistic and at most simply untrue. New approaches to employee motivation are needed.

THE INTERNAL APPROACH TO EMPLOYEE MOTIVATION

The internal approach attempts to look inside of people to find out what motivates them. The discussion in Chapter 12 indicated that needs are internal deficiencies that drive a person toward a goal. These needs may be power, achievement, affiliation, or self-actualization. These needs come from within the individual and help to explain people's behavior.

The catch with the internal approach to motivation is that no one has ever seen a need. When the supervisor observes an employee enter the company cafeteria and is asked why the employee is behaving this way, the answer will invariably be: "Because he is hungry." In other words, the supervisor attributes the observable behavior (walking into the cafeteria) to an unobservable, internal need (hunger). This may or may not be the reason the employee is behaving as he is. Maybe he is not hungry at all. Maybe the reason he is going into the cafeteria is to meet some friends (affiliation) or to check out the pretty new waitress (sex) or for any of a number of other possible reasons. The same is true of the employee who is diligently working on a task. The supervisor says to herself: "Joe is really achievement-motivated." In fact, Joe may be working hard on the task because he is fearful that the supervisor will jump on his back if he does not; this has nothing to do with achievement. In other words, the attribution of observable behaviors to inner needs leaves much room for error.

Yet, despite these limitations of the internal approach, it has dominated the recent study and application of work motivation. Most work-motivation theorists search for the inner causes of employee behavior. The suggested techniques include finding out the things that will appeal to the inner needs. Such an approach can certainly help us better understand employee behavior and should be able to help supervisors to be more effective in motivating their people toward better performance.

Maslow's Hierarchy of Needs

One of the first and most popular theories of internal work motivation comes from the famous humanistic psychologist Abraham Maslow. Over thirty years ago, he wrote a paper outlining an overall theory of motivation. In essence, he said that a person's motivation could be best explained in terms of a hierarchy of needs, and that once a given level of need is satisfied, it can no longer motivate the person. The following example clarifies what Maslow was proposing:

> If a carrot is held out in front of someone who has not eaten for a couple of days, this person will lunge at the carrot and devour it. He is very motivated by carrots. He has not eaten for a long time and carrots are very appealing to him. If a second carrot is held up after he has devoured the first one, he will just take it and eat it very deliberately. In other words, he is no longer as motivated by carrots. If a third carrot is then held up, the person may simply walk over slowly, eat about half the carrot, and throw the other half on the ground. He is no longer highly motivated by carrots. If still another carrot is now held up, he will walk away and say, "I'm full of carrots. Give me something else."

This example simply shows that once a person's need for carrots is satisfied, they can no longer be used to motivate that person. Yet, this is exactly what is happening in our efforts to motivate today's employees. We are holding the same carrots up to employees year after year and expecting them to be motivated. A few more cents an hour, another day off, and better health insurance are the "carrots" we are repeatedly holding up to employees, and they are telling us, "I'm full of these, what else do you have?" It makes employees feel permanently full. They are always going to want more money and better fringe benefits. But what Maslow's concept says is that once these needs are basically met, you have to appeal to a higher level of need in order to motivate employees.

Maslow, now deceased, did not intend his theory to be applied directly to work motivation. Yet management writers such as Douglas McGregor saw its applicability and popularized it in the field of human resource management. The five levels that Maslow identified and their counterparts in terms of work motivation are shown in Figure 15-1 and discussed in the following sections.

Physiological needs This is the most basic level of needs. Food, water, sex, and sleep are some of the common physiological needs that people have. They are needed to sustain life and usually take precedence over the other needs. In other words if a person is hungry, the other motives, such as security or esteem, will have little impact. There are, of course, exceptions to this; for example, celibacy among priests or fasting for a political belief. But by and large these physiological needs must be met before others will serve to motivate.

Applied to work motivation, this basic level can be equated with the wages and salary that a person makes. Money is used to feed, clothe, and shelter the employee. The money that one makes takes care of the basic physiological needs. Importantly, once these needs are taken care of—once the employee earns enough to take care of the physiological needs—then there must be an appeal to the next level in order to motivate that employee. Once again, however, it should be remembered that just as money cannot be equated with overall motivation, it should also not be equated with the physiological needs. Money has definite implications for the upper-level needs as well. For example, money has an important role in security and esteem.

Safety needs According to Maslow, the second level of the hierarchy consists of needs for emotional and physical safety. Once the

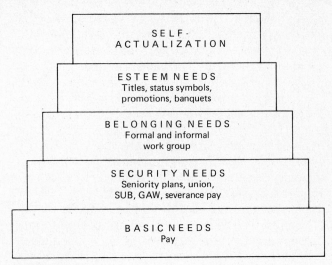

FIGURE 15-1
Maslow's hierarchy of needs.

physiological needs are taken care of, the person seeks out safety.

Applied to work motivation, this level can be best thought of as security. Job security in terms of seniority and fringe benefits (medical, savings, severance pay, etc.) represent this level for employees in modern organizations. Generally speaking, like pay, these security needs are pretty well taken care of in most organizations. This does not mean that being laid off or being replaced is not a constant fear of employees, because it is. In surveys asking employees what is important to their jobs, security constantly falls at or near the top of the list. But, like pay, security is not the end-all of work motivation. Higher-level needs must come into play in order to motivate today's employee.

Love needs This intermediate level identified by Maslow is the need for affection and to belong to the group. In this instance, Maslow is probably guilty of a poor choice of words, because "love" has many misleading connotations in our society. For example, it may imply sex, which is actually a first-level physiological need. As used here, "love" is most closely associated with the need for affiliation discussed in Chapter 12.

This need to belong, to be part of the group, is very intense in most employees. Going as far back as the famous Hawthorne studies (discussed in Chapters 1 and 13), it has been repeatedly shown by systematic research and everyday observation that being part of the informal work group and following its norms and rules for behavior is as important or even more important to employees than are some of the things supervisors can do for or to employees. For example, most employees would rather be accepted by their coworkers than have the opportunity to make a few more dollars a week. This latter example is evident in the relatively common occurrence of the deliberate restriction of output even in the face of incentive wages for more production. If supervisors want to motivate their employees, they will have to appeal to this need to belong.

The approach of the pioneering scientific manager Frederick W. Taylor to this motive was to break up the group. Let people operate as isolated individuals, Taylor said, because when they get together, they will "systematically soldier" (restrict output). We now know that the tight, highly cohesive group can help as well as hinder performance. By letting employees take breaks together and socialize on the job, and by encouraging them to socialize off the job, supervisors can help fulfill this need. The challenge for the supervisor is not only to encourage this type of group activity but also to make sure that the group will, as a result, work toward rather than against the unit's objectives.

Esteem needs This is the beginning of the so-called higher-level needs. Maslow said that this level contains both self-esteem and esteem from others. The needs for power and achievement discussed in Chapter 12 as well as the need for status can be considered part of this level.

These higher-level needs are those that are largely unmet in efforts to motivate today's employees. As has been indicated in the discussion so far, the lower-level needs are largely taken care of and, according to Maslow's theory, their further use will not motivate. In order to motivate today's employees, supervisors must depend more on the higher-level needs. Opportunities for achievement, power, and status will motivate employees. Ways of presenting such opportunities have been mentioned throughout this book. In particular, supervisors can involve employees in the decision-making and goal-setting processes and hold them accountable for the results. This will give employees the chance to achieve and grow in their jobs. The discussion in the next section, on Herzberg's two-factor theory and job enrichment, will suggest specific ways to appeal to these higher-level needs of employees.

Self-actualization needs This level represents the culmination of the other needs in Maslow's hierarchy. In essence, it represents the pinnacle of self-fulfillment. Having reached this level and become what he or she is capable of becoming, the person has realized his or her full potential. Obviously, self-actualization is a very healthy psychological state to have reached. It is something the person should strive to attain. It may represent $1 million for one person or a worthless but beautiful painting for another.

Applied to work motivation, self-actualization would represent the ultimate level of motivation. Realistically, few employees, at least at the lower levels of the organization, can expect to achieve self-actualization from their jobs. Yet, this also helps explain why employees never seem to be satisfied. They always seem to want more.

Analysis of Maslow's theory Maslow formulated his theory of motivation on the basis of clinical observation and did not test it through systematic research. Yet it does make a lot of sense, at least superficially, and has a great deal of applicability as a content theory of work motivation. It helps explain why employees do not seem to be motivated by continual increases and improvements in the traditional incentives of wages, working conditions, and fringe benefits. Maslow's answer is that once these lower-level needs have been pretty well satisfied, they no longer serve to motivate. According to Maslow, if supervisors want to motivate their employees, they would have to appeal to the higher-level needs (esteem and self-actualization).

Supervisors can certainly benefit from Maslow's theory. They must give emphasis to the higher-level needs that have generally been overlooked or deliberately ignored in the past. But, like the scientific-management ideas on economic motivation and those of the early human relations movement—which stressed money, working conditions, and security—Maslow's higher-level needs are not the end-all of work motivation. Recent research does not wholly support Maslow's theory. The number and names of his levels and even the hierarchial concept is open to question. Yet despite the lack of research support, Maslow correctly emphasized that people have diverse motives, some of which represent higher-level needs. Supervisors can greatly benefit from this understanding in their attempts to motivate their employees.

Herzberg's Two-Factor Theory

Frederick Herzberg extended the work of Maslow and aimed his work directly at employee motivation. His theory is currently the most popular in the actual practice of human resource management. Unlike Maslow, Herzberg developed his theory on the basis of empirical research. He went out and asked people in organizations two basic questions: (1) What is it about your job that really turns you on, that really motivates you? (2) What is it about your job that really turns you off, that really makes you unhappy and dissatisfied?

The answers that Herzberg and his colleagues obtained from this method of research were very interesting and fairly consistent. Employees were generally "turned on" by job experiences and job content. Most employees related incidents such as the following:

> The thing that really turned me on was the day the boss called me into her office and said, "Charlie, I'm finally going to take that month-long trip to Europe and I want you to take charge while I'm gone. I'm going to give you complete responsibility for the whole operation and it will give you a chance to show me what you can do." You know, that really made me feel good. She recognized I could do the job, gave me a great deal of responsibility and the opportunity to achieve and grow in the job.

In other words, Herzberg found that people were turned on by recognition, responsibility, achievement, advancement, and the work itself. Such job-content factors he called "the motivators."

Reported bad feelings also turned out to be fairly consistent. Employees were turned off by the things surrounding the job, the job context. In this regard, employees made reports such as the following:

> You know what really turns me off is that the guy down the hall from me is making more money than I am. If you can imagine, that idiot actually has a higher salary than I do.
> This company doesn't care about us. Last summer, the hottest time of the year, the air conditioning broke down. They didn't get it fixed for three days.
> Do you see that crack in the ceiling? Well, plaster drips down on my desk all the time. The conditions around here are lousy.

In other words, bad feelings were associated with the job context (salary and working conditions especially, but also company policies

401

and technical supervision). Herzberg labeled these job-context factors "dissatisfiers" or "hygiene factors." The term "hygiene," in the medical sense, implies prevention. Herzberg's hygiene factors *prevent* dissatisfaction; they do not lead to satisfaction.

Significantly, most employees did not mention that a raise in salary or improved working conditions turned them on. They did not mention that a raise in wages made them feel good or motivated, but they were very upset over the raise they did not get. For example, Herzberg says that if you give an employee a $1,000 raise one year and $500 the next, he or she has, psychologically, taken a $500 cut in pay. People always feel they deserve the raise they get; it does not motivate them. Employees did not mention that redecorating their offices or getting a new locker room turned them on; but if they had poor facilities, they were certainly turned off. In other words, Herzberg found that the traditional "motivators" of money and working conditions really did not motivate people. Instead, people were simply unhappy if money and working conditions were not taken care of.

Herzberg's theory can answer the question that supervisors have constantly been asking themselves in recent years:

> Our wages are as high as those paid by any organization in the area and they permit our people a very high standard of living. The working conditions are tremendous. We have air conditioning, pastel-colored walls, and soft music playing. Our fringe benefits are out of sight. We have major medical, three weeks' vacation, a liberal sick-leave policy, and free tuition for those who want to attend night school. With all this, our people are still not motivated. What in the world do they want?

What they want and what they are not getting, according to Herzberg, are the motivators of recognition, responsibility, achievement, advancement, and the work itself. The things that have been emphasized over the years (money and working conditions) turn out not to motivate people but only become sources of annoyance if they are inadequate. In the above example, the employees may not be dissatisfied or leaving their jobs because they apparently do have good wages, working conditions, and fringe benefits. On the other hand, they are not motivated because there are no opportunities for recognition, responsibility, or growth in the job.

The Herzberg two-factor theory (motivators and hygiene factors) makes a lot of sense for modern human resource management. It is similar to Maslow's theory in that Herzberg's hygiene factors are roughly equivalent to the lower-level needs and the motivators are similar to the upper-level needs. In addition, as in Maslow's theory, the hygiene factors serve as a floor; they must be taken care of before the motivators are activated. Once again, the hygiene factors do not motivate. They lead to dissatisfaction if they are not taken care of; if they *are* taken care of, they merely prevent dissatisfaction. Only recognition, responsibility, achievement, advancement, and the work itself lead to employee motivation according to the Herzberg two-factor theory of employee motivation.

How Can Supervisors Apply the Herzberg Theory of Motivation?

Herzberg's theory is not without criticism. In fact, most scholars of motivation agree that Herzberg oversimplified the complex motivational process; when different methods of research have been attempted, other results have been obtained. Despite this legitimate criticism, few would question that Herzberg's theory has had a new and important impact on the study and application of work motivation. What Maslow started, Herzberg was able to deliver. Up to the time of Maslow and Herzberg, human resource management had concentrated on wages, working conditions, and fringe benefits to motivate employees. But as was pointed out earlier, the traditional approach has fallen far short. Maslow's and Herzberg's theories help explain why. By concentrating only on the low-level hygiene factors, it can be expected that employees will not be motivated.

Herzberg's hygiene factors are usually beyond the direct control of the individual supervisor. Supervisors seldom have much to say about the level of wages, the working conditions, and especially the fringe benefits of their people. However, they do have much more direct control over the factors that Herzberg identified as the motivators. In other words, motivating factors such as recognition, responsibility, achievement, advancement, and the work itself are largely up to the supervisor. The supervisor can enrich the jobs of employees by incorporating the motivators. Thus, the applied aspects of Herzberg's two-factor theory has become known as job enrichment.

Job Enrichment

Sometimes job enrichment is confused with the older concept of job enlargement. The latter goes back to the 1950s, when a few enlight-

Even though it is very difficult to enrich some jobs, some employees show a great deal of creativity in even the most boring jobs (Winston Vargas/ Photo Researchers, Inc.).

ened companies such as Maytag and IBM became concerned with the overspecialization of jobs. Their response was to enlarge the job, which essentially amounted to expanding the number of operations performed by the employee. Thus, before job enlargement, the employee may have put on one bolt in assembling a machine as it moved past on a conveyor belt; now, under job enlargement, the employee puts on several bolts and spot welds a couple of places before the machine is sent on to the next work station. This approach was a step in the right direction and did alleviate some of the boredom associated with highly specialized jobs, but it fell short of motivating employees.

Job enrichment is an extension of job enlargement. Whereas job enlargement expands the number of operations performed (sometimes described as "loading horizontally"), job enrichment loads the job vertically by incorporating the motivators of recognition, responsibility, achievement, and growth. Job enrichment does not depend merely on expanding the number of operations but instead attempts to include a greater variety of work content. It usually requires a higher level of knowledge and skill in the job and gives employees more independence and responsibility for planning, directing, and controlling their own work. The purpose of job enrichment is to design jobs so that employees have the opportunity for personal growth and meaningful work experience.

Table 15-1 gives some examples of job enrichment. In one company, the productive process consisted of the typical assembly-line procedure. The first worker set up the work, the second performed a couple of simple operations, the third performed a couple more simple operations, and a fourth worker put the finishing touches on the product. The completed product was then passed on to an inspector, who checked it out. It was then packaged and sent to the customer. Unfortunately, too many of these products were being sent back because they were defective. There was an obvious quality problem. At first the supervisor in this situation reacted by bawling out the workers and chiding the inspector to tighten up standards and be more conscious of quality. After this approach failed to solve the problem, the supervisor tried job enrichment. She talked the head of the production department into letting her redesign the job. She set it up so that each worker now performed the production process from beginning to end. In other words, each worker now set up his or her own work, performed all the necessary operations, and completed the finishing touches. This, of course, was simply job enlargement. The number of operations was expanded. But the supervisor went

TABLE 15-1
EXAMPLES OF JOB ENRICHMENT

Old situation	Situation after job enrichment
Each employee rotated among all machines.	Each employee assigned to only two machines.
When machine failure occurred, operator called on maintenance group.	Each operator given training in maintenance; each conducts preventive and corrective maintenance on the two machines for which he is responsible.
Operator changes the slicing blade (the most important component of the machine) following a rigid rule contained in a manual.	Operator given authority to decide when to replace blade, based on his judgment.
Supervisor monitors operator and corrects unsatisfactory performance.	Performance feedback system developed that provides daily information on their work quality directly to operators.
Individual performs specialized task on units passing by him.	Three- to five-man teams build entire unit.
Supervisor decides who should do what.	Team decides who should do what.
Inspectors and supervisor test output and correct performance.	Team conducts own quality audits.

Source: Ross A. Webber, *Management,* Richard D. Irwin, Inc. Homewood, Ill., 1975, pp. 124–125. These examples were provided to Webber by David R. Sirota, Wharton School, University of Pennsylvania.

one step further. She eliminated the inspector and made each of the workers accountable for his or her own work. Now, after the worker had completely assembled the product from beginning to end, an identifying number had to be attached to it. Thus, if the product was returned, the supervisor knew exactly who had assembled it. This latter part was the job enrichment, giving the worker recognition and responsibility.

Significantly, the quantity of production under the above example of job enrichment remained about the same. When the supervisor backed off from high degrees of specialization and allowed the workers to work on a complete module of work, productivity did not suffer. But the quality of work improved dramatically. There were very few, if any, defects after the job enrichment was installed. The initial reaction of the workers was: "We don't want this kind of responsibility. We're not getting paid enough to take on that kind of responsibility." But after they tried it, they liked it. They became motivated to do a good job. As one of the workers said, "At first I didn't think I would like it. But after I got used to it I felt more worthwhile, that I was contributing to the company. It made me feel good and I began to try as hard as I could not to make any mistakes. I began to feel proud that I could make something on my own and not have any defects."

The same type of results from job enrichment have been demonstrated in office situations, hospital work, and in virtually every type of organization and at every level in the organization. Job enrichment generally seems to pay off in terms of increased motivation and improved performance. However, like the other concepts and techniques discussed in this book, a word of caution is in order. Like money, job enrichment is not the final word on motivation. Some employees will simply not respond to job-enrichment techniques. Some studies have shown that job enrichment does not work. It greatly depends on the values and needs of the employees and the nature of the job. For example, some job-enrichment designs decrease the opportunities for the employee to interact with coworkers. This trade-off (increased responsibility for decreased interaction) is not worthwhile to employees with high needs for affiliation. Yet despite the need for a contingency approach to job enrichment, supervisors can certainly motivate their employees better through an understanding and, in many cases, an application of the motivators of recognition, responsibility, achievement, and growth.

The importance of recognition There are several ways that supervisors can use recognition to motivate employees. The simplest, of course, is to recognize, verbally and/or in writing, an employee for a job well done. Recognition is usually effective if done publicly. For example, an "Employee of the Month" recognition could be given in the in-house publication, or specific recognition for some meritorious work could be given at a staff meeting or on a bulletin-board type of display. A few employees may find such public recognition embarrassing, or the informal group may not accept such behavior. It is up to the supervisor to find these exceptions and act accordingly. All employees, however, should respond favorably to private recognition from their supervisor for a job well done. This is discussed further in the last part of this chapter, on reinforcement.

Granting employees additional responsibility The use of this motivator basically involves making employees accountable for their own work. Too often, as soon as employees complete a task or a particular phase of an operation or process, they are absolved of all responsibility for what they have done. As in the detailed example discussed earlier, employees in manufacturing almost invariably pass their work on to inspectors. It is the inspector's responsibility to catch any defects in the work, not the employee's. The supervisor in the previous example overcame this situation by having workers attach an identifying number after they had completed a product. In doing this, the employees became responsible for their own work. When a product was returned for being defective, the supervisor knew exactly who to go to. Employees may sometimes rebel at such strict accountability, but at least for high-growth-need employees working on relatively complex tasks, research has shown that this will lead to motivation and improved performance.

Giving employees the opportunity to achieve The achievement motivator goes hand in hand with improved performance. Supervisors can best provide the opportunity to achieve by giving their employees a challenge. They can introduce new and/or more difficult tasks or make the goals more difficult to attain. This is sometimes referred to as "stretching," that is, giving the employees more than they are currently doing. Supervisors, of course, must be very careful that this does not turn into a good old "job speedup" or that they do not make the jobs so difficult that their people become frustrated.

The chance to advance and grow in the job It is very difficult for employees to maintain a status quo over the years. They either grow or they decline and become apathetic and give up. Unfortunately, as has been repeatedly brought out in this book, most employees have seemed to go the latter route. Survey after survey indicates that the productivity and quality of work of employees in the private and public sectors is low by any set of standards and seems to be getting worse. Why is this the case? Is it because employees are no darn good and are getting worse (McGregor's theory X assumptions about people) or because they are simply reacting to the way they are treated (theory Y assumptions about people)? Most psychologists and enlightened supervisors would say the latter. People will respond favorably and work hard on jobs under the proper conditions if given the chance. One of the best ways of doing this is to let employees grow in their jobs. Nothing will cause an employee to become apathetic and lazy faster than a dead-end job. Sadly, most of the jobs we have created for people in modern organizations are highly specialized, simplistic jobs with no opportunities for growth and advancement.

Importantly, with this motivator, we are not talking about continually promoting everyone up the hierarchical ladder of the organization. Obviously, there is just so much room at the top and, according to Lawrence Peter's principle, people would eventually reach their level of incompetency. What we are talking about is supervisors allowing their people to advance and grow in existing jobs. This can be done by giving the employee recognition, increased responsibility, and opportunities to achieve. In other words, supervisors should attempt to enrich jobs by incorporating Herzberg's motivators whenever conditions permit.

THE EXTERNAL APPROACH TO EMPLOYEE MOTIVATION

The external approach to motivation is environmentally based. Employees are extremely complex. The internal approach attempts to deal with that complexity by better understanding the needs of employees and determining whether they respond to self-actualization (Maslow) or responsibility (Herzberg). The external approach, on the other hand, concentrates on the environment in which employees operate. In particular, the external approach is concerned with the environmental consequences of employee behavior.

The external approach is based on the premise that employee behavior is a function of the environment's consequences. This premise comes from operant learning theory in psychology (operant conditioning is discussed in Chapter 12). The law of effect states that behavior followed by a positive consequence will tend to increase and behavior followed by a negative consequence will tend to decrease. Behavior followed by no consequence will also tend to decrease or extinguish in the long run. Based on this law, one can begin to predict and control human behavior by managing the consequences. If a negative consequence is applied to the behavior, it will decrease. If a positive consequence is applied, the behavior will increase. In this manner, supervisors can modify their subordinates' behaviors. They do not have to guess at the hidden need behind a given behavior, nor do they have to deal with the extreme complexities of their people. In the external approach, they simply manage the environmental consequences to encourage desirable behaviors and discourage undesirable behaviors.

Catch-23: What Is a Positive/Negative Consequence

Unfortunately, there are a couple of catches to the external approach to motivating employees. "Catch-23" in using this approach is: "What is a positive consequence?" The answer is: "Anything that increases behavior." This, of course, is a circular definition of a positive consequence. But it still has value, because only observables are being dealt with. If a supervisor attempts to supply a positive consequence, there is really no way of knowing whether or not it is positive until the results (subsequent behavior) appear. Yet in terms of predicting and controlling behavior, it may be hard for the supervisor to decide between possible positive consequences because of the individual differences among employees. What is positive for one employee may not be positive for another.

The problem associated with Catch-23 can be overcome by trying various consequences with individual employees and by following a couple of simple guidelines. Research to date indicates that practically all employees respond positively to attention/recognition and objective job feedback. A supervisor is on pretty safe ground in using these as positive consequences to increase desirable behaviors on the part of his employees. Thus, Catch-23 is a concern, but it certainly does not prohibit the effective use of the external approach.

Catch-24: Only the Contingent Consequence Has an Impact on Subsequent Behavior

There are many consequences of human behavior in organizations. Catch-24 says that only the contingent one has an impact on subsequent behavior. In laboratory experiments, where the law of effect was largely determined, the consequences of behavior can be isolated and readily controlled. In complex organizational settings, there are many competing consequences of employee behaviors. Only the one that links up with the behavior, usually the one that is most immediate and dominant, is the one that counts. The contingent consequence is the one on which the behavior depends. In complex settings, this is not always easy to identify or control.

The contingent consequence poses more of a problem for the external approach than does Catch-23. The solution to this problem lies in the ability of the supervisor to manage the contingent environment (both antecedent and consequent) of employee behavior. This is where supervisors must assume the role of "contingency managers." They must manage their people's environment instead of just managing the people themselves.

An Example of Catch-23 and Catch-24

A realistic example will help clarify what is meant by Catch-23 and Catch-24. Suppose, in an office situation, that one of the employees is rude to a customer. A supervisor who is using the external approach would apply a negative consequence to this undesirable employee behavior. Catch-23 says: "What is a negative consequence?" Let us say that in this case the supervisor goes over to the employee and chews him out as follows: "If I ever catch you treating one of our customers that way again, so help me there won't be a next time. Do you understand me?" The employee listens attentively and nods his head. Over the next week, he continues to treat customers rudely again and again. What happened here? Catch-23 says the supervisor did not provide a negative consequence by chewing him out. The behavior actually increased after the chewing out. In other words, the observable behavioral data suggests that the chewing out could have been a positive rather than a negative consequence. This could be explained by the fact that by chewing out the employee, the supervisor is giving him attention. And attention is very positive for people. Treating customers rudely is the only way this employee can get any attention from his supervisor.

The same example could also demonstrate Catch-24. Maybe the chewing out was not the contingent consequence at all. When the employee treated a customer rudely and the supervisor bawled him out, another consequence may have been involved when a coworker whispered: "Nice going—you really showed that customer a thing or two, and I loved the way the boss got all riled up." In other words, the contingent consequence was the positive recognition and attention given to the employee by a coworker. And it was this latter consequence that influenced the subsequent behavior.

"Catch an Employee Doing Something Right"

The above example is typical of how most supervisors manage people. They are on the lookout for something wrong and then jump on it. Unfortunately, as in the above example, this rarely has the desired effects. Negative control of behavior (punishing undesirable

411

behavior or threatening people in order to obtain desirable behavior) is very ineffective. One problem is that negative control is only temporary. As long as supervisors are around to keep constant watch over employees, they may get desired results from negative control. But as soon as they turn their backs or leave the area, the undesirable behaviors tend to surface again. In addition, a negative-control approach has many undesirable side effects. People do not like to be punished or threatened. They become upset and resentful. Such treatment leads to all kinds of counterproductive behaviors such as quitting, absenteeism, and a low quantity and quality of work.

The alternative to negative control is a positive approach. Instead of trying to catch employees doing something wrong and punishing them for it, supervisors should be trying to catch employees doing something right and rewarding them for it. The supervisor in the office example could have tried to catch the same employee treating a customer courteously. By applying a positive consequence to this behavior (e.g., recognition and feedback) the supervisor could increase it. This, of course, assumes that the consequence was actually positive and contingent; only by observing subsequent behavior can this be verified. If it *is* positive and contingent, then the desirable behavior will begin to replace that which is undesirable. Such positive control tends to be long-lasting and healthy for the individual and the organization. Supervisors should follow the slogan that says: "Catch Employees Doing Something Right Today."

ORGANIZATIONAL BEHAVIOR MODIFICATION

Supervisors can apply the concepts of the external approach through organizational behavior modification (or simply O.B. Mod.). Like the role that job enrichment plays in the internal approach, O.B. Mod. is a systematic application technique for the external approach. Figure 15-2 shows the five-step O.B. Mod. model. Supervisors can follow the guidelines provided in this model to manage their human resources more effectively. The remainder of this chapter discusses the five steps of O.B. Mod. and the way in which supervisors can apply them to improve performance of their departments.

Step 1: Identifying the Critical Behaviors

The first step is to identify the critical behaviors that influence performance. Like any problem-solving model, this first step is vital to

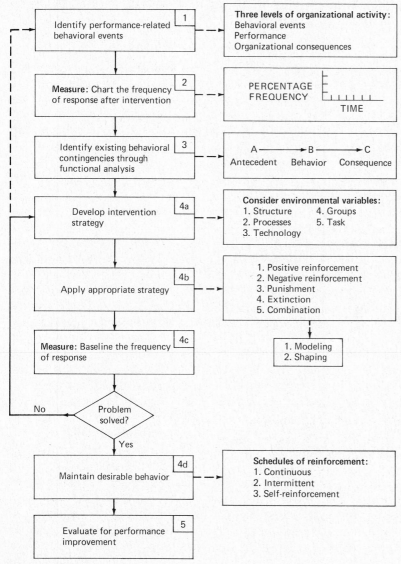

FIGURE 15-2
Organizational Behavior Modification.
(*Source:* Fred Luthans and Robert
Kreitner, "The Management of
Behavioral Contingencies," *Personnel,*
July–August 1974, p. 13.)

everything else that follows. This step is also not as easy as it may appear. Most supervisors have numerous solutions for everything that is going wrong. But very few truly understand what the real problems are. The same is true in O.B. Mod. There are a lot of obvious behaviors that supervisors would like to change, but the question is whether these behaviors are really critical to performance. For instance, a supervisor may be very irritated with a chronic complainer. Nothing is right with this person, and it is driving the supervisor "up the wall." Under O.B. Mod., the question this supervisor must ask is whether the complaining behavior has anything to do with performance. If the complainer is a good worker and contributes to the goals of the department, then this behavior should probably not be considered a critical behavior for step 1 of O.B. Mod. In other words, the supervisor should put up with the complaining behavior and concentrate on performance-related behaviors. On the other hand, if the complaining behavior is so disruptive that it is significantly affecting the performance of the department, then it probably should be given attention.

The critical behaviors can be thought of as "20-80" behaviors. This simply means that supervisors should concentrate on identifying the 20 percent of behaviors that influence 80 percent of performance rather than wasting time and effort trying to identify the 80 percent of behaviors that influence only 20 percent of performance. This, of course, is not always easy to accomplish. The supervisor can probably best identify critical behaviors by working backward from key performance areas. For example, if quality is a key performance area, what are the critical behaviors that go into it? The answer may be getting a certain individual to make a particular adjustment, having a particular employee in the right place at the right time, or receiving a necessary item from another department. All these can be expressed in behavioral terms that make them observable and measurable.

It should be noted that behaviors are not the only input into performance. Technology certainly plays a role. The machines and technological processes obviously have a significant impact on performance in all types of organizations. The same is true of training. Do the people know how to do their jobs? The ability of the people also has an impact. But, as previous chapters have pointed out time after time, technology, training, and ability do not necessarily explain poor performance. Generally speaking, our machines and technological processes are excellent. On a societal level, this amazing technology is what landed a man on the moon. But the major problems of contemporary society are the people problems

414

here on earth (e.g., poverty, war, disease, prejudice, etc.). This situation carries down to the organizational level. Most performance problems can be attributed to people, not technology. The same can be said of training and ability. People generally know how to do their jobs and, if anything, their abilities are being underutilized. The margin for improving performance lies in employee behaviors, in encouraging desirable, performance-related behaviors and discouraging behaviors that detract from performance.

Step 2: Measuring the Behaviors

After the critical behaviors have been identified, the next step is to determine how often they are occurring under existing conditions. This measurement step separates O.B. Mod. from an "off-the-cuff" type of approach. Systematic measurement is required to determine the frequency of the identified behavior.

Normally, existing records can be used to determine the frequency of the critical behavior. Production records, quality-control records, industrial engineering data of all kinds, cost-accounting data, time cards, and absenteeism records are some examples of data that are available to most supervisors. If these records are not available for certain types of behaviors, the supervisor may have to generate direct observation measures. In these latter measures, the supervisor should attempt to make the recording of data as simple as possible (e.g., "yes the person is at the work station" or "no she is not") and use time-sampling techniques (e.g., get representative samples of times during the day so that one can safely generalize to the whole day). Supervisors using observational techniques should also be careful not to let their presence influence the behaviors they are recording. Common sense is called for here, not sneaking around, being secretive, and invading privacy.

Usually the data that are collected through existing records or through observational techniques should be transferred to a simple frequency chart. Charts such as the one shown in Figure 15-3 give the supervisor a quick visual picture of the situation. Instead of raw frequency, percentage frequency is generally used; thus, if the supervisor missed gathering data at a certain time, the data would not be distorted. The charts can be constructed on graph paper or simply roughed out on a piece of scratch paper. The important point is that there is systematic measurement of the critical behaviors.

Often, the measurement in and of itself is very revealing to the

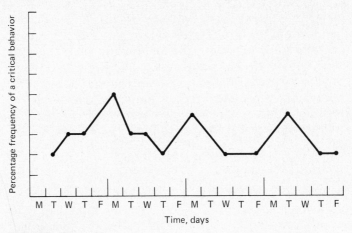

FIGURE 15-3
An example of a frequency chart for
organizational behavior modification.

supervisor. Sometimes the data indicates a much bigger problem
than was previously thought and sometimes the supposed problem
turns out to be no problem at all on the basis of the objective
information. In one case, a supervisor felt that his work group was
performing a critical behavior about 90 percent of the time. "After
all," he reasoned, "they were thoroughly trained to do this and were
constantly reminded of its importance." Upon objective measurement, however, it was found that the critical behavior was occurring
only 45 percent of the time, half of what the supervisor had thought.
On the other end, another supervisor felt that her people were
"never" on time and that it was getting to be a real problem. First of
all, this supervisor had to define carefully what she meant by being
tardy. She decided that those who were not at their assigned work
stations five minutes after the official starting time were tardy. When
she measured this tardiness behavior, it turned out to be so insignifi-
cant that she decided it really was not a problem at all.

Step 3: Analyzing the Critical Behaviors

After the critical behaviors have been identified and measured, they
then are systematically analyzed. As shown in Figure 15-2, this
analysis can be depicted as A-B-C. The A stands for antecedents, the

things that precede the behavior (B), and the C stands for the consequences of the behavior. The antecedents can control the behavior; they serve to prompt or cue the behavior. However, the antecedents do not cause the behavior. The consequences, on the other hand, are the key to the analysis. They are maintaining the behavior.

One supervisor who was using the O.B. Mod. approach identified unscheduled breaks as being a critical performance-related behavior for his department. In the measurement step, he determined that these unscheduled breaks represented a significant amount of lost time or irrecoverable production. It was costing the department considerable money. In the analysis step, he found an interesting pattern. The employees came to work at 8 A.M., had a scheduled break at 10 A.M., knocked off for lunch at 12 A.M., came back at 1 P.M., had a scheduled break at 3 P.M., and quit at 5 P.M. The supervisor discovered that almost precisely at 9 A.M., 11 A.M., 2 P.M., and 4 P.M. his workers were wandering off the job and going down to the rest room. In other words, they were taking a midbreak break. The antecedent cue was the clock. For example, at 9 A.M., a worker glanced at his watch and took off for the rest room. Importantly, it should be remembered that the clock did not cause the behavior. The time simply served as a cue for the behavior to occur. The consequences are what is maintaining the behavior. In this case, the supervisor determined that the consequences resulting from the unscheduled breaks his people were taking included escape from a dull, boring job, having a cigarette, and talking about the ballgames with their friends who were gathering down at the rest room at the same times.

Identifying the existing antecedents and consequences is in line with a problem-solving approach. With the knowledge of antecedents and consequences gained from the analysis, the supervisor can more effectively intervene with an appropriate strategy that will lead to performance improvement.

Step 4: Intervening for Performance Improvement

The first three steps of O.B. Mod. are preliminary to the action step of intervention. This is the step where the supervisor tries to change the behavior. The basic strategy is to accelerate the desired behaviors and decelerate the undesired behaviors. Based on the analysis made in step 3, the supervisor can change behaviors by changing either the

417

antecedents or the consequences. In most cases, it is very difficult to change antecedents. For example, it would be very difficult, if not impossible, for the supervisor who had the problem with unscheduled breaks to change the antecedent of time. Common antecedents for employee behaviors include home life, coworkers, and job/ organization design. Obviously, these are difficult for an individual supervisor to deal with. In general, supervisors should concentrate their interventions on behavioral consequences.

Positive reinforcement strategy To increase performance-related behaviors, a positive reinforcement strategy is recommended. As previously discussed, a reinforcer is a consequence that strengthens the behavior, so that the behavior tends to increase in subsequent frequency. Although Catch-23 says that supervisors do not know whether they are applying a positive reinforcer until they have a chance to see what actually happens to subsequent behavior, it is generally safe to assume that attention/recognition and feedback are positive reinforcers. Normal employees find these very reinforcing. In other words, if supervisors want to increase performance-related behaviors, then they should apply attention/recognition (e.g., "I noticed how you handled that problem, that is exactly what we are trying to get done in that area") and/or feedback (e.g., "Today you produced 85 percent of standard. This represents an improvement from your average, but don't forget that our agreed upon goal is 100 percent.")

Table 15-2 suggests some other rewards that supervisors may be able to apply as positive reinforcers. However, once again, supervisors should not assume that any "reward" is actually a positive reinforcer until the impact on behavior is observed. For example, praise or a pat on the back may seem like a logical positive reinforcer to use, but this may wear very thin very quick with many employees. Sugar-coated praise or a pat on the back may be interpreted as a phony gesture and actually turn out to be a negative consequence.

Money as a positive reinforcer Money, like praise, also comes quickly to mind as a reinforcer. The problem with money is that it is usually administered on a noncontingent basis. Money may decide whether the employee stays or quits for a better-paying job, but it really has little, if any, impact on day-to-day job behaviors. The paycheck at the end of the month or every two weeks is too far removed (noncontingent) from day-to-day behavior. The pay will certainly reinforce opening the envelope containing the check or

TABLE 15-2
CLASSIFICATIONS OF ON-THE-JOB REWARDS

Contrived on-the-job rewards				Natural rewards	
Consumables	**Manipulatables**	**Visual and auditory**	**Tokens**	**Social**	**Premack**
Coffee-break treats	Desk accessories	Office with a window	Money	Friendly greetings	Job with more responsibility
Free lunches	Wall plaques	Piped-in music	Stocks	Informal recognition	Job rotation
Food baskets	Company car	Redecoration of work environment	Stock options	Formal acknowledgment of achievement	Early time off with pay
Easter hams	Watches	Company literature	Movie passes	Invitations to coffee/lunch	Extended breaks
Christmas turkeys	Trophies	Private office	Trading stamps (green stamps)	Solicitations of suggestions	Extended lunch period
Dinners for the family on the company	Commendations	Popular speakers or lecturers	Paid-up insurance policies	Solicitations of advice	Personal time off with pay
Company picnics	Rings/tiepins	Book club discussions	Dinner and theater tickets	Compliment on work progress	Work on personal project on company time
After-work wine and cheese parties	Appliances and furniture for the home	Feedback about performance	Vacation trips	Recognition in house organ	Use of company machinery or facilities for personal projects
Beer parties	Home shop tools		Coupons redeemable at local stores	Pat on the back	Use of company recreation facilities
	Garden tools		Profit sharing	Smile	
	Clothing			Verbal or nonverbal recognition or praise	
	Club privileges				
	Special assignments				

Source: Fred Luthans and Robert Kreitner, *Organizational Behavior Modification*, Scott, Foresman and Company, Glenview, Ill., 1975, p. 101. Used with permission.

419

walking up to the pay window, but everyday behaviors depend on more immediate consequences.

Supervisors often make the mistake of saying to themselves, when one of their employees exhibits a desirable behavior: "Well, it's about time! Now he's doing what he's getting paid to do." If the supervisor lets it go at that and says nothing (i.e., gives no attention/recognition or feedback), there is no consequence for the desirable behavior, and this leads to a decrease in the desirable behavior. Supervisors should not assume that the money an employee makes is a contingent, positive consequence that will accelerate critical performance behaviors.

Please note that the above discussion does not deny that money is a positive reinforcer. It simply says that the way money is currently administered, it turns out to have little, if any, impact on everyday job behaviors. Most employees do not view money as a contingent consequence of their behaviors. If supervisors could make money contingent, then it might be a very positive consequence. For example, the supervisor who was having a problem with the unscheduled breaks his workers were taking had a seemingly impossible chore of changing the behavior. He could not change the antecedent (time), and if he changed the consequence by locking up the bathrooms between breaks, he would be inviting more trouble than he had before. This supervisor solved the problem by pointing out to his workers a heretofore ignored consequence. He calculated that every time any one of the work group took an unscheduled break, it cost each of them approximately $1.75 in lost group incentive pay from the lost-time production. In other words, the supervisor made money a contingent consequence of staying on the job. Once the supervisor pointed this out to his employees, there were no more unscheduled breaks. The supervisor did not have to admonish his people for taking unscheduled breaks or sheepishly tell them they could not go to the bathroom except on breaks. In addition, the work group enforced the rule of no unscheduled breaks themselves. Coworkers, in no uncertain terms, would let a person who started to wander off the job know that it was costing them money.

Significantly, in the above example the worker had always been on a group incentive system. In terms of making money a reinforcer for performance behaviors, incentive systems are much superior to day-rate pay schemes. But, as in the example, most incentive systems do not turn out to be contingent enough. They are usually so complicated that the employee is not able to determine what the payoff will be when he or she produces a certain amount. This is especially true in industrial situations. As in the example, if supervisors would simplify the incentive system and point out exactly what the payoffs are, money would become a more contingent consequence and thus an effective positive reinforcer. In a few instances, supervisors have actually tried handing out money on the spot to people who exhibited desirable critical behaviors; as a result, their performance increased significantly. The same is true in the sales area. Sales commissions are generally pretty well understood by the salespersons involved, and this helps explain why sales personnel are generally well motivated (at least relative to other types of work) and perform at high levels. Since they work on commission, money is a contingent reinforcer for them. Although wage and salary administration is beyond the control of most supervisors, it is possible to encourage performance by making money as contingent as possible on the exhibition of desirable critical behaviors. In general, however, supervisors will have to depend on nonfinancial rewards (attention/recognition and feedback) to positively reinforce critical behaviors for performance improvement.

Strategies to decrease behaviors It is much more effective for supervisors to exercise positive control over employee behavior than to impose negative control. For example, it is better for an employee to be rewarded for good attendance instead of being punished for absenteeism. Supervisors could wisely follow one of "Grandma's laws"—the one which says to "accentuate the positive and eliminate the negative." There are just so many behaviors that an employee can exhibit, and if the desirable ones are encouraged through positive reinforcement, they will begin to replace the undesirable behaviors. In other words, an effective strategy to decrease undesirable behaviors is to encourage desirable behaviors. This is called replacement.

Unfortunately, in many cases supervisors may not be able or willing to use a replacement strategy to decrease problem behaviors. In these cases an extinction or punishment strategy is the only alternative. In an extinction strategy, the supervisor tries to remove the reinforcing consequence that is currently maintaining the undesirable behavior. For example, maybe coworkers are providing reinforcing consequences for a worker's undesirable behavior. In that case, the supervisor might move the individual to another location so that the coworkers are no longer a contingent consequence.

As a last resort, the supervisor may have to punish undesirable behavior. This strategy is much overused, but in certain instances—especially those, such as unsafe behaviors, requiring immediate action—it may be the only alternative. If punishment is contingently applied to decrease undesirable behaviors, the supervisor should always carefully point out the desired alternative and vigorously reinforce it as soon as it appears. In this way, the undesirable side effects of punishment can be minimized.

Step 5: Evaluating for Performance Improvement

This final step emphasizes the importance of evaluating for performance improvement. Unlike other motivational schemes through the years, O.B. Mod. insists on this evaluation step. Supervisors must make sure that this systematic approach to behavior management does in fact lead to performance improvement.

Supervisors should not be satisfied with changing employee behaviors simply for the sake of behavioral change. The changes must improve the effectiveness of individual employees' performance and upgrade overall departmental or unit performance. Supervisors must continually monitor objective measures of performance to make sure that the O.B. Mod. is having its intended effect. The measurement that was initiated in step 2 helps in this regard. This measurement helps the supervisor to determine whether the intervention tried in step 4 is working or not. If performance is not improving, then—as shown in Figure 15-2—the supervisor must try another intervention and/or redefine the problem.

The ultimate goal of the O.B. Mod. process is more effective human resource management and performance improvement. If supervisors systematically follow the O.B. Mod. model in conjunction with the other motivational approaches discussed in the first half of the chapter, these goals can be reached.

■ KEY CONCEPTS

Internal motivation
Maslow's hierarchy of needs
Herzberg's two-factor theory
Job enrichment
External motivation
Law of effect
Contingent consequence

Organizational behavior modification (O.B. Mod.)
Positive reinforcement
Punishment

■ PRACTICAL EXERCISES

(These can be performed by individuals or by groups.)

1 Take a specific job that you are very familiar with (e.g., one that you are currently involved with or one from your past experience) and enrich it. How would you redesign this job to incorporate Herzberg's motivators? Give the details of this enriched job. What do you think the impact would be on employee satisfaction and performance?

2 Step 1 of the O.B. Mod. approach is to identify critical ("20-80") performance-related behaviors. From your present or past job experience, identify two or three such behaviors. Step 3 of O.B. Mod. is to functionally analyze the critical behavior, i.e., identify the antecedents and the consequences of the behavior. In retrospect, what do you think were some of the possible antecedents and consequences of the behaviors you identified? Step 4 of O.B. Mod. is to intervene to change the behavior(s). What are some possible interventions you could make to change the behavior(s) you have identified and functionally analyzed? What impact do you think these interventions would have on the behavior? Why?

■ DISCUSSION INCIDENTS

Jim Bock had worked his way up through "the school of hard knocks" and had been a supervisor for the past few years. Jim had just completed a human relations training program put on by the personnel department. Over coffee, one of his cosupervisors asked him what his reaction was to the program. Jim replied, "Well, I'll tell you one thing. Those personnel guys are dreamers. They tried to tell us that money wasn't important to our people. They told us that in order to motivate our people we should appeal to things like esteem, responsibility, and even something called self-actualization. What a bunch of baloney. I've dealt with people all my life and I've found that the only thing they are interested in is the bucks! Money is what motivates them, not this other junk."

1 How would you respond to Jim Bock? Was the trainer justified in saying that money is not important to people? Where does money fit into the Maslow theory? Into the Herzberg theory?

2 Why do you suppose Jim Bock feels they way he does? It is true that he has had experience with people all his life, yet should he feel this way? Why?

3 From an external approach to motivation, what role does money play? What role could it play to make it a more effective reinforcer?

Jane Hardy, a departmental supervisor for several years, really got into O.B. Mod. She read all the books and articles about it she could get her hands on and attended a couple of training seminars devoted to the background and application of O.B. Mod. She closely followed the five-step model in managing her human resources. The results were even better than she had anticipated. For the first time in the history of her department, both quantity and quality standards were exceeded, and tardiness and absenteeism were virtually eliminated. Jane was elated. Then her boss called on her and said, "Jane, I don't know what has gotten into your department lately, but I'm going to have the engineers go in and up your standards. We can't afford to pay incentive wages for that level of productivity. I know your people will be upset, but use that O.B. Mod. approach you are so thrilled with and see if you can smooth things out."

1 From an external motivation standpoint, what is the boss doing by upping the piece rate? Do you think the boss understands the O.B. Mod. approach? Could Jane use O.B. Mod. on her boss?

2 Is there any way that Jane could use the O.B. Mod. approach, as suggested by her boss, to handle the increased standards of performance? If you were Jane, how would you go about trying to motivate your people in light of the boss's action?

LEADING
EMPLOYEES

16 CHAPTER

It was a typical busy night at Duffy's tavern. Everyone was buying drinks for and offering advice to their old buddy Ed Falcon. Ed had just been promoted to supervisor of maintenance. The group at Ed's table consisted of Hank, the old retiring supervisor of maintenance; Ken, the supervisor of production; and Bob, the manager of personnel. At first, most of the advice came from old Hank. He stressed the quality of the work crew Ed would inherit, saying, "They're good boys. You just let them stay loose and don't meddle with them and you'll find that they do all right by you." Ken, the production supervisor, did not quite agree with old Hank's philosophy. He stressed a more hard-line approach, emphasizing things like gaining the respect and control of the employees. In particular, Ken stressed that it would be good for Ed to hand out fairly severe discipline to at least one employee early so that his people would know who the boss was. Finally, there was Bob's advice. Bob really didn't say much until the other two had left. Then the personnel manager took Ed aside for a little fatherly advice. Essentially, what he said was that the other two managers were very traditional in their thinking. In these times, he stressed, you have to treat employees with confidence and respect. You have to solicit their ideas and provide opportunities for their participation.

The next morning Ed had a tremendous headache. He wasn't sure if it was because of the beer or the prospect of becoming maintenance supervisor. For the first time, he realized he had some awfully big decisions and choices to make. The conversation last night left him more confused than confident. He knew that each of the supervisors was very successful, but he had very little idea of who was right. He wished he could get a little more knowledge of this thing called leadership so he could select his own style for supervising his people effectively.

■ LEARNING OBJECTIVES

After reading this chapter, you should have:
An understanding of traditional views of leadership styles and functions
An awareness of the wide variety of possible leadership styles available
The knowledge and ability to analyze and develop an effective leadership style
The necessary analytical skills to identify your particular leadership situation
The skill to combine the peculiarities of leadership style and situation for maximally effective performance

The dilemma faced by the new supervisor in the opening case is one of the central themes of this chapter, which focuses on leadership and the qualities, characteristics, circumstances, and behaviors that help to make it effective. This chapter should help supervisors select and develop appropriate leadership styles and behaviors for their particular circumstances and situations.

Although leadership has probably been given more attention through the years than any other single subject, very little is known about it. There is still much disagreement on the factors and circumstances of effective leadership. It is not possible to recommend a single approach that will work for all supervisors in all situations. Therefore, the approach taken here will be to present several different theories and styles of leadership. We will begin with a brief discussion of the traditional approaches to the study of leadership. Next, the results of three important studies will be reviewed briefly in order to gain a more realistic picture of the problems of determining effective leadership styles. This will be followed with a discussion of two of the most recent approaches to leadership: the behavioral and contingency approaches. Finally, the last section will provide a comprehensive review of leadership that will emphasize the practicalities supervisors must take into consideration when choosing their own leadership styles.

TRADITIONAL APPROACHES TO LEADERSHIP

The traditional approaches to the study and explanation of leadership can be summed up under the "great man" syndrome, which evolved into the search for traits or characteristics of effective leadership.

The "Great Man" Approach

In a nutshell, the "great man" approach says that leaders are born, not made. The proponents of this theory believe that there is very little to be gained from the study of leadership or leadership training because the traits and characteristics of effective leadership are present at birth and nothing can be done about it. Famous figures from history—for example, Alexander the Great, Queen Elizabeth, Napoleon, and John F. Kennedy—are used to support the "great man" theory. The argument is that these individuals would have emerged as leaders out of any situation. At best, the proponents of the theory suggest that studying the traits of famous leaders will help in the early identification and selection of effective leaders.

The "great man" approach applied today would emphasize the selection process and deemphasize training and development activities. The "great man" approach would suggest that people either have it or they do not. Why spend time and effort on job training, coaching, counseling, organizational development, or other such activities? Fortunately, this perspective does not dominate. Although many people feel this way about leadership, it is now generally recognized that there are many other variables that enter into the leadership process.

The Trait Approach

Trait theories are an outgrowth of the "great man" approach. As the great leaders of history were studied, some common traits seemed to emerge. This search for traits dominated leadership research from about 1920 to 1950. During this time, researchers attempted to build long lists of traits that supposedly led to effective leadership. Some of the traits and characteristics which were identified are shown in Table 16-1. Despite the wide variety and large number of traits, it soon became evident that the trait approach was not going to work. No two lists seemed to agree. Moreover, the lists uncovered almost nothing that people did not already know through their common sense. It was not until the appearance of the landmark research described in the next section that new and more realistic views of leadership emerged.

Despite the disappointing results of trait research, there is still some value in it and many still believe in it. For example, in selecting people for positions of leadership, the trait approach would stress a limited number of physical, mental, or personal characteristics such as physical size, intelligence, and personality. Unfortunately, this

TABLE 16-1
EXAMPLES OF LEADERSHIP TRAITS

Need for success	Self-confidence	Popularity
Concern for status	Enthusiasm	Decisiveness
Alertness	Persistence	Unselfishness
Tactfulness	Extroversion	Goal orientation
Social awareness	Insight	Physical stamina
Intelligence	Verbal skills	Physical health
Dependability	Social maturity	Analytical ability
Cooperativeness	Concern for people	Persuasive ability
Initiative	Socioeconomic status	Sympathy
Integrity	Ambition	Honesty
Sense of fair play	Adaptability	Strength

approach sometimes results in misplaced personnel and correspondingly unproductive and dissatisfied employees. In recent years, more realistic theories of leadership have been developed and implemented. The basis for these modern leadership theories is contained in some landmark research studies which are briefly summarized in the following section.

LANDMARK RESEARCH ON LEADERSHIP

Among the numerous studies on leadership that have been conducted through the years, three stand out. Much of modern leadership theory, research, and practice can be traced to the Iowa, Ohio State, and Michigan studies.

The Iowa Studies

The studies conducted at the University of Iowa in the late 1930s were the first to systematically analyze the effects of leadership styles on the behavior of the group. These studies were conducted by psychologists Ronald Lippitt and Ralph White under the general direction of Kurt Lewin, the recognized father of group dynamics. The study examined the effects that three different leadership styles had on a group of boys belonging to a hobby club. After a period of several weeks, the leadership of the group changed, until all three leadership styles had been experienced. The styles of leadership can be summarized as follows:

1 *Democratic.* This leader helped to organize the group and to determine the group's activities through voting. He assisted the group to achieve its goals through a helping, participative style.

2 *Autocratic.* This leader took full responsibility for deciding on the group's projects by assigning tasks to members and permitting little or no participation in the decision-making process.

3 *Laissez Faire.* This leader provided no direction at all for the group, neither praising nor criticizing members' behaviors. Thus, the group had almost no control over their activities and there was very little discipline.

During the group's experiences with the different leaders, the experimenters carefully observed and recorded the boys' behaviors. It was found that the democratic leadership style was almost unanimously preferred over either the laissez faire or authoritarian styles. In addition, it was found that even the laissez faire style was much preferred over the authoritarian style. Thus, these studies clearly indicated that, when given a preference, democratic styles of supervision were preferred.

A second finding of interest was that there was frequent hostility and aggression in both the laissez faire and autocratically led groups. On the other hand, hostility and aggression were much less frequent in the democratic groups. Another important finding was that in certain autocratically led groups, the boys became very apathetic and lethargic rather than aggressive. In other words, it appears that the autocratic supervisory style can have two effects: it can produce very aggressive and antagonistic individuals or it may lead people to become subdued and apathetic.

These pioneering studies are sometimes criticized or dismissed in discussions of supervision because they used young boys for subjects instead of mature employees. However, despite these legitimate criticisms, the studies were able to effectively demonstrate two important aspects of leadership which have definite implications for modern supervision:

1 Autocratic leadership styles have a definite impact on group behaviors such as aggression and hostility.

2 Democratic styles are generally preferred by the group over other leadership styles.

Importantly, however, the Iowa studies did not directly investigate or demonstrate the impact that leadership style has on group productivity. Although the researchers were able to demonstrate that the boys preferred democratic supervision and were less aggressive under this type of leadership, it was left to later studies to investigate the effect of leadership styles on productivity.

The Ohio State Studies

The Ohio State studies began right after World War II. Their major objective was to identify the functions that leaders perform. The researchers asked people in all types of organizations to describe the behavior of their leaders. Through mathematical techniques, the researchers were then able to identify two important classes of behaviors associated with the leadership function. These behaviors are described as follows:

1 *Initiating Structure.* Initiating behavior is directed toward defining, structuring, and determining group behavior and interactions. Performing this function, leaders define group goals, assign tasks, evaluate performance, and administer sanctions when necessary.

2 *Consideration.* Consideration is almost synonymous with human relations skills and attitudes. Consideration behavior would include things such as counseling, listening, and offering helpful suggestions to group members.

The implications of the Ohio State studies for effective supervision lie in the performance of both task-oriented (initiating) and human relations (consideration) behaviors. After the Ohio State studies, there was wide recognition and acceptance of task and human relations behaviors as the starting point for understanding and effectively applying leadership. Now the emphasis is placed on finding the proper balance between task and human relations behaviors.

The Michigan Studies

The Michigan studies concentrated on the systematic and scientific investigation of the effects of leadership style on employee productivity and satisfaction. The initial study was conducted after World War II at the home office of the Prudential Life Insurance Company in Newark, New Jersey. The study examined the leadership styles of the supervisors of twelve high-producing units and twelve low-producing units. By examining the differences between these high- and low-producing supervisory groups, the researchers believed that they would be able to isolate the behaviors and characteristics of effective supervisors. There were three important differences between the supervisors of the high- and low-producing groups:

1 The high-producing supervisors tended to be employee-centered or oriented toward human relations, whereas the low-producing supervisors were relatively more production-centered or task-oriented. For example, if a worker came to a supervisor who was employee-centered and complained of a headache, the supervisor would respond, "Don't worry about it, take it easy, the rest of us will cover for you." The production-centered supervisor would respond, "Oh darn it, there goes our production. 'Gut' it out so we can get the job done today."

2 The high-producing supervisors spent more time in face-to-face contact with their people than did the low-producing supervisors.

3 The low-producing supervisors had close styles of supervision, where they were actively involved in and critically analyzed employees' day-to-day operations. On the other hand, the effective supervisors used a more general style, where they helped employees plan, set objectives, and establish goals but gave the employees freedom and latitude in their daily operations.

The findings of the Michigan studies are particularly important because they provide evidence that the people-oriented styles of supervision in the workplace seemed to be more effective than task-oriented approaches. Today, the advocates of people-oriented supervisory styles still point to these pioneering studies as primary support. As will be discussed in later sections, there is now some doubt that this finding applies to *all* circumstances and situations faced by supervisors.

BEHAVIORAL THEORIES OF LEADERSHIP

Bolstered by the Iowa, Ohio State, and Michigan studies, attention in leadership shifted from a concern about the characteristics and traits of leaders to what leaders do (i.e., their behaviors). This new behavioral approach to leadership emphasized the analysis and description of the behaviors related to effectiveness and productivity. Most of the behavioral theories of leadership emphasized participative and democratic styles. Moreover, rather than just ignoring the need for task-oriented behavior, many of these theories viewed task and human relations behaviors as competing with and opposing one another. The behavioral theories of leadership more or less advocated that the human relations behaviors were effective whereas the task-oriented behaviors were ineffective. Figure 16-1 illustrates the various leadership styles along a continuum of effectiveness. Those who subscribe to the behavioral leadership theories advocate the styles on the right (human relations, employee-centered, democratic, participative, and "Y" styles). Figure 16-2 gives some specific examples of how the leadership style would be carried out in some basic elements of supervision discussed in other chapters in the book.

The behavioral theories have made a significant contribution to leadership effectiveness. As was noted in the last section, the Iowa studies provided considerable evidence that democratic styles are preferred over autocratic and laissez faire styles. More importantly, the Michigan studies were able to demonstrate, in an organizational setting, that supervisors who used a general style and were oriented toward human relations had more productive work groups than did the task-oriented, close supervisors.

Despite the findings from the classic studies, many questions have recently emerged regarding the validity of the behavioral approaches. Much of the questioning is based on practical considerations. For example, everyone can cite at least one leader who is very task-oriented and autocratic yet is exceedingly effective. General George S. Patton, the famous hero of World War II, was such a leader. In addition to common observations, recent research has revealed that at least in some particular circumstances, approaches oriented toward human relations may be less effective than task-oriented approaches. Thus, there is now a generally recognized need for a new approach to leadership.

Ineffective	Moderately Effective	Effective
Task orientation		Human relations orientation
Concern for production		Concern for employees
Autocratic		Democratic
Directive		Participative
Theory X		Theory Y

FIGURE 16-1
An effectiveness continuum of leadership styles.

CONTINGENCY LEADERSHIP APPROACH

Like the contingency approach to supervision described in the first chapter of this book, the contingency approach to leadership recognizes the importance of the situation. Briefly, the contingency approach says that effective leadership style depends on the situation. In other words, human relations, task-oriented, and even middle-of-the-road styles may be effective under the appropriate conditions. The key to this approach is to identify the situations in which a particular style will be effective.

Professor Fred Fiedler of the University of Washington, who

Elements of Supervision	Directive ⊢—————— Task-Oriented Ineffective	Moderate ——┼——————	Nondirective ——————┤ Human-Relations-Oriented Effective
Planning	Supervisor determines plans, objectives, and goals independently.	Supervisor solicits input from others but makes the final planning decisions.	Major goals, objectives, and plans are arrived at through group consensus.
Organize	Supervisor assigns positions and arranges organizational structure as he or she sees fit.	Supervisor solicits input regarding organization structure and job assignments but may or may not use this information in the decision.	Employees help to determine where their talents are best utilized. Major criteria come from position and assignments and are based on group acceptance.
Command	Directives are issued in an authoritative and no-nonsense manner.	Supervisor is careful in issuing commands, trying to make sure that employees are not alienated.	Commands are usually not necessary; members assume responsibility and take appropriate action.
Communication	Most communication flows from the supervisor downward.	The supervisor does not issue strong directives and occasionally solicits information from the lower levels.	Input is solicited from lower levels and is a major determinant of upward communication.
Control	Supervisor strictly rewards and punishes employees for conformance or nonconformance to standards.	Supervisor is fairly lenient in the control process, realizing that outside factors play an important role.	If the group is functioning appropriately, group sanctions and self are the most appropriate methods of control.

FIGURE 16-2
Examples of the way leadership styles would impact on the elements of supervision.

Leadership can determine the
difference between success and
failure (Magnum Photos).

developed some tests to identify leadership styles and situations, has
been able to identify some contingency relationships from his extensive research on leadership. The styles range from task-directed to
human relations. The leadership situation questionnaire assesses the
situation in terms of three fundamental dimensions: (1) the leader's
perception of the group's liking for her or him (called "leader-
member relations"); (2) the amount of structure inherent in employee's jobs (called "task structure"); and (3) the supervisor's power in
terms of the authority to hire, fire, reward, and punish employees

(called "position power"). Based on careful research in a wide variety of organizations, Fiedler has developed a model that relates the situational variables to leadership styles that lead to effective performance. His model is shown in Figure 16-3 and can be summarized as follows:

1 In extremely unfavorable circumstances (i.e., where there are poor relations between the supervisor and the subordinates, there are few guidelines for performing the work, and the leader has little or no authority to sanction employees), a task-directed style is the most effective.

2 Under extremely favorable circumstances, the task-directed leadership style is most effective. Extremely favorable circumstances occur when the supervisor is highly respected and liked by subordinates, the tasks and objectives are clear and well defined, and the leader has a great deal of authority to reward and punish employees.

3 Under moderately favorable or unfavorable conditions, the human relations style of supervision is most effective. These moderately favorable or unfavorable situations are where leader-member relationships are OK, task structure is moderate, and the supervisor may be able to recommend sanctions for employees and perhaps administer some sanctions independently.

To clarify the contingency model of leadership effectiveness, the following examples are presented:

1 *The Airline Maintenance Supervisor.* A good example of a very favorable leadership situation might be found in the airline industry. Jim Clancy, our hypothetical supervisor, heads a maintenance crew in which leader-member relations are very favorable. He has had the same crew for years and has built a loyal, mutually respectful relationship with the members. The task is very structured. There is a definite checklist of procedures that he and the crew follow in servicing the planes. Finally, he has a great deal of authority. Because they are dealing with life-and-death matters, Clancy has complete authority to give orders and reward and punish his crew members. Under these conditions, the Fiedler model would say that this supervisor should have a very task-oriented style of leadership to be effective. He should be a no-nonsense person who gives direct orders and does not ask for participation and involvement from the group members.

2 *The Leader of a Small Infantry Unit in the Vietnam War.* Consider the situation facing Jim Eaton, the leader of a typical, small unit of infantry men during the Vietnam war. The leader-member relations in this unit were generally poor because the men had been drafted

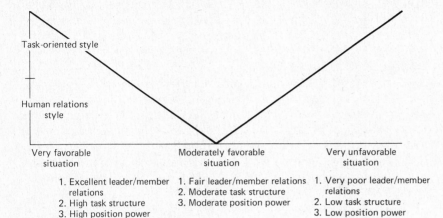

Task-oriented style

Human relations
style

Very favorable situation	Moderately favorable situation	Very unfavorable situation
1. Excellent leader/member relations	1. Fair leader/member relations	1. Very poor leader/member relations
2. High task structure	2. Moderate task structure	2. Low task structure
3. High position power	3. Moderate position power	3. Low position power

FIGURE 16-3
The Fiedler model on the relationship
between leadership style and
leadership situations.

reluctantly into a war that most of them did not want to be in, and they often took their frustrations out on Eaton. The task at hand was also not clearly defined. This was a different kind of war requiring a different approach. But no one was really sure how to go about it. Finally, the position power of the leader was poor. Because of the poor attitudes and fear of things like "fragging," many leaders like Eaton were not sure of their authority. Under these very unfavorable conditions, Fiedler's model would suggest that the leader should assume a very task-oriented, nonparticipative style in order to be as effective as possible. For instance, consider the squad leader who had to organize and carry out night patrols against the enemy. If such a leader had asked the soldiers how they felt about their duties and had solicited participation, he would undoubtedly have received many negative reactions. This would have made the job even more difficult and led to ineffective performance. On the other hand, responsiveness from the men was probably much higher for those leaders who simply issued their orders without opening up opportunities for discussion. Thus, Fiedler's suggestion that task-oriented leadership is effective in extremely poor leadership situations seems to make sense in this example.

Most supervisor's situations do not approach the extreme conditions described in these two examples. Although there are obviously exceptions, most supervisors are faced with moderately favorable or unfavorable situations. They have fair leader-member relations, adequate task structure, and some position power. Thus, according to the Fiedler model, the appropriate style for these supervisors is a human relations style.

Careful consideration of the contingency model also helps to explain the previous approaches to leadership. For example, although the Iowa and Michigan studies support the use of human relations over a task style of leadership, these findings are consistent with the contingency model if the situations investigated were moderately favorable. One could argue that this was, in fact, the case. In other words, a contingency view need not necessarily conflict with other theories of leadership.

There are several other, similar approaches in addition to the Fiedler contingency model of leadership. One of the more popular (e.g., Blake and Mouton's managerial grid and William Reddin's 3-D approach) is a grid approach such as the one illustrated in Figure 16-4. Each of the styles described in the figure is based on a different emphasis and combination of task versus human relations orientations. These various styles can be further described as follows:

1 *The Abdicator.* This style is characterized by a laissez faire approach. There is minimum concern for both people and task. Under this style, the leader allows members almost complete freedom, interacts with group members infrequently, and is not concerned about getting the job done.

2 *The Helper.* This style is characterized by the leader's genuine concern for the employees but minimum concern for the task. If necessary, the leader is willing to sacrifice getting the job done to ensure that employees are satisfied and content.

3 *The Driver.* This leader is primarily concerned with getting the job done and has minimum concern for people. If achieving the task causes human hardship and problems, the leader is willing to sacrifice the people for the task.

4 *The Compromiser.* This leader sincerely attempts to achieve both task and human relations goals. However, when difficulties arise, he or she readily sacrifices one goal for another. The result is that this leader tends to be expedient or "wishy washy."

5 *The Ideal.* This leader is able to integrate both task and human concerns into a consistent and rational style of leadership. Rules and guidelines for integration are developed over years of supervisory experience.

Although the ideal style is implied to be the best, some leadership

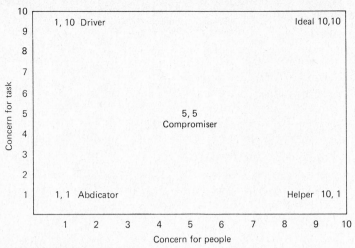

FIGURE 16-4
A two-dimensional grid for leadership.

theorists such as William Reddin, a Canadian writer and management consultant, recognize that the other styles can also be effective under certain conditions. Some possible situations where each of the styles may be effective are illustrated in Table 16-2. It is also important to remember that the relationship between styles and situations suggests that normally effective styles, such as the ideal one, may actually be ineffective under some conditions and situations. For example, the ideal style may not provide effective leadership in an organization that places almost exclusive emphasis on either people (e.g., a human services agency in the government) or tasks (e.g., a wartime military unit or a construction firm). The effectiveness of leadership styles is highly dependent upon the specific circumstances. The next section will discuss a practical approach to the evaluation of circumstances and the application of the most effective leadership style.

LEADERSHIP APPLIED

Despite the large amount of research and theory on leadership, there is, as mentioned before, no universally accepted approach. This lack of agreement is largely due to the complexity of leadership. As has been discussed so far, effective leadership is a function of many

Table 16-2
CIRCUMSTANCES WHERE EACH STYLE CAN BE EFFECTIVE

Style	Possible situations where the style may be effective
The abdicator	The organization contains highly motivated and achievement-oriented individuals who resent efforts to channel or direct their efforts, and there is little pressure or concern for task-oriented goals. Professional or research-oriented organizations such as a laboratory or a university may be examples.
The helper	The organization's major goals are human, not task concerns. Examples are many social and/or mental rehabilitation agencies.
The driver	The organization places a high value on production and employees are low-skilled individuals who can easily be replaced. Most manufacturing organizations would be examples.
The compromiser	The organization's plans, goals, and objectives frequently change. Examples are political organizations and organizations having highly volatile technologies.
The ideal	The organization is stable and has an equally balanced program emphasizing both human and task goals. Many large, successful organizations are in this category.

important personal, organizational, and job-related variables. Each of the approaches tries to account for the differing situations and circumstances, but the sheer number of factors makes a universally applicable leadership approach virtually impossible. Yet these variables must be taken into consideration by supervisors who wish to lead effectively.

The purpose of this section is to describe some of the most important variables that should influence the supervisor's choice of leadership style. Some of these variables have been suggested by research on the contingency approach previously discussed. Others are simply commonsense considerations that cannot be ignored. This discussion should help supervisors to analyze, develop, and apply more effective leadership styles.

Individual and Group Variables

There are several personal and group variables which should influence a supervisor's choice of leadership style. Among the more important of these are the following:

1 *Education.* It is generally recognized that more highly educated employees prefer and respond better to human relations styles of leadership than to task-oriented styles. The opposite is not necessarily true. There is little evidence to suggest that a task-oriented style is more effective with less educated employees.

2 *Age.* All other factors being equal, many believe that younger employees with today's values prefer and respond better to participative, human relations styles of supervision. On the other hand, a smaller number of people feel that older employees with more traditional values accept and respond better to more directive, task-oriented styles. Unfortunately, there is little research supporting either of these opinions. Supervisors should be aware that there are definitely exceptions to these generalities.

3 *Size of Groups.* The size of the group being led effects the type of style that is most effective. Because a human relations style requires large amounts of personal contact, it is extremely difficult to use with large groups. Therefore, directive, task-oriented styles may be more effective when the span of control is large.

4 *Employee Characteristics.* Employees differ on a wide variety of personal characteristics (e.g., self-esteem, motivation, values, attitudes, interests, personality, intelligence, abilities, and aptitudes). Each employee's unique combination of these personal characteristics complicates the leadership problem. Each characteristic may require a different style. Unfortunately, the research offers little guidance as to the relationship of these personal characteristics to the effective leadership style. A general guideline, however, would be that employees who are intelligent, self-motivated, and have positive self-esteem should respond better to participative, human relations styles of supervision. On the other hand, with all other conditions being equal, the more directive, task-oriented styles will probably work better with employees having more limited aptitudes, low self-esteem and lower self-motivation.

5 *Group Characteristics.* Besides personal characteristics, there are also certain characteristics of groups which may help determine the appropriate leadership style. Possible group characteristics would include cohesiveness, stability, and goal-orientation. Although very little research has been done to determine the precise effects that group variables have on style and effectiveness, some general guidelines can be offered. For example, supervisors should probably be more directive and task-oriented the more the leader and the group share the same goals. On the other hand, groups that are very stable and cohesive might require a more participative, human relations type of approach because it enables the group to sanction the supervisor.

6 *Personal Interest.* The amount of personal interest and direct impact that an individual employee has on the outcome of a decision or task may have a bearing on the leadership style that should be used. If the outcome can result in considerable personal gain for a particular employee or a group of employees, supervisors should probably take a more active, directive role. An extreme example would be decisions about promotions, raises, and transfers. Obviously, here the supervisor should not use a participative approach. However, in cases where employees can be trusted to base their decisions on organizational considerations, more participative approaches would be appropriate.

7 *Personal Cooperation.* A final important individual/group variable is the amount of cooperation required. Where supervisors must greatly depend upon employee cooperation in order to operate or complete a task successfully, participative human relations styles are probably preferable. The idea here is that if the employees are asked to participate, they are more likely to support the supervisor and to be more committed to the task. If they are not allowed any input (e.g., with a directive style), they are much less likely to be committed and give the necessary cooperation.

Job Characteristics Affecting Style of Supervision

Besides individual/group variables, there are many aspects of the job that affect leadership style. Both research and common sense bear out the importance of the job itself. Listed below are some important job characteristics that may have the biggest influence on supervisory style:

1 *Task Clarity.* When job tasks are very unclear and ambiguous, a directive style may be more appropriate, as the leader can then help to clarify procedures, methods, and goals. On the other hand, if the supervisor has no particular technical expertise concerning the job, then a human relations style may be more appropriate. In the latter situations the supervisor must utilize employee inputs to develop work procedures and complete the task successfully. All other factors being equal, tasks which are well defined and understood by employees probably do not require directive leadership.

2 *The Content of the Task.* There is little question that the nature of the work affects the type of leadership style that should be used. The problem is that there are mixed results and opinions regarding the relationship between job content and leadership style. For example, some argue that because routine jobs are boring and possibly distasteful, a task-oriented, directive approach is needed to make sure the work gets done. Another argument, however, suggests that the lack of job stimulation in routine jobs can be overcome by a participative human relations style. With the latter style, at least the factors surrounding the job are more appealing and, it is hoped, the employee will be motivated not to disappoint the supervisor. A third argument suggests that the supervisor carefully explain to the employee the relationship between performance of the routine task and the outcomes the employee desires, such as increased pay, promotion, or a better job. In this way, the supervisor uses a human relations approach to link the routine job with more desired outcomes. There is at least some research evidence demonstrating that this last approach toward routine work can be effective. Although there is much diversity of opinion regarding routine jobs, there is very little controversy on the appropriate style for demanding, stimulating jobs. Almost everyone agrees that a participative human relations style is most appropriate for these types of jobs.

3 *Low-Skill versus Professional Jobs.* Most experts would agree that the level of skill required in a job will affect the type of style that is effective. For example, a supervisor dealing with professionals may find it effective to find a common goal to unify the group and then to allow the professionals relatively free rein in achieving their goals. This would call for a participative human relations style. On the other hand, supervisors may find more directive styles appropriate for employees performing jobs requiring few or no skills.

4 *Information Availability in the Job.* Information concerning the job and its procedure is another factor which may influence the type of effective leadership style. When supervisors possess all the relevant information, they can usually be more directive. On the other hand, where the employees have the relevant information to do the job and the supervisors do not, it makes good pragmatic sense to assume that a participative style which utilizes the employee's information and expertise will be most effective.

Organizational Variables

Besides personal/group and job variables, the characteristics and features of the organization itself can also influence the effectiveness of different types of leadership styles. Listed below are some of the organizational variables that may influence supervisory style:

1 *Product/Service Orientation.* An organization which produces tangible products is more likely to be appropriate for fairly task-oriented supervisory styles. Examples of these types of organizations would include steel mills, auto assembly plants, and machine shops. On the other side of the coin, organizations which have a service orientation may be more successful with human relations styles. Examples of the latter would include health-care and educational institutions, social service agencies, and recreational facilities. It must be remembered, however, that these guidelines, like the others that have been suggested so far, involve many exceptions and should not be accepted at face value.

2 *Organizational Goals.* The goals of the organization can also exert some influence on supervisory styles. For example, organizations which emphasize quantity, profit, or sales tend to be more task-oriented, and thus the directive styles may work better for them. On the other hand, organizations which tend to emphasize quality and/or service may find a style that is oriented toward human relations to be more effective. Again, there are obviously exceptions to these general guidelines.

3 *Top-Management Leadership Style.* Many studies have shown that supervisors' leadership styles are greatly influenced by the way in which they are led by their bosses. In many cases, supervisors appear to imitate or model their bosses' styles. For example, task-oriented upper-level managers tend to have task-oriented first-line supervisors. Upper-level managers oriented toward human relations tend to have supervisors who are oriented in the same way, and so on. It is critical that supervisors analyze their own bosses' styles and make sure that their own choice of style is the best for their particular circumstances and not merely an imitation of the boss's approach.

I All other factors being equal, directive, task-oriented leadership seems most appropriate when:

A The supervisor:
1 Is a technical expert
2 Has an extremely favorable or unfavorable situation

B Group members:
1 Lack motivation
2 Are large in number

C The job is:
1 Boring
2 Very unstructured

D Employees:
1 Will make decisions based on personal considerations
2 Have goals in direct conflict with the organization
3 Have traditional values and expect task-oriented supervision

E The organization is:
1 Task-oriented
2 Product-oriented
3 Upper management favors a task-oriented style

II All other factors being equal, a participative human relations style seems most appropriate when:

A The supervisor wishes:
1 To have satisfied employees
2 To be liked by the employees

B The group members are:
1 Well educated
2 Professional
3 Relatively young
4 Self-motivated
5 Few in number

C The job is:
1 Stimulating
2 Clearly understood

D Employees:
1 Must contribute important job information
2 Can be trusted to base solutions on organizational rather than personal considerations

E The organization is:
1 Service
2 Employee-oriented
3 Managed at the upper levels in a human relations approach

FIGURE 16-5
Guidelines for effective leadership.

Concluding Comment on Applying Leadership

These personal, job, and organizational considerations represent only a few of the many factors influencing the supervisor's choice of an effective leadership style. Most assuredly there are many other factors, but these are either very specific or cannot be accurately identified at present. In addition, it must be emphasized that the list of factors and their suggested effects on leadership style are based on some research and experience, but this is still largely speculative. There is still a great need for more research in this area before recommendations can be made with confidence. Yet, it is hoped that the theories and factors reviewed here will serve as a realistic point of departure for supervisors who are striving to apply effective leadership. Figure 16-5 provides an overall summary of many of the important considerations that have been discussed in this chapter.

■ KEY CONCEPTS

"Great man" theory
Trait theory
Democratic style
Autocratic style
Laissez faire style
Initiating structure
Consideration
Human relations style
Task-oriented style
Contingency theory

■ PRACTICAL EXERCISES

(These can be performed by individuals or by groups.)
1 Complete the leadership test which follows. Included are instructions for scoring the test and then interpreting the results. Discuss the results in terms of the theories and styles of leadership presented in this chapter. Is your own style appropriate for your leadership situation?
2 Using the factors from Figure 16-5, analyze your own and/or any other relevant organizational environment and supervisory position. Which style appears to be most appropriate? Why?

446

T-P LEADERSHIP QUESTIONNAIRE:
AN ASSESSMENT OF STYLE

GOAL
To evaluate oneself in terms of task orientation and people orientation.

GROUP SIZE
Unlimited.

TIME REQUIRED
Approximately forty-five minutes.

MATERIALS
I   T-P Leadership Questionnaire for each participant.
II Pencil for each participant.
III T-P Leadership-Style Profile Sheet for each participant.

PHYSICAL SETTING
Participants should be seated at tables or desk chairs.

PROCESS
I   Without prior discussion, you are asked to fill out the T-P Leadership Question-
    naire. Do *not* read the rest of this until you have completed the test.
II In order to locate yourself on the Leadership-Style Profile Sheet, you will score
    your own questionnaire on the dimensions of task orientation (T) and people
    orientation (P).
III The scoring is as follows:
    1 Circle the item number for items 8, 12, 17, 18, 19, 30, 34, and 35.
    2 Write the number 1 in front of a *circled item number* if you responded S
       (seldom) or N (never) to that item.
    3 Also write a number 1 in front of *item numbers not circled* if you responded A
       (always) or F (frequently).
    4 Circle the number 1's which you have written in front of the following items: 3,
       5, 8, 10, 15, 18, 19, 22, 24, 26, 28, 30, 32, 34, and 35.
    5 *Count the circled number 1's.* This is your score for concern for people. Record
       the score in the blank following the letter P at the end of the questionnaire.
    6 *Count the uncircled number 1's.* This is your score for concern for task. Record
       this number in the blank following the letter T.
IV Next look at the Leadership-Style Profile Sheet and follow the directions on the
    sheet.

Source: Reprinted with permission from J. William Pfeiffer and John E. Jones (eds.), *A Handbook of Structured Experiences for Human Relations Training,* University Associates Publishers, 1974, La Jolla, Calif., vol. 1. The questionnaire was adapted from Sergiovanni, Metzeus, and Burden's revision of the Leadership Behavior Description Questionnaire, *American Educational Research Journal,* vol. 6, pp. 62–79, 1969.

VARIATIONS

   I Participants can predict how they will appear on the profile prior to scoring the questionnaire.

  II Paired participants already acquainted can predict each other's scores. If they are not acquainted, they can discuss their reactions to the questionnaire items to form some bases for this prediction.

 III The leadership styles represented on the profile sheet can be illustrated through role-playing. A relevant situation can be set up, and the "leaders" can be coached to demonstrate the styles being studied.

 IV Subgroups can be formed of participants similarly situated on the shared leadership scale. These groups can be assigned identical tasks to perform. The data generated can be processed in terms of morale and productivity.

LEADERSHIP QUESTIONNAIRE

Name _____ Group _____

Directions: The following items describe aspects of leadership behavior. Respond to each item according to the way you would most likely act if you were the leader of a work group. Circle whether you would most likely behave in the described way: always (A), frequently (F), occasionally (O), seldom (S), or never (N).

A F O S N	1	I would most likely act as the spokesman of the group.
A F O S N	2	I would encourage overtime work.
S F O S N	3	I would allow members complete freedom in their work.
A F O S N	4	I would encourage the use of uniform procedures.
A F O S N	5	I would permit the members to use their own judgment in solving problems.
A F O S N	6	I would stress being ahead of competing groups.
A F O S N	7	I would speak as a representative of the group.
A F O S N	8	I would needle members for greater effort.
A F O S N	9	I would try out my ideas in the group.
A F O S N	10	I would let the members do their work the way they think best.
A F O S N	11	I would be working hard for a promotion.
A F O S N	12	I would tolerate postponement and uncertainty.
A F O S N	13	I would speak for the group if there were visitors present.
A F O S N	14	I would keep the work moving at a rapid pace.
A F O S N	15	I would turn the members loose on a job and let them go to it.
A F O S N	16	I would settle conflicts when they occur in the group.
A F O S N	17	I would get swamped by details.
A F O S N	18	I would represent the group at outside meetings.
A F O S N	19	I would be reluctant to allow the members any freedom of action.
A F O S N	20	I would decide what should be done and how it should be done.

A F O S N   21 I would push for increased production.
A F O S N   22 I would let some members have authority which I could keep.
A F O S N   23 Things would usually turn out as I had predicted.
A F O S N   24 I would allow the group a high degree of initiative.
A F O S N   25 I would assign group members to particular tasks.
A F O S N   26 I would be willing to make changes.
A F O S N   27 I would ask the members to work harder.
A F O S N   28 I would trust the group members to exercise good judgment.
A F O S N   29 I would schedule the work to be done.
A F O S N   30 I would refuse to explain my actions.
A F O S N   31 I would persuade others that my ideas are to their advantage.
A F O S N   32 I would permit the group to set its own pace.
A F O S N   33 I would urge the group to beat its previous record.
A F O S N   34 I would act without consulting the group.
A F O S N   35 I would ask that group members follow standard rules and regulations.

T _____   P _____

T-P LEADERSHIP-STYLE PROFILE SHEET

Name _____ Group _____

Directions: To determine your style of leadership, mark your score on the *concern for task* dimension (T) on the left-hand arrow below. Next, move to the right-hand arrow and mark your score on the *concern for people* dimension (P). Draw a straight line that intersects the P and T scores. The point at which that line crosses the *shared leadership* arrow indicates your score on that dimension.

Shared Leadership Results from
Balancing Concern for Task and Concern for People

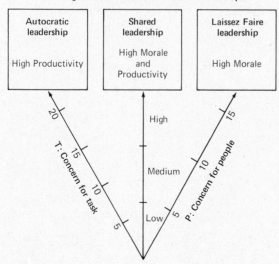

■ DISCUSSION INCIDENTS

Sandra Smith is the head of Pediatrics in General Hospital. She has a large department with almost thirty nurses. Sandra is described by her people as opinionated, directive, and strict. She is known to run a very "tight ship." Yet Pediatrics is viewed by both doctors and employees as one of the most effective departments in the hospital. Turnover is low and nurses from other areas often request transfers to Pediatrics.

Al Wilson is the head of the neurophysiology laboratory at General Hospital. His department is full of sophisticated technical equipment and highly skilled professionals. He is described by his people as being democratic, patient, understanding, and likeable. Like Sandra's department, Al's is considered one of the most effective in the hospital. The turnover in this department is low and both doctors and employees think very highly of it.

1 How do you explain the fact that Sandra and Al have such different styles of leadership but both seem to be effective? If the two switched departments, what do you think would happen?

2 Have you ever had a boss like Sandra? In retrospect, do you think this person was effective? How about a boss you have had who was like Al? What was the effectiveness of this person? Do you think he or she could have been more effective? How?

FUTURE PERSPECTIVES AND CAREER DEVELOPMENT

"Things are really starting to change in this old world. The future is definitely going to be a new ballgame. If only I had done things a little bit differently," said Charlie, "I could be a heck of a lot further along than I am today. It wouldn't even have taken a lot more effort, just a little bit of planning and foresight." Diane Gleason was listening carefully. She respected Charlie's wisdom and sage advice greatly. Moreover, she was eager to learn what would lie ahead and how she should plan her own career as effectively as possible. When the conversation with Charlie was over, Diane felt that Charlie had made some interesting and relevant points. He talked about how, in his time, a college education would have benefited him greatly. He also mentioned that, had he been more aware of certain opportunities that were opening up, he could have been much more successful. Both labor relations and computer services were areas where Charlie had been offered opportunities, but he had refused them. Now, in retrospect, he regretted his lack of foresight. At the conclusion of the discussion, Diane was more convinced than ever that she must begin, by some systematic method, to look into the future and plan her career. Yet even with all Charlie's experience and wisdom, he was not able to provide her with any real idea of the future or any concrete guidelines for career planning. Diane had a thirst for knowledge of the future and knew there must be some system or method one could follow to plan a career. She made up her mind to keep looking until she found some help.

After reading this chapter, you should be able to:

Comment on the future, including technological advances, computers, government regulation, nature of the work force, activism, accountability, and professionalization

Grasp the career planning process

Conduct a self-assessment

Utilize techniques to assist in identifying career goals

Establish paths to career goals

Assess career progress

The first part of this final chapter attempts to look into the crystal ball of the future. Some of the major changes that should affect supervision are summarized. If the rate of change of the coming years is anywhere close to that experienced in the recent past, many radical changes will be forthcoming. It is hoped that some of the projections of the future offered here will enable supervisors to be better prepared for coming changes and to find ways of adapting to change and progress while also improving their work.

The second part of the chapter gives some specific recommendations that potential or present supervisors can follow to prepare for change. This involves primarily the procedures and methods by which present or future supervisors can project and plan for their own futures and the development of their own careers.

THE CHANGING ENVIRONMENT FACING SUPERVISORS

There is no question that, in the future, supervisors will be facing a different environment than the one they are facing today or have faced in the past. The second chapter of this book spelled out the turbulent environment currently facing supervisors and hinted at some of the things to come. Knowledge of the future and the capacity to anticipate this change—as well as the ability (and in many cases the willingness) to adapt to and manage this change—can make the difference between effective and ineffective performance.

Technological Advances

The advance of technology can be thought of in terms of a speeding car where the surrounding landscape becomes more and more

453

obscure and finally ends in a blur. Each technological discovery opens the way for many more new discoveries. As a result, the environment facing supervisors in the future will reflect ever greater technological sophistication.

In many organizations, supervisors will be unable to understand all aspects of their employees' jobs. As a result, two trends in supervision which have already appeared should become more pronounced in the future. First, participative supervisory styles will become more relevant and necessary. Only through cooperative, participative styles will supervisors be able to obtain the information necessary to make their decisions. Second, supervisors are going to have to place more trust in their employees and give them more autonomy. In many cases, the supervisor will simply not have the facts or expertise to make important job-related decisions. As a result, supervisors will have to delegate more decision-making responsibility to employees and will have to place confidence and trust in them. In summary, as technological sophistication increases and the resulting gap between supervisors' authority and their knowledge of subordinates' jobs widens, more participation and trust will become necessary.

The Greater Influence of Computers

Computers are being more widely used in all organizational activities. For example, the airlines use computers for passenger reservations, and retail stores keep track of inventory by computer. Even health care is becoming more dependent on computers. Thus, supervisors in many different kinds of organizations have already experienced or can expect to see some definite changes in their jobs because of the computer.

The most important changes brought about by the computer can be summarized as follows:

1 *Information Gathering and Record Keeping.* Supervisors have traditionally been focal points for collecting and assembling information. In the future, supervisors will increasingly be asked to supply the input data for computerized information systems. Where possible, supervisors should delegate data-gathering activities, so that they will not become merely glorified file clerks.

2 *Problem Solving.* Both the speed and accuracy of the computer can be of very decided help to supervisors in solving problems. Calculations that used to take weeks to make can now be done in a matter of seconds. Importantly, however, the computer's major function should always be viewed as that of providing data and information. The decision itself should always be made by the person interpreting the information.

3 *Communications Link.* As computers are used more frequently to store, retrieve, and process information, supervisory positions will be viewed by many as the focal point for distributing this information. In many ways, this is not a great change from traditional communications patterns. However, the computer will provide supervisors with much more information and they will have to become much more skilled in analyzing and interpreting it.

4 *Loss of Power.* Some experts who study the impact of computers argue that it may result in the loss of power by many supervisors. For example, the computer would enable all personnel records to be centralized and thus to become the responsibility of the personnel department. The personnel manager could then be given the authority to handle all disciplinary matters relating to areas such as absenteeism. This approach would have the advantage of ensuring that all discipline would be uniform and nondiscriminatory. Unfortunately, it would also seriously erode the power of the first-line supervisor who traditionally handled these matters. As was pointed out in the first chapter, supervisory authority has already been eroded in many functions such as wage and salary administration, promotions, and job design. The computer should speed up this process. Thus, in the future, supervisors may find that even more of their important responsibilities are being stripped away from them.

5 *Centralized Control.* Because the computer is capable of processing information rapidly, it is becoming much easier for top management to keep close tabs on lower-level operations. Already it is possible in some organizations for top management to determine the exact, instantaneous output of a particular unit by merely punching a few keys on a remote terminal. Access to this type of information will become much more common in the future and will undoubtedly make for more top-management control decisions that were formerly handled by supervisors.

Government Regulation

The government is becoming increasingly involved in all aspects of organizational activity, and this trend will undoubtedly hold for the future. Areas already greatly affected by government regulations include (1) safety, (2) emissions and waste disposal, (3) product liability, (4) labor relations, and (5) employment practices. In many cases, the laws and their interpretations (probably the best current example is the Occupational Safety and Health Act or OSHA) have become so complex that only highly specialized experts can be sure that the organization is in compliance. As a result, these specialized staff experts replace the supervisor in interpreting and implementing government regulations. Accordingly, these specialists are often given "functional authority" over these areas. That is, these OSHA experts (or perhaps an equal opportunity compliance expert) may need to have almost absolute authority in order to do an effective job. This type of authority not only erodes the supervisor's own authority but also often places the supervisor in a subordinate position to these specialists.

The Changing Nature of the Work Force

Chapter 2 brought out the shift in composition and values of today's work force. A few decades ago, the stereotype of the working person was a white male about 35 years old. Today, if anything, there is no typical worker. Workers may be female, black, Oriental, Spanish-speaking, handicapped, under 21, or over 65. To an extent, of course, the increased participation of these minority groups in the work force is a function of government legislation. Yet it must be remembered that the laws really reflect the changes in our society. For example, many households cannot secure the things they want unless both the husband and wife work. This has forced many former housewives into the workplace, and they are rightfully demanding equal oppor-tunity. Now, with the protection of the law, they are beginning to compete with men on an equal basis for many jobs that were traditionally "male only." Similarly, many other minority work-force participants are now competing for traditional "white male only" jobs.

While the merits of these changes in the composition and accom-panying values of the work force are still debated, the trend is clear and definite. There will be much more participation from all types of people in the work force of the future. Supervisors, of course, will need to adapt to these new people and their values.

The Age of Activism and Participation

One outstanding development of the last two decades has been the American people's growth in awareness of, concern over, and involvement in affairs that affect them and the country. It has become an age of activism, where groups of people have vigorously attempted to put an end to a war, the building of nuclear power plants, the pollution of water and air, discrimination in employment, and prosecution for smoking marijuana. In some instances, they have been successful. Although the merit of some of these causes is still debated, it is clear that an increasing number of people will actively demand a voice in their fate. Much of this increased awareness and activism can be attributed to two important factors: education and mass-media communications. An increased level of education has brought about one of the biggest forces for change ever known in this country. In 1960, only about 12 percent of the population had some college education; now, however, almost half the population over 18 has had some college exposure. With the trend toward continuing and adult education, these effects are being and will continue to be felt in the workplace.

The other major force for change, mass-media communications (television in particular), has had a dramatic impact on all aspects of modern life. The world is no longer viewed as mysterious. Many of the employees supervisors deal with today feel that they are as aware and intelligent as their bosses. In many instances this may be true; even if it is not, the result will be increased demand for opportunities to participate in all aspects of the job. This, of course, coupled with the increased education of employees, can be a very healthy development for the performance of organizations.

Increased Accountability

News stories of recent years such as Watergate, the Korean bribery scandals, the My Lai massacre in Vietnam, and medical and law malpractice suits all had one thing in common. People were eventually nailed with the blame and held accountable for their actions. The outcome of these events indicate that the American public is becoming much less patient with the kind of buck-passing that occurred in previous times. Today, it is becoming more and more apparent that people will continue to demand responsible action from public officials and will hold these officials directly accountable when their actions are not appropriate. Correspondingly, supervisors can be viewed the same way by their people. Employees are beginning to demand that supervisors be held accountable for their actions. In some cases (e.g., college student-professor relations), subordinates are demanding the right to rate and appraise their leaders' effectiveness. In one case, the employee actually sued his supervisor for violating his legal rights. The supervisor's company in this case could neither provide a legal defense nor help pay the supervisor's resulting fine. This type of case seems to be a warning signal that supervisors will be held responsible by their people if they fail to perform their responsibilities appropriately. One possible result is that supervisors in the future may have to take out malpractice insurance, much the same way as doctors are doing presently. One hopes that responsible actions by practicing supervisors will make such drastic measures unnecessary.

Increased Professionalization of Supervisors

Other likely developments in the future include more closely knit professional organizations and a professional orientation for supervisors. This trend probably stems from the increasing pride in being a supervisor, increasing educational requirements for becoming a supervisor, and the growing split with top management on the one hand and the rank-and-file employees on the other.

The first factor, pride resulting in professionalism, comes from the growing recognition that supervisory positions are very demanding and require special knowledge and abilities. As supervisors become more aware of this, they begin to see themselves as professionals.

A second factor resulting in increased professionalization is the higher level of education for supervisors and its greater standardization. With the level of education going up for everyone, some supervisory jobs are currently requiring a college degree (associate or bachelor's), and more employers will undoubtedly be making such demands in the future. It is also becoming increasingly apparent that there is a common body of knowledge that supervisors should have assimilated and be able to apply. The subject matter of this book represents this body of supervisory knowledge and contributes to the professionalization of supervisors regardless of the type of organization they work for.

Finally, increased pressures from both the top and bottom levels of organizations are literally forcing supervisors to unify and identify themselves as a distinct professional group. In several large organizations, for example, wages paid to unionized hourly workers have equaled and even surpassed the salaries of their supervisors. In reaction, supervisors can unionize themselves, and in a few cases they have done so. The other approach is to adopt a more professional viewpoint and to demand the rewards that go with professionalism. In the long run, the latter route would seem to be in the best interest of individual supervisors, their organizations, and society. Supervisors must become professionals in terms of outlook, but this, of course, does not or should not prevent them from unionizing.

A Final Word on the Changing Environment and the Future Role of Supervisors

Thus far this chapter has provided a summary of some of the more obvious environmental factors that will affect the role of the supervisor in the future. While some of the developments precipitating these changes can be viewed in a negative context, there are also some very positive outcomes. In particular, these factors indicate that supervisors in the future will have a much more challenging and complex job than they have had in the past. If supervisors are able to respond to these challenges, they should be able to retain a position of importance in the organizations of the future. If not, they will become useless cogs in bigger and bigger machines.

The following section describes some specific techniques and procedures that supervisors can use for self-development and career planning. Present and potential supervisors utilizing these techniques should find that they will be better prepared to meet the dynamic challenges of the coming years.

CAREER PLANNING AND DEVELOPMENT FOR THE FUTURE

In many respects effective career planning and development follows good common sense coupled with some awareness and self-discipline. The individual should set goals, evaluate methods for achieving the goals, and then carefully chart a path that will result in

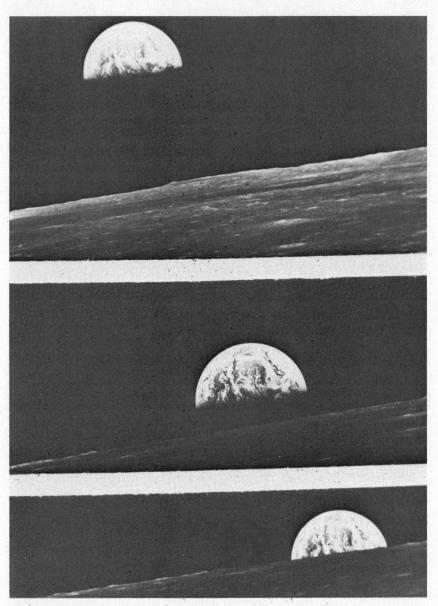

Time is passing and one should chart
the future through effective career
planning (NASA photo).

achieving the goals. Yet despite the apparent simplicity of such career planning, there are some difficult issues that must be resolved, and an effective career plan calls for some serious thinking. Present or future supervisors must ask themselves a number of questions in order to come up with effective career plans. These include the following:

1 There are many career goals available to me; how do I determine which ones are right for me?

2 I don't really know what my interests are. How do I find out?

3 What resources are available to help me assess my strengths and weaknesses?

4 How can I possibly know what I will be doing or what I want to be doing many years down the road?

5 How do I know where my organization will be in the future? More importantly, how do I know whether or not it will have the position and/or type of job I want in the future?

6 Is it unrealistic to try to prepare for and achieve a specific position or job that is still many years in the future?

The following sections will discuss ways that these issues and questions can be dealt with so as to build a realistic and sensible base for career planning.

The Career Planning Process

The model presented in Figure 17-1 illustrates the career planning process. The model shows four important and interrelated steps to effective career planning. First is a careful assessment of one's present skills, abilities, knowledge, and motivation. Based on this assessment, realistic career goals can be decided on. In order to achieve these goals, however, there must be some intermediate objectives. These intermediate, shorter-range objectives represent a series of related events outlining the path to the more important, longer-range goals. In this intermediate phase, the individual should develop some very specific plans and programs to meet his or her overall career goals. The final step in the model indicates the assessment and readjustment that must take place as unforseen opportunities or disappointments occur. Importantly, the loops indicate that the career planning model involves interrelated and interdependent steps. The following sections will provide detailed

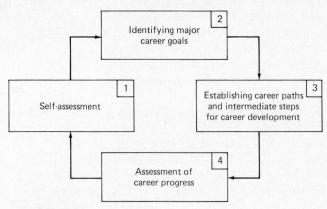

FIGURE 17-1
A model for career planning.

information to help present or potential supervisors gain a more comprehensive understanding of each of the important stages in the career planning process.

Step 1: Self-Assessment
The first step in designing a realistic career plan is to assess one's present knowledge, skills, abilities, and motivation. Described below are several different ways that this can be accomplished.

1 *Performance Appraisal.* Through the aid of the employer's appraisal process, an employee should be able to get an idea of his or her present knowledge, skills, abilities, and motivation. If a formal appraisal plan does not exist, most employees will find their superiors to be very cooperative in providing an assessment if asked to do so. One might initiate such a meeting with a remark such as: "Jim, I've been thinking about my career plans and I'm wondering if you would be willing to help me. I will need about an hour of your time in which I would like you to provide me with a detailed list of the areas where you think I need improvment and where you think my strengths lie."

2 *Self-Evaluation.* Another method whereby present strengths and weaknesses can be assessed is to do a self-evaluation of performance in one's present job. An example of how a supervisor in a print shop might conduct this self-evaluation is shown in Figure 17-2. In order to construct a self-evaluation form like the one shown in the figure, the duties and responsibilities from the job description are simply listed and broken down into major categories for evaluation. If this self-evaluation reveals that the individual is particularly strong or weak in a given area, then this information can be very useful for the career planning process. If no formal job descriptions exist, it will suffice simply to list for oneself one's major duties and responsibilities. Similarly, there is a wide range of meaningful categories that can be used to analyze the job (e.g., the basic elements of effective supervision covered in this book, such as planning, organizing, controlling, communicating, motivating, and leading).

3 *Subordinate Assessments.* People who are somewhat venture-

Major Job Category	Job Description of Print Shop Supervisor	Self Evaluation		
		Knowledge	Performance	Motivation
Administration	1. Order paper, ink, and other supplies	High	High	Medium
	2. Process time sheets daily and weekly	High	High	Low
	3. Budget for new equipment and supplies on a monthly basis	Medium	Medium	Medium
Supervisory	1. Assign work to operators on a daily basis	High	High	High
	2. Train new employees	High	High	High
	3. Establish and enforce quality control procedures	High	High	Medium
	4. Discipline employees for infractions of rules	High	High	Low
	5. Serve as the first step in the grievance procedure	High	Medium	Low
	6. Conduct appraisals of employee performance	Low	Medium	Low
Technical	1. Evaluate new methods and equipment	High	High	Medium
	2. Assist customers in designing and laying out projects	High	High	High
	3. Maintain performance and maintenance records for selected equipment	Medium	Low	Low
	4. Assist employees when technical problems arise	High	Medium	High

FIGURE 17-2
Example of a self-assessment form for a print shop supervisor.

some and who really want an accurate assessment may want to have the people who work for them analyze their (the supervisors') strengths and weaknesses. There are two important ideas behind asking subordinates to assess their boss. First, because subordinates work very closely with the boss, they are in an ideal position to spot the strengths and weaknesses in supervisory functions and skills. Second, supervisory strengths and weaknesses are frequently closely tied in to the subordinates' own behaviors. If supervisors are to develop and reach their career goals, they need the support and cooperation of their subordinates. There are a number of different ways to obtain such a subordinate assessment, one of the most popular of which is the work group survey. This approach consists of asking the subordinates a number of relevant questions about their supervisors. An example of the types of questions that might be asked are provided in Figure 17-3. If these questionnaire surveys are treated confidentially, subordinates will not feel that they are "on the spot" in having to evaluate their boss. In addition, the survey can be conducted with open-ended questions of the type shown in Figure 17-4. Although commercial surveys and questionnaires are available, supervisors can frequently construct very effective surveys themselves. In larger organizations, the personnel department will frequently help in the design and administration of the questionnaires. Finally, if the employee assessment process is used, the supervisors should be prepared to discuss the results and their corresponding plans of action with their employees. Most supervisors are capable of doing this themselves, but frequently a neutral representative from the personnel department who is experienced with these types of meetings can be of great help in setting up and conducting the assessment meeting.

4 *Professional Assessments.* There are a number of consultants, professional counselors, and university services which are able and willing to assess your present capabilities. One of the best bets is the psychology department or student services center of your local college or university. A typical assessment might include a personal interview; intelligence, achievement, and aptitude tests; personal preference or interest tests; personality assessments; and perhaps some interviews with relatives, close friends, and/or coworkers. At the conclusion of this type of assessment, a confidential interview is conducted which profiles the person's likes and dislikes, aptitudes, abilities, and personality characteristics. Although this type of information is very useful in helping people establish their career plans, in most cases these assessments do not result in a specific recommen-

1. What is your authority in carrying out your responsibilities?
   a. I do not know what my authority is.
   b. I am not sure of my responsibilities.
   c. I am not sure of a few responsibilities.
   d. I have a good idea about what authority I can exercise.
   e. I have a definite idea about the authority I can exercise.

2. Are you informed of the goals and activities of your entire department?
   a. I am not informed.
   b. I am rarely informed.
   c. I have some idea of what is going on in the department.
   d. I have a pretty good idea of what is going on.
   e. I am well informed on most departmental activities and objectives.

3. Does your supervisor give you the information you need to do your job?
   a. He(She) often withholds important information.
   b. Sometimes he(she) withholds important information.
   c. I have to ask for it.
   d. He(She) usually tells me what I need to know.
   e. He(She) always tells me what I need to know.

4. How significant does your work seem to your overall department's effort?
   a. My work seems unnecessary much of the time.
   b. While my work is necessary it doesn't seem significant in light of overall department objectives.
   c. My work makes some contribution to overall department objectives.
   d. I get involved in a number of significant assignments.
   e. Most of my work adds significantly to overall department objectives.

5. Does your supervisor respond to questions that affect you (such as leaves of absence) in a reasonable amount of time?
   a. She(He) always puts things off.
   b. She(He) avoids a reply if she(he) can.
   c. It depends on how she(he) feels.
   d. It takes a while, but I usually get an answer.
   e. She(He) answers the request immediately or within the next day.

6. Does the supervisor listen to your point of view?
   a. He(She) avoids discussing things if he(she) can.
   b. He(She) avoids discussing things.
   c. He(She) listens but nothing ever comes of it.
   d. He(She) listens and sometimes he(she) will change his(her) mind.
   e. He(She) listens and makes changes when it's appropriate.

7. How much challenge and learning experience does your job allow you?
   a. My job is very routine and boring.
   b. My work is routine, although there are still a few things for me to learn.
   c. Occasionally my job allows me to learn new things; there is some challenge.
   d. Frequently my job allows me to learn new things; I am periodically challenged.
   e. I am always learning new things and feel a constant challenge in my job.

8. How fair is your supervisor in handling disciplinary matters?
   a. She(He) is not at all fair.
   b. She(He) gets emotionally involved and is frequently unfair.
   c. She(He) is generally fair but occasionally reacts before she(he) gets all the facts.
   d. She(He) is consistent and fair most of the time.
   e. She(He) is always fair.

9. Does your supervisor seem to understand your needs and wants?
   a. He(She) does not understand my needs at all.
   b. He(She) probably understands some of my needs.
   c. He(She) seems to sense my needs but doesn't do anything about it.
   d. He(She) understands some of my needs and makes some effort to provide an environment to meet them.
   e. He(She) always seems to understand my needs and is able to provide an environment to satisfy them.

10. Do you get the credit you deserve on your performance?
    a. I almost never get credit.
    b. I usually do not get the credit I deserve.
    c. Sometimes.
    d. I usually get the credit I deserve.
    e. I always get the credit I deserve.

FIGURE 17-3 (continued on p. 466) Possible questions that can be asked of subordinates for self-assessment.

465

11. Does your supervisor tell you what he(she) thinks of your performance?
   a. He(She) never discusses what he(she) thinks of my performance.
   b. He(She) rarely is complete in telling me what he(she) thinks.
   c. He(She) tends to be general in telling me what he(she) thinks.
   d. He(She) is fairly complete but avoids some issues.
   e. He(She) fully discusses my performance.

12. Do you participate in planning your own work?
   a. No participation. I am told what to do.
   b. I participate some, but only on minor details.
   c. Occasionally I have a significant input on planning my work.
   d. I have a fair amount of participation regarding how things are to be done.
   e. I participate a great deal, both in planning and carrying out the plans.

13. How often does your supervisor offer suggestions on how to improve your performance?
   a. He(She) never gives me suggestions.
   b. He(She) rarely offers me suggestions.

   c. Occasionally he(she) will give me some general suggestions.
   d. He(She) usually offers suggestions when it seems appropriate.
   e. He(She) always offers suggestions and constructive criticism when it seems appropriate.

14. To what degree does your supervisor help you on your job?
   a. I do it all on my own.
   b. He(She) provides little help.
   c. He(She) provides some help.
   d. He(She) provides a great deal of help.
   e. He(She) goes out of his(her) way to help me.

15. Is your supervisor's method of supervision right for you?
   a. No, it is much too close. I have very little freedom in my job.
   b. He(She) is a bit too close. I do not have enough freedom.
   c. About right. He(She) still gives me enough room.
   d. A little too loose. He(She) doesn't provide enough guidance.
   e. Much too loose. He(She) hardly gives me any guidance at all.

dation for a career path. These methods are simply not developed to the extent that they can or should be allowed to provide specific recommendations.

5 *Assessment Centers.* An increasingly popular source of assessments is the assessment center. These programs usually last for a period of a couple of days to a week or so. During this time, besides taking part in tests and interviews, the person being assessed progresses through a series of exercises, cases, role-plays, games, and problems that closely imitate actual working conditions and situations. The end-of-chapter exercises and cases in this book would be representative of the types of things used in assessment centers. Throughout the program, the progress and behavior of the person is carefully rated and assessed by a panel or group of experienced assessors. At the conclusion of the program, each participant is given detailed feedback regarding strengths and weaknesses. Assessment centers are usually conducted by large organizations (e.g., American Telephone and Telegraph has been successfully using them for years) for the selection and development of their supervisors. However, many counsulting firms and universities are now establishing similar programs, where attendance is open to supervisors from a variety of organizations. These programs can be particularly useful in helping potential supervisors to decide whether or not they are equipped to handle a full-time supervisory career.

6 *Informal Feedback.* An often overlooked but invaluable source of information for self-assessment is the informal feedback provided daily by coworkers, peers, and bosses. Each day—through questions, comments, observations, criticisms, and compliments—individuals can receive valuable feedback that, if handled openly and constructively, can help them assess their strengths and weaknesses. Of particular interest are compliments or criticisms that are repeated by several different individuals, since they are usually more reliable. Rather than discouraging this type of feedback, astute people encourage and analyze this information so that they may achieve a more realistic assessment of their abilities.

These suggestions are representative of the variety of techniques that can be used to assess career potential. Most people should use these techniques in combination to develop realistic assessments of their abilities. Once they feel that their assessments are reasonably valid, they are ready to begin setting overall career goals.

---

1. Describe two things which your supervisor does that are particularly helpful to you in your job.

2. Describe two things which your supervisor does which particularly hinder or hurt your job performance.

3. Discuss at least two strong points of your supervisor.

4. Discuss at least two areas where your superior needs improvement.

5. Can you list some specific suggestions that would help your supervisor improve her or his performance?

FIGURE 17-4
Possible open-ended questions that can be asked of subordinates for self-assessment.

Step 2: Identifying Major Career Goals

Because of the wide variety of career possibilities and individual differences, there is no single process of goal setting that will work for everyone. However, there are some practical guidelines that can be followed by most people in setting career goals. The following sections suggest a couple of ways that present or potential supervisors can use to arrive at career goals more expeditiously.

The obituary approach to setting career goals Many people have considerable difficulty projecting themselves into the future. Although somewhat gruesome, the obituary technique can help some people overcome this type of problem. The approach is very straightforward. The people participating simply imagine that today is the last day of their lives. As objective observers, they are asked to write their own obituaries. They are asked to include several major categories, such as (1) career accomplishments, (2) educational achievements, (3) hobbies and pastimes, and (4) major disappointments and unfulfilled dreams. The participants are asked to make the obituary as comprehensive and detailed as possible. After the first obituary is complete, they are asked to write their obituaries for five, ten, and twenty years into the future. If the participants take the task seriously, implicit in each of the obituaries will be each individual's major career objectives and goals.

The flash-forward technique of setting career goals Another unique way of helping one to identify career goals is the flash-forward method. The basis of this approach is to create visual images of the future to help identify career goals. Essentially, it is the opposite of the flashback used in moving pictures. The technique is very simple and can be best described by steps such as the following:

First, the individuals are asked to identify at least three important places where they spend their time (e.g., house, workplace, and weekend cabin).

Second, they are asked to imagine each place five, ten, and twenty years from now and to take a quick snapshot of these future scenes.

Third, the participants are asked to provide a written description of each future scene.

Fourth, each future scene is compared with the present scene and major differences are identified.

Fifth, the required activities to attain the future picture are identified. *Sixth,* the participants set realistic and specific goals to accomplish the required activities.

Like the obituary method, the flash-forward method is only an aid to help identify goals for the career planning process; it does not determine what the goals will be.

Major considerations for all career goals In addition to specific techniques such as the obituary and flash-forward techniques, there are several important considerations which all career planners should consider. Some of these are outlined below.

1 *Be realistic.* Assuming that individuals have identified some general areas for career goals, they then need to do some serious thinking about what they can realistically accomplish. It would probably be unrealistic, for example, for a middle-aged employee with a large family who had only a high school education to go back to college to take a five-year architecture program. Although this person could possibly accomplish such a goal if sufficiently motivated, other career goals would be much more realistic and would not require such great sacrifices. Each individual, of course, must determine what is realistic. Importantly, however, research has clearly demonstrated that people who set goals that are either too high or too low do not perform as well as those who set realistic but challenging goals.

2 *Set priorities.* Another important consideration is personal priorities. Apart from their career goals, people also have important social, family, moral, religious, health, recreational, and financial objectives. In many cases, these personal objectives compete with each other and with job-related goals. This is illustrated in Figure 17-5, which depicts the weekly schedule of a typical full-time employee. As can be seen, only Monday and Wednesday nights are free. Although Saturdays and Sundays appear to be relatively free, there are important family, social, religious, and recreational commitments on these days. Thus, realistically, the individual in this case has only about eight hours of "free time" per week. If this individual decided to go to night school to meet educational qualifications for a promotion, to work extra hours to earn more money, or establish a program of personal development reading, some of the personal time in the weekly schedule would have to be sacrificed. Thus, time allocations and competing goals must be carefully considered before a career development program is undertaken. In some cases, people may

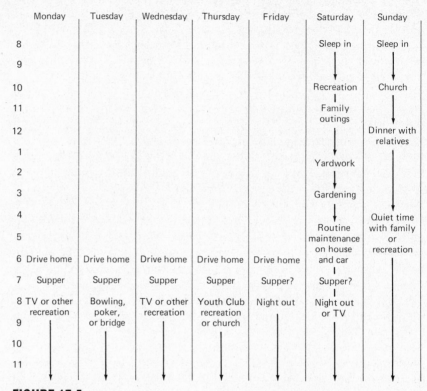

	Monday	Tuesday	Wednesday	Thursday	Friday	Saturday	Sunday
8						Sleep in	Sleep in
9						↓	↓
10						Recreation	Church
11						Family outings	↓
12						↓	Dinner with relatives
1							↓
2						Yardwork	
3						↓ Gardening	
4						↓	Quiet time with family or recreation
5						Routine maintenance on house and car	
6	Drive home	Drive home	Drive home	Drive home	Drive home		
7	Supper	Supper	Supper	Supper	Supper?	Supper?	
8	TV or other recreation	Bowling, poker, or bridge	TV or other recreation	Youth Club recreation or church	Night out	Night out or TV	
9	↓	↓	↓	↓	↓	↓	
10							
11	↓	↓	↓	↓	↓	↓	↓

FIGURE 17-5
A typical week for an employee.

legitimately decide that the personal sacrifices are not worth the gains. Others may decide that work toward most of the development goals must occur during working hours. Even in these cases, however, a person may discover that the established goals may compete with his or her ability to perform adequately on the present job. Thus, goals for career development must be carefully weighed against other job-related and personal objectives and all these must be ranked in order of priority.

3 *Deal with strengths and weaknesses.* There are two ways to consider strengths and weaknesses in relation to career goals. The first and more traditional perspective is that weaknesses are probably detriments and barriers to career objectives. It follows that career plans should emphasize ways to overcome these weaknesses. Recently, this approach is undergoing reexamination. The new viewpoint emphasizes capitalizing on strengths rather than concentrating on weaknesses. The idea is that habitual weaknesses and problems are indications of areas where the individual has little aptitude or ability. Therefore, career paths and goals should be designed to steer around or avoid situations which hit on these weak points. On the other side of the coin, areas where people continually demonstrate strength are usually areas of exceptional aptitude and ability. Therefore, effective career planning should attempt to take advantage of these proven areas.

4 *Maintain flexibility.* The last and perhaps most important consideration in establishing career goals is flexibility. Flexibility, in this context, is the willingness to change and adapt plans and goals to either take advantage of opportunities or avoid and compensate for failures. People who lack flexibility usually do not bother to establish career plans because they feel that something in the future will change and destroy their plans. Flexible and adaptable people are also aware that unexpected circumstances can change their plans, but their attitude is much different. First, flexible people know that there are many possible paths to their goals. Thus, when an unexpected or unwanted circumstance is forced upon them, they may have already considered an alternative strategy to achieve their goal. In addition, flexible persons are also more willing to consider the possibility that their goals need to be changed or adjusted. That is, as unexpected events occur, many find that they have set their sights either too high or too low. Previous planning and consideration of alternative goals, however, makes the adjustments of goals and priorities a much easier process. Thus, regardless of setbacks and defeats, career planners with flexibility know and appreciate the value of a plan, even if it has to be changed occasionally. They feel that the process of career planning helps them establish their course of action, and they consider possible mishaps and setbacks before they occur. They recognize that the relatively small amount of time invested in planning can help them ward off future setbacks or at least minimize their impact by allowing people to plan for these possibilities.

These considerations in setting career goals are not intended to be exhaustive. Instead, they are merely some of the most important considerations for setting overall career goals.

Step 3: Paths and Intermediate Steps

The third step in career development is to establish paths and intermediate steps which can accomplish overall career goals. There are several options available to a person in developing and pursuing these paths and intermediate steps.

The path-goal strategy The process of setting career goals should not be viewed as a singular act of the achievement of a single goal. Rather, the goal-setting process should be viewed from a multiple-goal perspective, with a series of subgoals leading to the major overall goal. For example, a young person with some college work behind him whose overall career goal is to become the head of an engineering department for an industrial organization would need to set some interim objectives regarding education and relevant technical and broad-based managerial experiences. An example of this career path and its intermediate objectives is shown in Figure 17-6. A similar example is in the career path established by a nurse's aide, shown in Figure 17-7.

Alternative paths for reaching career goals People planning for career goals should be aware of the many options that are available. While it would be impossible to list and describe all the alternatives, the following represent some of the most important:

1 *Job Changes.* A change in jobs can result from promotions, transfers, or even quitting one organization and joining another. Each of these can lead to upward mobility. Some people feel that they must be either transferred or promoted every couple of years in order to maintain their progress toward career goals. If the expected changes do not occur, many decide to jump to other organizations in order to make the expected progress. Of course, this strategy depends heavily on the person's career goals. Many would not feel comfortable changing organizations and, if their career goals are not agressively upward mobile, they may feel comfortable staying put. Moreover, the time for promotion or transfer varies from organization to organization. For some the critical period may be one year, while for others it may be ten years or longer.

2 *Formal Education.* Today, many organizations have provisions for refunding tuition costs to employees attending school. If formal education is consistent with people's career goals, they may wish to examine this alternative. Many of you reading this book have taken this course of action. Besides efforts by employers to make education

472

I. Educational Objectives	Target Dates
A. A bachelor's degree in electrical engineering	June, 1983
B. A master's degree in engineering or business administration	1987
C. Attend professional seminars and meetings to keep up to date	Annually
D. Certificate of professional engineering	1985
II. Managerial Experience*	
A. Serve on relevant committees to gain experience and understanding of total operations	Serve on at least one committee every two-year period after 1985
B. Try to get a lateral transfer to a personnel function for a period of a year	Before 1988
C. Try to get a lateral transfer as a production supervisor for a year	Before 1990
III. Probable Promotion Route and Career Path	
A. Engineering aide	Present
B. Engineer	1983
C. Senior engineer	1986
D. Group leader	1988
E. Engineering supervisor	1993
F. Head of engineering	2000

*Options: (1) At any time, lateral transfers to areas such as personnel, finance, and manufacturing will be desirable to gain experience; (2) If promotions are not granted or if similar advancements are available earlier in other organizations, consider changing organizations.

FIGURE 17-6
A career path to reach the goal
of head of engineering.

more attainable, many academic institutions are making greater efforts to accommodate full-time employees. Many community colleges, universities, and technical schools have established entire curriculums for degree programs on a nightime, part-time basis. Thus, if people are concerned with gaining additional formal education, they can expect most employers and educational institutions to be supportive.

3 *Additional Training.* Most large organizations offer a wide curriculum of courses or workshops for training and development. Usually

I. Educational Goals	Target Dates
A. Registered nurse	1981
B. Bachelor's degree in nursing	1983
C. Master's degree in nursing administration	1986
II. Professional and Job Experience Goals	
A. Professional organizations—Participation in the American Nursing Association (ANA) and the National League of Nursing Educators (NLNE)	Ongoing
B. Service on broad-based hospital committees such as management training and auditing	1981, then ongoing
C. Job experience in all major areas of nursing service through job rotation	Ongoing
D. Publications—At least two publications in either the *American Journal of Nursing* or *Registered Nurse*	1990
III. Probable Promotional Route and Career Path	
A. Nurse's aide	Present
B. Registered nurse	1981
C. Group leader	1982
D. Charge nurse	1983
E. Head nurse for a floor/ward	1984
F. Nursing supervisor of a major service	1986
G. Director of nursing services	1995

FIGURE 17-7
A career path to reach the goal
of director of nursing services.

the courses are relatively short, often lasting only a day or meeting for an hour a week over several weeks. Typical course topics include Basic Supervision, Accident Prevention, Finance for Nonfinancial Managers, Interviewing, Decision Making, Time Management, and Human Relations. When the individual works for a smaller organization, a similar curriculum of courses may be presented by a local university, community college, management consulting firm, or professional association. These courses are usually reasonably priced and the employer almost always pays the tuition. If one has difficulty finding such courses, try a call to the local Chamber of Commerce, the local Jaycees, the college(s) in the locale, or even the training department of a larger organization. Usually these people will be very cooperative in referring the interested person to appropriate courses, workshops, or programs.

4 *Gaining Experience Outside the Job.* Every community has a host of organizations that provide excellent opportunities for people to gain valuable experience in supervising and working with others on challenging tasks. Examples are the Jaycees, Toastmasters, Rotary, Chamber of Commerce, YMCA, YWCA, PTA, and church organizations. When opportunities to gain needed experience in the work environment are not available, people can usually turn to volunteer organizations and serve the community at the same time.

5 *Professional Organizations.* Another alternative for reaching career goals is through the various professional societies and organizations. Like the volunteer organizations, professional membership and involvement offers people opportunities to gain leadership experience within their relevant fields. In addition, professional organizations frequently sponsor various activities and programs. Examples of general professional organizations include The Society for Advancement of Management (SAM) and The Administrative Management Society (AMS). Each specialty generally has its own professional group, such as the American Society of Training and Development (ASTD) and the International Word Processors Association (IWPA). Very large private or public organizations may also have in-house associations. Everyone should be able to locate at least one appropriate professional association to join and become active in.

6 *Self-Development.* Self-development, of course, is available to everyone. Formal correspondence courses (from colleges and universities or professional associations) are readily available, or one can undertake an organized independent reading program. There are a variety of books, periodicals, and journals oriented toward practicing supervisors that provide up-to-date explanations of current supervisory theory and practice. Examples of such journals would include *Personnel Journal, Supervisory Management, Personnel, Organizational Dynamics, Public Personnel Management, Human Resource Management, Advanced Management Journal, Training and Development Journal,* and *Training Magazine.* In addition, there are a number of journals directly related to particular specialties, ranging all the way from heating and air conditioning to marketing research. A reading list for further self development in supervision and management is given at the end of this chapter.

Again, this is only a partial list of the many alternatives available for

475

career development. Everyone must study all options carefully and choose the combination which is most effective for meeting his or her particular career goals.

Step 4: Assessing Career Progress

The fourth major phase of career planning is the assessment of progress. Conceptually, this step is very simple. The career plan simply matches present progress with previous projections of progress. Thus, if the engineer and the nurse discussed earlier (see Figures 17-6 and 17-7) compared their progress in 1985 to the plans they made when they started, they would be making career assessments. A person's attainments or the discrepancy between projections and present status indicate progress or lack of progress toward achieving an ultimate career goal. If there is very little discrepancy, an individual will probably elect to go on following the same plan of action. On the other hand, if there are large discrepancies, either favorable or unfavorable, some adjustments will have to be made.

Several possible adjustments may result from assessment. First, intermediate objectives may be adjusted so that the ultimate goal can be achieved. For example, if the nurse falls a couple of years short in meeting her objective of being supervisor of a major service, she would probably have to make some radical alterations in her intermediate plans in order to reach her ultimate goal. It may be, for example, that she was held back because of difficulty in supervising people at the charge-nurse level. Thus, she might plan to attend a course or take specialized training in supervising and motivating people. In addition, of course, she would have to readjust the time schedule for meeting her other intermediate goals.

The second option after assessment is to alter or modify the ultimate career goal. Using the example of the nurse, she might decide that her goal of becoming director of nursing services was an unrealistic one. Her final decision might be to modify the ultimate career goal. Because of what has transpired in her personal and/or vocational life, she may now decide that being a supervisor of a major service is a desirable and obtainable career goal. Then, of course, she would begin working her way back through the model to make sure that her intermediate objectives focused on the achievement of this new career goal.

Finally, it may be appropriate to modify both one's intermediate objectives and the ultimate goal. If, for example, the nurse found that

476

she had advanced to director of nursing service a few years ahead of schedule, she might want to set some additional goals for herself. She would then proceed to work through the career planning model step by step.

A Final Word on Career Planning

Before we end the discussion of career planning, several features of the model should be reemphasized. First is that all phases of the career planning process are highly interrelated and interdependent, and the division of the process into four phases is largely artificial. In reality, many effective career planners actually work through all phases of the model simultaneously. For example, if a person saw a very attractive position open up that was not included in his career plan, he might immediately assess his ability to fill this position. If he decided that he was qualified and that the postion was consistent with his personal goals, he might apply for the new position with the idea of substituting it for one of the others currently on his career path. Thus, within a matter of minutes, this individual would have worked through the steps of the model.

A second characteristic of career planning which needs added emphasis is that it is a continuous, never-ending process. Most successful people are continuously comparing their present positions and opportunities with their career plans to make sure that they are making maximum progress in achieving their ultimate goals. Thus, career plans are in an ever-changing, dynamic state, and career planning cannot be viewed as a once-a-year activity. Rather, it is continuous, and it actively channels and integrates a person's performance so that he or she will maximize career benefits.

In the final analysis, however, it is still the thinking, hard-working person who gets ahead. As in every other life situation, a person gets out of a career whatever he or she puts in. It is hoped that by understanding and using the concepts and skills presented in this book, the reader will become a more effective supervisor and have a rewarding, fulfilling career.

◼ KEY CONCEPTS

Technological advances
Influence of computers

Government regulations

Changing work force

Age of activism

Accountability

Professionalism

Career planning process

Self-assessment techniques

Assessment centers

Career-goal-identification techniques

Obituary approach

Flash-forward technique

Path-goal strategy

Assessments of career progress

■ PRACTICAL EXERCISES

(These can be performed by individuals or by groups.)

1 Write your obituary for the present and for five years from now according to the process described in the chapter. By yourself or in a group, discuss some of the discrepancies between the one- and five-year obituaries. Discuss possible career paths to the goals that are implicitly stated in the obituaries.

2 Using the flash-forward technique discussed in this chapter, take a "snapshot" of yourself today and five years from now. Discuss goals and career paths for achieving these goals.

3 Independently predict technological and legal changes that will occur in the near future in an organization with which you are familiar. You may want to use the Delphi or NGT techniques discussed in Chapter 13 to make these predictions. What are the implications of these predictions for your career development?

■ DISCUSSION INCIDENTS

In the cutting room at United Packing, a meat cutting and processing company, two of the meat cutters were discussing their supervisor, Frank Williams. "That Frankie Williams is really something," said Johnny Morgan; "He's only 32 years old and he's already the top supervisor in the packing plant." "Yeah, he sure is," remarked Willie Steele. "But you know, he's always had it made. He grew up in the right neighborhood, his old man is a lawyer, he had the best grades in high school, played

Joe College for a while, and his old man used to golf with our general manager. So what do you expect? He's had it made all his life. Guys like us never get any breaks. We've got to sweat it out our whole lives." Johnny's head bobbed up and down in agreement, and he said, "Yeah, guys like us never get any breaks."

1 What kinds of faulty assumptions are Johnny and Willie making? How will these assumptions keep them from progressing?

2 How did Frank really get his "breaks"? Discuss the degree to which luck and breaks (e.g., whom you know) influence career progress. Can Frank still fail?

Ed Nagl was the supervisor of the housing assembly unit for Nichols Manufacturing, a small electronics assembly firm. Ten years ago he had received a degree in aeronautical engineering and was employed by a major defense contractor. He worked for the defense contractor only three years before being laid off in 1970, with thousands of other aeronautical engineers. His move to the electronics manufacturing firm was made in desperation. Now, several years later, he is extremely dissatisfied. The scene is his own home and he is talking with his wife, Rachel. She is being very supportive by letting Ed know that she will stand by whatever career decision he makes. "If you want to go back to school, change jobs, whatever you want, I'll make every effort to support you in that decision. But *please,* you have to make up your mind. You've been unhappy now for five years and we've simply got to make a change now." Ed replied, "I just don't know what to do. The last time I went to school, I wound up with an education for a field without any opportunities. The entire field went right down the drain. And, if you'll remember, at that time everybody was saying how we needed more engineers. No thanks, I'm not for any more of that school stuff. Besides the job I have is pretty steady and it pays well. There is no guarantee that any other job is going to be any better."

1 Could Ed have avoided his disappointment in his engineering career by careful planning? How?

2 Is there any way Ed could be more certain about the future? Discuss the implications of risk taking for career planning.

SOME SUGGESTED BOOKS
FOR SELF-DEVELOPMENT OF SUPERVISORS

Bittel, Lester R.: *What Every Supervisor Should Know,* 3d ed., McGraw-Hill, New York, 1974.

Davis, Keith: *Human Behavior at Work,* 5th ed., McGraw-Hill, New York, 1977.

Dowling, William F., and Leonard R. Sayles: *How Managers Motivate,* 2d ed., McGraw-Hill, 1978.

Drucker, Peter F.: *Management,* Harper & Row, New York, 1974.

Koontz, Harold, and Cyril O'Donnell: *Essentials of Management,* 2d ed., McGraw-Hill, New York, 1978.

Lorsch, Jay W., J. P. Baughman, J. Reece, and H. Mintzberg: *Understanding Management,* Harper & Row, New York, 1978.

Luthans, Fred: *Introduction to Management: A Contingency Approach,* McGraw-Hill, New York, 1976.

Luthans, Fred: *Organizational Behavior,* 2d ed., McGraw-Hill, New York, 1977.

Newport, Gene M. (ed.): *Supervisory Management,* West, St. Paul, 1976.

Ritti, R. Richard, and G. Ray Funkhouser: *The Ropes to Skip and the Ropes to Know,* Grid, Columbus, Ohio, 1977.

Sartain, Aaron Q., and Alton W. Baker: *The Supervisor and the Job,* 3d ed., McGraw-Hill, New York, 1978.

This, Leslie E.: *A Guide to Effective Management,* Addison-Wesley, Reading, Mass., 1974.

GLOSSARY

Accounting A system for recording, balancing, and reconciling financial transactions. Accounting is a widely used control technique.

Achievement The motivational need characterized by those who take moderate risks, want immediate feedback, and tend to be loners.

Adult ego state In TA, this is the source of rational and objective behavior. It underlies the behavior of the mature person.

Affiliation The motivational need to belong to the group and be accepted by others.

Affirmative action Taking specific actions and making specific plans to correct discrimination in all aspects of organizational life. It is not enough to simply say "we do not discriminate." Under an affirmative action approach, specific steps are taken to ensure opportunity for all employees.

AFL An acronym for the American Federation of Labor, which consists of craft unions. In 1955, the AFL merged with the CIO.

Agenda A schedule for a meeting.

Aggression A reaction to frustration where the person attempts to injure, physically or symbolically, or do harm to the barrier that stands in the way of goal attainment.

All-channel network A communications pattern in which all members interact freely with one another.

Appraisal by results A rating technique used in performance appraisal which concentrates on employee progress in achieving job-related objectives and responsibilities rather than emphasizing the employee's personality characteristics.

Arbitration The settling of a grievance by the decision of a neutral third party who has been selected by the conflicting parties. The decision of the arbitrator is binding to both parties in the dispute.

Assessment center A program designed to help assess supervisory potentials and skills through the use of practical exercises and experiences such as role-plays, in-basket exercises, self-tests, and case situations.

Autocratic A style of leadership in which a person makes decisions without the input or consultation of subordinates.

Balance-sheet accounting A method of accounting designed to show the financial status of an organization by categorizing all financial transactions into assets and liabilities.

Bank wiring room experiment A famous study conducted at the Hawthorne Works of Western Electric Company which demonstrated the power of the informal work group. One of the first comprehensive analyses that looked at human behavior in organizations.

BFOQ (bona fide occupational qualification) An acronym used in staffing, referring to qualifications directly related to job performance.

Body language The information transmitted intentionally or unintentionally through body movements, facial expressions, and/or voice inflection.

Brainstorming A creative decision-making technique which emphasizes the production, by a group, of many diverse ideas. A way of obtaining creative solutions from a group.

Budget A systematic statement of resources for a specified period of time, usually expressed in financial terms but also expressible in terms of hours, equipment, or raw materials.

Bureaucracy The theory of organization first proposed by Max Weber, a German sociologist, which is based on the ideas of specialization, rules, hierarchical organization, and impersonality. It was proposed as the ideal form of organization but today is recognized to have dysfunctions (faults) as well as positive functions for efficient operations.

Career path A set of objectives leading to a major overall career goal.

Case situation A learning/training strategy situation in which the participants read, analyze, and provide recommendations for action in a hypothetical but realistic situation.

"Catch-23" In an O.B. Mod. approach, refers to the problem of determining what is a positive/negative consequence for predicting and controlling employee behavior.

"Catch-24" In an O.B. Mod. approach, refers to the fact that only the contingent consequence (i.e., the one that links up) has an effect on subsequent behavior. In a complex setting like an organization, there are many consequences of employee behavior, but only the contingent one affects behavior.

Chain network A linear communications arrangement.

Child ego state In TA, this is the source of purely emotional responses. It underlies impulsive, immature behavior such as one would expect of a child.

CIO An acronym for Congress of Industrial Organizations, which is a federation of industrial unions. In 1955, the CIO merged with the AFL.

Classical conditioning A type of learning in which a neutral stimulus (e.g., a bell) is paired with a stimulus that will naturally lead to the response. After a number of pairings, the neutral stimulus will lead to the response.

Closed shop A shop in which only union members may be hired and employed.

Collective bargaining The negotiation, interpretation, and administration of a written agreement between labor and management over wages, hours, and conditions of employment.

Conciliation The process whereby, in a grievance dispute, a neutral, disinterested outside person tries to get the parties together and explore ways of resolving the grievance. The conciliator does not render a binding decision.

Contingency An if–then relationship. The contingency approach to management is directed toward identification of the situations and circumstances under which various management practices and principles apply most effectively.

Correlation The degree of relationship between two variables expressed in mathematical terms ranging from -1 to $+1$ where $+1$ is a perfect positive correlation, zero indicates no relation, and -1 indicates a perfect negative relationship.

Cost accounting An accounting method oriented toward controlling costs by assigning all transactions to particular categories for analysis and comparison.

Credibility gap The gap between what a person says and what a person does.

Critical incident technique A rating technique used in performance appraisal where the rater evaluates an individual through a series of important behaviors that have been observed during the rating period.

Critical path The most time-consuming chain of events within a network plan.

Crossed transaction In TA, an incompatible communication exchange where the person receives an unanticipated response from the other person.

Decentralization The degree to which decision-making responsibility and authority is delegated to the lower levels of the organization.

Decision making The process of selecting from among a group of alternatives. A major function of supervisors.

Decoding The process of interpreting a communication.

Delegation The process of assigning to subordinates tasks, duties, and responsibilities which are normally retained by the boss.

Delphi A planning/forecasting/problem-solving technique characterized by anonymous input and composite feedback to the members of the Delphi panel.

Departmentation A principle of organization that establishes division of labor and the organization of any given horizontal level of an organizational structure.

Discipline A technique of controlling employee behavior through either positive or punitive approaches; is imposed by self or others and aimed at the accomplishment of organizational objectives.

Distribution errors Rating errors resulting in underrating, overrating, or failure to discriminate among employees in the evaluation process.

Division of labor Another term for departmentalizing and organizing work.

Dynamics Stands for power and change. Used in reference to group processes.

EEOC (Equal Employment Opportunity Commission) An acronym for a powerful agency that is charged with maintaining compliance with the equal opportunity laws.

Ego state In TA, a consistent pattern of feelings or beliefs. The three ego states identified in TA are the Parent, Adult, and Child.

Elastic A word used in economics to characterize a demand curve which is greatly affected by price.

Equal opportunity The notion that all persons—regardless of race, color, creed, sex, and national origin—should receive equal treatment with regard to organizational practices such as hiring, tenure, use of facilities, transfer, promotion, and dismissal. The Equal Pay Act and the Civil Rights Act are among the major pieces of legislation enforcing equal opportunity.

External environment The external organizational factors—such as changing technology and attitudes toward work—which influence the effectiveness of supervision.

Facilitator A person who serves as a catalyst by helping a group perform its functions.

Featherbedding An unfair union practice which forces the employer to pay for services that are not actually performed.

Federation The top level of the union structure. Today the federation for most unions is the merged AFL-CIO.

Feedback control A method of control based on the assessment of data about outputs.

Feed-forward control A method of control which emphasizes the proactive control of inputs rather than after-the-fact control of outputs.

Fixation A reaction to frustration where the person pretends that the barrier that stands in the way of goal attainment does not exist.

Flash-forward technique A method of identifying major career goals by projecting one's thoughts into the future.

Forced choice A rating technique used in performance appraisal in which the rater is required to mark one and only one of several possible categories.

Free-form organization An organization with an implicit rather than explicit structure. There is no hierarchically structured organization chart. The free-form approach is most often used in rapidly growing or changing organizations.

Frustration This occurs when a motivated drive is blocked before the intended goal is reached. It can result in aggression, withdrawal, fixation, and/or compromise.

Functional authority The formal authority which takes precedence over managerial or supervisory decisions within clearly but narrowly defined functional areas such as personnel, marketing, or purchasing. For example, a policy that forbids supervisors to purchase without approval equipment costing more than $100 is an example of the functional authority of the purchasing department.

Functional departmentation The process of organizing work according to various functions such as sales, manufacturing, and finance.

Future shock A condition resulting from too much social change in too short a time.

Game In TA, a series of apparently parallel transactions which actually contain a hidden agenda or ulterior transaction that eventually surfaces. These are very common but are usually destructive to the players involved.

Gantt chart A mechanism used by scientific management pioneer Henry Gantt to plan in relation to time. A widely used planning tool.

Grapevine A common word used to describe the informal system of communication within an organization.

Great-man approach An approach to leadership theory which asserts that leadership qualities are hereditary. The person is born a leader.

Grievance A disagreement regarding the interpretation of a labor contract. Employees who feel they have been treated unfairly can file a grievance.

Grievance procedure A formal appeal process through which employees can express their complaints and see them resolved fairly. There are usually several steps in this process.

Group dynamics The study of the forces and changes which shape group processes.

Halo effect A rating error in which the entire rating of an employee is based on a single, overriding trait or attribute.

Herzberg's two-factor theory A theory of work motivation that identifies the dissatisfiers or hygiene factors as salary, working conditions, company policies, and technical supervision and the motivating factors as recognition, responsibility, achievement, advancement, and the work itself.

Heterogeneity The degree to which the characteristics of a group's members are dissimilar.

Hidden agenda The intent, purpose, or implicit message in a communication which is transmitted through body language or voice intonation and is inconsistent with the spoken or surface-level meaning of the words.

Homogeneity The degree to which the characteristics of the members of a group are similar.

"Hot stove" principle An approach to discipline which recommends that, like a red-hot stove, disciplinary policies should tell employees what is expected, be consistent, provide a warning, and be immediate, nondiscriminatory, impersonal, and fair.

Human relations approach The management philosophy based on the assumption that attention to human concerns and problems will result in greater employee satisfaction and productivity.

Hygiene factors In Herzberg's theory of motivation, the factors that prevent dissatisfaction but do not lead to satisfaction. Included would be salary, working conditions, company policies, and technical supervision.

Identification process In psychological development, the process whereby the 5- to 9-year-old child identifies with a model (e.g., the father or mother).

Inelastic A word used in economics to characterize a demand curve which is not greatly influenced by price.

Informal organization All relationships, communications, and group processes which occur outside the formally prescribed organizational structure.

In-process control A method of control which is capable of providing feedback during an activity rather than after it is completed.

Internal environment Factors within an organization (e.g., its private- or public-sector status, technology, size, and goals) which influences the effectiveness of supervision.

Job description A document which outlines an employee's major duties and responsibilities.

Job enlargement Often confused with job enrichment, job enlargement loads jobs horizontally by expanding the number of operations performed but does not enrich them with opportunities for recognition, responsibility, achievement, and growth.

Job enrichment An applied technique based on Herzberg's two-factor theory of motivation that loads jobs vertically by incorporating recognition, responsibility, achievement, and growth.

Jurisdictional strike An unfair union practice which involves forcing an employer to assign work to employees belonging to a particular union.

Laissez faire An approach to leadership whereby the leader exerts no control and allows subordinates to direct their own activities. Actually a form of no leadership.

Landrum-Griffin Act The Labor-Management Reporting and Disclosure Act which resulted from a Senate investigation that uncovered racketeering, violence, and collusion in unions. It gives the government more direct power to regulate and control labor relations.

Law of effect From operant learning theory, this law states that behavior followed by a positive consequence will tend to increase and behavior followed by a negative consequence will tend to decrease. This makes possible the prediction and control of behavior.

Learning The psychological process, based on reinforced practice or experience, that involves a change in behavior.

Leveling Bringing a hidden agenda to the surface; telling another person your interpretation of what he or she is doing to you.

Life position In TA, a person's feelings regarding his or her relationships with others. There are four possible positions: I'm OK—you're OK (the most healthy); I'm OK—you're not OK; I'm not OK—you're OK; and I'm not OK—you're not OK (the least healthy).

Life script In TA, the role of an individual, taken from earlier feelings and experiences, which specifies his or her method of interacting with the world.

Line authority The formally sanctioned authority of a position. Line personnel have the authority to give orders and make decisions.

Linking pin Key person linking the communications and contributions of one group to those of another. Supervisors link the contributions of their group to those in the rest of the organization.

Management by exception A control technique, sometimes abbreviated MBE, which states that supervisors should deal only with exceptional matters and have their subordinates handle things that are routine.

Maslow's hierarchy of needs A theory of motivation that starts at the basic physiological level and moves up through safety, love, esteem, and self-actualization. The basic premise is that once a level of need is satisfied, it can no longer serve to motivate.

Matrix structure A specialized form of project organization which has both horizontal and vertical lines of authority and communication and violates the principle of unity of command.

MBO (management by objectives) An acronym for a planning and control approach of setting of objectives and appraising by results.

Mediation In a grievance dispute, the process whereby a neutral third party gets the parties together to discuss and analyze the issues, makes specific recommendations, and renders a decision. Neither party, however, is forced to accept the decision of the mediator.

MIS (management information system) An acronym for generally designating a computerized information system that integrates important organizational information for use in decision making.

Modeling process In psychological development, the process whereby the very young child imitates the model (e.g., the father or mother).

Motivation A psychological process which is the driving force or energizer behind human behavior. The process can be depicted as a need setting up a drive aimed at a goal.

Motivators In Herzberg's theory of motivation, the factors that lead to motivation. Included would be recognition, responsibility, achievement, advancement, and the work itself.

Negative discipline A disciplinary practice, either rewarding or punitive, which is commonly used but generally hinders or at least does not help an employee achieve organizational goals.

Network planning A planning technique which demonstrates the interdependent relationships of goals. Examples are the program evaluation and review technique (PERT) and the critical path method (CPM).

NGT (nominal group technique) An acronym for a problem-solving process for groups involving the silent generation of ideas, round-robin input, discussion, and decision.

Nondirective interviewing An interviewing technique which uses broad open-ended questions to obtain information. This approach lets the interviewee do most of the talking.

Nonverbal communication The information transmitted, intentionally or unintentionally, through body movements, posture, facial expressions, and/or voice inflection. An often unrecognized but very important form of communication.

Norm An expectation for individuals based on tradition, past practices and/or an implicit agreement. Norms for supervisors may include wearing a shirt and tie or a dress, eating at particular times of the day, and working overtime without extra pay.

Obituary technique A method of identifying major career goals by writing one's own obituary.

OJT An acronym for on-the-job training, a practical and widely used training approach to teach employees their everyday responsibilities and tasks.

Open-door policy A systematic policy encouraging employees to bring any complaints or disagreements to their supervisor or manager at any time. A form of upward communication.

Operant conditioning A type of learning whereby the person operates on (or manipulates) the environment so as to bring about a desired consequence. This type of learning suggests that behavior is a function of its consequences.

Operational planning Day-to-day short-range planning.

Organizational behavior modification Termed O.B. Mod., this is an external approach to human resource management that is based on operant learning theory and involves the following five steps: identify, measure, analyze, intervene, and evaluate.

Organization development Often abbreviated as OD, this is a planned change process which uses behavioral science technology to help improve the health and effectivenss of organizations. A total OD strategy often includes a number of specific techniques such as job enrichment, organizational behavior modification, and team building.

OSHA (Occupational Safety and Health Act) A law designed to ensure safe working conditions.

Parallel transaction In TA, a compatible communication exchange where the person receives the anticipated response from the other person.

Parent ego state In TA, this is the source of critical and supportive behavior. It reflects the behavior of the dominant parent.

Perception The psychological process that people use to select, organize, and interpret the world around them.

Performance analysis A procedure for analyzing performance deficiencies which tells whether or not a problem stems from a deficiency in skill and then provides specific recommendations for analyzing the problem and developing strategies to solve it.

Performance appraisal A comprehensive, systematic, and planned approach to appraising and evaluating employee performance.

Policy A broad guideline which suggests appropriate procedures under a given set of circumstances.

Positive discipline Discipline which serves to help an employee achieve organizational objectives.

Power The motivational need to manipulate others.

Primacy error Rating an employee on the basis of his or her previous ratings.

Private sector Organizations that are not supported by local, state, or federal taxes. Private-sector organizations are most often privately owned, profit-oriented businesses such as local stores, supermarkets, steel mills, and gas stations.

Problem employee An employee whose personal problems are affecting or may affect his or her *work-related* performance.

Profit-and-loss accounting A method of accounting oriented toward determining the profits or losses of an organization or an identifiable subunit over a specified period of time.

Progressive discipline A policy of discipline which becomes increasingly more severe if infractions continue. Typical steps include a verbal warning, written warning, disciplinary layoff, and dismissal.

Project organization A modern organizational structure usually designed for one-of-a-kind projects. These structures often violate traditional principles of organization such as equal authority and responsibility.

Public sector Organizations that are supported by local, state, or federal taxes. Typically they are nonprofit organizations such as schools, hospitals, military units, government agencies, and churches.

Punisher Any consequence of behavior that tends to weaken it and lead to a decrease in frequency.

Random sampling An unbiased way of selecting or assigning which is accomplished by using a table of random numbers or drawing from a hat.

Real-time system A system of recording and feedback which is able to process inputs and provide feedback almost simultaneously. Real-time computer systems are used in areas such as airline reservations and retail inventory control.

Recency error Rating an employee on the basis of his or her most recent behavior.

Reinforcer Any consequence of behavior that tends to strengthen it and leads to an increase in frequency.

Requisition A form which documents a request. A supervisor would use an employment requisition, for example, to specify the qualifications needed in the person to be hired.

Right to work Laws prohibiting closed shops (shops requiring union membership as a prerequisite to employment). Such laws exist in 40 percent of the states.

Role A set of personal expectations. Typical roles are supervisor, housewife, union steward, leader, and counselor.

Role-play A learning/training strategy in which two or more people act out a contrived situation in order to examine their inter- and intrapersonal feelings and skills.

Sanctions Positive or negative events that are designed to enforce conformity to group norms.

Scalar principle This term is synonymous with the organization principle of hierarchy and implies that organizations should be structured in a hierarchical manner, indicating the chain or command, the levels of responsibility and authority, and the reporting relationships.

Scaling A rating technique used in performance appraisal in which the rater evaluates an attribute by placing a mark on a continuum.

Scientific management The philosophy of Frederick W. Taylor, one of the most important historical contributors to management. His approach emphasized the scientific design and analysis of the job.

Secondary boycott An unfair union practice of forcing an employer to cease doing business with or handling the products of another employer.

Self-actualization The pinnacle of Maslow's hierarchy of needs— the need or desire to realize one's potentials, to become whatever one can and wishes to become.

Simulation A contrived situation designed to approximate real conditions (e.g., a computer stimulation may be designed to approximate the actual financial conditions and relationships within an organization).

Skills analysis A technique of matching employee skills with required job skills in order to identify training needs.

Socialization process In psychological development, the process whereby the social adaptation of the older child and adult is shaped by parents/peers/friends.

Span of control The number of persons who report directly to a supervisor or manager.

Specialization A type of work simplification. The recognized advantage is greater efficiency. The major criticism is that it makes jobs boring and unchallenging.

Staff A person or group of persons serving in an advisory function. Staff personnel do not have direct line authority. In a manufacturing firm, personnel and engineering functions usually have a staff relationship to production-line supervisors.

Stamps In TA, feelings (e.g., anger, purity, or depression) which are saved up until a person earns the "right" to cash them in.

Standard A specific and measurable objective or output for achievement. This is the first step of the control process.

Status The relative ranking of a person in a group, organization, or society. Status often depends on some attribute such as sex, intelligence, or occupation.

Stereotype Evaluating a person according to a single attribute or trait which places the person within a particular group. Usually also implies that the group and thus the individual within the group is unfairly perceived in a negative manner.

Steward Sometimes called the committeeperson, this is the supervisor's counterpart on the union side of labor relations.

Strategic planning Long-range planning designed to optimize long-term rather than short-term goals.

Stroke As used in TA, it refers to any action which provides recognition (positive or negative) for another person.

Supervisor A person who performs functions such as planning, organizing, staffing, training, controlling, disciplining, or appraising; is directly responsible for understanding, communicating, motivating, and leading others; but does not normally take part in performing the physical or manual work.

Surface agenda The apparent meaning of a communication as transmitted by the meaning of words that are used.

Taft-Hartley Act The Labor-Management Relations Act which favored management by spelling out certain unfair practices of unions.

Team development or building A deliberate process (an OD technique) of building a cohesive work unit through the use of interventions such as survey feedback and group discussions of organizational problems.

Theory X A set of assumptions about human nature that leads to a task-oriented, autocratic leadership style.

Theory Y A set of assumptions about human nature that leads to a human relations, participative leadership style.

Trait approach A theory of leadership proposing that effective leadership depends on certain key traits and characteristics.

Transactional analysis Commonly called TA, it is a method, based on psychoanalytic theory, of analyzing interpersonal communications and relations. The three ego states in TA are the Parent, Adult, and Child.

Trend analysis A mathematical technique of forecasting which bases predictions on the slope and shape of a mathematical curve.

Tripartite board A group specified in a labor union contract to settle grievances and consists of a management representative, a union representative, and an agreed-upon neutral third party.

"Twenty/eighty" behaviors Those critical behaviors that should be identified in the first step of O.B. Mod. The 20 percent of behaviors affect 80 percent of performance.

Ulterior transaction In TA, a communication exchange in which one of the transmissions has both a surface or apparent meaning and a hidden or implied meaning.

Union shop A shop in which the employer can hire a nonunion person with the understanding that the employee will join the union within a stated period of time.

Unity of command The organization principle that an individual should have one and only one person to report to. The "one boss" principle.

Universal approach The management philosophy of Henri Fayol, which advocated the identification and application of universal management functions and principles such as planning, organizing, commanding, coordinating, and controlling.

Wagner Act The National Labor Relations Act, which was prolabor and gave unions the legal right to organize; to bargain collectively over wages, hours, and conditions; and to strike.

Wheel network A communications pattern where one person serves as the communications center or "hub" for the others.

SELF-REVIEW GUIDE

The purpose of this Self-Review Guide is to help you better understand and study the concepts and terms used in the text. There are four sections for each corresponding chapter in the book. Part A contains completion questions for the key concepts of the chapter. Part B has ten true-false questions, and Part C has ten multiple-choice questions. Answers are provided for the questions in these three parts. Part D contains four or five essay or discussion questions. In total, we hope that this material will help you better master the concepts and techniques of effective supervision and management.

THE ROLE OF THE MODERN SUPERVISOR

A COMPLETION QUESTIONS

a Scientific management
b Human relations
c Universal principles
d Contingency management
e Role expectations

From the above list, select the letter for the term that best completes each statement below.

1 The _____ approach stresses that there is a single set of rules and guidelines that apply to the management of all efficient organizations.
2 Every supervisor receives a set of _____ from his or her people which specifies the type of supervisory behavior that is anticipated.
3 The assembly line is a good example of the application of the principles of _____.
4 The results of the Hawthorne studies helped to usher in the _____ approach to management.
5 A supervisor who carefully examines the situation and circumstances in order to determine the appropriate course of action is practicing _____.

B TRUE-FALSE QUESTIONS

1 The scientific management approach is rarely used today.
2 The human relations role of a counselor suggests that supervisors should be willing to help employees with both personal and work-related problems.
3 The majority of supervisors fail because they lack the necessary technical skills and abilities.
4 As supervisors are promoted, their jobs usually become more technical and human relations oriented.
5 The universal approach is preferable because the principles apply under all circumstances.
6 It is extremely important that supervisors identify and adopt a role which best suits their job.
7 The Hawthorne studies began as a typical scientific management study designed to increase worker efficiency.
8 The most important factors contributing to the increased productivity at Hawthorne were the novelty and attention provided by the experimenters.

9 The principles advocated by the universal approach can serve as useful guidelines if circumstances are carefully considered.

10 Supervisors become increasing more conceptual as they are promoted.

C MULTIPLE-CHOICE QUESTIONS

1 The number of individuals who can be effectively supervised
   a is three.
   b is five.
   c is seven.
   d depends on the situation.

2 The scientific management approach
   a is the most scientific method.
   b is the most useful method.
   c was suggested by Frederick Winslow Taylor.
   d all the above

3 The pig-iron handling experiments of Taylor increased productivity approximately
   a two times.
   b four times.
   c eight times.
   d ten times.

4 The human relations approach suggested that productivity can be increased by
   a better wage incentives.
   b better pay.
   c more fringe benefits.
   d a concern and interest in workers.

5 In the experiments at Hawthorne, productivity increased when
   a light intensity was increased.
   b lunch breaks were changed.
   c light intensity was decreased.
   d all the above

6 The universal approach advocates
   a universal principles.
   b the function of planning.
   c uniform guidelines for supervision.
   d all the above

7 Most supervisors fail because they lack
   a technical skills.
   b human relations skills.
   c conceptual skills.
   d both b and c

8 The role(s) which is (are) characteristic of the universal approach is (are)
   a leader.
   b organizer.
   c planner.
   d all the above

9 The contingency approach may include
   a the scientific management approach.
   b the human relations approach.
   c the universal approach.
   d all the above

10 According to Kahn's study, almost _____ percent of the skills required of top management are conceptual in nature.

  a 50   **c** 100

  b 90   **d** 20

D ESSAY QUESTIONS OR CLASS DISCUSSION QUESTIONS

1 Of the various approaches to supervision, which do you feel is the most effective and realistic? Why?

2 In a discussion, a colleague says to you that the universal principles approach is outdated, old-fashioned, and useless. Agree or disagree with this person and state your reasoning.

3 In an orientation program for new supervisors, the discussion leader repeatedly emphasizes the need for supervisors to assume the role of the controller and the planner. When Jack Robbins, a new supervisor, asks the discussion leader about the need for human relations skills, the leader replies: "The last thing you have to worry about is human relations. The employees are tough, and they expect you to be tough too. So forget about the textbook human relations stuff you learned in school and assert your authority or you're going to lose it." Agree or disagree with the discussion leader and explain your reasoning.

4 In a discussion with her manager, Cindy Ross, the director of sales, is told that the one thing that gets people ahead in the company is their ability to plan. Cindy decides to deemphasize her visits to salespeople in the field in order to concentrate more on long-range forecasts and planning. Discuss the possible pitfalls in her reaction.

■ ANSWERS

A Completion Questions: **1** c   **2** e   **3** a   **4** b   **5** d

B True-False Questions: **1** F   **2** T   **3** F   **4** F   **5** F   **6** F

                       7 T   **8** T   **9** T   **10** T

C Multiple-Choice Questions: **1** d   **2** c   **3** b   **4** d   **5** d

                       6 d   **7** d   **8** d   **9** d   **10** a

②CHAPTER

A COMPLETION QUESTIONS

a Elastic demand	**e** Private sector
b Inelastic demand	**f** EEOC
c OSHA	**g** Craft technology
d Public sector	**h** Mass production technology
	i Process technology

From the above list, select the letter for the term that best completes each statement below.

1 Working conditions for health and safety are regulated by _____.
2 A good example of _____ is the assembly line.
3 When demand fluctuates depending upon economic conditions, it is said to be a (an) _____.
4 _____ organizations usually have greater continuity of leadership and agreed-upon goals.
5 _____ organizations are characterized by changing goals and elected officials.
6 High levels of skill and individual responsibility are characteristics of workers in a (an) _____.
7 A demand that is relatively stable despite changing economic and social conditions is a (an) _____.
8 A (An) _____ is characterized by a highly automated production system and highly skilled and technologically trained employees.
9 The _____ has the power to investigate charges of discrimination in employment practices.

B TRUE-FALSE QUESTIONS

1 People's attitudes and values toward work are entirely shaped by the era in which they grow up.
2 The EEOC has the power to fine companies and/or impose quotas if they violate the Equal Employment Opportunity laws.
3 Companies that manufacture products such as recreational vehicles and cosmetics usually have a relatively elastic demand.
4 The growth of technology is expected to continue at a faster rate in the future.
5 The public sector is usually considered a very stable environment in which goals are consistent.
6 A person's style of supervision is a personal choice and should not be influenced by the organization's technology.

7 As organizations grow, many supervisory functions are handled by staff and functional specialists.

8 It is generally agreed that organizations with long time spans produce climates conducive to employee satisfaction.

9 Status symbols such as parking places, company cars, and office furniture are relatively unimportant.

10 The Occupational Safety and Health Act (OSHA) gives the Secretary of Labor the powers to set standards for safety and health within most industries.

C MULTIPLE-CHOICE QUESTIONS

1 The recent law which governs health and safety is abbreviated
   a EEOC.
   b SAFE.
   c OSHA.
   d FSLA.

2 People who grew up during the 1940s can often be characterized by a (an) _____ value system.
   a conformist
   b opportunistic
   c social
   d future shock

3 An inelastic demand
   a is very stable.
   b is experienced by most utility industries.
   c supports traditional management styles.
   d all the above

4 An elastic demand
   a is stable.
   b changes frequently.
   c is desirable.
   d occurs very infrequently.

5 The public sector is characterized by
   a elected officials.
   b changing leadership.
   c changing goals.
   d all the above

6 The private sector is characterized by
   a private ownership.
   b large organizations.
   c flamboyant leadership.
   d all the above

7 Mass production technology is often associated with
   a assembly lines.
   b manufacturing.
   c worker dissatisfaction.
   d all the above

8 Craft technologies are characterized by
   a large capital investments.
   b worker dissatisfaction.
   c highly skilled workers.
   d all the above

9 Staff and functional specialists may
   a reduce supervisory authority.
   b increase efficiency.
   c help avoid costly lawsuits.
   d all the above

10 Economic measures on supervisors will probably
   a not play a large role in most of their lives.

b continue to increase.

c continue to decrease.

d remain about the same.

D ESSAY QUESTIONS OR CLASS DISCUSSION QUESTIONS

1 Alice Perkins receives two new people to supervise from the personnel department. One is a 63-year-old man and the other is an 18-year-old woman. Both people are being assigned to the same task. What differences in performance can she expect?

2 List the major laws designed to ensure that all people have an equal opportunity for employment. Describe how these and other laws affect policies and practices in organizations.

3 Which organization's product demand would be considered more elastic: a feed store or a jeweler? Describe the impact that elasticity of demand can have on organizations.

4 Discuss the differences between the supervisor's environment in public sector versus private sector organizations.

5 Discuss the impact that staff and functional specialists are likely to have on the authority structure of the supervisor's job. Include a description of some of the functional areas which are likely to be affected.

■ ANSWERS

A Completion Questions: **1** c **2** h **3** a **4** e **5** d
6 g **7** b **8** i **9** f

B True-False Questions: **1** F **2** T **3** T **4** T **5** F **6** F
7 T **8** T **9** F **10** T

C Multiple-Choice Questions: **1** c **2** b **3** d **4** b **5** d
6 a **7** d **8** c **9** d **10** b

A COMPLETION QUESTIONS

a Budgeting   **e** Trend analysis
b Management by objectives   **f** Correlation
c Network planning   **g** Simulation
d Statistical projection

From the above list, select the letter for the term that best completes each statement below.

1 The result of _____ is a statement of the financial resources required for a specified period of time.

2 The major disadvantage of _____ is that it assumes that future conditions will be identical to past conditions.

3 A _____ is a contrived situation which is designed to depict characteristics of a realistic situation.

4 _____ is characterized by a process of setting goals and appraising by results.

5 Although a _____ may indicate that two variables are related, it does not indicate that one variable causes or controls the other.

6 A planning method which helps to determine how to schedule competing resources so that time is conserved is _____.

7 In _____ the levels of an index are plotted over time on a graph.

B TRUE-FALSE QUESTIONS

1 Planning ensures that all events will follow in a predetermined order.

2 Most organizational plans are in a continual process of change.

3 It is desirable to budget more money than required so that the budget is not exceeded later in the year.

4 Management by objectives is a popular planning technique stressing goal setting and evaluation by results.

5 PERT, CPM, MCP, PEP, and PROPS are essentially similar planning techniques.

6 The critical path is the least time consuming chain of events in a network planning process.

7 Statistical projections based on historical data are almost always accurate.

8 Correlations are important because they indicate which variable needs to be manipulated to cause a change in the other variable.

9 A supervisor should make use of as many planning aids such as desk calendars, wall calendars, pocket calendars, and notebooks as possible.

10 A Gantt chart is an effective method of scheduling work and maintaining a running record of progress.

C MULTIPLE-CHOICE QUESTIONS

1 The features of the planning process include
   a unpredictability.
   b flexibility.
   c goal setting.
   d all the above

2 Budgets
   a should never be exceeded.
   b are a valuable planning tool.
   c always refer to financial plans.
   d all the above

3 Long-range planning
   a is also called strategic planning.
   b is often inaccurate.
   c is often time consuming.
   d all the above

4 The characteristics of MBO include
   a results orientation.
   b evaluation of attitudes.
   c evaluation of effort.
   d all the above

5 MBO
   a should always originate at the top.
   b must be an organizationwide process.
   c is too complex to implement without a skilled consultant.
   d none of the above

6 The critical path is
   a the most time consuming chain of events.
   b the least time consuming chain of events.
   c the path with most obvious opportunities for error.
   d the most visible route to the goal.

7 Trend analysis
   a takes into consideration recent changes of events.
   b can be done through mathematical analysis.
   c is usually more accurate than projections made by averaging.
   d all the above

8 Gantt charts
   a were named after the great race horse -A-Gantt.
   b illustrate planning in relation to time.
   c are an outdated mechanism.
   d are rarely accurate.

9 Forecasting
   a is filled with risks.
   b is time consuming.
   c can be very costly.
   d all the above

10 Real-time systems
  a are an invaluable time-keeping device.
  b use time-in-minutes as input.
  c are too costly.
  d provide almost instantanious updating after each transaction.

D ESSAY QUESTIONS OR CLASS DISCUSSION QUESTIONS

1 Pretend that you have been appointed director of sales for a new company that will deal in solar heating products. Describe and explain some of the decisions that you will need to make in planning for your sales strategies and your new sales force.

2 Describe some of the major advantages of an MBO approach to planning.

3 During the previous ten years, you have seen a dramatic increase in the number of people needed in your area of responsibility. The figures for the past ten years are 10, 11, 11, 12, 13, 14, 16, 18, 21, 26. Write a brief letter to the personnel department showing your anticipated need for the next one- and five-year periods.

4 Explain the concept of "real-time system". Speculate on how such a system could revolutionize the way retail stores operate.

■ ANSWERS

A Completion Questions: **1** a **2** d **3** g **4** b **5** f
  6 c **7** e

B True-False Questions: **1** F **2** T **3** F **4** T **5** T **6** F
  7 F **8** F **9** F **10** T

C Multiple-Choice Questions: **1** d **2** b **3** d **4** a **5** d
  6 a **7** d **8** b **9** d **10** d

④CHAPTER

A COMPLETION QUESTIONS

a Time management	**d** Job analysis
b Delegation	**e** Prioritizing for time management
c Time wasters	**f** Planning for time management

From the above list, select the letter for the term that best completes each statement below.

1 Two good methods for _____ are activities checklists and random sampling procedures.

2 Analyzing the job and establishing priorities are important aspects of _____.

3 Establishing a routine wherein the bulk of a supervisor's activities are concerned with priority job issues that have a high payoff is effective _____.

4 Some of the most irritating _____ are paperwork, unnecessary conversations, telephone interruptions, procrastination, unnecessary reading, and meetings.

5 The assignment of tasks and duties that are normally considered the responsibility of supervisors is _____.

6 Analyzing jobs for time consumption, importance, and authority are important aspects of _____.

B TRUE-FALSE QUESTIONS

1 The notion that good supervisors always have time is more fact than myth.

2 Many supervisors have difficulty delegating because they have not defined their own levels of responsibility and authority.

3 Random sampling is the easiest method of job analysis because it allows the supervisor to analyze the job whenever it is convenient.

4 In establishing the importance of supervisory activities, needed activities are those activities which are critical if the group is to achieve its basic goals.

5 Employees should never be delegated complete authority for an important job objective.

6 Phased delegation is a process of gradually allowing an employee more authority until it is completely delegated.

7 One possible way of dealing with paperwork is to ignore it.

505

8 The major reason why most people cannot manage their time is that other people waste it.

9 Delegation is an important method of training and employee development.

10 All systems designed to help supervisors manage time require an initial investment of time.

C MULTIPLE-CHOICE QUESTIONS

1 The difference between the average strokes of the PGA's leading money winner and the fortieth place finisher is

  a extremely small.   **c** five strokes.

  b very large.   **d** ten strokes.

2 A myth about time and time management is

  a time can be saved.

  b other people waste time.

  c good supervisors always have time.

  d all the above

3 Assigning employees authority to complete tasks which are normally supervisory in nature is

  a a very serious but necessary responsibility.   **c** delegation.

                              d all the above

  b part of good time management.

4 What is *not* one of the recommended procedures for dealing with paperwork?

  a write answers and replies on letters   **c** handle papers, at maximum, three times

  b ignore the paperwork   **d** use form letters

5 To stop unnecessary conversations, supervisors can

  a excuse themselves and go to the bathroom.

  b schedule appointments in the other person's office.

  c stand up before the conversation begins.

  d all the above

6 The third of the four levels for phased delegation is

  a act and then report.   **c** action after approval.

  b total responsibility.   **d** none of the above

7 Many supervisors do not delegate because

  a they do not trust their people.

  b they like the work too much.

  c they don't know their own level of authority and responsibility.

  d all the above

8 What is the most preferable method of analyzing the job for time usage?

  a the activities checklist   **c** use of a consultant

  b random sampling   **d** none of the above

9 A good time-management program requires
  a careful job analysis.
  c establishing priorities.
  b an initial investment of time.
  d all the above

10 Meetings are
  a always unnecessary.
  b often called without a purpose.
  c an ineffective method of using time.
  d none of the above

D ESSAY QUESTIONS OR CLASS DISCUSSION QUESTIONS

1 Delegation is a relatively simple concept, yet many supervisors fail to delegate properly. Describe some of the reasons why managers fail to delegate.

2 One common reason for not delegating is that supervisors do not know which authority level should be assigned to a particular task. Describe a process for analyzing and overcoming this problem.

3 At some time, most supervisors realize the need to do a thorough analysis of how they use their time. Describe the general process which you would follow in analyzing your time usage.

4 Imagine that your boss conducts weekly meetings which are both time consuming and poorly organized. What are some of the things that you, as a participant, could do to improve the meetings?

■ ANSWERS

A Completion Questions: **1** d   **2** a   **3** f   **4** c   **5** b   **6** e
B True-False Questions: **1** F   **2** T   **3** F   **4** F   **5** F   **6** T
  7 T   **8** F   **9** T   **10** T
C Multiple-Choice Questions: **1** a   **2** d   **3** d   **4** c   **5** d
  6 a   **7** d   **8** b   **9** d   **10** b

A COMPLETION QUESTIONS

a Bureaucratic theory
b Departmentation
c Specialization
d Span of control
e Hierarchy
f Equal authority and responsibility

g Unity of command
h Functional authority
i Staff structure
j Project organization
k Matrix organization
l Free form organization
m Informal organization

From the list above, select the letter for the term that best completes each statement below.

1 A (An) _____ is a structure where the unit members serve in an advisory capacity but have no formal authority.

2 The _____ often makes up for the inadequacies of the formal organizational structure.

3 The number of employees reporting directly to a supervisor indicates the supervisor's _____.

4 According to the _____ principle, authority and responsibility go from the top down.

5 Max Weber was the pioneering sociologist who proposed the ideal form of organization which is described by _____.

6 The basic idea of the _____ principle is that people become more efficient as their work is subdivided.

7 When a supervisor is responsible for completing a job and lacks the required authority, the principle of _____ is violated.

8 The concept that a person should have only one boss is the idea of _____.

9 Staff personnel such as employment offices, purchasing agents, and engineers often have _____ over line personnel.

10 Customers and clients, numbers, alphabetical order, types of products, time, and different kinds of machinery can all help form natural lines by which to practice _____.

11 In a _____ a person often has more than one boss.

12 An organization formed to accomplish a specific purpose or goal is called a (an) _____.

13 An organization with a constantly changing structure, which responds to environmental demands is a (an) _____.

B TRUE-FALSE QUESTIONS

1 Most people today accept Weber's concept of bureaucracy as the ideal form of organization.

2 Functional departmentation is probably the most commonly used method of departmentation.

3 Most organizations are departmentalized in several ways such as time, function, and product.

4 Specialization always results in more efficient work processes.

5 There is no universally accepted way of determining an appropriate span of control.

6 According to the scalar principle, members of an organization without a common supervisor should not be directly engaged in formal communications.

7 The principle of equal authority and responsibility should never be violated.

8 Functional authority is formal staff authority within a specified functional area.

9 Staff persons "carry little weight" in organizations because of their lack of formal authority.

10 The informal organization can and should be viewed as an indispensable aid to the formal organization.

C MULTIPLE-CHOICE QUESTIONS

1 An appropriate method for departmentalizing is
   a alpha-numerical.   **c** time.
   b functional.   **d** all the above

2 Specialization is closely related to
   a hierarchy.   **c** departmentation.
   b staff functions.   **d** none of the above

3 The span of control should usually be
   a five employees.
   b dependent upon the situation.
   c no more than ten employees.
   d examined by an organizational specialist.

4 Matrix organizations
   a are a special type of project organization.
   b directly violate unity of command.
   c are characterized by frequent conflicts.
   d all the above

5 The principle which states that a person should have one and only one boss is
   a unity of command.
   b hierarchy.

    c equal authority and responsibility.

    d specialization.

6 The most important characteristic of staff personnel is

    a they are usually engineers.   **c** they are usually young and

    b their authority is only   better educated.

       advisory in nature.   **d** their special privileges and

                              powers.

7 An organization formulated to achieve a specified goal within a particular time period is a _____ organization.

    a project   **c** free form

    b bureaucratic   **d** matrix

8 The informal organization

    a often aids the formal organization.

    b is made of people outside the formal organization.

    c is not a legitimate concern.

    d none of the above

9 A bureaucracy is

    a an inefficient way of organizing.

    b characterized by red tape.

    c theoretically impossible.

    d none of the above

10 A supervisor of a purchasing department usually possesses

    a little authority.   **c** line authority.

    b staff authority.   **d** both b and c

D ESSAY QUESTIONS OR CLASS DISCUSSION QUESTIONS

1 Describe and discuss the relative advantages and disadvantages of work simplification and specialization.

2 Your department is much overworked and you desperately need additional help. Your boss refuses to grant your request for additional people and, as her rationale, she states that your span of control (six people) has already become too large. How would you respond to this objection?

3 In coordinating a special project, for ease of communication, you suggest to another supervisor that he allow you to issue instructions directly to his people. The other supervisor replies that this would violate unity of command and that no effective supervisory stratgey can be effective when it violates this principle. How might you reply?

4 Differentiate between line and staff authority. What is meant by the concept of functional authority?

5 Discuss the advantages and disadvantages of the informal organization.

■ **ANSWERS**

A Completion Questions: **1** i   **2** m   **3** d   **4** e   **5** a   **6** c
7 f   **8** g   **9** h   **10** b   **11** k
12 j   **13** l

B True-False Questions: **1** F   **2** T   **3** T   **4** F   **5** T   **6** T
7 F   **8** T   **9** F   **10** T

C Multiple-Choice Questions: **1** d   **2** c   **3** b   **4** d   **5** a
6 b   **7** a   **8** a   **9** d   **10** d

CHAPTER 6

A COMPLETION QUESTIONS

a Employment process
b Selection
c Bona fide occupational qualification
d Employment requisition
e Lawful employment inquiry

f Unlawful employment inquiry
g Affirmative action
h Nondirective interviewing
i Orientation process

From the above list, select the letter for the term that best completes each statement below.

1 Asking an applicant if he or she is married is an _____.
2 One of the major objectives of the _____ is to alleviate any initial fears the employee may have regarding the job.
3 A (An) _____ is a requirement that is directly related to the applicant's ability to perform the job.
4 A good _____ should state the specific qualification required of applicants for the job.
5 _____ is the idea that an organization will take positive action to ensure that its personnel practices are nondiscriminatory.
6 During a (an) _____ process, the objective is to provide the applicant with a maximum opportunity to supply information about his or her qualifications.
7 Asking applicants whether or not they can submit a birth certificate or proof of citizenship is a _____.
8 The _____ includes many aspects of an employee's career, including the selection interview, orientation, goal setting, and planning.
9 The objective of the _____ process is to match the applicant's abilities with the requirements of the job.

B TRUE-FALSE QUESTIONS

1 Bona fide occupational qualifications are the officially sanctioned qualifications of the EEOC.
2 A good way to start a selection interview is with a topic of mutual interest such as a recent ballgame.
3 A common problem in interviewing is that interviewers talk too much.
4 The age discrimination act ensures that young people may seek employment even though they may not be 16 years of age.

5 An important goal of the orientation is to provide an employee with as much information about the job and personal benefits as possible.

6 It is probably unlawful to ask a female applicant how many children she has.

7 Supervisors can be held directly responsible by the courts for violations of employment laws.

8 A nondirective interview is an interview where the goal is constantly changing.

9 Staffing involves both the selection and orientation processes.

10 Affirmative action plans are quotas imposed by the federal government.

C MULTIPLE-CHOICE QUESTIONS

1 Which of the following is a lawful employment inquiry?
a How many children do you have?
b Have you ever been arrested?
c Do you have any distinguishing physical characteristics?
d How old are you?

2 Which of the following is an illegal employment inquiry?
a What type of military discharge do you have?
b Do you have any handicaps?
c Where were you born?
d all the above

3 During a nondirective interview
a the interviewer changes goals constantly.
b the interviewer asks specific and pointed questions.
c the interviewer does most of the talking.
d none of the above

4 The major objective of the employment interview is to
a make the candidate feel at ease.
b match candidate skills with job qualifications.
c sell the organization.
d pick the most intelligent and skilled candidate.

5 A bona fide occupational qualification is
a a real qualification.
b approved by the EEOC.
c directly related to job performance.
d an unrealistic objective.

6 The orientation process is directed toward
a training the employee.
b making the employee feel at ease and familiar with the work setting.
c explaining employee benefits.
d none of the above

513

7 An employment requisition

    a states job requirements.

    b is a notice announcing the need to fill a job.

    c can be an important document for interviewing.

    d all the above

8 Affirmative action

    a sets quotas.

    b is synonomous with the EEOC.

    c is required of some companies by federal law.

    d none of the above

9 The Civil Rights Act of 1964 makes it unlawful to discriminate on the basis of

    a religion.

    b age.

    c race.

    d all the above

10 The preemployment interview is

    a unlawful according to the Civil Rights act of 1964.

    b one of the least effective methods of selecting employees.

    c a process which makes organizations vulnerable to charges of discrimination.

    d an outdated selection technique.

D ESSAY QUESTIONS OR CLASS DISCUSSION QUESTIONS

1 During a selection interview for a job as a laborer, a supervisor asks an applicant who is a minority race member whether or not he has an arrest record. The individual admits that he has been arrested once for loitering. Later the individual is denied employment. What are some possible implications of this situation?

2 In a conversation with a co-supervisor from another department, Alice James admits that she is having a difficult time in determining what questions can be legally asked during an employment interview. Can you give her some guidelines?

3 Provide a brief description of the procedure you would follow in interviewing a job applicant.

4 What are some of the major considerations in orienting a new employee?

■ ANSWERS

A Completion Questions: **1** f   **2** i   **3** c   **4** d   **5** g   **6** h
                             7 e   **8** a   **9** b

B True-False Questions: **1** F   **2** T   **3** T   **4** F   **5** F   **6** T
                          7 T   **8** F   **9** T   **10** F

C Multiple-Choice Questions: **1** c   **2** d   **3** d   **4** b   **5** c
                           6 b   **7** d   **8** c   **9** d   **10** c

⑦CHAPTER

A COMPLETION QUESTIONS

a Training needs
b Skills analysis
c Performance analysis
d Lecture method
e Case approach

f Role-playing exercise
g Vestibule method
h On-the-job training (OJT)
i Coaching
j Organizational development

From the above list, select the letter for the term that best completes each statement below.

1 The model of Mager and Pipe is a very helpful aid in conducting a (an) _____.

2 The advantage of the _____ is that a great deal of information can be communicated in a relatively short period of time.

3 Prior to developing a training program, a thorough analysis of employee _____ should be conducted.

4 Instruction, information, and experience at the job site should be considered _____.

5 A simple way of conducting the _____ is to develop a checklist of tasks and duties and evaluate each employee according to this list.

6 The advantage of the _____ is that it is a very close approximation of a real life situation.

7 The _____ gives employees experience with the actual work task in a sheltered environment under the direction of a qualified trainer.

8 A planned process of changing the organization through diagnosis, possible use of a consultant, and the use of behavioral science interventions such as team building is called _____.

9 The _____ allows participants to examine real life situations in a nonthreatening environment.

10 A good guideline for _____ is a list of characteristics of effective and ineffective feedback.

B TRUE-FALSE QUESTIONS

1 The training department has the bulk of the responsibility for training a supervisor's employees.

2 Every organization needs a good course in time management.

3 Skills analysis checklists are a very simple method of analyzing training and development needs.

4 In the Mager and Pipe model, the lack of a skill deficiency indicates that there is something wrong with the employee's environment.

5 The lecture method is probably the most effective method of covering a large volume of material in a relatively short period of time.

6 The advantage of the case approach is that individuals act out the feeling and emotions of individuals in realistic situations.

7 On-the-job training occurs in the natural course of an employee's job.

8 The public performer's abilities and problems are known by both the supervisor and the performer.

9 A consultant should always be used during an organizational development process.

10 Effective feedback is intended to be helpful, timely, and general in nature.

C MULTIPLE-CHOICE QUESTIONS

1 The primary responsibility for employee training rests with
  a the training department.   **c** the employee.
  b the supervisor.   **d** all the above

2 The first step in developing a training program is
  a identifying training needs.   **c** finding the physical facility.
  b identifying an instructor.   **d** determining the training method.

3 A good method of identifying training needs is
  a a skills analysis.
  b a performance analysis.
  c both a and b
  d neither a or b

4 According to the performance analysis model, a performance deficiency that occurs when employees already have the required skills may be the result of
  a poor training.
  b lack of practice.
  c punishment of performance.
  d all the above

5 The lecture method
  a communicates a large volume of information.
  b if preferred by most trainees.
  c is the most efficient training method.
  d all the above

6 Discussion groups are advantageous when
  a time is limited.
  b participant agreement is essential to adopting a course of action.
  c people know each other well.
  d people do not know each other.

7 On-the-job training includes
  a preparation.   **c** practice.
  b presenting the big picture.   **d** all the above
8 A good training program usually
  a is centered around the instructor.
  b uses several different training methods.
  c lasts one day.
  d incorporates role-playing.
9 Employees who do not know their own deficiencies and needs, but the supervisors are aware of them, are
  a public performers.
  b private performers.
  c blind performers.
  d unknown performers.
10 The most effective organizational development technique probably is
  a team building.
  b job enrichment.
  c feedback and reinforcement.
  d dependent upon the situation.

D ESSAY QUESTIONS OR CLASS DISCUSSION QUESTIONS

1 A supervisor in one of the major departments approaches you, the supervisor of training, and states that he wants you to develop a training program to help him reduce the absenteeism in his department. How should you respond to this request?
2 Discuss the advantages and disadvantages of using lectures versus discussion groups to train employees.
3 Describe the process of on-the-job training.
4 Briefly describe the process of organization development. How is the OD approach to performance problems different from traditional training approaches?

■ ANSWERS

A Completion Questions: **1** c   **2** d   **3** a   **4** h   **5** b   **6** e
                7 g   **8** j
B True-False Questions: **1** F   **2** F   **3** T   **4** T   **5** T   **6** F
                7 T   **8** T   **9** F   **10** F
C Multiple-Choice Questions: **1** b   **2** a   **3** c   **4** c   **5** a
                6 b   **7** d   **8** b   **9** c   **10** d

A COMPLETION QUESTIONS

a Objectives	**g** Feedback control
b Standards	**h** Personal observation
c Activities	**i** Accounting controls
d Feed-forward control	**j** Budgeting
e Policies	**k** Management information systems
f In-process control	**l** Performance appraisal
	m Management by exception

From the above list, select the letter for the term that best completes each statement below.

1 A process which projects expected resources is _____.

2 _____ are a good example of feed-forward control.

3 The control process begins with the establishment of _____.

4 Control which occurs during an activity is called _____.

5 When supervisors respond to only the most important level of decisions, they are practicing _____.

6 _____ occurs after an activity is completed and is therefore less effective than other methods.

7 The third step in the control process is the _____ which are performed.

8 The most used and adaptable control technique is probably _____.

9 _____ are a specific yardstick which indicates whether or not an objective has been achieved.

10 The advantage of _____ is that the situation is corrected before the damage is done.

11 Although _____ sometimes seem more rigorous than necessary, they are critical to the financial success of an organization.

12 _____ are a computerized system which can provide supervisors with important information on all aspects of their operation.

13 The _____ is a technique of controlling and providing feedback for individual employee performance.

B TRUE-FALSE QUESTIONS

1 Standards and objectives are essentially the same thing.

2 Feedback control is the single most effective method of controlling activities.

3 The last step of the control process is the control decision.

4 In reality the processes of setting objectives, setting standards, doing activities, and making control decisions are extremely difficult to isolate into discreet components.

5 A stop-sign is an example of feed-forward control.

6 A speeding ticket is an example of in-process control.

7 Persons who write policies must be careful not to make them too specific.

8 Cost accounting divides all transactions into assets and liabilities.

9 It is a myth that all accountants wear white shirts, bow ties, and garters on their sleeves.

10 Network planning is most often an ineffective control technique.

C MULTIPLE-CHOICE QUESTIONS

1 The control process is best characterized by
  a setting objectives.
  b setting standards and activities.
  c the control decision.
  d all the above

2 Feed-forward control is control which occurs
  a before the action.
  b during the action.
  c after the action.
  d all the above

3 Policies should be worded so that
  a they are not too general.
  b they are not too specific.
  c both a and b
  d neither a nor b

4 Conceptually, an objective is about the same as
  a a standard.
  b a goal.
  c a strategy.
  d a place.

5 An example of feedback control is
  a automatic switches.
  b numerical counters.
  c performance appraisals.
  d all the above

6 Self-reporting is a reliable method of measurement if
  a employees are rewarded for turning in correct reports.
  b employees are reprimanded for turning in poor reports.
  c employees are rewarded even when performance is poor.
  d it is used only once.

7 Balance sheet accounting
  a sorts transactions according to account numbers and cost.
  b divides all financial transactions into assets or liabilities.
  c is concerned with profit and loss.
  d is an outdated accounting method.

8 Management by exception is
  a responding to crises as they arise.
  b an unrealistic way to supervise.
  c is a valuable control technique.
  d is similar to MBO.

9 In projecting their budgets, supervisors should

     a overbudget to ensure they get enough resources.
     b be as accurate as possible.
     c underbudget so that they will be rewarded for efficiency.
     d none of the above
10 Management information systems
     a provide data on all aspects of an organization.
     b can be an invaluable planning tool.
     c are more theory than reality for most organizations
     d all the above

D ESSAY QUESTIONS OR CLASS DISCUSSION QUESTIONS

1 The control process incorporates the four major elements of objectives, standards, activities, and the control decision. What are the possible decision alternatives available to the supervisor when employees do not achieve standards?

2 Explain and provide an example of the concept of feed-forward control. Why is feed-forward control preferable to feedback control?

3 Explain the concept of cost accounting. How is it used to help control costs?

4 Define and explain the concept of management by exception. How does management by exception differ from management by crisis?

■ ANSWERS

A Completion Questions: **1** j   **2** e   **3** a   **4** f   **5** m   **6** g
                          7 c   **8** h   **9** b   **10** d   **11** i
                          12 k **13** d

B True-False Questions: **1** F   **2** F   **3** T   **4** T   **5** T   **6** T
                        7 T   **8** F   **9** T   **10** F

C Multiple-Choice Questions: **1** d   **2** a   **3** c   **4** a   **5** c
                            6 a   **7** b   **8** c   **9** b   **10** d

⑨ CHAPTER

A COMPLETION QUESTIONS

a Positive discipline
b Negative discipline
c Punitive discipline

d Red-hot stove principle
e Progressive discipline
f Counseling interview
g Problem employee

From the above list, select the letter for the term that best completes each statement below.

1 A _____ is an employee whose problems are affecting or may have a potential effect on work-related performance.
2 Discipline is considered _____ when it succeeds in helping employees correct their problems.
3 The _____ attempts to provide guidelines for administering punitive discipline in a fair and impartial manner.
4 Discipline is considered _____ when it is not directed toward helping employees solve their problems.
5 _____ is undesirable because it has so many negative side effects.
6 During a _____ the supervisor should never directly accuse an employee of having a personal problem such as alcoholism.
7 A system of _____ is important because it ensures that employees have an opportunity to correct their mistakes before severe discipline is administered.

B TRUE-FALSE QUESTIONS

1 Positive discipline is never punitive.
2 Discipline implies the use of punitive sanctions.
3 Negative discipline is not necessarily punitive in nature.
4 According to the red-hot stove principle, the administration of punitive discipline should be as consistent and nondiscriminatory as the burn people receive when they touch a hot stove.
5 One of the biggest problems with punitive discipline is that it is often so nonspecific that people do not know why they are being punished.
6 The effects of punishment on behavior are usually only temporary.
7 Progressive discipline is most often considered unfair because it increases the penalty for the same offense.
8 If an employee has violated work rules or procedures, the employee's previous record should be of little consequence in deciding disciplinary action.

521

9 The second step of a progressive discipline program is a formal verbal warning.

10 A supervisor has no right to question an employee's personal behavior unless it is severely affecting the employee's performance.

C MULTIPLE-CHOICE QUESTIONS

1 Negative discipline involves
  a punitive action.
  b lack of concern for improvement.
  c bad feelings by the supervisor.
  d all the above

2 Positive discipline involves
  a concern for improvement.
  b possible reinforcement and rewards.
  c possible punitive actions.
  d all the above.

3 Punitive discipline can be
  a positive.
  b negative.
  c both a and b
  d neither a nor b

4 In the long run, punitive discipline is often ineffective because
  a the effects are only temporary.
  b it is nonspecific.
  c it limits the ability of the supervisor to reward.
  d all the above

5 What is *not* a characteristic of the red-hot stove approach to discipline?
  a It is discriminating.
  b It is consistent.
  c It is expected.
  d It is immediate.

6 What is *not* one of the steps of a progressive discipline program?
  a verbal warning
  b formal verbal warning
  c written warning
  d mandatory layoff

7 In deciding on disciplinary action, it is important to consider
  a the employee's history.
  b other similar disciplinary actions.
  c alternative disciplinary procedures.
  d all the above

8 In dealing with a problem employee the supervisor
  a should not directly confront a person with his or her problem.
  b should carefully observe productivity.
  c should not get directly involved, but try to refer the person to an appropriate counseling agency.
  d all the above

9 One of the most important objectives of the counseling interview is
  a to get the employee to recognize and accept responsibility for his or her problem.
  b to discipline the employee.

c to solve the employee's problem.

d to build a progressive discipline case.

10 If any employee will not admit a problem or accept help, the supervisor should

    a confront the employee.

    b discuss the problem with the employee's spouse.

    c set up an appointment with a qualified professional.

    d deal with the problem on a performance-related basis.

D ESSAY QUESTIONS OR CLASS DISCUSSION QUESTIONS

1 Define the concept of discipline. What is the difference between positive and negative discipline.

2 During lunch, the supervisor of data processing justifies the use of punitive discipline as the only effective way to gain employee respect. Take an adversary role and explain the case against punitive discipline.

3 Describe the process of how a supervisor might decide what appropriate disciplinary actions to take.

4 Explain the differences between nondirective and directive counseling approaches. What are the advantages of each?

5 Discuss the process of dealing with personal problems of employees such as drug abuse and alcoholism.

■ ANSWERS

A Completion Questions: **1** g   **2** a   **3** d   **4** b   **5** c   **6** f
        7 e

B True-False Questions: **1** F   **2** F   **3** T   **4** T   **5** T   **6** T
        7 F   **8** F   **9** F   **10** F

C Multiple-Choice Questions: **1** b   **2** d   **3** c   **4** d   **5** a
        6 b   **7** d   **8** d   **9** a   **10** d

A COMPLETION QUESTIONS

a Appraisal functions
b Timing of appraisal
c Performance rating

d Appraisal by results
e Appraisal interview
f Appraisal errors

From the above list, select the letter for the term that best completes each statement below.

1 Recency, primacy, and halo effects are all different types of _____.
2 One important consideration in the _____ would be the length of time the employee has held the job.
3 Closely tied to the MBO process is _____.
4 Maintaining an open mind and being prepared for feedback are important aspects of preparing for the _____.
5 Several different types of _____ systems are the trait, forced choice, scaling, critical incident, and ranking techniques.
6 Feedback, recognition, and performance improvement are important _____.

B TRUE-FALSE QUESTIONS

1 Organizations without formal appraisal systems run the risk of violating the law.
2 Biannual appraisal interviews work well for most organizations.
3 The trait method is probably the most commonly used appraisal method.
4 Appraisal by results is a natural outcome of the MBO process.
5 Preparing a preliminary draft of the appraisal is not recommended since it may make the employee feel the supervisor is already biased.
6 A recency error occurs when a supervisor rates an employee according to his or her previous rating.
7 The halo effect is often based on traits unrelated to performance.
8 Emphasizing specific incidents of performance is dangerous because employees may feel that they are being picked on.
9 In general, the more frequently appraisals are administered, the better.
10 Using a mark on a continuum to rate an employee's performance with respect to a trait or category is called scaling.

C MULTIPLE-CHOICE QUESTIONS

1 The function(s) of a performance appraisal is (are)
  a feedback and recognition.   **c** planning.
  b fulfilling legal obligations.   **d** all the above

2 Appraisals should be conducted
  a at least twice a year.
  b once a year.
  c every two years.
  d none of the above

3 The use of specific behaviors which demonstrate an employee's performance is called
  a the critical incident technique.
  b ranking.
  c scaling.
  d forced-choice.

4 The appraisal by results technique
  a very closely follows the control model.
  b can be used with a trait appraisal form.
  c is closely related to MBO.
  d all the above

5 In general, the participative interview technique is
  a easier than the directive technique.
  b more effective than directive techniques.
  c less time consuming than directive techniques.
  d not recommended for inexperienced supervisors.

6 The purpose of the initial phase of a performance interview is to
  a summarize the evaluation.
  b relieve employee anxiety.
  c discuss measurement of performance.
  d establish a directive orientation with the employee.

7 During an appraisal interview
  a supervisors should concentrate on objective and measurable results.
  b feedback should concentrate on performance-related behaviors.
  c supervisors should consciously avoid discussions of the employee's attitude and personality traits.
  d all the above

8 An employee's failure regarding a particular area can be attributed to
  a the employee.
  b the supervisor.
  c external conditions and circumstances.
  d all the above

9 Ideally, the method for evaluation should be
  a forced choice.

b agreed on by the employee and supervisor before the appraisal.

c directive.

d none of the above

10 Underrating, overrating, or simply failing to discriminate among groups of employees is a

a halo effect.

b distribution error.

c recency error.

d job error.

D ESSAY QUESTIONS OR CLASS DISCUSSION QUESTIONS

1 Explain the process of appraisal by results. What are its particular advantages as opposed to other types of appraisal approaches?

2 There are several things a supervisor should do in preparation for conducting a performance appraisal. Explain the preparation and planning for the appraisal interview.

3 What is the distribution error? How can supervisors avoid distribution errors when appraising employees?

4 Discuss the purposes and advantages of a formal appraisal process.

■ ANSWERS

A Completion Questions: **1** f   **2** b   **3** d   **4** e   **5** c   **6** a

B True-False Questions: **1** T   **2** F   **3** T   **4** T   **5** F   **6** F

                        7 T   **8** F   **9** F   **10** T

C Multiple-Choice Questions: **1** d   **2** d   **3** a   **4** d   **5** b

                              6 b   **7** d   **8** d   **9** b   **10** b

LABOR RELATIONS AND THE GRIEVANCE PROCEDURE

A COMPLETION QUESTIONS

a	Wagner Act	**f**	Union steward
b	Taft-Hartley Act	**g**	Unionization process
c	Landrum-Griffin Act	**h**	Collective bargaining
d	Prounion attitudes	**i**	Grievance procedure
e	Union federation	**j**	Arbitration

From the above list, select the letter for the term that best completes each statement below.

1 The _____ resulted from the growing public disenchantment with the labor movement and attempted to restore a balance of power to labor relations.

2 Strength in numbers is an example of the reason many employees have _____.

3 During the _____, supervisors should avoid asking employees to talk in private about the union.

4 An important phase of the _____ process that is relevant to supervisors is the grievance procedure.

5 The _____ is a formal appeals process through which employees can have their complaints expressed and fairly resolved.

6 After the passage of the _____, if a majority of the employees of a defined unit wanted a union to represent them, the employer had to recognize the union and bargain in good faith.

7 At the top of the internal structure of unions is the _____.

8 The supervisor's counterpart on the union side of labor relations is the _____.

9 Almost all labor contracts call for _____ as the terminal step in the grievance procedure.

10 The _____ was a direct result of a Senate investigation that uncovered some blatant racketeering, violence, and collusion in the internal affairs of certain powerful national unions.

B TRUE-FALSE QUESTIONS

1 Supervisors have a very political role to play in labor relations.

2 Unions have been in existence almost from the time the United States was founded.

3 The Taft-Hartley Act is usually considered to be the first major piece of labor legislation.

527

4 The Landrum-Griffin Act outlawed government interence in the private sector.

5 In an open shop the employer can hire a nonunion person.

6 The two largest national unions are no longer members of the AFL-CIO.

7 Large nonunionized organizations seldom have a formal grievance procedure.

8 Supervisors represent management rights in the first step of the grievance procedure.

9 The decision of the conciliator is binding to both parties in a labor dispute.

10 As a rule, grievances are seldom settled at the first step.

C MULTIPLE-CHOICE QUESTIONS

1 Which of the following was *not* a provision of the Wagner Act?
- **a** to organize employees
- **b** to bargain collectively
- **c** to force supervisors to join a union
- **d** to allow employees to strike

2 Which of the following acts of labor legislation gave the government more direct power over labor relations?
- **a** Wagner Act
- **b** Taft-Hartley Act
- **c** Sherman Act
- **d** Landrum-Griffin Act

3 Probably the biggest reason why some people are so antiunion is because
- **a** unions run counter to widely held values of individualism and free enterprise.
- **b** unions exploit employees.
- **c** unions cause employees to lose their self respect.
- **d** unions are dominated by foreign influences.

4 Which of the following organize workers by industry?
- **a** AFL
- **b** CIO
- **c** KIA
- **d** CRM

5 Which of the following union personnel conducts the day-to-day business of the union and is generally employed full time?
- **a** president
- **b** secretary-treasurer
- **c** business agent
- **d** steward

6 During the unionization process the supervisor can safely
- **a** talk to employees in private about the union.
- **b** threaten employees if they vote for the union.
- **c** spy on employees' union activities.
- **d** attempt to correct any obvious untruths or misleading statements by the union.

7 Which step of the grievance procedure is of greatest impact and concern to supervisors?

a first   **c** third

b second   **d** fourth

8 Which of the following does not give specific recommendations or make a decision?

a mediator

b arbitrator

c conciliator

d tripartite board

9 The counterpart to the union steward on the management side of labor relations is the

a personnel manager.

b first-line supervisor.

c top manager.

d the head of production.

10 What is true of a "union shop"?

a The employer must hire a member of the union.

b It is the same as a "closed shop."

c A new employee must join the union.

d It only existed in the old days.

D ESSAY QUESTIONS OR CLASS DISCUSSION QUESTIONS

1 In your own words, briefly summarize the major acts of labor legislation.

2 What are some of the more widely held, important reasons why employees belong to unions?

3 Going from top to bottom, briefly describe the internal structure of unions.

4 What is a grievance? Briefly describe the major steps in the grievance procedure.

■ ANSWERS

A Completion Questions: **1** b   **2** d   **3** g   **4** h   **5** i   **6** a
                        7 e   **8** f   **9** j   **10** c

B True-False Questions: **1** T   **2** T   **3** F   **4** F   **5** T   **6** T
                     7 F   **8** T   **9** F   **10** F

C Multiple-Choice Questions: **1** c   **2** d   **3** a   **4** b   **5** c
                       6 d   **7** a   **8** c   **9** b   **10** c

A COMPLETION QUESTIONS

a Personality	**e** Perception
b Modeling	**f** Learning
c Identification	**g** Motivation
d Socialization	**h** Frustration

From the above list, select the letter for the term that best completes each statement below.

1 _____ represents the entire person psychologically.

2 Friends and the social group become especially important to the _____ process of older children and adults throughout their lives.

3 _____ results when a motivated drive is blocked before the intended goal is reached.

4 _____ involves the way people select, organize, and interpret the many things around them.

5 The _____ process takes place with very young children and involves imitation.

6 Usually the parent of the same sex serves as the model for the _____ process.

7 Simply defined, _____ is a change in behavior that is based on reinforced practice or experience.

8 _____ is the driving force, the energizer behind human behavior.

B TRUE-FALSE QUESTIONS

1 In a recent Gallup poll, all wage earners admitted they could accomplish more each day.

2 One extensive survey of supervisors across the country found that their employees have less pride in their work.

3 The psychological subsystem is more important than the physiological subsystem in the understanding of human behavior.

4 Classical conditioning explains most of human behavior.

5 Operant conditioning suggests that employee behavior depends on its consequences.

6 Motivational needs are observable.

7 Personal power is concerned with the means to attain desired group goals.

8 High achievers take high risks.

9 Frustration can explain simple or complex aggressive behaviors.

10 Withdrawal, rather than aggression, is more likely to be a reaction to frustration for most employees.

C MULTIPLE-CHOICE QUESTIONS

1 What is the most accurate statement concerning the identification process?

　a It takes place very early (between the ages of about 2 and 5).

　b It occurs before modeling.

　c Usually the parent of the same sex serves as a model in identi-fication.

　d It is merely imitation.

2 What is *not* a basic element of perception?

　a behavior　　　　　　　**c** organization

　b selection　　　　　　　**d** interpretation

3 Learning involves

　a changed or modified behavior.

　b reinforcement.

　c both a and b.

　d neither a nor b.

4 In operant conditioning

　a antecedent stimuli are the most important.

　b attitudes play the most important role.

　c consequences are most important.

　d personality characteristics dominate.

5 What is *not* a characteristic of high achievers?

　a taking moderate risks　　**c** not needing feedback

　b being a loner　　　　　　**d** gravitating into careers like sales

6 In reaction to frustration, regression is a form of

　a aggression.　　　　　　**c** fixation.

　b withdrawal.　　　　　　**d** compromise.

7 The plodder or bureaucrat is most close to the _____ reaction to frustration.

　a aggression　　　　　　　**c** fixation

　b withdrawal　　　　　　　**d** compromise

8 What is the most accurate statement concerning personality?

　a It consists of the whole person.

　b Most of the characteristics seem to be learned rather than in-born.

　c both a and b

　d neither a nor b

9 What is true of classical conditioning?

　a It helps explain reflexive behaviors.

　b The person operates on the environment in order to receive a reward.

c It stresses that behavior depends on its consequences.

d all the above

10 What reaction to frustration would occur when a person begins to pout and whine when faced with a barrier?

a aggression

b withdrawal

c fixation

d compromise

D ESSAY QUESTIONS OR CLASS DISCUSSION QUESTIONS

1 Personality is said to represent the psychologically whole person. What is meant by this statement and how does one's personality develop?

2 What is the essence of classical and operant conditioning and how do they differ from each other?

3 Why is it important for supervisors to understand human behavior and what are the major dimensions for this understanding?

4 Jeff Nelson has the highest sales record for Pine Insurance. An opening has just occurred for the sales manager's position. The president reasons that since Jeff had the best sales record he should become sales manager. How would you argue against the boss's reasoning?

■ ANSWERS

A Completion Questions: **1** a **2** d **3** h **4** e **5** b **6** c **7** f **8** g

B True-False Questions: **1** F **2** T **3** T **4** F **5** T **6** F **7** F **8** F **9** T **10** T

C Multiple-Choice Questions: **1** c **2** a **3** c **4** c **5** c **6** b **7** c **8** c **9** a **10** b

GROUP DYNAMICS, DECISION MAKING, AND MEETINGS

A COMPLETION QUESTIONS

a Group dynamics and power
b Group formation
c Group cohesiveness
d Norms
e Roles
f Sanctions

g Informal groups
h Decision-making process
i Brainstorming
j Delphi
k Status
l Nominal group technique (NGT)
m Meetings

From the above list, select the letter for the term that best completes each statement below.

1 The study of group forces and how they change is the study of _____.
2 Needs for affiliation, identification, and social support may all be reasons for _____.
3 A person's relative ranking within a group indicates his or her _____.
4 Silent generation of ideas in writing and deciding by voting are part of the _____.
5 Expectations for behavior are called _____.
6 Name calling, vicious horseplay, and fighting might all be forms of _____.
7 A freewheeling, supportive atmosphere is necessary for the _____ process to be effective.
8 The _____ process was named after a Greek shrine and is characterized by the anonymous inputs of the panel members.
9 Defining the relevant variables, evaluating alternatives, and making a choice are all parts of the _____.
10 The _____ can often aid supervisors in areas where they need help.
11 Factors which help to create _____ include isolation, size, external pressure, face-to-face contact, and similarity.
12 The _____ of supervisor, employee, and friend can cause conflicts within supervisors.
13 _____ are often viewed as an unnecessary waste of time.

B TRUE-FALSE QUESTIONS

1 Groups are simply a collection of individuals.
2 A good example of an informal sanction is the binging game discovered in the Hawthorne studies.

3 In Asch's study almost 40 percent of the people gave in to group pressure.

4 Groups with a great deal of face-to-face contact are usually not very cohesive.

5 Dress, titles, and productivity are all examples of roles.

6 A supervisor should decide on his or her role and then stick to it.

7 Sanctions can be both positive and negative.

8 The informal group has been traditionally viewed as a source of irritation and disruption.

9 Once a choice has been implemented, the decision process is complete.

10 The Delphi technique is characterized by the anonymous input of the group members.

C MULTIPLE-CHOICE QUESTIONS

1 An important function of a meeting leader is
- **a** enforcing the rules.
- **b** clarifying inputs.
- **c** assigning action steps.
- **d** all the above

2 The nominal group technique is characterized by
- **a** freewheeling.
- **b** deciding by voting.
- **c** creativity and humor.
- **d** all the above

3 The study of group dynamics implies
- **a** the study of power.
- **b** the study of change.
- **c** both a and b
- **d** neither a nor b

4 In the Asch conformity experiment, about _____ percent of the subjects gave in to group pressure.
- **a** 20
- **b** 40
- **c** 50
- **d** 60

5 In Kurt Lewin's famous decision-making study, women who made their decisions in groups were
- **a** more committed to the decision.
- **b** hostile to Lewin.
- **c** less likely to need support.
- **d** more independent than the others.

6 Groups form because of
- **a** close physical proximity.
- **b** financial needs.
- **c** needs for affiliation.
- **d** all the above

7 Isolation is often thought to
- **a** contribute to group strength.
- **b** create external pressure.
- **c** cause homogeneity.
- **d** both a and b

8 Expectations for dress, longer coffee breaks, and informal productivity standards are all examples of
- **a** group norms.
- **b** roles.
- **c** both a and b
- **d** neither a nor b

9 Status is indicated by
  a a person's relative position in a group.
  b telephones.
  c dress.
  d all the above
10 The informal organization can
  a support the formal organization.
  b make life for supervisors very miserable.
  c be an invaluable source of leadership.
  d all the above

D ESSAY QUESTIONS OR CLASS DISCUSSION QUESTIONS

1 Briefly define the following concepts: group dynamics; role; norms; informal group; status; and sanction.
2 There are a number of factors which contribute to group strength and cohesiveness. Describe at least four of these factors and explain how they influence cohesiveness.
3 Explain and provide an example of the concept of role conflict. How can role conflict be minimized and reduced?
4 There is a great deal of debate as to whether or not decisions should be made independently or in a participative manner. Name and describe some of the factors which should be considered when deciding on a group versus an individual method for problem solving and decision making.

■ ANSWERS

A Completion Questions: **1** a **2** b **3** k **4** l **5** d **6** f
  7 i **8** j **9** h **10** g **11** c **12** e
  13 m
B True-False Questions: **1** F **2** T **3** T **4** F **5** F **6** F
  7 T **8** T **9** F **10** T
C Multiple-Choice Questions: **1** d **2** b **3** c **4** b **5** a
  6 d **7** a **8** a **9** d **10** d

A COMPLETION QUESTIONS

a Organizational communication networks	**f** Open-door policy
b Top-down communication	**g** Grapevine or informal communication
c Horizontal communication	**h** Distorted information
d Upward communication	**i** Nonverbal communication
e Team development	**j** Transactional analysis

From the above list, select the letter for the team that best completes each statement below.

1 The grievance procedure, team development meetings, and open-door policies are all ways of getting more _____.

2 The _____ process involves the collection of data, analysis of that data, and the development of problem-solving strategies.

3 The parable, shotgun, and good times approaches are all ways in which supervisors can create _____.

4 In _____, communications are analyzed in terms of the interactions between peoples' ego states.

5 Channel, wheel, and chain arrangements are all different types of _____.

6 Nodding the head, smiling, and holding the door for another person are all types of _____.

7 When a hierarchy is bridged and a person talks directly to a peer in another part of the organization, he or she is engaged in _____.

8 Memos, directives, and instructions are all forms of _____.

9 The _____ is often more fiction than fact.

10 The _____ can be a very beneficial force and supplement the formal channels of communication.

B TRUE-FALSE QUESTIONS

1 There is very little chance of communication distortion when a long chain structure is used.

2 Wheel networks are usually very efficient for making simple decisions.

3 An increase in grievances can sometimes be a favorable indication of upward communication.

4 The grapevine should be watched closely and eliminated if possible.

5 The top-secret syndrome, needling, and information overload are all ways of stimulating horizontal communication.

6 Most of the communication in organizations is verbal.
7 The assignment of a job or office can be a very important status message.
8 The parent ego state is often critical and judgmental.
9 In a crossed transaction, the lines of communication are parallel.
10 Crossing a crossed transaction with the adult ego state is one method of eventually uncrossing it.

C MULTIPLE-CHOICE QUESTIONS

1 Organizational communication can be characterized by
   a all-channel networks.   c chain networks.
   b wheel networks.   d all the above
2 The method of upward communication which uses surveys and feedback of the survey information is
   a the grievance procedure.   c meetings.
   b team development.   d the Delphi technique.
3 Participation in the grapevine
   a is impossible to eliminate.
   b is the source of many supervisors' frustrations.
   c is more a function of position than personality.
   d all the above
4 Giving out bits and pieces of information without focusing on the big picture is a characteristic of
   a information overload.
   b the shotgun approach.
   c the parable approach.
   d the top secret syndrome.
5 Written communication should be used when
   a information is complex.
   b documentation is needed.
   c time is critical.
   d all the above
6 Nonverbal communication
   a is usually an ineffective technique.
   b accounts for a major portion of communications.
   c should be avoided.
   d is most often destructive.
7 The parent ego state is
   a critical.   c judgmental.
   b nurturing.   d all the above
8 In a complementary transaction
   a people remain in the same ego states.
   b the lines of communication are truthful.
   c the receiver gets the expected response.
   d nobody gets hurt.

9 To stop a crossed transaction a person can

   a stay in the adult.

   b cross the transaction with the adult.

   c remain calm and ignore the crossed lines.

   d all the above

10 Games are characterized by

   a an initial series of complementary transactions.

   b a hidden agenda.

   c a payoff where one party feels superior or inferior.

   d all the above

D ESSAY QUESTIONS OR CLASS DISCUSSION QUESTIONS

1 In a conversation with a co-supervisor, a supervisor mentions that he is going to fire Andy Evans because Andy has been very active in spreading rumors among his department. Will the rumors stop if Andy is fired? What can the supervisor do to end the rumors?

2 There are many ways in which supervisors can unintentionally communicate and/or distort information. Describe at least four ways that information is unintentionally distorted.

3 From transactional analysis, describe the concepts of the parent, adult, and child ego states. What ego state should supervisors strive for in order to communicate effectively?

4 Describe the types of communication channels that would probably exist in an interdepartmental meeting of supervisors from the same level in the organization.

■ ANSWERS

A Completion Questions: **1** d   **2** e   **3** h   **4** j   **5** a   **6** i
                            7 c   **8** b   **9** f   **10** g

B True-False Questions: **1** F   **2** T   **3** T   **4** F   **5** F   **6** F
                        7 T   **8** T   **9** F   **10** T

C Multiple-Choice Questions: **1** d   **2** b   **3** d   **4** b   **5** d
                                6 b   **7** d   **8** c   **9** d   **10** d

A COMPLETION QUESTIONS

a	Internal motivation	**f**	Law of effect
b	Maslow's hierarchy of needs	**g**	Contingent consequences
c	Herzberg's two-factor theory	**h**	Organizational behavior modification (O.B. Mod.)
d	Job enrichment	**i**	Positive reinforcement
e	External motivation	**j**	Punishment

From the above list, select the letter for the term that best completes each statement below.

1 _____ states that people are turned on by recognition, responsibility, achievement, advancement, and the work itself.

2 _____ is based on the premise that employee behavior is a function of the environment's consequences.

3 The catch with _____ is that no one has ever seen a need.

4 The _____ states that behavior followed by a positive (negative) consequence will tend to increase (decrease).

5 _____ states that once a given level of need is satisfied, it can no longer motivate the person.

6 The first step of _____ is to identify the critical behaviors that influence performance.

7 To increase performance-related behaviors, a (an) _____ strategy is recommended.

8 The applied aspects of Herzberg's two-factor theory has become known as _____.

9 Catch-24 means that only _____ have an impact on subsequent behavior.

10 As a last resort, the supervisor may have to use a (an) _____ strategy to decrease undesirable behaviors.

B TRUE-FALSE QUESTIONS

1 It is now generally recognized that people are mainly, if not solely, economically motivated.

2 The scientific-management pioneers can be legitimately accused of oversimplifying human motivation.

3 Motivational needs such as power or achievement are readily observed.

4 The most basic level of needs in Maslow's hierarchy is the safety needs.

5 The culmination of the other needs in Maslow's hierarchy is self-actualization.

6 The job context factors in Herzberg's theory are called the motivators.

7 Job enrichment involves horizontally loading the job.

8 Negative control of human behavior tends to be only temporary.

9 The first step of O.B. Mod. is to measure the frequency of the critical behavior.

10 A reinforcer is a consequence that strengthens the behavior.

C MULTIPLE-CHOICE QUESTIONS

1 Traditionally, what was given the least amount of attention in motivating employees?

a working conditions   **c** money
b responsibility   **d** fringe benefits

2 The third level of needs in Maslow's hierarchy is

a safety.
b love.
c physiological satisfactions.
d esteem.

3 What is the most accurate statement concerning Maslow's hierarchy of needs theory of motivation?

a It is the end-all of work motivation.
b There is a great deal of research to support the theory.
c The theory correctly emphasizes that people have diverse motives.
d It has no value for supervisors.

4 What is *not* an example of a Herzberg motivator?

a working conditions   **c** advancement
b recognition   **d** achievement

5 What is the *least* accurate statement about job enrichment?

a It loads the job vertically.
b It mostly depends on expanding the number of operations performed.
c Its purpose is to provide personal growth for the employee.
d Its purpose is to provide meaningful work experience.

6 The external approach to motivation is _____ based.

a emotionally   **c** subconsciously
b environmently   **d** Freudian

7 Under Catch-23 how is the question of 'What is a positive consequence?' answered?

a anything that works
b a reward
c anything that increases behavior
d anything that decreases problems

8 What is the fourth step of O.B. Mod.?

a intervention   **c** analyzing
b identification   **d** measurement

9 What is the most appropriate unit of analysis for improving performance under O.B. Mod.?

a technology
b training
c behavior
d ability

10 The strategy to decrease undesirable behaviors by encouraging desirable behaviors is called

a counterreward.
b cross punishment.
c second-order punishment.
d replacement.

D ESSAY QUESTIONS OR CLASS DISCUSSION QUESTIONS

1 Compare and contrast Maslow's theory with Herzberg's theory of motivation.
2 Describe the major dimensions of job enrichment. How does it differ from job enlargement?
3 How does the internal approach differ from the external approach to motivation?
4 In your own words describe the five steps of O.B. Mod.

■ ANSWERS

A Completion Questions: **1** c   **2** e   **3** a   **4** f   **5** b   **6** h
                         7 i   **8** d   **9** g   **10** j

B True-False Questions: **1** F   **2** T   **3** F   **4** F   **5** T   **6** F
                        7 F   **8** T   **9** F   **10** T

C Multiple-Choice Questions: **1** b   **2** b   **3** c   **4** a   **5** b
                          6 b   **7** c   **8** a   **9** c   **10** d

⓰CHAPTER

A COMPLETION QUESTIONS

a "Great man" approach
b Trait theory
c Democratic style
d Autocratic style
e Laissez faire style

f Initiating structure
g Consideration
h Human relations style
i Task-oriented style
j Contingency theory

From the above list, select the letter for the term that best completes each statement below.

1 Task-oriented upper-level managers tend to have _____ first-line supervisors.

2 The _____ maintains that leaders are born, not made.

3 The _____ leader would help to organize the group and to determine the group's activities through voting.

4 The Iowa studies found that a (an) _____ of leadership has a definite impact on group behaviors such as aggression and hostility.

5 In the Ohio State studies _____ is almost synonymous with human relations skills and attitudes.

6 The _____ of leadership recognizes the importance of the situation.

7 _____ is an outgrowth of the "great man" approach and dominated research from about 1920 to 1950.

8 The _____ of leader provides no direction for the group.

9 In the Ohio State studies _____ is the leader who is directed toward defining, structuring, and determining group behavior and interactions.

10 In contingency theory, under moderately favorable conditions, the _____ of supervision is most effective.

B TRUE-FALSE QUESTIONS

1 Leadership has probably been given more attention through the years than any other single subject.

2 The "great man" approach to leadership says that leaders are made not born.

3 The studies conducted at the University of Iowa in the late 1930s were the first to prove the validity of the "great man" approach.

4 The major objective of the Ohio State studies was to identify the functions that leaders perform.

5 In the Michigan studies the high-producing supervisors tended to be production-centered or task-oriented.

6 Briefly, the contingency approach maintains that effective leadership style depends on the situation.

7 It is generally recognized that a task-oriented style is more effective when employees have little education.

8 There is little question that the nature of the work affects the type of leadership style that should be used.

9 Directive, task-oriented styles may be more effective when the span of control is large.

10 Leaders' styles do not seem to be affected by the way in which the leaders, in turn, are led by their bosses.

C MULTIPLE-CHOICE QUESTIONS

1 All the following were styles of leadership evaluated in the University of Iowa studies *except*:

a democratic **c** autocratic
b "great man" **d** laissez faire

2 What were the two classes of behavior which were identified by the Ohio State studies as being associated with the leadership function?

a initiating structure and giving
b trust and friendships
c initiating structure and consideration
d environment and satisfaction

3 The high-producing supervisors in the Michigan studies

a tended to be production-centered.
b spent more time in face-to-face contact with their people.
c had close styles.
d critically analyzed employees' day-to-day operations.

4 Under Fiedler's contingency model of leadership, a task-directed style is most effective under

a no circumstances. **c** moderately favorable circum-
b extremely favorable cir- stances.
  cumstances. **d** moderately unfavorable circumstances.

5 Which of the following styles is characterized by a laissez faire approach?

a abdicator **c** driver
b helper **d** compromiser

6 With all other conditions beging equal, the more directive, task-oriented styles will probably work better with employees having

a more limited aptitudes. **c** high self-motivation.
b high self-esteem. **d** all the above

7 A directive style may be more appropriate

a when a supervisor has no particular technical expertise.

b when tasks are well defined.

c when tasks are clearly understood.

d none of the above

8 Which of the following is an accurate statement?

  a Supervisors may find more directive styles appropriate for employees performing jobs requiring few or no skills.

  b When job tasks are very unclear and ambiguous, a directive style may be appropriate.

  c both a and b

  d neither a nor b

9 Which of the following is an accurate statement?

  a Organizations which emphasize quantity, profit, or sales tend to be more effective with human relations styles.

  b Organizations which tend to emphasize quality and/or service tend to be more effective with a directive style.

  c both a and b

  d neither a nor b

10 Which approach would maintain that little can be gained from the study of leadership or leadership training?

  a contingency   **c** trait

  b "great man"   **d** behavioral

D **ESSAY QUESTIONS OR CLASS DISCUSSION QUESTIONS**

1 Two supervisors are arguing about an appropriate leadership style. One says that the "hard-line," authoritative approach is best. The other believes that an approach which respects the individual and responds to personal needs works best. If you were asked to join this debate, what would you suggest as being the best approach?

2 The Iowa studies are often cited as proof that the democratic style of leadership is best. Briefly summarize these classic leadership studies and critique the conclusion that the democratic style is best. Other relevant research should also be used to support your answer.

3 Diagram Fiedler's contingency model of leadership and explain the relationship among the components of the model.

4 From a practical perspective, describe some of the factors which influence a person's choice of leadership style.

■ **ANSWERS**

A Completion Questions: **1** i **2** a **3** c **4** d **5** g **6** j
                     7 b **8** e **9** f **10** h

B True-False Questions: **1** T **2** F **3** F **4** T **5** F **6** T
                     7 F **8** T **9** T **10** F

C Multiple-Choice Questions: **1** b **2** c **3** b **4** b **5** a
                        6 a **7** d **8** c **9** d **10** b

⒄CHAPTER

A COMPLETION QUESTIONS

a Technological advances
b Influence of computers
c Government regulations
d Changing work force
e Age of activism
f Accountability
g Professionalism
h Career-planning process

i Self-assessment techniques
j Assessment centers
k Career-goal-identification techniques
l Obituary approach
m Flash-forward technique
n Path-goal strategy
o Assessments of career progress

From the above list, select the letter for the term that best completes each statement below.

1 _____ open (opens) the way for many more new discoveries and will make the supervisor incapable of having all the facts or expertise to make important job-related decisions.

2 _____ is (are) reflected in groups of people vigorously attempting to put an end to a war, building nuclear power plants, and ending discrimination in employment.

3 In the _____ the people doing career planning are asked to imagine that today is the last day of their lives.

4 The basis of the _____ is to create visual images of the future to help identify career goals.

5 The _____ is (are) being felt in all organizations such as passenger reservations in the airlines.

6 Areas already affected by _____ include(s) safety, product liability, and labor relations.

7 The _____ has (have) four important and interrelated steps, including the final one indicating assessment and readjustment.

8 A (An) _____ involve(s) a multiple-goal perspective, with a series of subgoals leading to the major overall goal.

9 While the _____ is (are) still debated, there will be more participation from all types of people.

10 If _____ indicate(s) that a person is particularly strong or weak in a given area, then this information can be very useful for the career-planning process.

11 _____ use(s) a series of exercises, cases, role-plays, games, and problems that closely imitate actual working conditions and situations.

545

12 Employees are beginning to demand _____ for their supervisors' actions.

13 The pride resulting in _____ comes from the growing recognition that supervisory positions are very demanding and require special knowledge and abilities.

14 The fourth major phase of career planning involves _____.

15 Some _____ include(s) job changes, formal education, and professional organizations.

B TRUE-FALSE QUESTIONS

1 Supervisors will be facing essentially the same environment as in the past.

2 In the future, supervisors will not be asked to supply the input data for computerized information systems.

3 In the future, supervisors may find that even more of their important responsibilities are being stripped away from them.

4 In 1960, only about 12 percent of the population had some college education.

5 A supervisor has never been sued by an employee.

6 The first step of the career-planning process is to make specific plans.

7 Supervisory strengths and weaknesses are frequently closely tied to the subordinates' own behaviors.

8 Setting career goals should be viewed as a singular act to achieve a single goal.

9 Self-development is available to everyone.

10 Career planning is a continuous, never-ending process.

C MULTIPLE-CHOICE QUESTIONS

1 What is true concerning supervisors' information gathering and record keeping?
  a They have traditionally been focal points for collecting and assembling information.
  b In the future they will increasingly be asked to supply input data for computerized information systems.
  c They should delegate data-gathering activities.
  d all the above

2 What has been a major force for change in this country?
  a an increased level of education
  b mass-media communications
  c both a and b
  d neither a nor b

3 What is the least contributing factor to the increased professionalization of supervisors?

a pride

c pressures from top and bottom

b higher level of education

d unionization

4 What is the second step in the career-planning process?

  a self-assessment

  c identifying major career goals

  b paths and intermediate steps

  d assessment of career progress

5 People who are somewhat venturesome and who really want an accurate assessment may want to consider

  a self-evaluations.

  b performance appraisals.

  c subordinate assessments.

  d flash-forwards.

6 What method of identifying major career goals has a person imagine that today is the last day of his or her life?

  a flash-forward

  c assessment center

  b obituary

  d news headline

7 What is the *least* likely adjustment that may result from assessment of career progress?

  a changing the intermediate objectives

  b changing the ultimate career goal

  c quitting and starting over

  d reassessing strengths and weaknesses

8 What is true of the impact of education?

  a In 1960 about half of the population had some college education.

  b Increased education tends to promote the status quo.

  c Increased education should have a big impact on the workplace.

  d Today over three-fourths of the population has had some college.

9 What is the last step in the career-planning process?

  a self-assessment

  c establish career paths

  b identify major career goals

  d assess career progress

10 What method of identifying major career goals asks the person to create visual images of the future?

  a obituary

  c flashback

  b flash-forward

  d assessment center

D ESSAY QUESTIONS OR CLASS DISCUSSION QUESTIONS

1 One factor which will undoubtedly influence supervisors in the future is the computer. Speculate what you think the impact of the computer will be on the profession of supervision.

2 Diagram and briefly explain the career-planning process.

3 What is the assessment center? How can this approach aid supervisors?

547

4 Explain how the flash-forward technique of identifying career goals works and give a realistic example.

■ **ANSWERS**

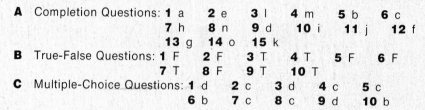

A Completion Questions: **1** a   **2** e   **3** l   **4** m   **5** b   **6** c
                            7 h   **8** n   **9** d   **10** i   **11** j   **12** f
                            13 g   **14** o   **15** k
B True-False Questions: **1** F   **2** F   **3** T   **4** T   **5** F   **6** F
                            7 T   **8** F   **9** T   **10** T
C Multiple-Choice Questions: **1** d   **2** c   **3** d   **4** c   **5** c
                               6 b   **7** c   **8** c   **9** d   **10** b

INDEX